Technology Roadmap for Energy Saving and New Energy Vehicles 3.0

China Society of Automotive Engineers

Technology Roadmap for Energy Saving and New Energy Vehicles 3.0

Springer

China Society of Automotive Engineers
Beijing, China

ISBN 978-981-95-2501-0 ISBN 978-981-95-2502-7 (eBook)
https://doi.org/10.1007/978-981-95-2502-7

This Springer imprint is published by the registered company Springer Nature Singapore Pte Ltd.
The registered company address is: 152 Beach Road, #21-01/04 Gateway East, Singapore 189721, Singapore

Preface

Currently, technological revolutions led by clean energy, artificial intelligence (AI), etc., are advancing in greater depth. Innovations in cutting-edge automotive technology are transforming rapidly, with disruptive innovations emerging frequently, leading to systemic transformation in the industrial development ecosystem. Faced with new changes and situations, domestic and international automotive industries are jointly calling for researching and revising *Roadmap 3.0* to chart the development path for automotive technology in the next 15 years and strengthen the top-level design of the new automotive industrial ecosystem. In this context, the China Society of Automotive Engineers (China SAE) officially launched the revision of the *Technology Roadmap for Energy Saving and New Energy Vehicles 3.0* in December 2023, with over 2,000 domestic and international experts from the automotive, energy, transportation, materials, communication, and AI sectors engaged. After 18 months of thorough research and systematic demonstration, the *Technology Roadmap for Energy Saving and New Energy Vehicles 3.0* that embodies broad industrial consensus was finalized.

Roadmap 3.0 further enhances the guiding principles of "forward-looking vision, systematic approach, scientific method, inheritance, openness, and public interest". Building upon the "1 + X" research framework of *Roadmap 2.0*, *Roadmap 3.0* reconstructs a "1 + 5 + X" research framework from the perspective of the emerging industrial transformation and novel industrial ecosystem and crafts the technology roadmaps for both "industrial products" and "automotive manufacturing". Meanwhile, driven by industrial demands, *Roadmap 3.0* establishes a cooperative mechanism, vertically connecting the general report with thematic studies and horizontally linking various thematic studies. The general report emphasizes industrial transformation and the construction of a new industrial ecosystem, focusing on top-level industrial planning, while the sub-roadmaps focus more on key technology development paths.

Roadmap 3.0 further clarifies the global development direction of "decarbonization, electrification and intelligentization" of automotive technology, vividly depicting the future of the automotive industry. Grounded in China and fostering global cooperation, it adopts Chinese practices as a model to propose that by 2040, the automotive industry's total carbon emissions will decrease by over 60% from their peak, new energy vehicle (NEV) sales will account for over 80% of new car sales and Level 4 autonomous driving vehicles will see widespread adoption. The automotive industry will have formed a low-carbon and sustainable modern industrial cluster and automotive manufacturing will fully achieve high-end, intelligent and green development.

Roadmap 3.0 further implements the principle of "openness, inclusiveness, cooperation, integration and joint development". It brings together global intellectual resources to establish an international expert advisory committee for top-level guidance, integrates the research capabilities of multinational corporations and international institutions to collaboratively advance research initiatives and yields outcomes that can lead China's industrial development and possess global reference value, aiming to contribute Chinese wisdom to the collaborative transformation and upgrading of the global automotive industry.

The revision of *Roadmap 3.0* has received robust support from government leaders, academicians, experts and key technical personnel of enterprises, as well as international partners and supporting organizations. We extend our sincere gratitude and respect to all contributors. We hope that all stakeholders in the global automotive industry can utilize the *Technology Roadmap for Energy Saving and New Energy Vehicles* as a platform to jointly foster a new ecosystem of open cooperation, promote synergistic technological progress in domestic and international automotive industries and fuel the prosperous development of the global automotive industry.

Beijing, China China Society of Automotive Engineers

Contents

Chapter 1
General Report of Technology Roadmap for Energy Saving and New Energy Vehicles

1.1 Global Trends in Automotive Technology and Industry Transformation

As the core engine of the emerging industrial and technological revolution, AI presents significant strategic development opportunities for the automotive industry and catalyzes systemic transformations in product forms, industrial ecosystems, and the automotive societal relationships. AI technology exhibits a prominent "leading effect", profoundly changing the development model of the automotive industry and technological development patterns and accelerating the decarbonization, intelligentization, and digitalization of the emerging industrial and technological revolution. It comprehensively empowers intelligent transformation across all stages in the automotive industry, elevating automotive intelligence from product functions to the innovation chain across the entire industry. This drives the evolution of product forms toward embodied intelligence terminals and reshaping the underlying logic of research and development (R&D), production, manufacturing, and services. In the meantime, the boundaries of the automotive industry are further expanding, deepening the cross-industry integration with energy, transportation, communication, AI, and other sectors. This has formulated a new mobility societal relationship centered on intelligent connected vehicles (ICVs) and deeply coupled with smart energy, smart transportation, and smart cities, driving the leap of the automotive industry from "technological iteration" to "ecological revolution".

Technology Roadmap for Energy Saving and New Energy Vehicles 3.0,
https://doi.org/10.1007/978-981-95-2502-7_1

1.1.1 AI is Accelerating the New Chapter of Automotive Technological Innovation and Industrial Transformation

With robust learning and generalization capabilities, large models can deconstruct in depth the knowledge system accumulated in the century-old automotive industry, expand the boundaries of the automotive industry's possibilities through disruptive innovation, enable large-scale applications of new products and scenarios, and accelerate the intelligent upgrade of automotive products and industry. More significantly, AI will also drive the innovation paradigm shift of the automotive industry from "incremental improvement" to "emergent breakthroughs" (Fig. 1.1).

1.1.1.1 AI Has Become a Core Driver in Enhancing the Intelligence of Automotive Products

New-generation AI technologies, represented by large models, are driving vehicles' evolution toward embodied intelligence agents centered on smart mobility services and characterized by intelligent mobile spaces. By restructuring the driving decision-making system, AI empowers vehicles with dynamic environment modeling and autonomous decision-making capabilities, promoting the evolution of vehicles from mechanical executors reliant on human experience into data- and algorithm-driven intelligent mobility agents, and progressively promoting driving capabilities that generalize from specific scenarios to all scenarios. On such a basis, the cockpit leverages the natural language understanding and generation capabilities of the large model to break through the limitations of traditional command-based interaction. It establishes a cognitive intelligence closed loop of "demand perception, intention reasoning, and service recommendation", transforming the cockpit

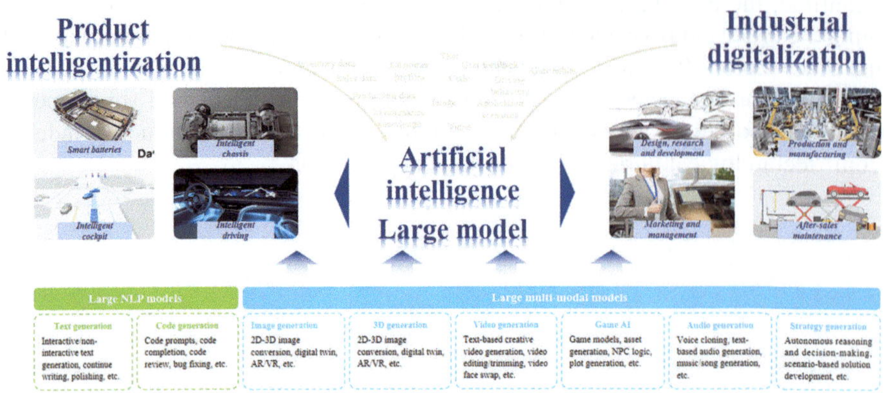

Fig. 1.1 AI empowers the intelligent transformation of automotive products and industry

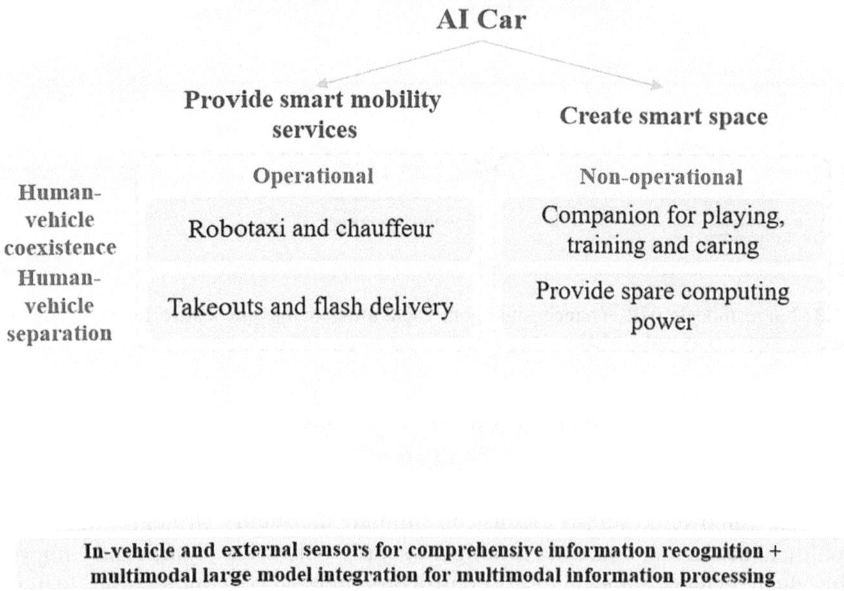

Fig. 1.2 Vehicles will evolve into embodied intelligent agents focusing on smart mobility services and possessing smart mobility space attributes

from a passive responder to a proactive service partner. Moreover, AI can facilitate the formulation of interconnected ecosystems between automotive intelligent agents and other smart terminals like mobile phones, computers, tablets, wearables, and smart homes. Through efficient resource management, task scheduling, and precise multi-terminal service distribution, this can create a all-scenario service ecosystem featuring multi-agent collaboration of "human-vehicle-environment" is realized, accelerating human's transition toward a deeply intelligent mobile lifestyle (Fig. 1.2).

1.1.1.2 "AI Revolution" Profoundly Empowers the Entire Process of the Automotive Industry

Based on numerous data accumulated within the industry and the integrated application of new technologies like the Internet of Things (IoT), 5G communication, and digital twins, AI is profoundly empowering the entire automotive manufacturing process, driving the intelligent and digital development of China's automotive industry. In R&D, AI has significantly accelerated product iteration, drives breakthroughs in product performance, and reduces R&D costs. In

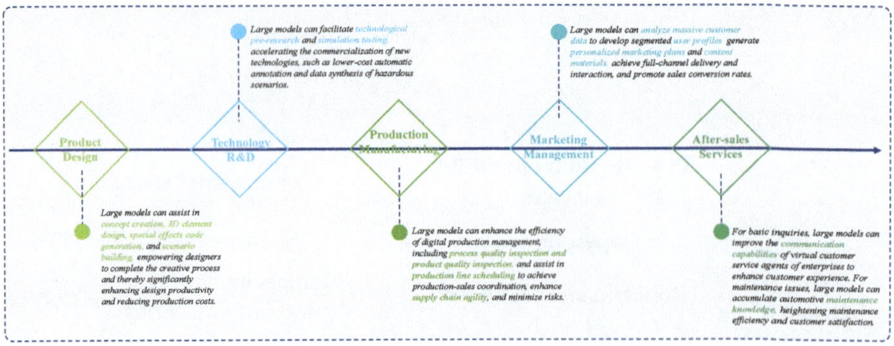

Fig. 1.3 Large models will enhance intelligent capabilities across the entire R&D, production, marketing, and service value chain

manufacturing, "AI + digital twin" operation systems can critically analyze historical order data, supply chain status, equipment wear curves, and other parameters to autonomously generate optimal production plans. Enhanced by digital twin technology, AI-empowered supply chains can simulate the supply strategies in different geopolitical scenarios, construct intelligent supply networks, significantly improve supply chain resilience, and precisely control procurement cost fluctuations. In digital marketing, the development of virtual reality and the metaverse has opened up new application scenarios, including virtual experiences, digital humans, and immersive online events, enabling brands to interact with consumers in more diversified and personalized manners and providing them with richer and more immersive marketing experiences (Fig. 1.3).

1.1.1.3 Automotive Technological Innovation is Embracing a Novel "AI-Driven" Paradigm

Revolutionary breakthroughs in the accuracy, emergent abilities, and generalization capabilities of large AI models are driving systemic revolutions in scientific research paradigms. In this context, "AI for Science (AI4S)" is integrating into the innovation system of the automotive industry at unprecedented speed, breadth, and depth. This will reshape the innovation ecosystem of the entire chain of the automotive industry, from basic and frontier research to engineering and industrial technology R&D, significantly elevating the efficiency of automotive technological innovation.

In terms of electrification, the traditional "trial-and-error" approach to NEV battery R&D is undergoing disruptive changes. Applying AI-powered high-precision modeling techniques and efficient intelligent optimization algorithms to battery design allows for more accurate establishment of structure–activity relationships between design parameters and key performance, as well as automatic identification of the optimal and fastest solutions for the design process, driving a quantum leap in battery R&D efficiency.

In terms of intelligentization, the vehicle-to-cloud closed data loop will reshape the traditional "rule"-based intelligent driving R&D system. For example, a closed data loop can enable full-process automation of "collection-annotation-training-verification-deployment", with data crowdsourcing and multi-source collection providing basic data resources, automated annotation tools (such as LiDAR point cloud semantic segmentation models) improving data annotation efficiency, imitation/reinforcement learning promoting the continuous iteration and evolution of intelligent driving models, and virtual-reality fusion testing guaranteeing basic performance. Based on the "vehicle-road-cloud integration" system and agile on-vehicle deployment via OTA, this has created a data-driven and self-evolving system and driving continuous surges in the performance of intelligent driving technology.

1.1.2 The Automotive Industry is Witnessing a Systemic Ecosystem Transformation

Coupled with the accelerated progress of carbon neutrality objectives, the current widespread and profound breakthroughs and applications of AI are comprehensively reshaping automotive product forms, the industrial ecosystem, and the vehicle-societal relationships. The scope, depth, and pace of this industrial transformation are unprecedented.

1.1.2.1 Reshaping "Embodied Intelligence" Automotive Products

Carbon neutrality objectives are driving accelerated development of decarbonization and electrification technologies in the automotive industry. AI is accelerating the continuous iteration of automotive intelligence technologies. The in-depth integration and innovative development of decarbonization, electrification, and intelligence technologies are fundamentally transforming the functions, forms, and applications of automotive products. **In terms of functions**, vehicles will evolve into embodied intelligence agents that can proactively provide personalized services to users while also functioning as distributed energy storage units, mobile computing nodes, information terminals, and intelligent living spaces. **In terms of forms**, multifunctional intelligent shared cars with replaceable mounted modules and flying cars supporting integrated air-ground transportation are emerging, profoundly altering traditional automotive forms. **In terms of applications**, vehicles will transcend the single purpose of "mobility" and engage in the construction of new power systems through vehicle-energy Interaction. Leveraging their functions as energy, information, and computing nodes, the vehicles can facilitate the realization of smart communities, smart government services, and other functions (Fig. 1.4).

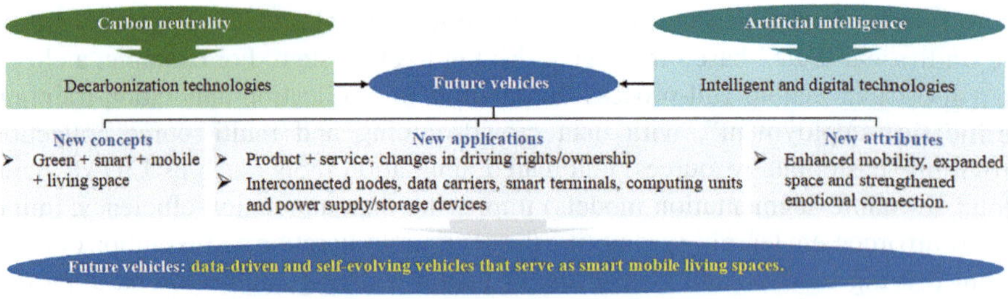

Fig. 1.4 Embodied intelligence in automotive product forms

1.1.2.2 Reshaping the "Cross-Industrial Integration" Ecosystem of the Automotive Industry

The emerging technological revolution is accelerating the automotive industry's transition from a traditional chain structure to a three-dimensional network, fostering a new ecosystem through in-depth cross-industrial integration. On the one hand, the industrial entities exhibits a diversified trend, encompassing traditional enterprises like vehicle manufacturers and spare part suppliers, as well as innovative powers such as integrated solution providers, information and communication technology providers and manufacturing startups. This also gives rise to novel business models like content operation and platform services. On the other hand, industrial boundaries continue to expand, accelerating the extension of the industrial ecosystem through in-depth integration with transportation, energy, AI, the low-altitude economy, and other sectors (Fig. 1.5).

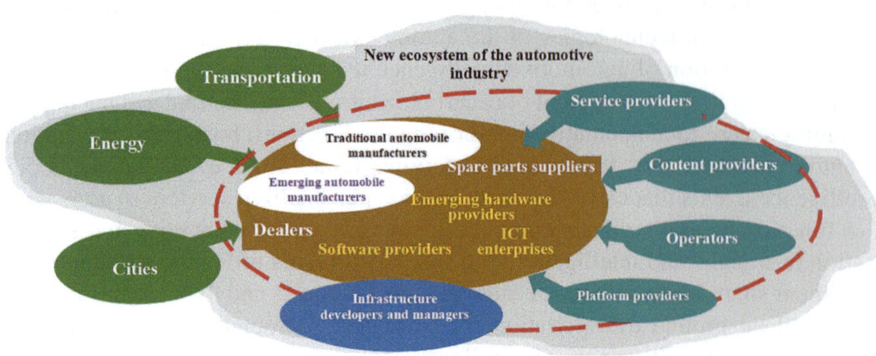

Fig. 1.5 The cross-industrial ecosystem of the automotive industry

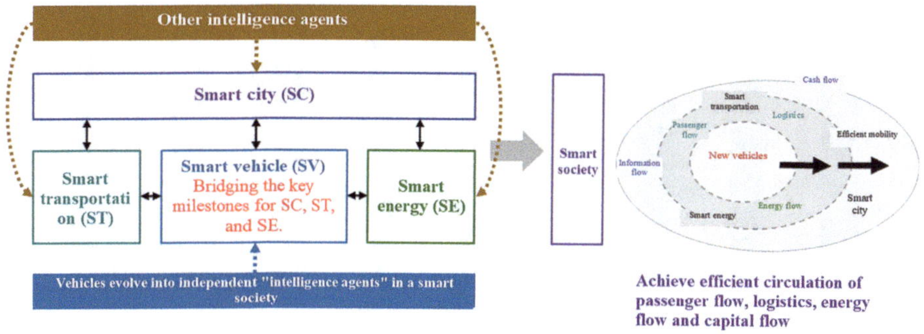

Fig. 1.6 Harmonious coexistence between human, vehicles and society

1.1.2.3 Reshaping the Automotive-Societal Relationships of "Harmonious Coexistence"

Empowered by AI technology, future smart vehicles (SVs) will exhibit new characteristics of collective intelligence and openness, becoming key nodes connecting smart transportation (ST), smart energy (SE), and smart cities (SCs), achieving in-depth coupling of the "4S". The permeation of automotive solutions into all areas of digital life will create a large intelligent ecosystem through further collaboration with intelligent terminals such as flying cars and humanoid robots, thus forming a new paradigm of human-vehicle-society relationships characterized by low-carbon, green and environmental protection practices, safe and efficient intelligence, as well as harmonious and friendly coexistence (Fig. 1.6).

1.2 Current Status and Development of Global Automotive Industry Technology

1.2.1 The Global Automotive Industry is Witnessing Stable Rebounding, with Emerging Productive Forces Serving as Key Growth Drivers

Over the past five years, the global automotive industry has overcome adverse factors such as the COVID-19 pandemic and geopolitical conflicts, with sales gradually rebounding from their low in 2020 to approximately 95 million units in 2024. Based on a comprehensive analysis of key factors such as global economic development trends, technological innovations in the automotive industry, and the unleashing of consumption potential in emerging markets, it is expected that the global annual automotive sales will exceed 100 million units after 2030 and enter a long-term stable plateau phase. In the long term, the transformative impacts of decarbonization,

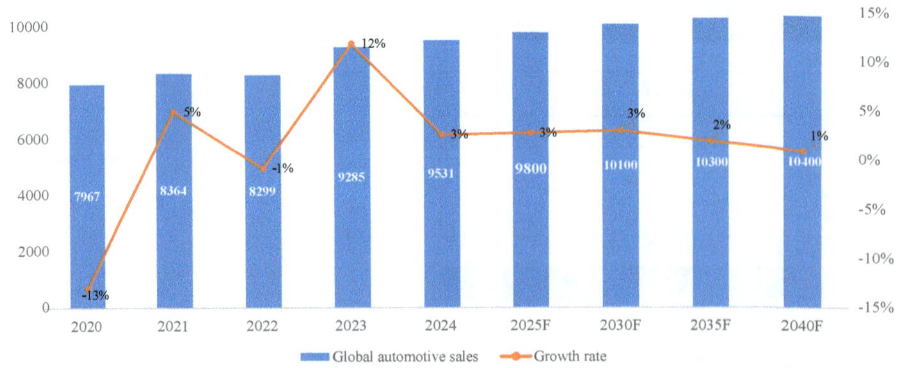

Fig. 1.7 Global vehicle sales and growth rate (2020–2040F). *Source* International Organization of Motor Vehicle Manufacturers (OICA) and China SAE

electrification, and intelligentization will disrupt the ownership and usage models of automotive products, potentially impacting global automotive sales by 20–30% (Fig. 1.7).

Automotive markets in developed countries have entered now in a stock-competition phase, while emerging markets are increasingly the core engine of global auto market growth. In recent years, automotive markets in developed countries, such as the United States, Japan, South Korea, and major European Union (EU) member states, have undergone slow growth or even slight declines. In terms of the sales over the past five years, the US saw a growth of approximately 10%, Germany and Japan witnessed declines of 2.3% and 3.9%, respectively, and South Korea experienced a significant decrease of 14.3%. China has continued to lead the global market, accounting for over 30% of the global share with a sales volume of 31.44 million vehicles and representing a growth rate of 24.2%. India has surpassed Japan and Germany to become the world's third-largest automotive consumer, with a growth rate as high as 77.9%, making it an exemplary representative of the rise of emerging markets (Fig. 1.8).

1.2.2 Automotive Decarbonization is Progressing Steadily, with Carbon Neutrality Driving Synergistic Development Across Multiple Technological Pathways

Major automotive markets worldwide are tightening their carbon emission and fuel economy regulations and strengthening policy constraints on the low-carbon transition of the automotive market. This has created a diversified landscape for green and low-carbon development in the global automotive industry.

Ranking	Country	Change in ranking compared with 2020	Growth rate	2024 automotive sales (ten thousand units)
1	China	→	24.2%	3144
2	United States	→	9.8%	1634
3	India	↑2	77.9%	523
4	Japan	↓1	-3.9%	442
5	Germany	↓1	-2.3%	319
6	Brazil	↑1	28.0%	263
7	United Kingdom	↑1	20.6%	237
8	France	↓2	2.6%	216
9	Canada	↑1	20.2%	191
10	South Korea	↓1	-14.3%	163

Fig. 1.8 Comparison of top 10 countries by automotive sales (2020 vs. 2024). *Source* OICA

Driven by the "zero-carbon" objective, the EU is promoting a low-carbon transition through the coordinated development of electrification and zero-carbon internal combustion engines. To achieve the 2050 carbon neutrality objective, the EU passed legislation in 2023 mandating a ban on the sale of new fuel-powered sedans and small passenger vehicles by 2035, and tightened the original 2030 average carbon emission reduction target for new passenger vehicles and light commercial vehicles from a 37.5% reduction in 2021 to a 55% reduction. In terms of technological structures, the market share of traditional fuel vehicles decreased to one-third in the EU in 2024, while the share of hybrid electric vehicles (HEVs) exceeded 30%, and NEVs exceeded 20%. However, compared to the objective proposed by ACEA, which requires electric vehicles to exceed 25% to meet 2025 carbon emission targets, the electrification transition falls short of expectations and faces multiple challenges such as cost, infrastructure, and consumer intentions. In this context, the EU has proposed to promote zero-carbon development through a combination of hydrogen-based zero-carbon fuels and electrification, encouraging companies like Volkswagen and BMW to explore the research and development of hydrogen-based and e-fuels.

The US emphasizes a goal-oriented approach to emission reduction, promoting energy the parallel development of efficiency improvements and diversified clean fuels. The US has established a comprehensive framework encompassing the *Clean Energy for America Act*, emission standards, and incentive policies, aimed at reducing the proportion of fuel vehicles and fostering the joint development of diversified energy saving solutions, such as electric vehicles (EVs), fuel cell vehicles (FCVs), hydrogen, plug-in hybrids, and renewable diesel. The 2022 *US Inflation*

Reduction Act incorporated plug-in hybrids vehicles, hydrogen-powered vehicles, and renewable diesel vehicles as eligible for subsidies. In June 2024, the US government proposed new fuel economy standards for passenger vehicles and light trucks, mandating a 2% annual increase in fuel economy for passenger vehicles from 2027 to 2031, and 2% for light trucks from 2029 to 2031.

Japan's automotive decarbonization features HEVs and hydrogen fuel cells, with a growing focus on EVs. According to the 2030 fuel economy standards for passenger vehicles released by Japan's Ministry of Land, Infrastructure, Transport and Tourism and the Ministry of Economy, Trade and Industry in 2019, the average fuel economy of new passenger vehicles shall reach 25.4 km/L (approximately 3.9 L/100 km) by 2030. Currently, the average fuel consumption standard for new passenger vehicles in Japan stands at about 20.3 km/L (approximately 4.9 L/100 km). Among the low-carbon fuel passenger vehicles on the market, HEVs account for 46.2%, EVs 1.6%, and plug-in hybrid vehicles (PHEV) 1.2%. According to the *Green Growth Strategy Through Achieving Carbon Neutrality in 2050*, Japan plans to achieve complete electrification of all new passenger vehicle sales by 2035. By then, the Japanese market will be dominated by HEVs, EVs, PHEVs, and FCVs. Over the past two years, major Japanese companies have increased their investment in NEVs. Toyota has invested over USD 10 billion in North America to produce electric vehicles and plans to launch 15 EV models by 2027 and secure an EV production volume of 1 million units. Honda announced a USD 65 billion investment in electrification by 2030, with plans to cease the sales of fuel vehicles by 2040.

China is pursuing low-carbon transition by collaboratively promoting energy saving and carbon reduction solutions and electrification strategy for traditional vehicles. To promote the low-carbon transition of fuel vehicles, the Chinese government is continuously tightening emission standards. In August 2024, the Ministry of Industry and Information Technology released a draft for the third revision of GB27999, "Method and Indicators for Fuel Consumption Appraisal of Passenger Vehicles," requiring the average fuel consumption of passenger vehicle manufacturers to be reduced to 3.3L/100 km by 2030. This objective represents an approximately 33% increase in stringency compared to the 2025 standard for vehicles of equivalent weight. Thanks to the joint efforts of all parties, in 2024, the average fuel consumption of passenger vehicles in China reached 3.78L/100 km, achieving Roadmap 2.0's 2025 target of 4.6 L/100 km ahead of schedule (Fig. 1.9).

1.2.3 Electrification Has Become a Global Consensus and NEV Marketization is Accelerating

Global sales of new energy vehicles continue to grow rapidly, with the pace of industrial transformation accelerating. Since 2012, global new energy vehicle sales have grown exponentially. Despite headwinds from high inflation, economic weakness, and geopolitical crises, global NEV sales still hit a record high in 2024,

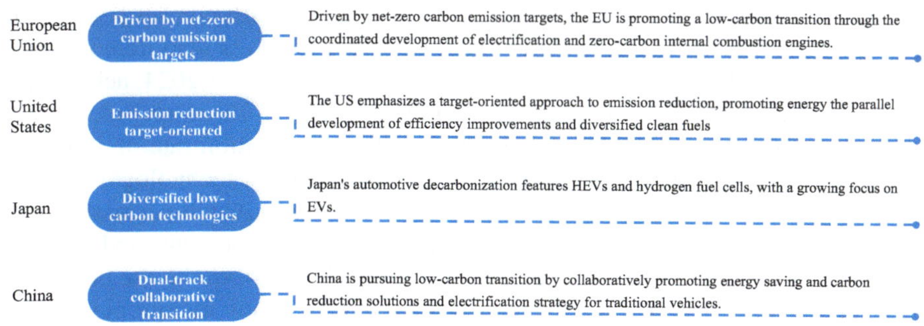

Fig. 1.9 Decarbonization technology solutions by country

amounting to approximately 17.71 million units, a year-on-year growth of about 15.8%, with a market penetration rate nearing 20%. With the global popularization of NEVs driven by policies and market strategies, and the industry chain is gradually maturing. The acceptance of NEVs continue to improve in most markets. It is expected that the global NEV penetration rate will exceed 30% by 2030, and approach 50% by 2040 (Fig. 1.10).

The US, China, and Europe are leading the electrification transition, with emerging markets rapidly closing the gap, driving an accelerated transformation of the global NEV landscape. Global NEV sales are concentrated in three major markets, namely China, Europe, and the US. In 2024, China accounted for nearly 70% of global sales, with a penetration rate of 40.9%. The US saw a NEV sales exceeding 1.5 million units in 2024, with a penetration rate of approximately 10%. The sales in seven European countries (Germany, France, the United Kingdom, Italy, Spain, Sweden, and Norway) exceeded 2 million units, with an average penetration rate of over 20%. Nordic countries such as Norway and Sweden have taken

Fig. 1.10 Current situations and forecasts of global NEV sales. *Source* OICA, Marklines and China SAE

the lead and entered an advanced stage of electrification, with current penetration rates approaching or exceeding 90%. Other emerging markets also demonstrated robust growth. India saw approximately 2.02 million EV sales in 2024, achieving a penetration rate of about 2% and year-on-year growth of 25%. Brazil recorded an EV sales of approximately 180,000 units in 2024, with a penetration rate of about 7% and year-on-year growth of 89%. Fueled by policy tailwinds, technological breakthroughs, and mature industry chains, the European and North American markets still hold significant growth potential. With favorable policy environments and substantial market potential, Eastern Europe and ASEAN will contribute to the continued acceleration of the global electrification process. China's new energy penetration rate is expected to reach 65–70% by 2030. Europe and the US are expected to rise to 40–45% and 25–30%, respectively, while India and Brazil are likely to surpass 15% and 10%. By 2035, with the expansion of China's combustion ban pilot programs, the EU's combustion ban taking effect, and the continued impact of the US IRA, new energy penetration in China, Europe, and the US will reach 75–80%, 60–65%, and 45–50%, respectively. Emerging markets will accelerate their catch-up, with India reaching 25–30% and Brazil reaching 20–25%. By 2040, the global NEV market will reach maturity, with projected penetration rates of 85–90% in China, over 80% in Europe, over 70% in the US, and over 50% and 40% in emerging markets like India and Brazil, respectively. Breakthroughs in battery and charging technologies, underperforming construction of charging infrastructure, policy fluctuations (such as subsidy reductions), and raw material supply risks may lead to an adjustment of approximately 10% to the aforementioned forecast.

From the perspective of technological solutions, BEVs will continue to dominate the global NEV market in 2024, with sales reaching approximately 11 million units, representing a year-on-year growth of 15.8% and accounting for 62.9% of global NEV sales. From 2020 to 2024, significant regional variations emerged in the market shares of BEVs and PHEVs. While BEVs remain dominant in the Chinese market, PHEVs have experienced significantly accelerated growth since 2021, steadily increasing their market share. In 2024, BEV sales in China's NEV market reached 7.72 million units, accounting for approximately 60.0% of the market shares, while PHEV sales reached 2.70 million units, accounting for approximately 40.0%. This exhibits an increase of over 20 percentage points compared to 18.3% in 2020. Initially, PHEVs held a similar share to BEVs in the EU market. However, since 2022, the focus has shifted towards BEVs, with their share of NEV sales in the EU rising from 51.4% in 2020 to 66.1% in 2024. The US NEV market structure is relatively stable, with PHEV and BEV experiencing similar year-on-year growth, maintaining a long-term "two-eight" structure. In 2024, U.S. BEV sales reached 1.2 million units, up 9.1% year-on-year, while PHEV sales reached 290,000 units, up 10.3% year-on-year (Fig. 1.11).

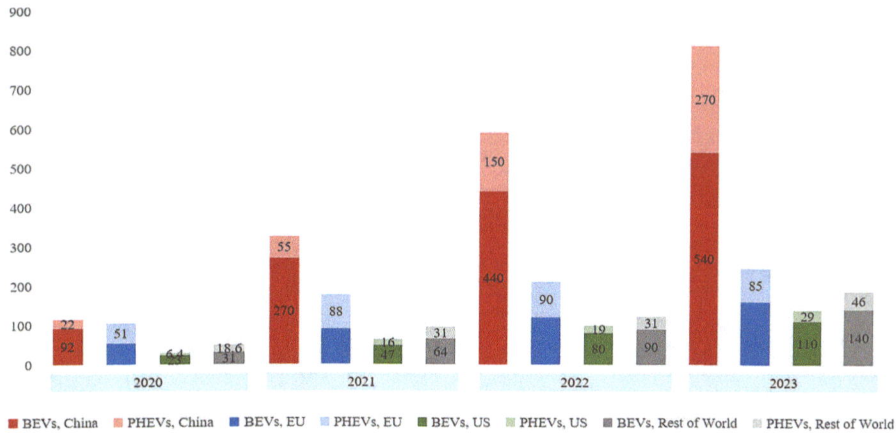

Fig. 1.11 Global new energy technology roadmap structure by country/region. *Source* IEA

1.2.4 ICVs Have Become a Strategic Priority for Many Countries, with Continuous Breakthroughs in Industrialization

ICVs have become a global strategic priority for the automotive industry. Various countries are promoting the innovative development and business application of ICVs by improving top-level design, supporting technological innovation, refining policies and regulations, and opening road tests. The US Department of Transportation continuously updates and releases plans such as the *Automated Vehicles Policy* and the *Automated Vehicles Comprehensive Plan* to strengthen cross-departmental and cross-industrial coordination, support industrial platform development, and encourage the commercial applications of autonomous driving. Europe is establishing a comprehensive policy framework across various levels, encompassing regulatory frameworks, standardization and interoperability, data governance, international cooperation, testing, and deployment. Strategic plans like the *Sustainable and Smart Mobility Strategy* has been released to facilitate the large-scale deployment of autonomous driving services by 2030. The Cabinet Office of Japan has coordinated with relevant ministries to implement the Cross-ministerial Strategic Innovation Promotion Program (SIP), aiming to achieve Level 4 autonomous driving for private vehicles and highway freight transport by 2025. China has released top-level strategic plans such as the *New Energy Vehicle Industry Development Plan (2021–2035)* and the *Intelligent Vehicle Innovation Development Strategy* to strengthen the safety management, technological R&D, demonstration and applications of ICVs, and specified that the large-scale application of L4 autonomous driving vehicles will be achieved by 2035.

The industrialization of ICVs has progressed significantly, with accelerated promotion and application of autonomous driving at various levels. The United

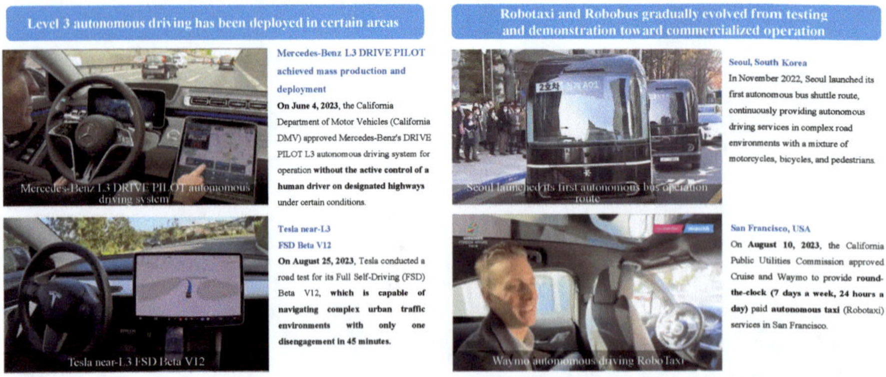

Fig. 1.12 Gradual rollout and application of various levels of autonomous diving across the globe

States has taken the lead in critical autonomous driving technologies. Tesla, for instance, pioneered the "BEV + Transformer" neural network algorithm and "end-to-end" model architecture. Leveraging "shadow mode" and significant sales volume, they have amassed substantial driving data to continuously validate and refine their models. As a result, their FSD System (currently still at L2 autonomous driving level) has improved its average safe disengagement mileage in urban environments from approximately 50 km in 2021 to nearly 200 km. Europe is strengthening the top-level design and demonstration applications of high-level autonomous driving. For example, Mercedes-Benz obtained the world's first international certification in Germany for a Level 3 conditional autonomous driving System, and the maximum speed supported has been increased from 60 to 95 km/h, making it the fastest Level 3 autonomous driving system in mass-production vehicles worldwide. Japan is steadily advancing high-level autonomous driving technology and vehicle planning. Honda has already obtained L3 certification and the *Road Traffic Act* has been revised, allowing L4 autonomous driving mobility services and automated delivery robot operations under specific conditions (Fig. 1.12).

AI-based end-to-end architectures and closed data loops that support imitation and reinforcement learning have become the mainstream solutions and research paradigms for autonomous driving. Driven by the ongoing advancements in general AI, a new paradigm for intelligent driving R&D powered by large model training, big data, and substantial computing power has become an industrial consensus. Domestic and global automotive manufacturers and autonomous driving companies are building and intentionally optimizing their algorithm networks based on BEV + Transformer architectures. They are leveraging supercomputing centers and hundreds of millions of kilometers of driving data to train end-to-end large models for autonomous driving and exploring the integration of cutting-edge technologies such as visual language models, vision-language-action models, and world models into end-to-end applications. Meanwhile, to address the potential risks of the unexplainability in data-driven solutions, the industry adheres to establishing a security and redundancy system based on rule-based algorithms and actively explores

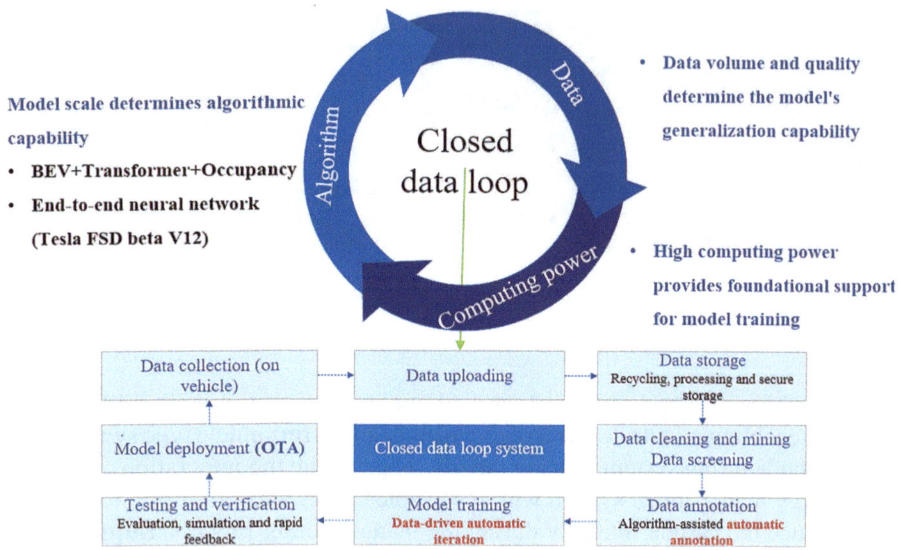

Fig. 1.13 AI-driven autonomous driving R&D paradigm

a technological framework driven by "rules + data". In terms of training methods, a closed-data-loop R&D paradigm of "self-supervised foundation + reinforcement learning optimization" is formulated. By interacting with virtual environments (such as long-tail scenarios constructed by generative AI), it can realize the autonomous evolution of driving strategies, ultimately leading to an explainable and evolvable intelligent driving system (Fig. 1.13).

1.2.5 The Accelerated Exploration of Intelligent Manufacturing in the Automotive Industry is Promoting Digital and Intelligent Transformation and Upgrades Throughout the Entire Value Chain

Currently, automotive enterprises are actively exploring new intelligent manufacturing systems, technologies, and models. Multiple innovations are emerging across various segments, encompassing R&D, production, supply, marketing, and services, driving the progress of the entire industry. **The R&D system is advancing in parallel with digital twins and cross-industrial integration**. The global automotive R&D system and digital design tools have achieved seamless connectivity across the entire process, from demand identification and concept development to virtual verification, drastically shortening the R&D cycle. **Production models are undergoing an accelerated shift towards flexible and sustainable manufacturing**. Industrial Internet of Things (IoT) have deeply penetrated all production segments, with the real-time

Fig. 1.14 BMW's actual manufacturing status and real-time digital twin results based on the NVIDIA Omniverse platform

interconnection of equipment, process, and quality data ensuring closed-loop optimization, enabling minute-level response in multi-platform vehicle type switching. A green manufacturing system is being rapidly shaped, with the integration of factory-level energy management system with renewable energy and smart grid to continuously reduce the carbon intensity during the manufacturing process. **Supply chain management is achieving dual improvements in resilient reshaping and intelligent collaboration**. Digital procurement platforms integrate in depth with upstream and downstream resources, enabling real-time visibility and control of orders, logistics, and inventory. **The service ecosystem is achieving enhanced empowerment through scenario-based solutions and value extension**. After-sales service is being upgraded toward predictive maintenance, with remote diagnostic systems enabling early warning and proactive intervention (Fig. 1.14).

In the future, the competitive edges of automotive intelligent manufacturing will hinge on three key dimensions, namely the in-depth application of digital tools, the dynamic adaptability of flexible manufacturing systems, and the closed-loop management of circular supply chains. The R&D focus will further shift towards "system-level innovation". Digital twin technology will evolve from isolated breakthroughs to collaborative modeling of the vehicle ecosystem. The popularization of modular development platforms will accelerate the cross-vehicle reuse of technological outcomes, achieving large-scale innovation effects. The concept of circular material design will be deeply integrated into the R&D system, promoting the controllable development of the environmental footprint throughout the entire life cycle. **The production system will evolve towards "distributed collaborative manufacturing**". Regional manufacturing networks will ensure dynamic balancing of global capacity. The iteration and upgrades of carbon neutral factories will promote the in-depth coupling between manufacturing processes and energy networks, forming a new production paradigm that achieves energy self-sufficiency. **The supply chain system will transform into a "networked ecosystem"**. Smart contract technology will enable collaborative autonomous decision-making across the entire chain. The in-depth integration of digital logistics systems and physical warehousing networks will create a dynamic inventory system that can precisely match the demand. The formation of the regenerative material circulation network will be accelerated, promoting the continuous evolution of the supply chain to fulfill the zero-waste objective.

1.3 New Demands for Leading High-Quality Development of the Automotive Industry in the New Stage

1.3.1 The Global Economic Recovery Requires the Automotive Industry to Act as a Fundamental Growth Driver

As the "pearl in the crown of modern industry", the automotive sector is a concentrated reflection of a nation's comprehensive strength and a vital pillar of its economic power. All major global automotive powerhouses, such as the US, the EU, and Japan, are leading economic powers, with their automotive industries contributing 12, 7, and 8% to their respective GDPs. In China, the automotive sector is a pillar industry of the national economy, generating an annual output value of over RMB 10 trillion and contributing approximately 7% of the total national industrial added value. Taxes from the automotive sector and related industries account for not less than 10% of the national tax revenue, and automotive sales constitute not less than 10% of the national retail sales of consumer goods.

Since 2020, frequent "black swan" and "gray rhino" events across the globe has resulted in a new normal of slow growth for global economy in the wake of repeated impacts. The United Nations projects a global economic growth rate of merely 2.8% in 2025, below the 3.0% average annual growth rate between 2001 and 2019. The World Trade Organization recently further lowered its growth forecast for the same period, underscoring the grim reality of weak global economic recovery momentum and increasing downward pressure. In this context, the automotive industry should give full play to its role as a fundamental driver of economic growth, leading consumption upgrades through technological innovation, strengthening investment expectations with industrial resilience, and boosting foreign trade through globalized deployment, thereby continuously injecting robust momentum into global economic growth.

Currently, green growth has become a core paradigm for economic development in economies such as the EU and Japan. Under the guidance of its carbon peaking and carbon neutrality goals, China is also accelerating its comprehensive green transformation of economic and social development. Meanwhile, the digital economy, a burgeoning engine of global economic growth, is developing rapidly, with its share in global GDP surging from 44% in 2020 to 60% in 2023. Faced with the new development opportunities arising from the combination of the green transition and the digital economy, the automotive industry should further strengthen technological R&D and innovation in decarbonization, electrification, and intelligentization. It should continuously cultivate new industries, types of operation, and models focusing on green decarbonization, intelligent connection, and digital-intelligent integration, striving to create new business growth drivers and further contribute to global economic development.

1.3.2 The Carbon Neutrality Vision Requires the Automotive Industry to Lead Green and Low-Carbon Transition in Economic and Social Development

Accelerating carbon–neutral development to meet the *Paris Agreement's* goal of limiting global warming has become a global consensus. So far, over 150 countries and regions worldwide, including the EU, Japan, and China, have proposed their carbon neutrality development goals. However, due to multiple various factors, the global progress of green and low-carbon development has fallen short of expectations in recent years. Notably, in 2024, the global average surface temperature once surpassed the 1.5 °C warming threshold, making it the hottest year on record. As the world's second-largest carbon-emitting sector (accounting for approximately one fourth of emissions), the transportation sector witnesses exceptional severe situations in emission reduction. In countries and regions such as the US and the EU, transportation is the only or the fastest growing sector in terms of carbon emissions. Specifically, road transportation, dominated by vehicles, contributes approximately 75% of global transportation carbon emissions. Faced with the current bottlenecks in global green and low-carbon development, the automotive industry urgently needs to leverage the transition towards decarbonization, electrification, and intelligentization to continuously step up its carbon emission reduction efforts. Meanwhile, it should fully utilize its constructive and leading roles endowed by its extensive industry chain, broad reach, and intensive cross-industry integration to drive collaborative among multiple relevant industries, such as the transportation, energy, and materials sectors, to achieve low-carbon development.

On the one hand, the automotive industry should persistently make breakthroughs in decarbonization and electrification technologies to continuously improve the fuel economy of energy saving vehicles and accelerate the all-weather and all-scenario deployment of NEVs. Meanwhile, the industry should leverage intelligent and connection technologies to improve vehicle operating efficiency, mitigate the risk of traffic accidents, and comprehensively promote carbon emission reduction in automotive products and road traffic. On the other hand, efforts should be made in various aspects, such as improving energy efficiency, promoting clean energy alternatives, upgrading process and equipment, and enhancing resource recycling, to further promote the green and low-carbon development of automotive manufacturing. Concurrently, green supply chain management should be strengthened, with additional emphasis on low-carbon development synergy with upstream material suppliers, to accelerate the alternative application of new automotive materials featuring low energy consumption and high performance. Furthermore, the industry should give full play to the role of NEVs as distributed mobile energy storage units in promoting renewable energy consumption and grid peak shaving and frequency regulation, thereby supporting the development of a clean, low-carbon, secure, and efficient new power system. Additionally, capitalizing on the cross-regional and large-scale promotion and deployment of FCVs, the industry should accelerate the coordinated development of the upstream and downstream segments of the clean hydrogen industry, facilitating broader application of green hydrogen.

1.3.3 Technological Transformation and Consumption Upgrade Are Driving the Reshaping of the Automotive Industry's Technology System and Product Forms

With accelerated evolution of the new technological and industrial transformation, global technological innovation has entered an unprecedented period of intensive activity. New energy technologies such hydrogen-ammonia-methanol integration and biomass energy, new computing technologies such as large models and cloud computing, and new material technologies such as nanomaterials and high-performance carbon fibers are blooming across multiple sectors, competing to achieve significant breakthroughs in fundamental theories and technological challenges from the origin and ground, and yielding innovative outcomes that drive significant performance improvements. These technologies are being rapidly deployed to integrated applications and interdisciplinary fusion on vehicles, creating an urgent demand for systemic restructuring of the automotive technology innovation system while fully tapping their "enabling" and "empowering" effects. To this end, the automotive industry needs to further develop and refine its cross-industrial integration and innovation system, strengthen forward-looking and leading deployment in basic science and interdisciplinary fields, and formulate new automotive technologies characterized by cross-disciplinary, cross-industrial and cross-sectoral breakthroughs, thereby empowering the automotive industry to continue leading global innovation and transformation.

In the meantime, with the current in-depth integration of the digital and real economies, the public's lifestyles and consumption habits are being rapidly reshaped. Consumers' perceptions, experiences, and expectations for "efficiency, intelligence, and convenience" are rapidly extending from smart terminals like computers, mobile phones, and consumer electronics to automotive products. The consuming demand, application scenarios, and usage of vehicles are becoming increasingly diversified. Consequently, accelerating the creation of "new automotive products" that serves more than mere transportation tools is an inevitable requirement for enterprises to address consumer upgrades. In this regard, the automotive industry should further develop automotive products into embodied intelligence agents with self-evolving and self-iterating capabilities, shifting from passively receiving work instructions to autonomously perceiving user demands and proactively providing personalized services, thus becoming users' intelligent companions. Meanwhile, through in-depth interconnection between vehicles and smartphones, computers, and smart homes, the industry should accelerate the transformation of vehicles into "intelligent mobile spaces" combining mobile spaces, workspaces, and living spaces to meet users' expectations for seamless transitions between travel and commuting, efficient work, and diversified lifestyle scenarios.

1.3.4 Intertwined Opportunities and Challenges Facilitate More In-Depth Global Collaboration in the Automotive Industry

The century-long evolution of the automotive industry has forged a highly globalized division of labor, which has become a pivotal cornerstone for the rise of automotive powerhouses and the development of multinational automakers. The global automotive industry is currently faced with major transformation unseen in a century. Characterized by intertwined opportunities and challenges, the transformation progress closely binds the fates of all stakeholders and poses more pressing and practical demands for global collaboration of the automotive industry. To this end, the global automotive industry should seize the opportunities for "incremental expansion" brought by the comprehensive reshaping of the industry chain, innovation chain, and value chain. It should focus on new demands and challenges such as cross-industrial integration, infrastructure construction, data regulation, cybersecurity, and traffic regulations to further strengthen communication and exchanges, enhance understanding and mutual trust, and deepen practical cooperation. Building on the foundation of countries leading in energy saving and NEVs, the industry should promote the efficient gathering of global innovation resources and development factors, jointly break through the bottlenecks restricting the high-level transformation and upgrading of the automotive industry, and establish a development model that can be replicated and promoted globally, driving the revitalization of the global automotive industry. Meanwhile, the industry should strengthen policy and regulation coordination and technical standard benchmarks, deepen and refine the division of labor and collaboration based on the advantages of various stakeholders, jointly create a new industrial landscape featuring openness, inclusion, cooperation, integration and common development. All stakeholders should collaboratively build a "community with a shared future on wheels" to better benefit people across the globe with the outcomes of innovative technological development.

1.4 Visions and Objectives of the Automotive Technology Development

1.4.1 Development Visions

1.4.1.1 Industrial Visions

As embodied intelligence agents of green and smart mobile spaces, future vehicles will center on smart mobility services to fulfill personalized, diversified, and integrated "point-to-point" mobility demands. They will form an open, interconnected, and shared ecosystem with other intelligent terminals, providing users with a green, safe, convenient, and comfortable service experience. The automotive industry will become an emerging industrial cluster characterized by the cross-industrial collaboration and integration of new energy, AI, and the low-altitude economy as well as sustainable development and prosperity, creating a new automotive-societal landscape featuring value symbiosis and global collaboration (Fig. 1.15).

1. **New technology: cross-industry collaboration and innovation**

Automotive innovation will be empowered by cutting-edge technologies such as new energy, AI, cloud computing, next-generation information technology, and new materials, leading to diversified automotive technological innovation methods and novel innovation paradigms of multidisciplinary convergence and cross-industry integration of multiple technologies.

2. **New product: embodied intelligence for mobility**

Vehicles will become embodied intelligence agents integrating electric drive, intelligent chassis, intelligent cockpit, on-board computing platforms, and cloud-based infrastructure platforms, enabling modular development, layered self-evolution, and integrated self-iteration.

Fig. 1.15 Blueprint for the future automotive industry and mobility

3. **New industry: synergistic and clustered aggregation**

The automotive industry will lead the shift from product intelligence to industrial intelligence, evolving into a new industrial cluster featuring cross-industrial collaboration and aggregation of multiple fields such new energy, AI, big data, the low-altitude economy, and embodied robotics, thereby creating numerous new trillion-yuan markets.

4. **New ecosystem: interconnected and networked intelligence**

The automotive industry will reshape the full-domain shared interconnection of smart transportation, smart energy, and smart cities through "autonomous driving + scenario-based services", creating a new ecosystem of multi-domain integration for smart mobility.

5. **New landscape: global opening-up and cooperation**

The global automotive industry continues to deepen the upgrading of industry chain, the reshaping of supply chain, and the reconstruction of value chain, striving for a new development paradigm featuring openness and inclusiveness, mutual benefits, and integration and cooperation.

1.4.1.2 Social Visions

1. **Green, low-carbon sustainable development**

The technological level of automotive decarbonization will continue to improve. Efficient resource utilization and environmental friendliness throughout the automotive production life cycle will be achieved through a green manufacturing system. As smart mobile energy storage units, vehicles will drive transportation and mobility, low-carbon energy, and other related industries toward green, low-carbon, and sustainable development.

2. **Safe, efficient, and smart mobility**

With vehicles as the central hub, the automotive industry will integrate in depth with smart cities, smart transportation, and smart energy sectors. This will drastically reduce traffic accidents, mitigate traffic congestion, and substantially improve transportation and urban operational efficiency, achieving safer, more efficient, and more convenient smart mobility.

3. **Cross-industry economic integration and development**

The automotive industry will achieve collaborative innovation with new technologies like new energy, AI, and big data as well as in-depth integration with emerging fields like flying cars, humanoid robots, and shared mobility services. This will promote industrial structure optimization and upgrades, create multiple cross-sector and trillion-yuan market opportunities, and build a more resilient and dynamic engine for national economic growth.

4. **Harmonious and friendly automotive society**

Coordinated development of vehicles and humans, other transportation modes, roads, and cities will be realized to meet the mobility demands of all populations of society. Vehicles will become an all-age-friendly smart living companion, seamlessly integrate into the urban rhythms, enrich the quality of life for every community, and build a harmonious and friendly automotive society that embraces technology for social good and human-centric symbiosis.

1.4.2 Overall Objectives of Industrial Development by 2040

By 2040, the total carbon emissions will peak before the national carbon emission reduction commitment of 2030, decreasing by over 60% from the peak. A transportation system dominated by ICVs will evolve toward "zero accidents, zero casualties, and high efficiency". NEVs will become mainstream products, achieving a penetration rate of over 80% and accelerating the comprehensive electrification of the automotive industry. A mature and robust vehicle–road-cloud integration ICV infrastructure ecosystem will be established, enabling the wide deployment of high-level autonomous driving vehicles. Automotive technological innovation will achieve coordinated development with education, technology, and talent sectors, becoming a global hub for original automotive technological innovation and leading the world in original innovation capabilities. A modern automotive industrial cluster led by innovation, driven by data, and characterized by collaboration, efficiency, resilience, safety, low-carbon development, and sustainability will be established, achieving high-end, intelligent, and green development. The global competitiveness of independent brands will be significantly enhanced, and key component enterprises will deeply integrate into the global industrial system, positioning China among the world's leading automotive powerhouses.

China's overall objectives and major milestones for automotive technology development are shown in Fig. 1.16.

1.4.3 Key Technologies

Driven by the decarbonization, intelligentization, and digitalization of technological transformation in the automotive industry, and the consequent restructuring of the industrial innovation chain, value chain, and industrial chain, the research framework of *Roadmap 3.0* is reshaped from the perspective of industrial transformation to deliver technology roadmaps for both "industrial products" and "automotive manufacturing". The Automotive Product Technology Roadmap encompasses four major technologies, namely energy saving technology, new energy technology,

			2030	2035	2040
Overall development objective			The total carbon emissions of the automotive industry will reach its peak around 2028, ahead of the national carbon reduction commitment, and the total emissions will drop by more than 60% from the peak by 2040;		
			A transportation system dominated by ICVs will evolve toward "zero accidents, zero casualties, and high efficiency";		
			The penetration rate of NEVs will exceed 80% by 2040, accelerating the comprehensive eletrification progress of the automotive industry.		
			Create a mature and sound vehicle-road-cloud integration ICV infrastructure ecosystem High-level autonomous driving vehicle products achieve large-scale application.		
			Ensure the coordinated and integrated development of education, technology, and talent in automotive technological innovation, positioning China as a global hub for original automotive technological innovation and global leader in original innovation capabilities.		
			An innovation-led, data- and AI-driven, collaborated, efficient, resilient, safe and sustainable modern automotive industrial cluster will be established, achieving high-end, intelligent, and green development.		
			The global competitiveness of independent brands will be significantly enhanced, and key component enterprises will deeply integrate into the global industrial system, positioning China among the world's leading automotive powerhouses.		
Major milestones	Passenger vehicle	product market	Passenger HEVs account for 80% of the sales of new traditional energy passenger vehicles; Fuel-powered passenger vehicles account for 20% of the sales of new traditional energy passenger vehicles.	Traditional energy passenger vehicles transition to complete hybridization.	Traditional energy passenger vehicles transition to complete hybridization.
			Passenger NEVs account for around 70% of the annual sales of new passenger vehicles, with a BEV to PHEV ratio of 5:5.	New energy passenger vehicles account for over 80% of the annual sales of new passenger vehicles, with a BEV to PHEV ratio of 6:4.	New energy passenger vehicle sales account for over 85% of the annual sales of new passenger vehicles, with a BEV:PHEV ratio of 8:2.
			Level 2 and above intelligent connected passenger vehicles shall achieve full popularization in new passenger vehicle sales; Intelligent connected passenger vehicles with Level 3/Level 4 (L3/L4) functionality shall account for over 35% of annual new passenger vehicle sales.	Level 2 and above intelligent connected passenger vehicles shall achieve full popularization in new passenger vehicle sales; Intelligent connected passenger vehicles with Level 3/Level 4 (L3/L4) functionality shall account for over 70% of annual new passenger vehicle sales.	Level 4 systems are comprehensively popluarized in ICVs and Level 5 ICVs begin to enter the market.
		Technological innovation	The average fuel consumption for new traditional energy passenger vehicles reaches 5.0 L/100 km (WLTC); The average fuel consumption of new hybrid passenger vehicles reach 4.5 L/100 km (WLTC).	The average fuel consumption for new traditional energy passenger vehicles reaches 4.0 L/100 km (WLTC); The average fuel consumption of new hybrid passenger vehicles reach 4.0 L/100 km (WLTC).	The average fuel consumption for new traditional energy passenger vehicles reaches 3.5 L/100 km (WLTC); The average fuel consumption of new hybrid passenger vehicles reach 3.5 L/100 km (WLTC).
			The average carbon emissions intensity for passenger vehicles decrease by over 30% compared with 2024.	The average carbon emissions intensity for passenger vehicles decrease by over 45% compared with 2024.	The average carbon emissions intensity for passenger vehicles decrease by over 60% compared with 2024.
			The energy consumption of typical technologically leading A-segment EVs under comprehensive working conditions is less than 10 kWh/100 km (CLTC).	The energy consumption of typical technological leading A-segment EVs under comprehensive working conditions is less than 9.5 kWh/100 km (CLTC).	The energy consumption of typical technological leading A-segment EVs under comprehensive working conditions is less than 9.2 kWh/100 km (CLTC).
			The average hydrogen consumption of passenger vehicles under comprehensive working conditions is less than 0.7 kg/100 km (CLTC).	The average hydrogen consumption of passenger vehicles under comprehensive working conditions is less than 0.65 kg/100 km (CLTC).	The average hydrogen consumption of passenger vehicles under comprehensive working conditions is less than 0.6 kg/100 km (CLTC).
			The mass energy density of high-energy-density NEV batteries is not less than 500 Wh/kg.	The mass energy density of high-energy-density NEV batteries is not less than 600 Wh/kg.	The mass energy density of high-energy-density NEV batteries is not less than 700 Wh/kg.
	Commercial vehicle	product market	Commercial HEVs accounted for 20% of the sales of new traditional energy commercial vehicles; Low- and zero-carbon solutions for commercial vehicles commence demonstration operation.	Commercial HEVs accounted for 40% of the sales of new traditional energy commercial vehicles; The penetration rate of low-carbon and zero-carbon ICEs account for over 8% of the annual sales of new traditional energy commercial vehicles.	Hybrid sales accounted for 65% of new commercial vehicle sales powered by traditional energy sources. The penetration rate of low-carbon and zero-carbon ICEs account for over 15% of the annual sales of new traditional energy commercial vehicles.
			Commercial NEVs account for around 30% of the annual sales of new commercial vehicles.	Commercial NEVs account for around 55% of the annual sales of new commercial vehicles.	Commercial NEVs accounted for 75% of the annual sales of new traditional energy commercial vehicles;
			Commercial ICVs with Level 2 and above autonomous driving systems account for over 50% of the annual sales of new commercial vehicles.	Commercial ICVs with Level 2 and above autonomous driving systems account for over 85% of the annual sales of new commercial vehicles, and vehicles with Level 4 functionality account for over 35%.	Level 4 systems are comprehensively popluarized in ICVs and Level 5 ICVs begin to enter the market.
		Technological innovation	Heavy-duty, long-haul fuel tractors (49 t) will achieve a decrease by 13% in fuel consumption as well as a decrease by 16% in average carbon emission intensity compared with 2024.	Heavy-duty, long-haul fuel tractors (49 t) will achieve a decrease by 22% in fuel consumption as well as a decrease by 29% in average carbon emission intensity compared with 2024.	Heavy-duty, long-haul fuel tractors (49 t) will achieve a decrease by 27% in fuel consumption as well as a decrease by 41% in average carbon emission intensity compared with 2024.
			The energy consumption of technologically leading heavy-duty long-haul EV tractors (49 t) under comprehensive working conditions is less than 135 kWh/100 km (CHTC).	The energy consumption of technologically leading heavy-duty long-haul EV tractors (49 t) under comprehensive working conditions is less than 128 kWh/100 km (CHTC).	The energy consumption of technologically leading heavy-duty long-haul EV tractors (49 t) under comprehensive working conditions is less than 122 kWh/100 km (CHTC).
			The energy consumption of typical technologically leading EV buses (12 m) under comprehensive working conditions is less than 58 kWh/100 km (CHTC).	The energy consumption of typical technologically leading EV buses (12 m) under comprehensive working conditions is less than 54 kWh/100 km (CHTC).	The energy consumption of typical technologically leading EV buses (12 m) under comprehensive working conditions is less than 51 kWh/100 km (CHTC).
			The average hydrogen consumption of medium and heavy-duty commercial vehicles under comprehensive operating conditions (CHTC) is less than 8kg/100km.	Medium and heavy-duty commercial vehicles have an average hydrogen consumption of less than 7 kg/100 km under comprehensive operating conditions (CHTC).	The average hydrogen consumption of medium- and heavy-duty commercial vehicles under comprehensive operating conditions (CHTC) is less than 6 kg/100 km.

Fig. 1.16 Objectives and major milestones for the development of China's automotive industry

intelligent connection technology, and common supporting technology. The Automotive Manufacturing Technology Roadmap incorporates an intelligent manufacturing technology roadmap.

This established the "1 + 5 + X" research framework for *Technology Roadmap 3.0*, which focuses on five major technologies and 26 key specialized technologies selected in key technology directions therein, as shown in Fig. 1.17.

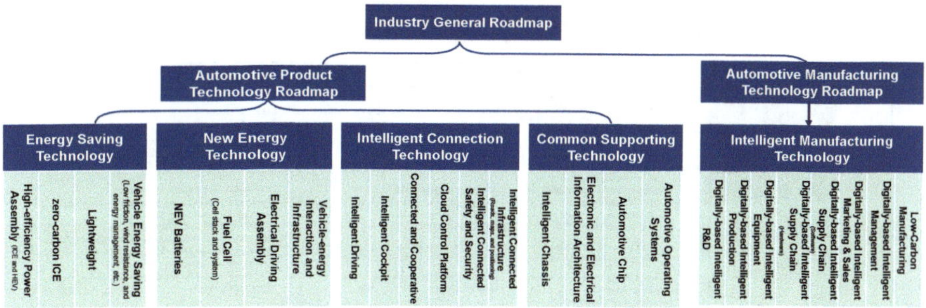

Fig. 1.17 "1 + 5 + X" Technological framework

1.5 Overall Roadmap for Industry Development

Based on *Technology Roadmap 2.0*, *Technology Roadmap 3.0* comprehensively considers the global trends of automotive transformation and technological innovation, as well as the emerging changes, demands, and missions in the development of China's automotive industry. Focusing on thematic research outcomes on five key technologies, it balances current situations with long-term visions to coordinate the overall progress and targeted breakthroughs. Adhering to the guiding principles of innovation, coordination, green development, openness, and sharing, it establishes an overall roadmap for China's automotive industry as well as roadmaps for key areas, as shown in Fig. 1.18.

			2030	2035	2040
Product Market	Market size		Annual automotive production and sales volume reached 38 million units.	Annual automotive production and sales volume reached 40 million units.	Annual automotive production and sales volume reached 41 million units.
	Market structure	Traditional energy vehicles	Passenger HEVs account for 80% of the sales of new traditional energy passenger vehicles. Passenger ICEs account for 20% of the sales of new traditional energy passenger vehicles.	Traditional energy passenger vehicles transition to complete hybridization .	
			Hybrid vehicles account for over 20% of the annual sales of new traditional energy commercial vehicles. Low- and zero-carbon solutions for commercial vehicles commence demonstration operation.	HEVs account for over 40% of the annual sales of new traditional energy commercial vehicles. The penetration rate of low-carbon and zero-carbon ICEs account for over 8% of the annual sales of new traditional energy commercial vehicles.	HEVs account for over 65% of the annual sales of new traditional energy commercial vehicles. The penetration rate of low-carbon and zero-carbon ICEs account for over 15% of the annual sales of new traditional energy commercial vehicles.
		NEVs	Passenger NEVs account for around 70% of the annual sales of new passenger vehicles; The BEV:PHEV ratio stands at 5:5.	Passenger NEVs account for over 80% of the annual sales of new passenger vehicles; The BEV:PHEV ratio stands at 6:4.	Passenger NEVs account for over 85% of the annual sales of new passenger vehicles; The BEV:PHEV ratio stands at 8:2.
			Commercial NEVs account for around 30% of the annual sales of new commercial vehicles.	Commercial NEVs account for around 55% of the annual sales of new commercial vehicles.	New commercial vehicle sales of new energy vehicles account for about 75% of the annual sales of new commercial vehicles.
			The ownership of hydrogen fuel cell vehicles reaches over 500,000 units.	The ownership of hydrogen fuel cell vehicles reaches over 1 million units.	The ownership of hydrogen fuel cell vehicles reaches over 4 million units.
		ICVs	Level 2 and above intelligent connected passenger vehicles shall achieve full popularization in new passenger vehicle sales, while Level 2 and above intelligent connected commercial vehicles shall account for over 50% of annual new commercial vehicle sales	Level 2 and above intelligent connected passenger vehicles shall achieve full popularization in new passenger vehicle sales, while Level 2 and above intelligent connected commercial vehicles shall account for over 85% of annual new commercial vehicle sales	
			Intelligent connected passenger vehicles with Level 3/Level 4 (L3/L4) functionality shall account for over 35% of annual new passenger vehicle sales, while commercially operated autonomous vehicles with Level 4 functionality (including robotaxis, ride-hailing vehicles, long-haul logistics vehicles, etc.) shall achieve new sales volumes reaching tens of thousands	Intelligent connected passenger vehicles with Level 3/Level 4 (L3/L4) functionality shall account for over 70% of annual new passenger vehicle sales, intelligent connected commercial vehicles with Level 4 functionality shall comprise over 35% of annual new commercial vehicle sales, and commercially operated autonomous vehicles with Level 4 functionality (including robotaxis, ride-hailing vehicles, long-haul logistics vehicles, etc.) shall achieve new sales volumes reaching millions	Level 4 systems are comprehensively popluarized in ICVs and Level 5 ICVs begin to enter the market.
			New vehicles with collaborative minding and early warning functions account for over 90% of the annual sales of new vehicles. C-ADAS is deployed in over 50% of the vehicles with driving assistance systems, and C-ADS is deployed in over 30% of autonomous driving vehicles.	C-ADAS/C-ADS become mainstream functions.	
Technological innovation	Energy saving technology		The average fuel consumption for new traditional energy passenger vehicles reaches 5.0 L/100 km (WLTC); The average fuel consumption of new hybrid passenger vehicles reach 4.5 L/100 km (WLTC); The energy consumption of typical technologically leading B-segment PHEVs (CS mode) achieve 3.4 L/100km (WLTC); The average carbon emissions intensity for passenger vehicles decrease by over 30% compared with 2024; The fuel consumption of heavy-duty, long-haul fuel tractors (49 t) will decrease by over 13% compared with 2024; The average carbon emission intensity of heavy-duty, long-haul tractors (49t) will decrease by over 16% compared with 2024.	The average fuel consumption for new traditional energy passenger vehicles reaches 4.0 L/100 km (WLTC); The average fuel consumption of new hybrid passenger vehicles reach 4.0 L/100 km (WLTC); The energy consumption of typical technologically leading B-segment PHEVs (CS mode) achieve 3.1 L/100km (WLTC); The average carbon emissions intensity for passenger vehicles decrease by over 45% compared with 2024; The fuel consumption of heavy-duty, long-haul fuel tractors (49 t) will decrease by over 22% compared with 2024; The average carbon emission intensity of heavy-duty, long-haul tractors (49t) will decrease by over 29% compared with 2024.	The average fuel consumption for new traditional energy passenger vehicles reaches 3.5 L/100 km (WLTC); The average fuel consumption of new hybrid passenger vehicles reach 3.5 L/100 km (WLTC); The energy consumption of typical technologically leading B-segment PHEVs (CS mode) achieve 2.9 L/100km (WLTC); The average carbon emissions intensity for passenger vehicles decrease by over 60% compared with 2024; The fuel consumption of heavy-duty, long-haul fuel tractors (49 t) will decrease by over 27% compared with 2024; The average carbon emission intensity of heavy-duty, long-haul tractors (49 t) will decrease by over 41% compared with 2024.
	New energy technology		The energy consumption of typical technologically leading A-segment EVs under comprehensive working conditions is less than 10 kWh/100 km (CLTC); The average hydrogen consumption of passenger vehicles under comprehensive working conditions is less than 0.7 kg/100 km (CLTC); The mass energy density of high-energy-density NEV batteries is not less than 500 Wh/kg; The energy consumption of technologically leading heavy-duty long-haul EV tractors (49 t) under comprehensive working conditions is less than 135 kWh/100 km (CHTC); The energy consumption of typical technologically leading EV buses (12 m) under comprehensive working conditions is less than 58 kWh/100 km (CHTC); The average hydrogen consumption of medium and heavy-duty commercial vehicles under comprehensive working conditions (CHTC) is less than 8 kg/100 km.	The energy consumption of typical technological leading A-segment EVs under comprehensive working conditions is less than 9.5 kWh/100 km (CLTC); The average hydrogen consumption of passenger vehicles under comprehensive working conditions is less than 0.65 kg/100 km (CLTC); The mass energy density of high-energy-density NEV batteries is not less than 600 Wh/kg; The energy consumption of technologically leading heavy-duty long-haul EV tractors (49 t) under comprehensive working conditions is less than 128 kWh/100 km (CHTC); The energy consumption of typical technologically leading EV buses (12 m) under comprehensive working conditions is less than 54 kWh/100 km (CHTC); The average hydrogen consumption of medium and heavy-duty commercial vehicles under comprehensive working conditions (CHTC) is less than 7 kg/100 km.	The energy consumption of typical technological leading A-segment EVs under comprehensive working conditions is less than 9.2 kWh/100 km (CLTC); The average hydrogen consumption of passenger vehicles under comprehensive working conditions is less than 0.6 kg/100 km (CLTC); The mass energy density of high-energy-density NEV batteries is not less than 700 Wh/kg; The energy consumption of technologically leading heavy-duty long-haul EV tractors (49 t) under comprehensive working conditions is less than 122 kWh/100 km (CHTC); The energy consumption of typical technologically leading EV buses (12 m) under comprehensive working conditions is less than 51 kWh/100 km (CHTC); The average hydrogen consumption of medium and heavy-duty commercial vehicles under comprehensive working conditions (CHTC) is less than 6 kg/100 km.
	Intelligent connection technology		Achieve Level 3 conditional driving automation on urban roads and Level 4 high driving automation in scenarios such as highways, urban expressways, and parking; Level 3 conditional driving automation achieves not more than 3 disengagements/10,000 km on highways (industry average) and not more than 30 disengagements/10,000 km under urban working conditions (industry average); Level 4 high conditional driving automation achieves not more than 0.1 system interventions/10,000 km on highways (industry average) and not more than 0.5 system interventions/10,000 km under urban working conditions (industry average); The intervals between accidents caused by IC systems should reach 1 million km on highways (industry average) and 500,000 km under urban working conditions (industry average); Integrated Safety design and development covers intelligent driving, networked communication, and other on-board critical systems and components, initially establishing an Integrated Safety design and development system; The onboard end-to-end driving system can cover not less than 95% scenarios (industry average) ; The onboard large intelligent driving models can interpret is not less than 20 types of driving scenarios (industry average);	Level 4 high conditional driving automation is achieved on highways, urban expressways, certain scenarios, and urban streets. Level 3 conditional driving automation achieves not more than 0.3 disengagements/10,000 km on highways (industry average) and not more than 3 disengagements/10,000 km under urban working conditions (industry average); Level 4 high conditional driving automation achieves not more than 0.01 system interventions/10,000 km on highways (industry average) and not more than 0.1 system interventions/10,000 km under urban working conditions (industry average); The intervals between accidents caused by IC systems should reach 2 million km on highways (industry average) and 1 million km under urban working conditions (industry average); Integrated Safety design and development covers vehicle-road-cloud integrated critical systems and components, basically establishing an Integrated Safety design and development and operational monitoring system; The onboard end-to-end driving system can cover not less than 98% scenarios (industry average) and achieve a computation execution frequency of not less than 20 Hz (industry average); The onboard large intelligent driving models can interpret is not less than 100 types of driving scenarios (industry average), with an accuracy of not less than 98% (industry average);	Integrated vehicle-road-cloud intelligent connectivity technological architecture achieves full maturity, with AGI deployed in automotive domains. Autonomous driving systems surpass professional human drivers across safety, adaptability, efficiency, and contextual comprehension capabilities.

Fig. 1.18 Overall roadmap for the development of China's automotive industry

Technological innovation	Common support technology	Comprehensive breakthroughs will be achieved in key technologies and performance of the intelligent chassis, exemplified by the distributed intelligent chassis with integrated drive and brake system; Integrated and collaborated control of the intelligent chassis in the X, Y, and Z directions will be achieved, comprehensively enhancing its key performance; The architectural form tends to be unified, evolving from a domain-centric pattern to a centralized pattern; Intelligent connected chips support Level 4 autonomous driving capabilities and highly integrated, multi-modal interactive cockpit functionalities. Onechip technology will become the mainstream solution for multi-domain fusion chips.	New forms of intelligent chassis products will emerge, exemplified by distributed intelligent chassis based on new driving units; Integrated new driving units with highly integrated driving, braking, steering, and suspension systems will achieve mass production; Integrated architecture ensures efficient vehicle-road-cloud connection; The intelligent connected chips support the integration of Level 5 autonomous driving into all scenarios as well as the in-depth integration of AI large model algorithms and multi-modal interaction for cockpit functions;	Major upgrades of intelligent chassis will be realized for unmanned driving and new modalities of air-ground collaboration, exemplified by the split-type reconfigurable intelligent chassis; The in-depth integration of intelligent chassis and autonomous driving enables complete servitization of functional units. A vehicle-cloud integrated architecture will be completely formed, enabling large-scale computing on the cloud; Intelligent connected chips support the leap from general AI to super AI, enabling safe and sustainable intelligent driving.
	Intelligent manufacturing technology	50% enterprises will reach iM-1 in intelligent automotive manufacturing; 50% enterprises will reach iM-2 and 5% iM-3;	65% enterprises will reach iM-2 in intelligent automotive manufacturing; 30% enterprises will reach iM-3 and 5% iM-4;	15% enterprises will reach iM-2 in intelligent automotive manufacturing, 45% will reach iM-3 and 40% iM-4.
Industrial integration	Automotive-energy integration	Vehicle-to-charging-point ratio reaches (2~1.8) :1; V2G bidirectional charging terminals account for at least 10% of newly installed charging piles; Vehicle-pile-cloud certificate deployment rate will reach 20%.	Vehicle-to-charging-point ratio reaches (1.5~1):1; V2G bidirectional charging terminals account for 50% of newly installed charging piles; Vehicle-pile-cloud certificate deployment rate will reach 50%.	Vehicle-to-charging-point ratio reaches 1:(1.2-1.5); V2G bidirectional charging terminals account for 80% of newly installed charging piles; Vehicle-pile-cloud certificate deployment rate will be not less than 70%.
		Megawatt-level fast-charging standards are largely mature, the V2G standard system is essentially in place, and business models are being scaled up, providing 10-12 million kW of regulating power and 40-60 million kWh of regulating energy, with green electricity consumption accounting for 55%-60%.	The frameworks for EV engeagement in spot markets, green electricity certificate markets, carbon trading, and suppporting services markets will be in place, providing 200-300 million kW of regulating power and 400-600 million kWh of regulating electricity, with green electricity consumption accounting for 65%-70%.	Automatic charging/discharging and V2G smart energy will be widely deployed, providing 2-2.5 billion kW of power and 800-1200 million kWh of regulable electricity, with green electricity consumption accounting for 75%-80%.
		3,000 hydrogen refueling stations enables commercialized demonstration of liquid hydrogen storage and refueling stations, with an average refueling capacity of 2 t/d and a hydrogen cost at the dispenser nozzle of RMB 25/kgH2@35MPa.	5,000 hydrogen refueling stations enables large-scale operation of liquid hydrogen storage and refueling stations, with an average refueling capacity of 3 t/d and a hydrogen cost at the dispenser nozzle of RMB 20/kgH2@35MPa.	10,000-20,000 hydrogen refueling stations enables large-scale promotion of liquid hydrogen storage and refueling stations, with an average refueling capacity of 4 t/d and a hydrogen cost at the dispenser nozzle of RMB 20/kgH2@35MPa&70MPa.
		Charging stations will be widely deployed on highways, with integrated energy supply stations combining PV-ESS-swap charging/PV-ESS-hydrogen swap charging accounting for 10%-20% of all new energy supply infrastructure on highways.	Integrated energy supply stations combining PV-ESS-swap charging/PV-ESS-hydrogen swap charging will account for 30%-40% of all new energy supply infrastructure on highways, forming a fast charging and swapping energy supply trunk line corridor for highway freight.	Integrated energy supply stations combining PV-ESS-swap charging/PV-ESS-hydrogen swap charging will account for 65%-80% of all new energy supply infrastructure on highways, enabling large-scale multi-energy complementary application along freight trunk lines.
	Automotive-transportation integration	The coverage rate of smart intersections will reach 90% in key first- and second-tier cities nationwide and smart highways will account for 20% of the national highway network;	The coverage rate of smart intersections will reach 90% in key first-, second- and third-tier cities nationwide and smart highways will account for 50% of the national highway network;	The coverage rate of smart intersections will reach 100% in cities at county level or above cities nationwide and smart highways will account for 70% of the national highway network;
		Flying cars will see demonstrative applications in scenarios like emergency rescue, urgent medical response, and material delivery, with an aerial flight range of no less than 300 kilometers. Technological breakthroughs in air-ground integrated energy and power systems will be achieved; meanwhile, the development of both a general technical standard system and a dedicated airworthiness standard system for flying cars will be completed	Flying cars will expand its application scenarios to early mass-adoption cases such as low-altitude tourism and official business travel, with an aerial flight range of no less than 500 kilometers. A cross-domain regulatory standard system will be established, domestic ownership will exceed 10,000 units, and a full-cycle standard system covering "R&D, production, operation, and recycling" will be put in place.	Flying cars will further expand its application scenarios to large-scale popularization cases such as urban commuting and logistics delivery, with an aerial flight range of no less than 1,000 kilometers. Domestic ownership will exceed 100,000 units. In addition, mutual recognition of international standard systems in areas such as airworthiness certification, component general technology, and operation will be achieved
	Automotive-information integration	Fusion perception target positioning accuracy ≤ 30 cm; speed detection accuracy ≤ 0.2 m/s; mean Average Precision (mAP) ≥ 96%; traffic event recognition accuracy ≥ 98%; basic scenario cooperative decision-making accuracy ≥ 99%.	Fusion perception target positioning accuracy ≤ 20 cm; mAP ≥ 99%; speed detection accuracy ≤ 0.15 m/s; traffic event recognition accuracy ≥ 99%; cooperative decision-making accuracy ≥ 99%.	Fusion perception target positioning accuracy ≤ 20 cm;mAP≥99.5%; speed detection accuracy ≤ 0.1 m/s; traffic event recognition accuracy ≥ 99.5%. Meeting the requirements of vehicles with different levels of intelligence and connectivity for diverse cooperative perception, decision-making, and control capabilities.
		Achieve vehicle communication applications with data rates of 1 Gbit/s-10 Gbit/s. Ethernet technology commences mass production. High-performance physical layer technology will be employed. The research and validation of technologies like TSN and DDS will be completed.	Achieve vehicle communication applications with data rates of 10Gbit/s-30Gbit/s. Vehicle optical communication technology will commence large-scale deployment. Wireless technology will be adopted on passenger vehicles. Direct satellite connectivity will be enabled.	Achieve vehicle communication applications with data rates of 30 Gbit/s-50 Gbit/s. The coverage of all-optical communication technology will expand from onboard systems to vehicle-road-cloud infrastructure. A vehicle-road-cloud integration communication architecture will be completed.
	Automotive-AI integration	AI-powered vehicles will evolve into embodied intelligent agents focusing on smart mobility services and possessing smart mobility space attributes.		
		AI will profoundly empower the entire automotive manufacturing process, driving the intelligent and digital development of China's automotive industry.		
		AI will reshape the automotive industry's innovation ecosystem throughout the entire industry chain, from basic and frontier research to engineering and industrialized technological R&D, dramatically boosting the efficienty of automotive technology innovation.		
Industrial base	Innovation system	Strengthen the construction of cross-industrial technological systems and enhance networked and matrix-based collaboration among various innovation entities.		
		Build shared and basic technological outcome and industrialization platforms to improve the efficiency of technological innovation outcome transfer.		
	Supply chain system	Bridge the gaps and strengthen advantages in core foundational spare parts (components), advanced manufacturing processes, key fundamental materials, industrial technology infrastructure, and basic industrial software, making major breakthroughs in key priority areas.		
		Build "collaborative, efficient, resilient, and secure" supply chains		
	Knowledge system	Establish a new automotive talent development ecosystem that features science-education-talent collaboration and integration, in-depth industry-education integration centered on energy saving, new energy, and intelligent connection, as well as cross-industrial collaboration.		

Fig. 1.18 (continued)

Chapter 2
Energy Saving Technology

2.1 High-Efficiency Power Assembly

2.1.1 Domestic and International Technical Status Comparison

2.1.1.1 High-Efficiency Hybrid Powertrain Technologies Have Diversified Significantly, Reshaping the Competitive Landscape

1. **Hybrid powertrain for passenger vehicles**

(1) **The maximum effective thermal efficiency of dedicated hybrid engines (DHEs) continues to improve**. The maximum effective thermal efficiency of DHEs achieves progressive breakthroughs through advanced technology integration such as high compression ratios and Atkinson/Miller cycle configurations. The maximum effective thermal efficiency for DHE of Chinese vehicle manufacturer Geely's Leishen EM-i hybrid powertrain achieves 46.5%, while BYD's DM-i hybrid powertrain reaches 46.06%. The maximum effective thermal efficiency for DHE of Japanese vehicle manufacturer Nissan's e-Power hybrid powertrain achieves 46.0%, and Toyota's THS hybrid powertrain attains 41.0%.

(2) **The topological configurations of dedicated hybrid transmissions (DHTs) have diversified significantly**. Toyota's THS hybrid powertrain and GM's Voltec hybrid powertrain employ single-mode/dual-mode power-split configurations, while European vehicle manufacturers like BMW and Mercedes-Benz primarily adopt ADD-ON parallel hybrid configurations, and Honda's i-MMD hybrid powertrain features a single-gear series–parallel configuration. The topological configurations of Chinese vehicle manufacturers' DHTs demonstrate a competitive landscape of technological diversity, establishing a distinctly

Technology Roadmap for Energy Saving and New Energy Vehicles 3.0,
https://doi.org/10.1007/978-981-95-2502-7_2

Chinese technical route dominated by multi-gear series–parallel configurations, exemplified by BYD's 1DHT, GAC's and GreatWall's 2DHT, Geely's and Chery's 3DHT, and Dongfeng's 4DHT.

(3) **Intelligent technologies continue to unlock the energy-saving potential of hybrid powertrain**. Data from the European Environment Agency (EEA) show that [1] plug-in hybrid electric vehicles (PHEVs) exhibit 250% higher real-world fuel consumption than certified values. Rule-based energy management strategy (EMS) in PHEV demonstrates poor adaptability to driving cycles, resulting in limited energy saving across diverse driving cycles. Chinese vehicle manufacturers have developed predictive intelligent EMS by integrating multi-source information, enhancing hybrid powertrain operating efficiency in complex driving cycles and releasing energy-saving potential.

2. **Hybrid powertrain for commercial vehicles**

The development of hybrid powertrain for commercial vehicles abroad has benefited from accumulated advantages in automated mechanical transmissions (AMTs), with parallel hybrid powertrain predominating. Chinese vehicle manufacturers successively introduced hybrid light-duty commercial vehicles in 2023, including Geely Farizon's methanol range-extended light-duty truck and BYD's plug-in hybrid light-duty truck. For heavy-duty commercial vehicles, GreatWall launched the 8-gear series–parallel hybrid powertrain called Hi4-G, while Foton, FAW, and Dongfeng introduced P2 parallel hybrid powertrain for heavy-duty trucks.

2.1.1.2 High-Efficiency Non-hybrid Powertrain Technologies Now Match the Global Advanced Levels

1. **Commercial vehicle engines**

In 2023, the maximum effective thermal efficiency of China's heavy-duty diesel engines achieved 48–49%. In 2024, Weichai Power launched the world's first diesel engine with the maximum effective thermal efficiency of 53.09%, setting a global record. Internationally, the maximum effective thermal efficiency of Navistar's non-mass production diesel engine reached over 51.6%. The maximum effective thermal efficiency of China's heavy-duty natural gas engines attained 42%, matching the international advanced level.

2. **Commercial vehicle transmissions**

China's commercial vehicle AMTs have gradually achieved independent innovation, including integrated designs, high-performance components, and advanced software with functional safety technologies. By optimizing transmission design and manufacturing, mechanical transmission efficiency of AMT is continuously improved. It is mainly distributed in the range of 97.0–98.9% under different gears, with the average mechanical transmission efficiency of 97.3%.

3. **Commercial vehicle drive axles**

China has successfully established a commercial vehicle drive axle product systems, achieving reliability, durability, lightweighting, and low noise, with comprehensive efficiency exceeding 98.5%. However, the key technologies such as real-time monitoring of main reducer oil temperature, axle vibration, and wear conditions still require further development.

2.1.2 Outlook on Technology Development Trends

2.1.2.1 High-Efficiency Hybrid Powertrains Are Evolving Toward High Efficiency, Integration, and Intelligence

1. **DHEs pursue high thermal efficiency**

Through adopting technologies such as lean combustion, high exhaust gas recirculation (EGR) rate, the improving compression ratio and stroke-to-bore ratio, the coordinated optimization design technology of combustion system, injection system and intake system, and the advanced thermal management and intelligent control methods, thereby improving the effective thermal efficiency and expanding high-efficiency operating range for DHEs.

2. **DHTs target high efficiency and integration**

The topological configuration of DHTs is optimized for different target vehicle models and application scenarios. Technologies like low-slip gears and low-drag wet clutches enhance comprehensive transmission efficiency of hybrid powertrains. Highly integrated multi-function systems featuring efficient oil-cooled motors and motor controllers enable more compact and lightweight DHTs.

3. **Dedicated hybrid batteries (DHBs) are developing towards high energy density and intelligent management**

The R&D and application of new high-energy-density materials and lightweight materials continuously improve battery mass energy density, enhancing PHEVs range at equivalent battery weight. Intelligent technologies enable comprehensive battery management, achieving real-time state monitoring and intelligent charge/discharge process optimization to extend battery service life.

4. **The intelligent energy management of hybrid powertrain aims at personalization and global optimization**

Building on real-time status information decision-making, it comprehensively processes multi-source information including static/dynamic traffic data, driver characteristics, and driving cycles. Centered on intelligent optimization algorithms, it matches optimal power output with energy recovery logics to maintain peak hybrid powertrain efficiency across complex driving cycles, achieving global, all-domain, and all-time intelligent EMSs.

2.1.2.2 High-Efficiency Non-hybrid Powertrains Are Evolving Toward High Efficiency, Integration, and Intelligence

1. **Commercial vehicle diesel and natural gas engines pursue higher efficiency and energy savings**

Advanced diesel engine technologies including Miller cycle, high-compression-ratio pistons, and electric accessories improve diesel engine effective thermal efficiency. Natural gas engines achieve comparable effective thermal efficiency to diesel engines through high-tumble combustion system, low-pressure EGR, and high pressure direct injection (HPDI). Diesel engines integrate burner/electric heaters with two-stage selective catalytic reduction (SCR), while natural gas engines enhance three-way catalyst conversion (TWC) efficiency or adopt HPDI lean-combustion strategy for emissions control.

2. **Commercial vehicle transmissions target high efficiency, intelligence and lightweight integration**

Transmission efficiency is improved through optimized drivetrain architecture design, full helical gear sets with ground tooth process, and macro-geometry optimization for heavy-duty gears. Advanced control algorithms and sensor technologies enable real-time monitoring and intelligent adjustment of transmission operation. Aluminum alloy casings produced via high-pressure die casting achieve weight reduction.

3. **Commercial vehicle drive axles advance in efficiency, lightweighting, and intelligence**

Friction pair resistance reduction is attained through precision low-friction bearings and low-friction seals, while fine gear design increases gear transmission efficiency. Application of high-strength steel and other new materials reduces drive axle weight. Intelligent drive axle functionalities aligned with vehicle operational requirements are developed, including real-time oil temperature/quality monitoring, as well as fault detection and early warning systems.

2.1.3 Development Goals and Milestones for 2040

Through continuous optimization, innovation and upgrading of high-efficiency powertrain technologies, the key breakthroughs are being achieved toward enhanced efficiency, integration, and intelligence.

By 2030, DHEs for PHEV/hybrid electric vehicle (HEV) and range extended electric vehicle (REEV) applications will reach the maximum effective thermal efficiency of 45% and 48% respectively, with the maximum oil-electricity energy conversion rate exceeding 3.8 kW · h/L, while the hybrid powertrains achieve the electromechanical coupling comprehensive efficiency under the Worldwide Harmonized Light

Vehicles Test Cycle (WLTC) of 90.0%. Innovative design of hybrid powertrains for commercial vehicles with different load capacities and application scenarios, with heavy-duty hybrid powertrains attaining the electromechanical coupling comprehensive efficiency under the China Heavy-duty Commercial Vehicle Test Cycle (CHTC) of 85% and exceeding the maximum fuel-to-electric conversion rate of 5.0 kW · h/L. For non-hybrid powertrains, heavy-duty diesel engines will achieve the maximum effective thermal efficiency of 51%, with the high-efficiency zone coverage of 65%, and heavy-duty tractor powertrains will demonstrate energy saving under the CHTC compared to 2024 baseline of 8%.

By 2035, DHEs for PHEV/HEV and REEV applications will reach the maximum effective thermal efficiency of 46% and 49% respectively, with the maximum oil-electricity energy conversion rate exceeding 3.9 kW · h/L. The intelligent EMSs fully incorporate personalized driving characteristic information, and the hybrid powertrains achieve the electromechanical coupling comprehensive efficiency under the WLTC of 90.5%. The heavy-duty hybrid powertrains achieve the electromechanical coupling comprehensive efficiency under the CHTC of 86%, with the maximum fuel-to-electric conversion rate exceeding 5.2 kW · h/L. For non-hybrid powertrains, heavy-duty diesel engines will achieve the maximum effective thermal efficiency of 54%, with the high-efficiency zone coverage of 65%, and heavy-duty tractor powertrains will demonstrate energy saving under the CHTC compared to 2024 baseline of 13%.

By 2040, passenger vehicles will achieve hybridization, with DHEs for PHEV/HEV and REEV applications reaching the maximum effective thermal efficiency of 48% and 50% respectively. These systems will demonstrate the maximum oil-electricity energy conversion rate exceeding 4.0 kW · h/L. Intelligent EMSs have self-evolution function, and the hybrid powertrains achieve the electromechanical coupling comprehensive efficiency under the WLTC of 91.0%. The heavy-duty hybrid powertrains achieve the electromechanical coupling comprehensive efficiency under the CHTC of 87%, with the maximum fuel-to-electric conversion rate exceeding 5.4 kW · h/L. For non-hybrid powertrains, heavy-duty diesel engines will achieve the maximum effective thermal efficiency of 55%, with the high-efficiency zone coverage of 65%, and heavy-duty tractor powertrains will demonstrate energy saving under the CHTC compared to 2024 baseline of 16%.

2.1.4 Technology Roadmap

The technical architecture of "high-efficiency hybrid powertrain + high-efficiency non-hybrid powertrain" is adopted. With the continuous development goal of advancing powertrains toward higher efficiency, integration and intelligence, we support the traditional energy passenger vehicles with hybridization and the commercial vehicles with energy-saving and low-carbon. The technology roadmap for high-efficiency powertrain is shown in Fig. 2.1.

		2030	2035	2040
Overall objectives of high-efficiency powertrain		The maximum oil-electricity energy conversion rate of passenger vehicle hybrid powertrain exceeds 3.8 kW·h/L.	> 3.9 kW·h/L	> 4.0 kW·h/L
		The heavy-duty hybrid powertrain attains the electromechanical coupling comprehensive efficiency under CHTC of 85%.	86%	87%
		The heavy-duty tractor powertrain demonstrates energy savings under the CHTC compared to 2024 baseline of 8%.	13%	16%
High-efficiency hybrid powertrain	Passenger vehicle hybrid powertrain	The hybrid powertrain attains the electromechanical coupling comprehensive efficiency under WLTC of 90.0%.	90.5%	91.0%
		The dedicated hybrid engine for HEV/PHEV attains the maximum effective thermal efficiency of 45% and the high-efficiency zone coverage of 40%.	46% 40%	48% 40%
		The dedicated hybrid engine for REEV attains the maximum effective thermal efficiency of 48%.	49%	50%
	Commercial vehicle hybrid powertrain	The maximum oil-electricity energy conversion rate of heavy-duty/ medium-duty/ light-duty hybrid powertrain exceeds 5.0/4.8/4.3 kW·h/L.	> 5.2/5.0/4.5 kW·h/L	> 5.4/5.2/4.5 kW·h/L
		The medium-duty/ light-duty hybrid powertrain attains the electromechanical coupling comprehensive efficiency under CHTC of 86%/87%.	87%/88%	88%/89%
		The heavy-duty/ medium-duty/ light-duty dedicated hybrid diesel engine attains the maximum effective thermal efficiency of 53%/51%/46% and the high-efficiency zone coverage of 68%/65%/63%.	55%/53%/47% 68%/65%/63%	56%/54%/47% 68%/65%/63%
high-efficiency non-hybrid powertrain	Commercial vehicle non-hybrid powertrain	The heavy-duty/ medium-duty/ light-duty diesel engine attains the maximum effective thermal efficiency of 51%/50%/45%. The heavy-duty/ medium-duty/ light-duty natural gas engine attains the maximum effective thermal efficiency of 45%/43%/41%.	54%/52%/46% 52%/50%/43%	55%/53%/46% 54%/52%/44%
		The heavy-duty/ medium-duty/ light-duty transmission attains the torque-to-weight ratio of 11.5/7.2/6.6 N·m/kg. The heavy-duty/ medium-duty/ light-duty transmission attains the comprehensive transmission efficiency of 97.5%/97%/96.8%.	12/7.3/6.8 N·m/kg 97.7%/97.3%/97%	13/7.5/7 N·m/kg 97.8%/97.5%/97.2%

Fig. 2.1 Technology roadmap for high-efficiency powertrain

For high-efficiency hybrid powertrain, the focus areas include dedicated hybrid engines/diesel engines, transmissions, batteries, and hybrid powertrain integration and energy management. Improve the maximum effective thermal efficiency and high-efficiency zone coverage of dedicated hybrid engines/diesel engines, promote highly integrated designs of DHTs, develop high-energy–density DHBs, and accelerate the evolution of hybrid powertrain EMS toward intelligent, personalized and globally optimized solutions. **For passenger vehicle DHEs**, development priorities include variable compression ratio technology, electric accessories, ultra-lean combustion technology with lean-combustion aftertreatment, thermal insulation spraying and thermal barrier coating technologies for cylinder liners, waste heat recovery technologies, and engineering applications of advanced intelligent thermal management systems. **For commercial vehicle dedicated hybrid diesel engines**, mastering combustion mechanisms and fundamental control theories; developing intelligent combustion chamber technologies with auto-sensing and adaptive adjustment capabilities; and devising integrated diesel particulate filter (DPF) and diesel oxidation catalyst (DOC) technologies to reduce emissions. **For electromechanical coupling devices**, pioneering multi-objective optimization design for multi-gear and multi-mode topological configurations, coupled with rapid application-scenario matching techniques; refining the housing structure and oil circuit design to enable integrated deployment of multiple components, thereby reducing the axial dimension; implementing an integrated and modular hydraulic system design, developing high-capacity electronic pump-based high-efficiency hydraulic systems, and enabling real-time monitoring and automated adjustment capabilities. **For motors**, engineering novel motor architectures with high torque output and superior efficiency, advancing technologies like low-harmonic windings and short-pitch distributed windings; spearheading the development and application of low-loss and high-performance silicon steel sheets, alongside permanent magnets characterized by high remanence, strong coercivity, and minimal heavy rare-earth content; developing insulation materials resistant to high frequencies and high voltages; developing intelligent control systems capable of real-time monitoring of motor operation and dynamically optimizing performance within the high-efficiency operational range. **For motor controllers**, developing high-temperature-resistant, low-loss semiconductor materials; devising variable boost and voltage platform adaptation technologies for motors and controllers, while innovating new solutions for NVH, EMC, reliability, and functional safety; pioneering novel double-sided module welding techniques, high-temperature encapsulation materials, and advanced packaging processes. **For DHBs**, undertaking research and demonstration applications of emerging battery systems, including solid-state lithium-ion batteries and sodium-ion batteries; designing battery packs with a module-free architecture and optimizing the structural strength of battery pack enclosures; developing battery liquid cooling systems integrated with phase-change material coverage, as well as self-sensing and intelligent temperature regulation technologies. **For hybrid powertrain integration and energy management**, developing and applying EMSs incorporating ultra-perceptive multi-source spatiotemporal data fusion, along with the global intelligent energy management optimization control technologies; advancing coordinated temperature control technologies across the entire operational temperature range of hybrid powertrain, enhancing engine warm-up efficiency and thermal retention during shutdowns; developing active noise reduction and intelligent control technologies for hybrid powertrain, breaking through the bottleneck of integrated active NVH control among engines, motors, and electromechanical coupling devices.

In the realm of high-efficiency non-hybrid powertrains, the emphasis lies on diesel engines, natural gas engines, transmissions, and drive axles. The key objectives include enhancing the effective thermal efficiency of diesel engines, minimizing exhaust pollutant emissions, driving the evolution of natural gas engines towards higher efficiency and energy saving, improving transmission efficiency and achieving integration, and promoting the enhanced efficiency and integrated development of drive axles. **For diesel engines**, developing high-explosion-pressure diesel engines, equipping heavy-duty models with an explosion pressure rating of 250–270 bar, and reinforcing the strength of engine blocks and cylinder heads; mastering high-pressure common-rail technology for electronically controlled diesel engine injection, with injection pressures of heavy-duty diesel engines reaching 2,000–2,500 bar; pioneering two-stage SCR technologies, and integrating DPF and DOC to significantly reduce emissions. **For natural gas engines**, pioneering intelligent combustion control technologies with variable thermodynamic cycles to boost explosion pressure capabilities; advancing intake manifold single-point injection (SPI) and multi-point injection (MPI) systems, elevating the compression ratio to levels comparable with diesel engines; developing natural gas oxidation catalysts (GOC), gasoline particulate filters (GPF) for natural gas engines, and ammonia slip catalysts (ASC), leveraging multi-catalyst combinations to minimize post-treatment emissions. **For transmissions**, developing transmission control technologies tailored to hybrid architectures and intelligent driving systems, and mastering the design principles of integrated transmissions; establishing a comprehensive theoretical framework for friction and lubrication, deploying low-friction bearings and oil seals, and innovating low-oil-churning-resistance technologies to optimize transmission efficiency; developing and implementing lightweight high-strength steel materials, and optimizing housing topologies based on specific load scenarios to meet vehicle matching requirements. **For drive axles**, pioneering low-friction and low-oil-churning-resistance technologies to create highly efficient lubrication systems; designing intelligent differential locks, developing intelligent cleanliness monitoring systems, and establishing fault detection and early warning mechanisms for drive axles; employing lightweight materials such as hollow half shafts and aluminum alloy housings, and innovating brake structures like wedge and disc brakes to enhance overall lightweighting.

2.2 Zero-Carbon ICE

2.2.1 Domestic and International Technical Status Comparison

2.2.1.1 In China, Hydrogen Engines Lag Behind International Counterparts but Show Strong Industrial Potential

International enterprises and research institutions have an early-mover advantage in hydrogen engine technology, with significant technical foundation and innovation experience. Germany, the U.S., and Japan lead in R&D and application, having conducted road and off-road testing for multiple hydrogen engine products. In the passenger vehicle sector, major OEMs globally are actively engaged in the development and deployment of prototype hydrogen engines. Notably, Toyota is conducting parallel research and demonstrations encompassing both hydrogen fuel cell and hydrogen engine technologies. While GAC, Geely, and FAW have initiated preliminary demonstrations and operation of hydrogen engine passenger vehicle. In the commercial vehicle sector, notable examples include the 7.8L hydrogen engine co-developed by Germany's Deutz and KEYOU, adopting port fuel injection technology, now ready for mass production, and Cummins' 6.7L hydrogen direct injection engine, which is soon to be deployed in Tata trucks in India. In China, companies like Weichai, Yuchai, and FAW are accelerating the development of 13–16L heavy-duty commercial vehicle hydrogen engines for demonstrations, with small-batch production planned around 2026. While international players maintain a first-mover advantage in hydrogen engine development, enterprises and research institutions in China are rapidly closing the gap under the nation's "Dual Carbon" strategic framework. Through industry-academia-research collaboration, policy incentives, and key R&D program support, China is narrowing the gap with global leaders.

2.2.1.2 In China, Ammonia Engines Have a Relatively Good R&D Foundation, Yet They Face Challenges in the Process of Industrialization

As the world's largest producer of liquid ammonia, China possesses abundant feedstock for ammonia engine commercialization, with a well-established industrial foundation and controllable production costs. Current R&D in ammonia engines primarily focuses on stable ammonia combustion, NOx emission control, and operational range expansion. Due to ammonia's low laminar burning velocity, applications are currently limited to low-speed engines, making them particularly suitable for marine engine applications. Ammonia engines require high ignition energy, with current research primarily focusing on high-energy spark ignition or pilot-fuel ignition using diesel or biodiesel. Chinese universities, including Tsinghua University, Tianjin University, and Shanghai Jiao Tong University, have made breakthroughs in ammonia engine combustion technology, successfully achieving stable operation of ammonia-fueled engines. In 2022, China's first ammonia-diesel heavy-duty vehicle engine, jointly developed by Dongfeng Trucks Technical Center and Tsinghua University, successfully achieved ignition. However, ammonia engines still face challenges in combustion stability, toxicity, corrosiveness, as well as NOx and NH_3 emissions, remaining significantly below automotive application requirements and necessitating further research on key technological breakthroughs. Globally, ammonia engine applications in Japan, Germany, and the United States are currently limited to marine and power generation sectors, with no existing implementations in automotive applications.

2.2.2 Outlook on Technology Development Trends

2.2.2.1 Hydrogen Engines Need to Break Through Key Technologies Such as Pre-ignition and Knock and In-Cylinder Direct Injection to Achieve Industrialization

Commercial vehicle hydrogen engines have achieved preliminary technological advancements, primarily adopting port fuel injection, flat-top combustion chambers, and spark-ignition combustions. Nonetheless, in practical applications, hydrogen engines still encounter a series of challenges, including insufficient power, backfiring, pre-ignition, and low thermal efficiency. Future technological development will mainly focus on the following aspects: (1) Hydrogen in-cylinder direct injection technology; (2) Hydrogen nozzle reliability technology; (3) High-efficiency high-pressure ratio supercharging technology; (4) Advanced exhaust gas aftertreatment technology; (5) High-performance hydrogen storage technology. Furthermore, specialized technological efforts are imperative for the ignition system, lubrication system, and dedicated engine oil of hydrogen engines.

The core technical routes for future automotive hydrogen engines will predominantly incorporate a combustion strategy that integrates in-cylinder direct injection, high-compression-ratio combustion chambers, ultra-high-pressure ratio supercharging, ultra-lean combustion, and spark-plug ignition. Under high compression and supercharging ratios, ultra-lean combustion of hydrogen fuel enables more complete heat release, thereby significantly enhancing the thermal efficiency and power output of hydrogen engines. The implementation of in-cylinder direct injection technology allows for precise control of hydrogen injection timing and volume, optimizing the combustion process, reducing thermal loads, and comprehensively improving the overall engine performance. Nevertheless, due to hydrogen's wide ignition range, issues such as pre-ignition & knock under high-load conditions and the durability of high-pressure hydrogen nozzles remain significant challenges. To address these, future technological development of hydrogen engines will focus on the following aspects: (1) Optimization of high-compression-ratio combustion chambers; (2) Fine-grained design of the hydrogen in-cylinder direct injection process; (3) Pre-ignition and knock suppression technologies; (4) Thermal management technologies.

2.2.2.2 Ammonia Engines Need to Overcome Key Technologies Including Stable Combustion and the Control of NOx and NH_3 Emissions, and Explore the Feasibility of Their Application in Vehicles

Currently, the technologies and key components of ammonia engines for commercial vehicles are still in the R&D phase. Since ammonia requires ignition assistance from other fuels, various technical routes, such as mixture formation and ignition modes of dual-fuel systems (e.g., ammonia-hydrogen, ammonia-gasoline, ammonia-diesel), are still being investigated, and core key technologies remain immature. For specific application scenarios, the technical routes for automotive ammonia engines are expected to be finalized and demonstrated between 2027 and 2030. There are currently two combustion modes for automotive ammonia engines: premixing of ammonia gas + ignition with an active fuel (e.g., ammonia-diesel engines); premixing of ammonia and hydrogen gases and spark-plug ignition (e.g., ammonia-hydrogen integrated engines). In ammonia engines ignited by active fuels, ammonia and the active fuels are mixed in a specific ratio. Given ammonia's low calorific value and slow combustion rate, the thermal efficiency of such engines is comparable to that of existing gasoline or diesel engines. In the future, efforts will be made to gradually increase the ammonia fuel substitution rate. Ammonia-hydrogen integrated engines adopt an ignition approach, with ammonia and hydrogen fuels mixed in a certain ratio. Thanks to the excellent anti-knock properties of ammonia and hydrogen, a high compression ratio can be employed to achieve superior thermal efficiency. Currently, the thermal efficiency of the ammonia port fuel injection mode is relatively low. In the future, the application of ammonia in-cylinder direct injection technology is expected to achieve higher thermal efficiency and lower emissions.

Coupled with pre-chamber jet ignition technology, high-supercharging-ratio intake technology, high-pressure exhaust gas recirculation (EGR) technology, and the Miller cycle, it can effectively address issues such as difficult ignition, slow combustion, and high-load knock in ammonia engines.

2.2.3 Development Goals and Milestones for 2040

By 2030, the passenger vehicle sector will achieve significant breakthroughs in high-efficiency combustion technologies and zero-carbon fuel production processes. Hydrogen engines are expected to reach peak effective thermal efficiencies of 45%, with high-efficiency zones (maintaining such efficiencies above 40%) covering 45% of their operational ranges. Concurrently, industrialization capabilities for key components will be progressively established in China. Policy support will encourage the production and consumption of dedicated hybrid engines utilizing zero-carbon fuels, while promoting demonstration programs for hybrid passenger vehicles powered by such engines. The commercial vehicle sector will achieve industrialized production of zero-carbon engines with breakthrough in high-efficiency combustion technologies that meet or surpass the world's most stringent emission standards. Hydrogen and ammonia engines will reach peak effective thermal efficiencies of 47% and 48% respectively, with high-efficiency zones (maintaining such efficiencies above 42% and 43%) covering 45% of their operating ranges. Demonstrating commercial vehicle applications in specific scenarios such as urban buses and logistics distribution to validate the viability of zero-carbon engine technologies.

By 2035, in the field of passenger vehicles, the technology of zero-carbon engines will be fully mature. Hydrogen engines shall achieve a peak effective thermal efficiency of 47%, with 50% operational coverage in the high-efficiency zone (maintaining such efficiency above 42%). The durability and reliability of key components will be significantly improved, and the emission levels will meet the requirements of the emission regulations of the same period. The technical standards and regulatory system for and zero-carbon fuels and engines will be improved. Zero-carbon engines will gradually achieve mass production and market launch. The market penetration rate of vehicles equipped with zero-carbon engines in the market of new advanced hybrid passenger vehicles will reach 5%. In the field of commercial vehicles, the peak effective thermal efficiency of hydrogen and ammonia engines will all reach 50%, with high-efficiency zones (maintaining such efficiencies above 45%) covering 45% of their operating ranges. Differentiated combustion technology routes will be explored and applied to achieve in-cylinder high-pressure direct injection of fuels, improve the system integration and intelligent level, and form a complete zero-carbon engine industry chain, including fuel production, supply, refueling, and services. Through large-scale production and technological progress, costs will be reduced, and market competitiveness will be enhanced. The market penetration rate of vehicles equipped with zero-carbon engines in the market of new traditional energy medium and heavy-duty trucks will reach 8%.

By 2040, in the field of passenger vehicles, zero-carbon engines will gradually achieve efficient integration and optimization of the industrial chain, forming strong competitiveness and risk resistance capabilities. The peak effective thermal efficiency of hydrogen engines will reach 50%. Among them, the high-efficiency zones (maintaining such efficiency above 45%) shall achieve 50% and 45% operational coverage respectively, while zero-carbon engines reach large-scale application. The market penetration rate of vehicles equipped with zero-carbon engines in the market of new advanced hybrid passenger vehicles will reach 8%. In the field of commercial vehicles, the peak effective thermal efficiency of hydrogen and ammonia engines will all reach 52%, with high-efficiency zones (maintaining such efficiencies above 47%) covering 45% of their operating ranges. The independent controllability and high reliability of key components will be achieved, reducing external dependence. The large-scale production and application of green fuels will be realized, supporting the environmental protection goals of zero-carbon engines. Zero-carbon engines will firmly establish their market leadership in multiple pivotal domains, including heavy-duty transportation and long-haul transportation. By then, the market penetration rate of vehicles equipped with zero-carbon engines in the market of new traditional energy medium and heavy-duty trucks will reach 15%.

2.2.4 Technology Roadmap

The application scenarios of engines using zero-carbon fuels vary between passenger vehicles and commercial vehicles. Passenger vehicles mainly use hydrogen fuel engines, with the emphasis on improving combustion efficiency and reducing emissions. Commercial vehicles predominantly center on the application of hydrogen engines, concurrently delving into the viability of ammonia engine applications. Paramount importance is attached to guaranteeing durability, emission control, and superior fuel economy amidst high-power outputs and protracted high-load operational scenarios.

In the field of passenger vehicles, the technical routes of zero-carbon fuel engines incorporate hydrogen engines. Hydrogen fuel, as a clean energy source, can provide power through efficient combustion in the engine while reducing carbon emissions, thus having broad application prospects in future passenger vehicles. By 2030, the application of hydrogen engines in passenger vehicles will achieve initial breakthroughs in combustion efficiency and emission control, aiming to reach an effective thermal efficiency of 45% and meet the emission standards of the same period. Concurrently, demonstration operations will be carried out in some typical scenarios to verify the technical feasibility and stability in real—world usage environments.

In the field of commercial vehicles, scenarios such as heavy-duty vehicles and long-haul transportation are key areas for the application of hydrogen engines. Leveraging its superior mass energy density and zero-carbon emission characteristics, hydrogen fuel is poised to become the cornerstone of commercial vehicle powertrains. The stringent requirements of commercial vehicles for power, durability, and

		2030	2035	2040
Overall objectives		Achieve commercialization of low-carbon and zero-carbon engines, drive breakthroughs in combustion technology, enhance product thermal efficiency, and conduct demonstration operations in specific application scenarios	Further improve the thermal efficiency of low-carbon and zero-carbon engine products, with vehicles equipped with such engines accounting for 5% of new advanced hybrid passenger vehicle sales and 8% new medium and heavy-duty truck sales in the traditional energy sector	Low-carbon and zero-carbon engines achieve peak thermal efficiency, with vehicles equipped with such engines accounting for 8% of new advanced hybrid passenger vehicle sales and 15% of new medium and heavy-duty truck sales in the traditional energy sector
Passeng er vehicle	Hydroge n engines	Hydrogen engines achieve a peak effective thermal efficiency of 45%, with high-efficiency zone coverage reaching 45%	Hydrogen engines achieve a peak effective thermal efficiency of 47%, with high-efficiency zone coverage reaching 50%	Hydrogen engines achieve a peak effective thermal efficiency of 50%, with high-efficiency zone coverage reaching 50%
		C-segment passenger cars equipped with hydrogen engines achieve a hydrogen consumption of 1.35 kg/100 km under the CLTC	C-segment passenger cars equipped with hydrogen engines achieve a hydrogen consumption of 1.15 kg/100 km under the CLTC	C-segment passenger cars equipped with hydrogen engines achieve a hydrogen consumption of 1.1 kg/100 km under the CLTC
		Hydrogen engines meet contemporary emission standards		
		Achieve breakthroughs in hydrogen engine combustion technology, and conduct demonstration operations in selected scenarios	Achieve productization and integration into applications for hydrogen engines, and progressively realize full commercialization	Hydrogen engines are progressively achieving large-scale application
Comme rcial vehicle	Hydroge n engines	Hydrogen engines achieve a peak effective thermal efficiency of 47%, with high-efficiency zone coverage (where BTE ≥ 42%) reaching 45%	Hydrogen engines achieve a peak effective thermal efficiency of 50%, with high-efficiency zone coverage (where BTE ≥ 45%) reaching 45%	Hydrogen engines achieve a peak effective thermal efficiency of 52%, with high-efficiency zone coverage (where BTE ≥ 47%) reaching 45%
		Master the high-efficiency combustion mechanisms of hydrogen engines	Master ultra-lean combustion technology and high-boost-ratio intake technology	Master hydrogen high-pressure direct injection (HPDI) diffusion combustion technology
		The hydrogen consumption of a 49-tonne tractor-trailer is less than 11kg/100km	The hydrogen consumption of a 49-tonne tractor-trailer is less than 10.5kg/100km	The hydrogen consumption of a 49-tonne tractor-trailer is less than 10kg/100km
	Ammoni a engines	Ammonia engines achieve a peak effective thermal efficiency of 48%, with high-efficiency zone coverage (where BTE ≥ 43%) reaching 45%	Ammonia engines achieve a peak effective thermal efficiency of 50%, with high-efficiency zone coverage (where BTE ≥ 45%) reaching 45%	Ammonia engines achieve a peak effective thermal efficiency of 52%, with high-efficiency zone coverage (where BTE ≥ 47%) reaching 45%
		Master the high-efficiency combustion mechanisms of ammonia engines, as well as ammonia gaseous fuel port injection technology and pre-chamber technology	Master ammonia in-cylinder low-pressure direct injection technology and ultra-lean combustion technology	Master liquid ammonia in-cylinder high-pressure direct injection and stratified ultra-lean combustion technologies
		The ammonia consumption of a 49-tonne tractor-trailer is less than 69kg/100km	The ammonia consumption of a 49-tonne tractor-trailer is less than 67kg/100km	The ammonia consumption of a 49-tonne tractor-trailer is less than 64kg/100km

Fig. 2.2 Comprehensive technology roadmap for zero-carbon engines

High-load operation makes hydrogen engines particularly critical for this sector. By 2030, commercial vehicles equipped with hydrogen engines will enter the demonstration phase, leveraging combustion optimization and emission control technologies to achieve efficient and environmentally friendly operation. Ammonia, as a burgeoning zero-carbon fuel, has garnered increasing attention for its application in commercial vehicles. Ammonia engines are primarily deployed in long-haul transportation and heavy-duty vehicle applications, particularly for commercial vehicles requiring sustained high-load operation. While ammonia fuel offers advantages in volumetric energy density and reduced carbon emissions, challenges remain in controlling NOx and NH_3 emissions. By 2035, the commercial vehicle sector is projected to achieve technological breakthroughs in ammonia engines through optimized combustion processes and enhanced emission control capabilities. By 2040, ammonia engines are expected to emerge as a viable powertrain option for commercial vehicles.

The comprehensive technology roadmap for zero-carbon engines is shown in Fig. 2.2.

2.3 Lightweight

2.3.1 Domestic and International Technical Status Comparison

2.3.1.1 Comparison of Automotive Lightweight Structure Design at Home and Abroad

(1) **Highly integrated design of component structure**

Against the backdrop of the increasingly severe global energy and environmental crisis, the automotive industry, as a key sector of energy consumption and carbon emissions, has become a key position for advancing the "dual-carbon" strategy, and at the same time is one of the key tasks for automotive manufacturers to fulfill their social responsibilities. At the same time, a series of cutting-edge technologies such as new automotive steel, high-strength magnesium alloy and aluminum alloy, basalt fiber composite material and multi-material body assembly structure, CTB/CTC new architecture design, highly integrated design of parts and components, and integrated molding process are constantly emerging. Driven by a new round of scientific and technological innovations such as electrification and intelligentization, it has given new connotation to the lightweighting of future automobiles.

Tesla took the lead in adopting one-piece die-cast aluminum alloy body part integration design technology globally, triggering a global research boom in highly integrated component design. In September 2020, the rear floor of Tesla Model Y took the lead in adopting this technology, reducing more than 70 parts and lowering the weight of body-in-white by about 20%. In May 2022, Volkswagen rolled off the production line of a one-piece die-cast aluminum alloy rear body part, which integrated more than 30 parts. This marked the first application for the development of pure electric vehicles under the Trinity project on the SSP platform, achieving a weight reduction of 10 kg. In June 2023, Toyota announced that the rear floor of a certain Lexus body adopted the one-piece die-casting aluminum alloy parts technology, integrating more than 80 parts. Since 2021, Chinese automakers including NIO, Ideal, Xiaomi, Geely and Chang'an and other automotive companies have adopted the technology and developed one-piece die-casting front and rear floors of passenger cars.

In terms of integrated design of ultra-high-strength steel parts, one-piece hot-formed steel door rings have been industrialized by Leapmotor, Great Wall Motor and other enterprises. Meanwhile, the Lightweight Alliance has joined hands with CITIC Metals, Baosteel, Ansteel, China Automotive Research Institute, Great Wall Motor, Ruilan Auto and other enterprises to jointly develop one-piece double door rings and floor longitudinal and transverse beams, which provide a new option for the integrated design and manufacturing of high-strength steel parts.

(2) **Body CTC/CTB new architecture innovation design**

In October 2021, Tesla took the lead in launching CTB body technology, which realizes the integration of the body with the top cover of the battery pack, pioneering the fusion of the body and the power battery system in innovative design. In May 2022, BYD released the Corsair model equipped with CTB technology, through the CTB integration of the battery pack of the blade battery module with the body, enables the body to reach a torsional stiffness of 40,500 Nm/°, the volume utilization rate of the power battery system reaches 66%, and the lightweight coefficient of the body reaches 1.75. The technology provides innovative ideas for the design of a new architecture for new energy vehicles. Since then, Leapmotor, Changan Auto, Dongfeng Motor, Li Auto and other enterprises have also developed CTB technology, which further enriches and improves the design method and evaluation system of the new architecture of the body and power battery system. In 2024, the world's first ultra-high-safety skateboard chassis applying CTC technology-"CATL Granite Chassis" was officially launched. "Granite Chassis", the world's first ultra-high safety skateboard chassis applying CTC technology, was officially released, which redefined the safety standard of intelligent chassis. A comparison of domestic and international developments in the field of lightweight design of automotive structures are shown in Table 2.1.

Table 2.1 Domestic comparison of lightweight design of automotive structures

Comparison program	Domestic situation	Situation abroad	Comparative results
Highly integrated design of component structures	Aluminum flooring, thermoformed steel sheets, double door rings and other parts have been industrialized and applied	First to industrialize aluminum alloy flooring, thermoformed steel single and double door ring components	Relatively backward in the country
Battery pack and body CTB integration design	Several automotive companies have industrialized CTB technology	Tesla first to industrialize CTB technology	Comparable domestic and international levels
Cell and chassis integrated CTC skateboard chassis design	PIX, Yojimbo and other car companies have already developed CTC models	RIVIAN, CANNO and others take the lead in developing CTC skateboard chassis models	Relatively backward in the country
Structural intelligent design	Structural intelligent design methodology and software under development	Structural AI design methodology under development	Comparable domestic and international levels

2.3.1.2 Automotive Lightweight Materials Comparison of Domestic and Foreign Technologies

Comparison of Domestic and Foreign Technologies for Automotive Steel

Cold-fomed steels at home and abroad have developed a quenching distribution QP steel, phase-change induced plasticity TRIP steel, twin-induced plasticity TWIP steel, excellent forming two-phase DH steel, excellent forming composite phase CH steel, phase-change-assisted bainite TBF steel and martensitic steel, ultra-fine grain coverings with UF steel and other new steels, the strength level of up to 1,300 MPa—1,700 MPa. Such as Baosteel developed 1,700 MPa roll forming steel, Japan developed 1,500 MPa cold-stamping steel, etc. For example, Baosteel has developed 1700 MPa roll forming steel, and Japan has developed 1500 MPa cold stamping steel.

Hot-formed steel is the current hot spot of steel research and application for lightweighting at home and abroad. Bare plate, aluminum–silicon coated, galvanized and uncoated hot forming steels of 500–2200 MPa level have been developed. Such as ArcelorMittal and Bensteel developed 2000 MPa hot forming steel, POSCO of Korea developed 1700 MPa hot forming steel, CITIC Metals, Beijing Institute of Technology and Tangshan Steel jointly developed 2000 MPa hydrogen embrittlement-resistant hot-formed steel HEROs2000, Suzhou Yucai Tong joint MaGang developed 500–2200 MPa high toughness aluminum–silicon coated hot forming steel, Sumitomo developed 1800 MPa hot forming steel and so on. 1800 MPa hot forming steel, etc., the United States plans to raise the tensile strength of hot forming steel to 2000 MPa by 2025. Ultra-high-strength steel materials at home and abroad, such as Table 2.2 shows.

Comparison of Domestic and International Technologies of Light Alloys for Automobiles

Along with aluminum, magnesium alloy in the automobile application continues to deepen, the body of large structural parts of one-piece die-casting aluminum alloy technology industrialization application development is rapid. In the field of die-casting equipment, the rapid development of large-scale die-casting machine of LiJin science and technology, YiZhiMi, Haitian metals and other with a maximum tonnage of 16000 tons, can meet the demand for large-scale die-casting equipment of automobile enterprises. In terms of basic materials, Lizhong Group, Chinalco and other enterprises actively layout, the development of Al-Mg and Al-Si series of high strength and toughness of aluminum alloys and other materials. In the parts manufacturing link, Guangzhou Hongtu, CITIC Dicastal and other enterprises have made inroads in the integrated die-casting field. At the same time, Shanghai Jiao Tong University and other institutions have developed rare earth aluminum alloys and ceramic aluminum materials, whose tensile strength reaches 600–800 MPa, providing

Table 2.2 Comparison of domestic and international technologies for ultra-high-strength steel materials

Comparison Program	National level	Foreign level	Comparative results
High-strength steel for the body Application ratio	Highest 81.5% in China (Great Wall Blue Mountains)	80% Of high-strength steel used in VW ID.UNYX bodies	Comparable domestic and international levels
Commercial vehicle cabs	The main use of Dc series, 340 grade, 510 MPa, 590 MPa, 1500 MPa hot-forming steel, high-strength steel and advanced high-strength steel, etc. accounted for about 40 percent	Mainly used 340 MPa, 510 MPa, 590 MPa, 700 MPa and 980 MPa, 1500 MPa level, high strength steel and advanced high strength steel, etc. 70% or more	Relatively backward
Hot forming steels	Developed 500-2200 MPa aluminum–silicon coating, bare plate and other products; 1500 MPa and 2200 MPa steel VDA cold bending angle of 60°, 45°, respectively	Developed 1500-2000 MPa bare plate, aluminum–silicon coated hot forming steel and other products; 1500 MPa steel VDA cold bending angle 55°-60°	World leader
	Mainly hot press molding process, supplemented by hot air uplift molding process	Mainly using hot stamping and molding process	World leader
Cold forming steels	1300 MPa, 1500 MPa, 1700 MPa, roll forming mainly	1300 MPa, 1500 MPa, 1700 MPa, roll and cold press molding	Considerable domestic and international
Plate spring steel	High strength up to 2000 MPa	High strength up to 1800 MPa	World leader

a new choice of high-performance aluminum alloys for automotive chassis structural components.

Magnesium alloy will also play an important role in automotive lightweighting. In 2021, Japan developed a tensile strength of 448 MPa, elongation of 15% of the magnesium alloy products, as well as tensile strength of more than 280 MPa high-pressure casting of magnesium alloy, elongation remains at 11%. The United States has developed AZ91D magnesium alloy for thin-walled parts, as well as AZ31B and AZ61A magnesium alloys for structural parts of the body. 2023, the National Engineering Research Center for Magnesium Alloys of Chongqing University developed high strength magnesium alloys with room temperature tensile strength of up to 330 MPa, yield strength of 285 MPa, and elongation rate of 11%. Vehicle magnesium, aluminum alloy materials and forming domestic and international comparisons such as shown in Table 2.3.

Table 2.3 Comparison of domestic and international technologies for magnesium and aluminum alloy materials

Makings	Comparison program	National level	Foreign level	Comparative results
Aluminum	Key properties of 6 series aluminum alloys	Maximum tensile strength of profile: 420 MPa, fatigue strength >150 MPa, elongation > 12%	Maximum tensile strength of profile: 400 MPa, fatigue strength >140 MPa, elongation > 10%	World leader
		Plate 6061-T6: Tensile strength 290 ~ 330 MPa, Yield strength 240 ~ 280 MPa, Elongation 10–15%	Plate 6061-T6: Tensile strength 310 ~ 350 MPa, Yield strength 250 ~ 300 MPa, Elongation 10–15%	Par
	Key properties of Al-Si casting alloys and molding process and equipment	Tensile strength 320 MPa, fatigue strength >130 MPa, elongation 8%; long filling test flow distance 1750 mm	Tensile strength 320 MPa, fatigue strength >102 MPa, elongation 8%; long filling test flow distance 1800 mm	Par
		Integrated die casting production efficiency of 120 s per piece	Tesla productivity is 80 ~ 90 s per piece	Relatively backward
		Forming equipment at 16,000 tons	Forming equipment under 10,000 tons	World leader
		Die-casting molding yield rate 90%	Tesla's die-cast molding yield is 95%	Relatively backward
	Stamping and forming	Mold life 4 million times	Mold life 10 million times	Relatively backward
	Extrusion molding	Extruded flat die life 20 ~ 30 tons/die	Extruded flat die life 50 tons/die	Relatively backward
Key properties of magnesium alloys	Die-casting magnesium alloy	Tensile strength 250 ~ 300 MPa, good flowability	Tensile strength 200 ~ 250 MPa, good flowability	World leader
	Casting magnesium alloy	(1) 350 MPa grade, 5 ~ 15% parts with a projected area of up to 2.2 m^2; (2) deformed magnesium alloy: 550 MPa grade, 10 ~ 20%	(1) 300 MPa level, 5 ~ 10%; (2) Deformed magnesium alloy: 500 MPa grade, 10–15%	World leader

Table 2.4 Domestic and international technology comparison of composites and engineering plastics

Comparison program	National level	Foreign level	Comparative results
Carbon fiber for automotive	12–24 K Tow and 300GPa high modulus carbon fiber have been applied in batch, and 48 K/50 K have industrialization conditions	Toray/Hersey and other 12–24 K and 300GPa high modulus carbon fiber industry has been applied in large quantities, and is developing 300/600 K	Large tow carbon fiber lags Behind in China
Carbon fiber composites for automotive applications	T300 Grade carbon fiber has been widely used, T700/T800 grade carbon fiber has been applied in mass production but the quality is not stable, and T1000 is applied in small quantities	T300–T800 Grade carbon fiber in bulk with good batch stability, T1000 grade CFRP in small batches	Relatively backward in the country
Carbon fiber composite molding and applications	Molding efficiency ≤5 min, fast curing resin within 5 min, mostly used for exterior parts	Molding efficiency ≤4 min, fast curing resin within 2 min, for structural and exterior parts	Relatively backward in the country
Engineering plastics	Polypropylene PP, polycarbonate PC, nylon PA, ABS and other engineering plastics for parts such as bumpers, wings and door guards	Polypropylene PP, polycarbonate PC, nylon PA, ABS and other engineering plastics for parts such as bumpers, wings and door guards	Considerable domestic and international
Glass fiber reinforced composites	PP-LFT, PA-LFT, SMC, etc., used for instrument panel frames, front-end modules, battery compartment covers, and commercial vehicle cab exteriors	PP-LFT, PA-LFT, SMC, etc., used for instrument panel frames, front-end modules, battery compartment covers, and commercial vehicle cab exteriors	Considerable domestic and international

Comparison of Domestic and International Technologies for Automotive Lightweight Non-metallic Materials

Non-metallic materials are pivotal to automotive lightweighting. A comparison of the current status of non-metallic materials and application technologies at home and abroad is shown in Table 2.4, for example.

In the application of automotive interior and exterior parts, there is a growing tendency to adopt high toughness of high-performance engineering plastics, such as bumpers, wings, door guards and other parts are often used polypropylene PP, polycarbonate PC, nylon PA, ABS engineering plastics and bio-based plastics.

For body and chassis structural components, key parts such as instrument panel frames, front-end module, battery compartment cover, etc. are now widely manufactured using glass-fiber reinforced composites, such as PP-LFT, PA-LFT and low-density SMC. European heavy-duty truck manufacturers such as MAN, Renault, Mercedes-Benz, etc. as well as domestic commercial vehicle enterprises are adopting SMC in a large number of cab exterior parts. In addition, parts such as body, hybrid structure steering brackets (CCB), and chassis brake discs are being actively promoted in the application of carbon fiber composites, and Tesla and Volvo are developing regenerative carbon fiber composites application technology.

2.3.1.3 Domestic and Foreign Technology Status and Comparison of Automobile Lightweight Dissimilar Materials Connection

Taking passenger car body as an example, the traditional steel-based body is evolving toward the material concept of steel/aluminum hybrid body and multi-material body. According to the way of material combination, the application scenarios of its dissimilar material joining are shown in Table 2.5:

2.3.2 *Outlook on Technology Development Trends*

2.3.2.1 Development Trend of Lightweight Structure Design for Automobiles

1. **Multi-material hybrid structural design**

Multi-material fusion design has emerged in response to the complexity and variability of automobile driving conditions and the differentiated performance requirements of components. This design gives full play to the characteristics of different materials to realize "rigidity and flexibility", but also faces challenges such as temperature adaptability, electrochemical corrosion and recyclability. In the future, the core of multi-material fusion design will lie in the establishment of material-connection-structure-performance-process synergistic design methodology, in order to realize the optimal matching and synergistic effect between different materials and the performance of the whole vehicle.

2. **Highly integrated design**

Highly integrated design is a key technology for automotive lightweight structural design. By integrating multiple parts or functions into a single part or structural unit, it can reduce the number of parts, material usage, weight and simplify the assembly process, significantly improving the overall performance of the vehicle. With the

Table 2.5 Connection process table for typical applications of dissimilar material connections

Material mix	High strength steel	Ultra high strength/hot forming steels	Die-cast aluminum	Die-cast aluminum/steel	Rolled aluminum alloy	Aluminum (magnesium)/ steel	Aluminum/ magnesium	Composite material
Resistance spot welding	•	•	•		•			
Self-Pierce Riveting (SPR)			•	•	•	•		
Rivetless riveting					•	•		
Hot Fusion Self Tapping Wire (FDS)			•	•	•	•	•	
Friction Stir Welding (FSW)					•			
Laser welding	•	•	•		•			
Arc welding	•				•			
Viscid composite connection	•	•	•	•	•	•	•	•
Bolt/pull-out connections			•	•	•	•	•	•
Resistance element welding (REW)				•		•		
Friction Electro Welding (FEW)				•		•		

rapid development of electrification, intelligentization and low-carbonization of automobiles, automotive architectures and structural forms are undergoing profound transformations, and Platform-based and modular design has further driven the in-depth development of structural integration.

3. **Artificial intelligence-based lightweight structure design**

Artificial intelligence (AI) technology significantly enhances the efficiency and accuracy of lightweight structural design, and becomes an inevitable trend for future structural design development. In order to meet the requirements of AI lightweight structure design, it is necessary to build a sound data architecture, mine and collect multimodal training datasets, including building a high-quality data collection path, establishing clear data specifications, and building an efficient big data platform and other key aspects. Meanwhile, it is necessary to algorithms and big models suitable for AI lightweight structure design are developed, covering including in-depth re-understanding of the design process, multi-expert system cooperative operation technology, redesign and self-learning mechanism, and optimization of intelligent human–computer interaction interfaces.

2.3.2.2 Development Trend of Automotive Lightweight Materials and Their Molding Process Technology

Steel is still one of the most important materials for automotive lightweighting, high strength, high plastic toughness, low carbon emissions is the hot direction of automotive steel research. Such as Baosteel developed 1800 MPa cold forming automotive steel, Baosteel, Anshan Iron and Steel and the University of Science and Technology Beijing, etc. developed a low-density steel, such as Baosteel developed a density of $\leq$7.4 g/cm^3 low-density high-strength steel.

Hot forming steel delivers a remarkable lightweighting effect, and is developing towards 2200 MPa or even higher strength. Domestic Northeastern University, Beijing University of Science and Technology and other units are developing 2200 MPa, 2500 MPa hot forming steel. Beijing Institute of Technology and Bensteel have jointly developed coating-free hot forming steels (e.g., high Cr-Si system) with an oxidation-resistant layer thickness of <0.6 μm and a tensile strength of 1500–2000 MPa. 2023 Northeastern University published a high-plasticity, high-toughness 2000 MPa steel with elongation of $\geq$15% in Science. In Jan. 2024 A research team at Tsinghua University developed a steel with a yield strength of up to 1.7 GPa, a tensile strength of about 2.0 GPa, a uniform elongation of about 9%, and a maximum elongation of about 16%. In Oct. 2024 CITIC Metal and partners released a new grade of super-hydrogen embrittlement-resistant HEROs2000, which dramatically improves the resistance to hydrogen embrittlement of thermoformed parts. Internationally, Japan has developed hot-forming steels with a tensile strength of 2,000 MPa, a material with an elongation of no less than 6% and a cold bending angle of $\geq$56.3°. Germany ThyssenKrupp and ArcelorMittal developed a tensile strength of 1900 MPa, 2000 MPa hot forming steel, the cold bending angle are $\geq$80°. In order to meet the requirements of carbon emissions, low-carbon row steel has also become a hot spot of general concern in the automotive industry, and the country is expected to realize a reduction of carbon emissions by about 70% in 2030.

Aluminum alloys are also advancing along the trajectory of high strength, high toughness and low carbon technology. On the one hand, the development of high-performance one-piece casting aluminum alloy materials, a case in point is high mobility, low shrinkage, etc., its yield strength >250 MPa, elongation >10%; on the other hand, aluminum alloys used for automotive chassis structural components tensile strength increased to more than 500 MPa, elongation control in more than 8%, its yield strength fluctuation control within ± 15 MPa, fatigue strength >150 MPa, such as the domestic Development of rare earth aluminum alloy tensile strength of 700–740 MPa, yield strength of 650–700 MPa, elongation of 8–10%; in addition, more than 300 MPa deformed aluminum alloys and high-modulus aluminum alloys (modulus up to $\geq$90GPa) will also be the key focuses of future research and development.

For magnesium alloy materials, the future development direction is mainly focused on two aspects: one is suitable for semi-solid one-piece molding of high-performance magnesium alloy, its room temperature tensile strength of up to 350 MPa, yield strength of 220 MPa, elongation of 15%, mainly used in passenger car floors and electric drive shells, etc.; the second is the development of magnesium alloy plate with a tensile strength of 300 MPa or more, mainly used in passenger car back door panels and other parts. The second is to develop magnesium alloy sheet with tensile strength above 300 MPa, which is mainly used in passenger car back door inner plate and other parts.

Interior and exterior products are an important part of automotive lightweighting. In the future, diversified technical routes will remain the development trend of lightweight automotive interior and exterior trim:

1. The development trend of interior and exterior parts is to continue to adopting high-fluidity, high-impact toughness engineering plastics and bio-based plastics (including recycled materials) and low-density materials.
2. The development trend of structural parts is to further expand the scope of application of (super) large tow carbon fiber composites, recycled carbon fiber composites and thermoplastic composite molding processes.

The U.S. is developing low-cost carbon fiber technology, for example, Oak Ridge National Laboratory is developing 300-600 K ultra-large tow carbon fiber to meet the automotive industry's future demand for low-cost carbon fiber composites. Basalt fiber reinforced composites is also one of the development directions for automotive lightweight, basalt fiber tensile strength has a of 2400-4000 MPa, modulus of elasticity of 90-110GPa, carbon emissions between 0.9–3.26, and in the process of production of no exhaust emissions. Owing to its environmentally friendly, green, high-performance fiber material characteristics, basalt fiber will become a new darling of automotive lightweight.

Low-density molding processes such as glass beads, physical foaming and chemical foaming will be adopted in the molding process, as well as high-efficiency

RTM, E-LFT (Enhanced Long Fiber Thermoplastic Materials), in-mold molding, blister molding, two-color molding, in-mold injection and other molding process technologies.

2.3.2.3 Development Trend of Automotive Lightweight Joining Technology

The widespread adoption of multi-materials will inevitably bring new joining challenges, requiring the development of more advanced joining technology, to meet the requirements for joining quality, efficiency, performance and low cost and other aspects. Future automotive joining technology will show the following trends:

(1) Welding is a key method for automotive lightweight joining and continuous innovation. Laser welding due to the concentration of energy, deformation and other advantages, the future application of a wider range. Other technologies include, friction stir welding, resistance spot welding and other technologies;
(2) The adhesive joining process will become increasingly important. Adhesive process and mechanical joining, welding and other combinations, the first glue to increase the tightness, and then supplemented by other joining to enhance the strength, to achieve the quality and durability of the joining.
(3) Mechanical joining technology innovation. Lightweight fasteners are adopted to ensure joining strength and achieve weight reduction. At the same time, through the mechanical-solid-phase composite technologies such as self-punch friction self-piercing riveting (F-SPR), as well as mechanical-metallurgical composite technologies such as resistance riveting welding (FRW), etc., in order to improve the efficiency and quality of the joining.
(4) Automation and intelligence boost automotive joining process. Robot welding, automated adhesive application equipment to achieve precise automatic operation, improve joining efficiency and quality consistency, and reduce costs. Combined with artificial intelligence, Internet of Things, sensor monitoring parameters, and intelligent regulation, to achieve 100% monitoring and control of the joining quality, to ensure optimal joining quality.

2.3.3 Development Goals and Milestones for 2040

2.3.3.1 Vision for the Development of Automotive Lightweighting

By 2040, establish a technical system of performance characterization, forming, and application of automotive high-strength steel, aluminum alloys, magnesium alloys and composite materials, establish methods for connecting parts of dissimilar materials and inhibiting electrochemical corrosion, and boost the development and application of multi-material lightweight hybrid structure auto parts; break through the key technologies of integrated design, manufacturing and evaluation of large auto parts, and push forward the research and development and application of platform, modularized and assembled lightweight auto body and skateboard chassis structure research and development and application; promote the application of big data and artificial intelligence multi-modal model in the lightweight design of automobile structure, focus on the research and development of artificial intelligence-enabled automobile lightweight AI design methodology and software, and significantly improve the efficiency and accuracy of automobile structural lightweight design; build a low-carbon emission, high-efficiency vehicle and parts manufacturing and production mode, elevating China's automobile lightweight technology to an international leading level. This will enable China's automotive lightweight technology to be among the international leading level, and boost the development of automobile electrification, intelligence and low-carbonization.

2.3.3.2 Automotive Lightweighting Goals and Milestones

This roadmap continues to follow overall vehicle lightweight coefficient as the evaluation index of vehicle lightweighting when formulating automotive lightweighting targets at different phases, and with the help of the lightweighting evaluation method specified in the new group standard of the Society of Automotive Engineers (SAE) for trucks, three-axle tractor-trailers and buses, classifies vehicle models according into the electric passenger cars, fuel passenger cars, trucks, tractor-trailers and buses, and formulates the lightweight development targets of the whole vehicle for the next 15 years, relative to the year 2024, as shown in Fig. 2.3. The three phases of vehicle lightweight development goals are shown in Fig. 2.3.

In order to achieve the vision and goals outlined in the Lightweighting Thematic Roadmap 3.0, the overall plan for automotive lightweighting over the next 15 years will be divided into three phases for phased advancement.

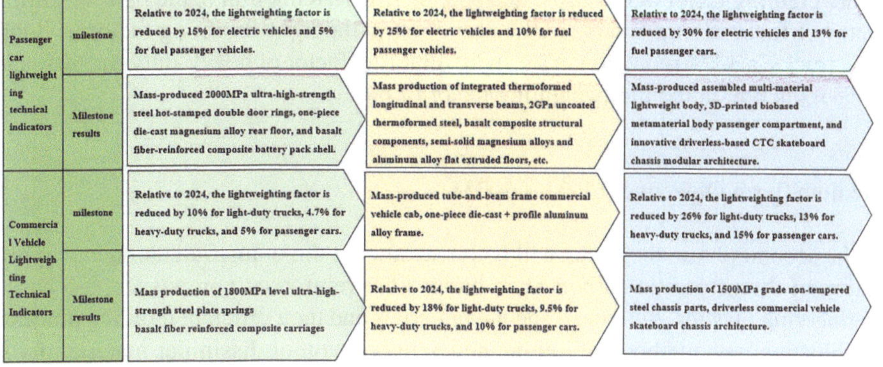

Fig. 2.3 Overall technology route for automotive lightweighting in 2025 ~ 2040

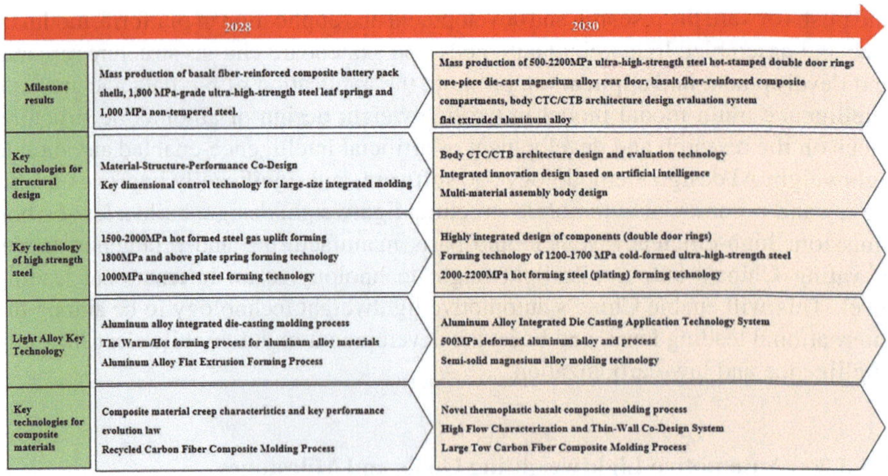

Fig. 2.4 2025 ~ 2030 Automotive lightweighting technology route

Immediate Goals (2026 ~ 2030)

In the first phase, further expand the industrialized application of ultra-high-strength steel, aluminum alloy, magnesium alloy, high-performance fiber-reinforced composite materials and their advanced forming processes, break through the key technologies of integrated design, manufacturing and evaluation of large aluminum alloy and magnesium alloy die castings, laser splicing and welding of thermoformed steel double-door rings and other parts, and develop the technological route of automobile lightweighting with high-strength steel as the main component and light alloys as the supplementary component., and form the aluminum and magnesium alloy Material application technology system, lightweight landmark achievements and technical routes as shown in Fig. 2.4.

Compared with 2024, by 2030, we will achieve a 15% reduction in the lightweighting factor of electric passenger cars, a 5% reduction in the lightweighting factor of fuel passenger cars, a 10% reduction in the lightweighting factor of light-duty trucks, a 4.7% reduction in the lightweighting factor of heavy-duty tractors, and a 5% reduction in the lightweighting factor of buses.

Medium-Term Objectives (2031 ~ 2035)

In the second phase, the focus will be on advancing the industrialization and application of thermoplastic carbon fiber, basalt fiber reinforced composites, bio-based engineering plastics, functional special materials and their efficient molding process, establishing new methods of joining and anticorrosion of dissimilar material parts, developing the lightweight technology route of lightweight material-based multi-materials mixing and application, promoting the hybrid structural design and new

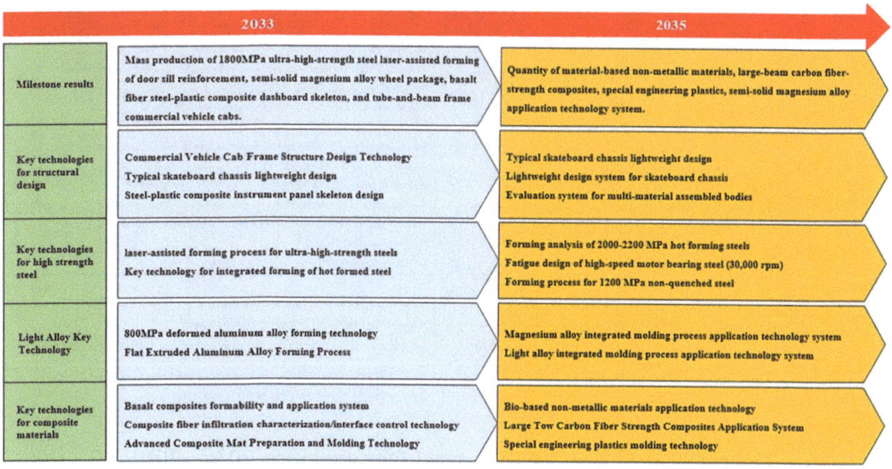

Fig. 2.5 2031 ~ 2035 Automotive lightweighting technology route

technology of integrated molding process, and completing the composite automotive composite material application technology system. The lightweight landmark achievements and technical routes are shown in Fig. 2.5. By 2024, the lightweight index of electric passenger cars will be reduced by 25%, that of fuel-fired passenger cars by 10%, that of light-duty trucks by 18%, that of heavy-duty tractors by 9.5%, and that of buses by 10%.

Forward Targets (2036 ~ 2040)

In the third phase, efforts will focus on promoting the application of big data and AI multimodal big models in the lightweight design of automobile structures, research and develop automotive lightweight AI design methods and software, and improve the efficiency and precision of lightweight design of automobile structures; promote the application of low-carbon materials and recycled materials in automobiles, build a technical system of diversified automobile materials and integrated design and manufacturing, and promote the research and development and application of platform-based, modular, and assembly-oriented lightweight automotive bodies and skateboard chassis structures research and development and application, and boost the development of automobile electrification, intelligentization and low-carbonization.

Relative to 2024, the goal of reducing the lightweighting factor of electric passenger cars by 30%, light-duty trucks by 26%, heavy-duty tractors by 13%, and buses by 15% will be achieved (Fig. 2.6).

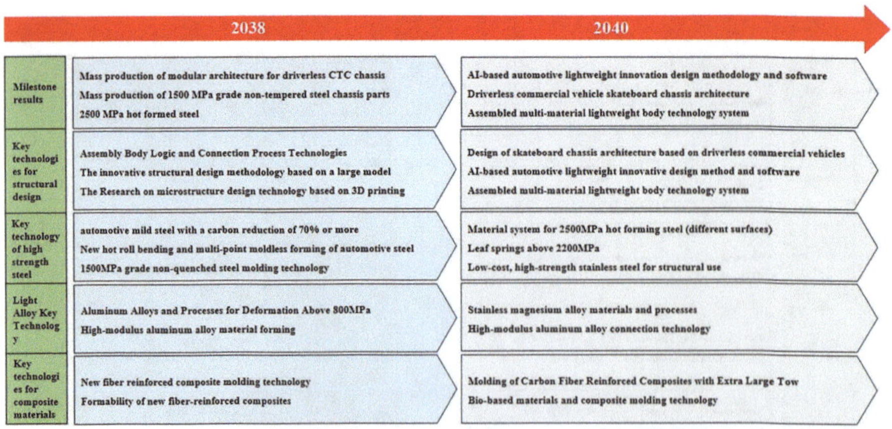

Fig. 2.6 Lightweighting technology routes for multi-format vehicles, 2036 ~ 2040

2.3.4 Technology Roadmap

2.3.4.1 Technology Roadmap for Lightweight Structural Design of Automobiles

With the continuous advancement of structural design theories and methodologies, automotive lightweight design has gradually evolved in the direction of multi-objective and multi-disciplinary collaborative optimization. With the diversification of materials used in automobile structure, the joining of dissimilar materials and the continuous development of advanced manufacturing technology, the integrated design method of structure-materials-process-joining-performance has been widely used, and has played an increasingly important role in the lightweight research and development of automobile products. In recent years, the integration of automotive components has developed rapidly, and the integrated design of large component structures, reinforcement optimization and performance simulation and evaluation have attracted much attention from the automotive industry, and have become an important means of automotive structural design and development. With the rapid development of artificial intelligence technology, big data and large models, the traditional automotive structural design and development methods mainly based on numerical calculation and analysis are increasingly not adapted to the needs of the R&D of automotive products with rapid updating and iteration due to the many types of application software, difficult to master, low computational efficiency and poor accuracy, and the AI design methods and software based on the multi-modal and large models of automotive structural lightweight design of big data and artificial intelligence will significantly improve the efficiency and accuracy of the automotive lightweight design. Based on big data and artificial intelligence multi-modal large model automobile structure lightweight AI design methods and software will significantly improve the efficiency and accuracy of automobile lightweight design, and

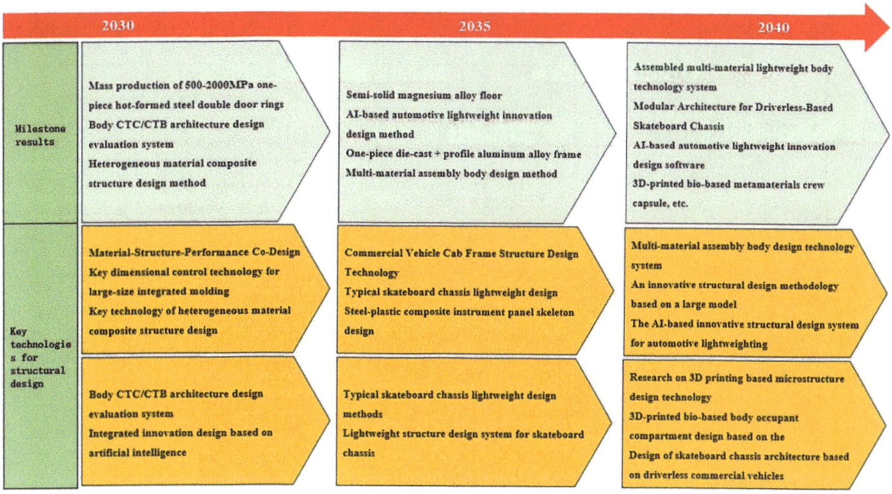

Fig. 2.7 Technology roadmap for automotive lightweight structure design topics

is the development direction of the future automobile structure design. In summary, the future automotive lightweight design technology roadmap is shown in Fig. 2.7.

2.3.4.2 Automotive Steel Technology Roadmap

The future development of automotive steel focuses on two major trends of decarbonization and high strength and toughness. Low carbonization, the use of ESP, PSF, hydrogen smelting and other technologies, carbon emissions in 2030 compared with traditional automotive steel to reduce more than 70%, short-flow rolling process to speed up the hot-rolled steel will be more alternative to cold-rolled steel. High strength and toughness, the development of tensile strength of 2000 MPa, elongation of more than 12% of the ultra-high-strength steel, tensile strength of up to 2,500 MPa hot-forming steel, 1,300 MPa non-tempered steel, 2,000 MPa cold-forming steel, high fatigue/strength ratio (>45%) of 700 ~ 800 MPa beam steel and high-speed motor bearing steel. Ultra-high-strength steel two-dimensional and three-dimensional roll forming, cold press forming and laser-assisted local heating forming is the future direction of development of low-carbon forming, automotive steel thematic technology routes shown in Fig. 2.8.

2.3.4.3 Technology Roadmap for Lightweight Materials for Automobiles

Lightweight materials used for automotive lightweighting include aluminum alloys, magnesium alloys, engineering plastics, fiber-reinforced composites and specialty

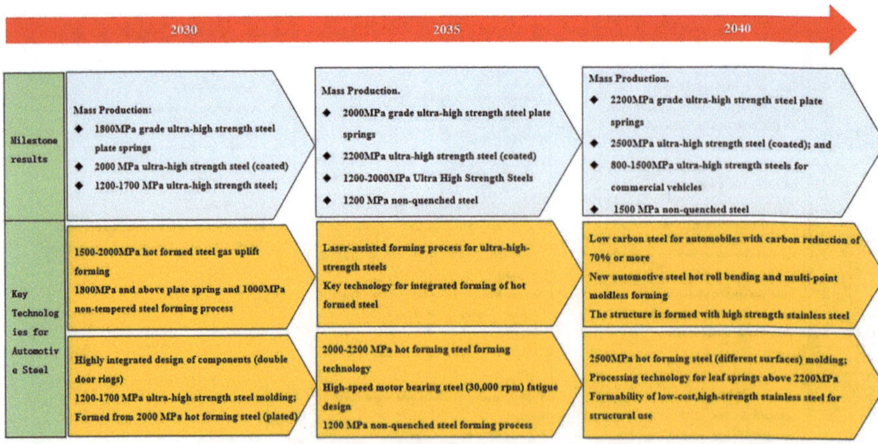

Fig. 2.8 Thematic technology roadmap for automotive steel

plastics. With the automotive energy saving and consumption reduction on lightweight requirements and the development of new technologies, high-toughness deformable aluminum and magnesium alloys, high mobility casting aluminum, magnesium alloys will be widely applied in the automotive body and chassis structural parts. In addition, high flow, high toughness engineering plastics and glass fiber reinforced composites will continue to play a role in automotive interior and exterior lightweight parts; Looking ahead of low-cost carbon fiber and basalt fiber reinforced composites, intelligent membrane materials, special engineering plastics, polydicyclopentadiene (PDCPD) materials, bio-based materials, natural fiber-reinforced composites, high-weather-resistance non-metallic materials, etc., the use of the dosage will be increasing. The integrated molding technology of composite materials and metal hybrid structure will expand the application scope, and the molding efficiency of thermoplastic fiber-reinforced composites will be further improved. Lightweight material technology route for automobile is shown in Fig. 2.9.

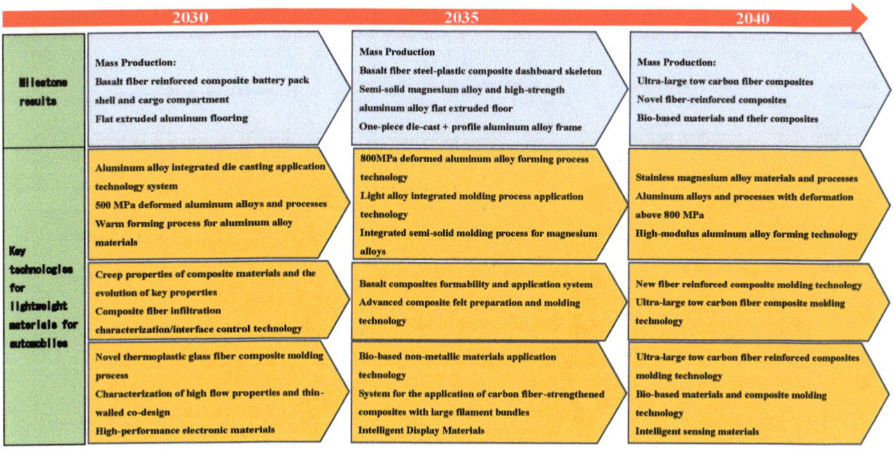

Fig. 2.9 Technology roadmap for lightweight materials for automobiles

2.3.4.4 Automotive Lightweight Connectivity Technology Roadmap

With the diversification of automobile lightweight materials, the demand for dissimilar material joining technology has become increasingly urgent, new joining methods such as bonding, self-punching riveting (SPR), flow drill screws (FDS), Clinching, friction stir welding (FSW) and friction self-piercing riveting (F-SPR) and so on are constantly emerging and maturing, and the quality and efficiency of the joining equipment are has achieved continuous improvements and their application in the field of automobile The application in the field of automobile manufacturing is more extensive. Future artificial intelligence technology will help automotive dissimilar material parts joining process precision selection and process parameters automatically generated and dynamically optimized, new joining technology will be constantly updated and iterative, the joint performance prediction accuracy is getting higher and higher, with the development and application of digital simulation and digital twin technology, the whole process of connecting the process of on-line quality monitoring and virtual reality fusion of the twin control will be practical, the digitization of automotive connection technology will be The digitalization of automotive joining technology will boost the rapid development of automotive lightweight technology. The technical route of automobile connection technology is shown in Fig. 2.10.

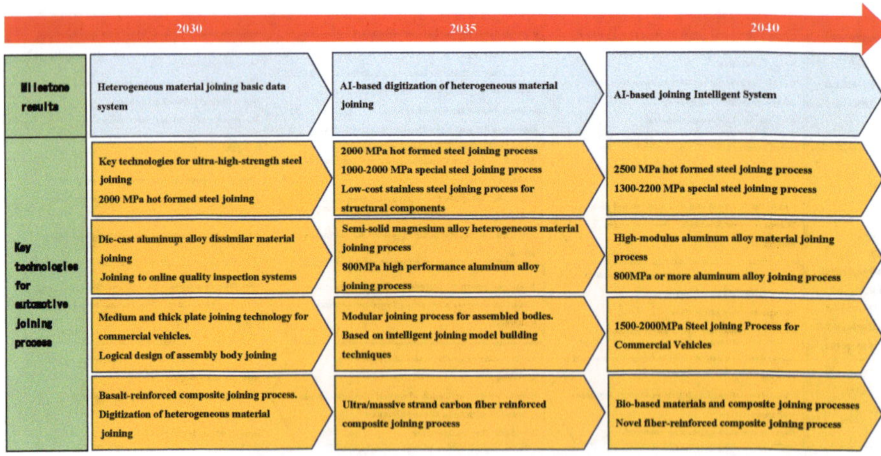

Fig. 2.10 Automotive lightweight joining process technology roadmap

2.4 Vehicle Energy Saving

2.4.1 Domestic and International Technical Status Comparison

2.4.1.1 Optimized Vehicle Energy Consumption

(1) Development trends of power consumption of battery electric vehicles (BEV) and fuel consumption of hybrid electric vehicles (HEV) among passenger vehicles

Equipped with high-efficiency powertrains as well as low aerodynamic drag and low drag and other generic technologies, passenger vehicles evidently achieved remarkable progress in energy consumption. According to the *2023 Annual Report on the Implementation of Parallel Management of Average Fuel Consumption and New Energy Vehicle Credits of Passenger Vehicle Enterprises*, the average energy consumption of passenger vehicles is generally on a downward trend. By September 2024, the fuel consumption of BEVs averaged 12.49 kW·h/100 km, while average fuel consumption of HEVs declined to 5.9L/100 km. In particular, the segment-A BEV model Toyota bZ3 and the segment-B BEV model Starry Era had power consumption as low as 11.0 kW·h/100 km and 11.7kWh/100 km respectively within CLTC range, while the segment-B HEV model Qin L achieved CS fuel consumption as low as 3.8L/100 km under WLTC condition, establishing total supremacy in the industry.

Note The fuel consumption refers to the CS (Charge Sustaining) fuel consumption of plug-in hybrid vehicles (PHEV).

(2) Development trend of fuel consumption of commercial vehicles

At present, the average fuel consumption of China's heavy-duty commercial vehicles (HCV) is 2 ~ 5% better than the three-phase fuel consumption limits, but that of foreign semitrailer tractors is 4.7% above China's limits and 2.7% better than China's homemade semitrailer tractors; and less than 2% of foreign trucks are above China's limits on average. In a word, China's own commercial vehicles are basically on a par with foreign commercial vehicles in terms of fuel consumption. Though the regulation on single vehicle fuel consumption limits now applies to China's HCVs, the four-phase fuel consumption standard is expected to speed up application of conventional energy-saving technology. For the HCV industry, the European Union (EU) adopts the pattern of mean corporate administration, while the United States (US) sets goals of carbon emissions reduction under mean fleet regulation mechanism. The EU, US and Japan have laid down regulations on carbon emissions reduction for 2025, 2030, 2035 and 2040. Looking forward, China may draw on the experience of the EU and US, regarding the administration of HCV fuel consumption. By incorporating it into corporate average fuel consumption (CAFC) requirements, China aims at a lower energy consumption of HCVs and progress towards clean low-carbon energy technology, thus helping attain the strategic goals of "carbon peaking and neutrality".

2.4.1.2 Higher Lightweight Vehicle Level

European vehicle models apply advanced lightweight materials and processes, with a focus on overcoming challenges in multi-material joining technologies and emphasizing the application and promotion of environmentally friendly materials. The United States and Japan are continuously expanding the application of high-strength steel and light metals, while actively promoting the development of advanced materials and innovation in processing technologies. In China, the "carbon peaking and neutrality" policy is accelerating the lightweight process. Compared to 2019, the lightweighting coefficients of China's fuel vehicles, BEVs, and commercial vehicles decreased by 7.5%, 30.7% and 18.3%, respectively.

The global industry is rapidly advancing the research & development (R&D) of advanced lightweight vehicle materials, including high-intensity steel, aluminum alloys, magnesium alloys, and carbon fiber. Against the backdrop, it is imperative for China to make breakthroughs in high-performance technologies and processes, such as multi-phase steel and medium manganese TRIP steel, along with advancements in high-intensity and high-tenacity aluminum alloys, aluminum-steel jointing technologies, and overcoming the cost and technological challenges associated with carbon fiber materials. These efforts will enable broader application of lightweight materials.

2.4.1.3 Industry-Leading Low Wind Resistance Technology

The rapid development of the ultra-low aerodynamic drag vehicle is credited to the improved new energy vehicle (NEV) industry standards and regulations, aerodynamic drag reduction theories and wind tunnel testing technologies. For passenger vehicles, as shown in the Fig., from 2020 to 2024, the average drag coefficient of electric sedans dipped from 0.264 to 0.230. Among them, pioneering models such as the Arcfox Alpha, Xpeng MONA 03, Xiaomi SU7, and Yangwang U7 stood out with the drag coefficient knocking down to 0.1925 ~ 0.195. For commercial vehicles, the all-electric HCV Windrose WH11 set a new record among all HCV models, with a drag coefficient as low as 0.276.

2.4.1.4 Narrower Gap from Top Notch in Tire Rolling Resistance

Shifting from benchmarking to independent R&D, China's tire makers are significantly narrowing the gap from top international brands, by optimizing tire compounds and structure through material optimization, rolling resistance simulation and tension control technology. The rolling resistance coefficient of passenger vehicles fell from 7.5‰ in 2021 to 6.0‰ in 2024, approximating the 5.8‰ of top foreign brands. For commercial vehicles, the rolling resistance coefficient of tires used in heavy-duty trucks, medium-duty trucks, light-duty trucks and buses exceeded 5.5‰.

2.4.1.5 Fast-Growing Low-Drag Calipers and Low-Friction Hub Bearing Technologies

By refining piston and brake lining retraction, China's passenger vehicle caliper suppliers have been aligned with world leading drag standards; Low-drag brake calipers for commercial vehicles are still under research in China, European enterprises have set about working on active resetting technology for brake linings.

Additionally, though China's suppliers have begun optimizing structural design for low-friction hub bearings, they see a noticeable gap from world industry leaders, owing to reliance on imported production and manufacturing equipment and incompetence in bearing grease R&D.

2.4.1.6 Groundbreaking Energy-Saving Technology for Thermal Management System

NEV thermal management systems are breaking new ground, with characteristics of high efficiency, integration and intelligence. High-efficiency air source/water source heat pump systems become mainstream, compared with traditional electric heating modules; For integration, integrated energy flow management technology has been unveiled, featuring centralized deployment of thermal requirements and sources for cockpit, batteries, e-motors and electric control; As for intelligence, vehicle energy efficiency and performance have been brought to a new level, by dint of artificial intelligence (AI) and big data technologies, auto passenger sensing and vehicle state adjustment and thermal management strategies.

2.4.1.7 Initial Industrialization of Intelligent Energy Management Technology

Using intelligent energy management technology, passenger vehicles can access multi-source information, make intelligent predictions about power requirements throughout the full drive, and apply the sequence of energy management decisions to the vehicle and its powertrain, so as to attain optimal allocation and utilization of energy. Used in mass-produced models by a host of Chinese manufacturers, the technology now has brought down fuel savings by 5–15% and made relevant models ranked among the top the world in terms of energy savings and built-in settings.

Through analysis of GPS and slope information, the predictive cruise technology for commercial vehicles enables dynamic speed adjustment and consequently optimizes engine efficiency and gear control, thus saving fuel and slashing emissions. Since 2012, major commercial vehicle companies in Europe have been working on the R&D and mass production of fuel-efficient models. China's commercial vehicle companies, such as Foton Auman EST and FAW Jiefang, have stepped up the work of technology R&D in recent years, to roll out models with 1% fuel savings and 4.48% fuel savings on plain and hilly expressways respectively.

2.4.2 Outlook on Technology Development Trends

2.4.2.1 Development of Vehicle Energy Conservation Towards Intelligence and New Architecture

Auto intelligence is an unstoppable trend, and new technologies, such as intelligent drive, intelligent cockpit and intelligent chassis, are rapidly put into extensive use in NEVs. Through driving behavior analysis and road condition prediction, these technologies enable dynamic energy scheduling and saving under actual user operating conditions. Nevertheless, mounting high computing power controllers, sensors and control mechanisms poses a challenge of power consumption in vehicle accessories. Leading car makers define a surge of 0.5 kW·h/100 km in power consumption induced by autonomous vehicle accessories in configuration.

Besides, as high-performance vehicles, off-road vehicles and medium- and large-sized vehicles are more demanding on the performance and features of electric drive systems, multi-motor distributed drive structure becomes a prevalent power system program for premium NEV models; Relative to vehicles built with centralized electric drive, the structure increases vehicle energy consumption by approximately 2 kW·h/100 km, owing to higher assembly mass, higher drag resistance and waning efficiency.

2.4.2.2 Breakthrough and Extensive Application of Lightweight Materials

In the future, lightweighting technology is projected to make advances in three dimensions: novel materials, structural design and manufacturing process optimization.

(1) Through disruptive development and processing of aluminum/magnesium alloys and carbon fiber composites, new materials featuring high strength, toughness and cost-effectiveness will be developed and widely applied.
(2) Topology optimization, as well as modular and integrated design, will help reduce material consumption. Intelligent jointing technologies and optimizated connections between lightweight and dissimilar materials will help balance vehicle rigidity and crash performance.
(3) By advancing industrialization of advanced forming technologies, such as precision laser welding, integrated pressure casting, semi-solid-state casting, high-efficiency rolling/squeezing, and hot stamping—mass production technologies for large, sophisticated lightweight parts will be developed, increasing the proportion of lightweight materials in vehicles.

2.4.2.3 Platform-Based, Intelligent and Collaborative Development of Aerodynamic Drag Reduction Technology

The platform-based design has shifted its focus from aerodynamic drag reduction of individual components to investigating inter-component aerodynamic coupling mechanisms, aiming to achieve superior aerodynamic performance. Key research priorities include aerodynamics integrated design, multi-scale complex flow mechanism for vehicle flow, etc. Through real-time information interaction with road conditions, traffic patterns, and ambient wind environments, intelligent optimization algorithms enable dynamic optimization of drag reduction solutions. Future advancements will leverage artificial intelligence and big data to incorporate multi-disciplinary considerations including aerodynamics performance, fuel efficiency, and manoeuvrability, ultimately realizing multi-objective collaborative optimization design.

2.4.2.4 Sweeping Development and Design of Energy-Saving and Environment-Friendly Tires with Low Rolling Resistance

The "carbon peaking and neutrality" initiative and demand for long range of NEVs drive tires towards low rolling resistance, green and intelligent development. The use of key technologies, such as new materials, intelligent tires, advanced mixing and vulcanization technology brings low rolling resistance tire compound and structural design to a reality; Meanwhile, the wider use of biomass and other sustainable materials helps with production of green and premium tires.

2.4.2.5 Coordinated Design and Intelligent Development of Low Friction Technology

Under the trend of ultimate energy-saving design, low-friction technology will move towards integrated design and intelligent control of parts systems. Integrated piston roll-back design based on the entire caliper structure will be a priority in low-drag caliper development; The development of low-resistance, high-seal structure design and high-performance lubricating grease will be an important direction for low-friction hub bearings.

2.4.2.6 Highly Integrated and Intelligent Development of Thermal Management System

The focus of new heat pumps with wide temperature range will lie in the development of efficient and environment-friendly refrigerants, which, coupled with enhanced vapor injection technology, will improve heating performance of heat pump systems under extreme cold environment. With compressors at the core, integrated thermal management design, as a mix of heat exchanger, valve body and other parts, will help mitigate system flow resistance and thermal dissipation and enable compact and energy-saving design. Using the model prediction method, the vehicle-mounted thermal management system will coordinate with systems for control of waste heat, temperature regulation in the passenger compartment, battery temperature control, etc., for high-efficiency utilization of vehicle energy through energy interaction.

2.4.2.7 More Intelligent Energy Management System

With advances made in intelligent & connected vehicle (ICV) technology and car networking infrastructure, vehicle controllers are capable of forecasting future traffic conditions, and plotting out the best route and speed for drivers. On the ground of vehicle intelligence, the vehicle-road-cloud-integrated technology enables coordinated control of ICVs from a higher dimension and consequently safe, green and efficient operation of urban transport systems. The technology roadmap necessitates coordinated development of high-speed radio communication system, intelligent road system, transport information network, etc. Initially piloting in ports, coal mines and other enclosed transport scenarios, it will gradually apply to high-speed enclosed scenarios, urban low-speed open scenarios.

2.4.3 Development Goals and Milestones for 2040

On the basis of lightweighting, electric drive, high-efficiency powertrain and other advanced technologies, the vehicle energy conservation project places emphasis on making technical advances in low resistance, low friction, thermal management and energy management, for the purpose of low-carbon and intelligent transition of NEVs. By 2030, the BEVs will achieve a leading power consumption down to 8 kW·h/100 km, followed by HEVs with fuel consumption of 3.1L/100 km. Traditional new energy, hybrid and all-electric commercial vehicles will see a decline of 10, 24 and 8.5% in energy consumption from 2024. By 2035, BEVs will retain supremacy in the auto industry with power consumption down to 7.7 kW·h/100 km, followed by HEVs with fuel consumption of 2.8L/100 km. Traditional new energy, hybrid and all-electric commercial vehicles will have energy consumption further declined by 15%, 33% and 13.5% from 2024. By 2040, BEVs will still stay ahead in the auto industry with power consumption further down to 7.5 kW·h/100 km, followed by HEVs with fuel consumption of 2.6L/100 km. Traditional new energy, hybrid and all-electric commercial vehicles will embrace sinking energy consumption by 20, 38 and 17% from 2024.

2.4.4 Technology Roadmap

The roadmap covers BEVs, PHEVs, HEVs and fuel-powered vehicles. Underpinned by vehicle lightweighting, resistance and friction reduction, thermal management and energy management technologies, it is intended to bring down energy consumption of both traditional and new energy vehicles, with phased power consumption/fuel consumption goals defined; Indicators and technology roadmaps pertinent to key areas are also identified to help achieve the overarching vehicle goals.

Lightweighting technologies will focus on coordinated innovation of lightweight materials, structural optimization and manufacturing processes: (1) With a focus on R&D of high-intensity and low-cost lightweight materials, it is advised to break the bottleneck in the use of magnesium–aluminum alloys in structural parts and accelerate the development and industrialization of new composite materials. (2) Structural efficiency will be increased in all respects, leveraging integrated design of materials and topology optimizationy. Deep integration of vehicle systems will help reduce redundant structures. The development of modular and standardized design methods will help enhance scalability. (3) With a focus on intelligent manufacturing, endeavors will be made to promote automated mass production of large-sized sophisticated and lightweight parts; Improved technological stability and precision will help attain high-efficiency processing and assembly of lightweight materials.

The platform-based, intelligent and multi-objective collaborative evolution of low aerodynamic drag technology: At the platform level, efforts will focus on researching multi-component aerodynamic coupling mechanisms and establishing systematic drag reduction frameworks to achieve a leap in vehicle aerodynamic performance. From the intelligence perspective, data-driven methodologies enable the construction of digital closed-loop systems that integrate parametric modelling, simulation, and optimization design; Dynamic active drag reduction can be further realized through adaptive aerodynamic kits combined with real-time spacing control technologies, such as those applied in commercial vehicle platooning.. The collaborative aspect involves establishing multi-physics field coupled analysis systems to achieve integrated optimization of energy efficiency, stability and safety performance.

With regard to low rolling resistance technology, the tire rolling resistance technology remains in rapid progress, indicating continuously lowering rolling resistance coefficient. With enhancements made to the development of new materials and relevant manufacturing technologies, ultra-low-temperature vulcanization technology and low-heat-generated rubber will be put into full use by 2030; By 2035, high-dispersion nanofillers and ultra-high-intensity framework materials will come into use; By 2040, comprehensive use of wet mixing in mass production and platform-based technology of low rolling resistance design is expectable.

In terms of low friction technology, the system design and intelligent control of brake calipers and hub bearings will pave the way for the development and application of brake calipers and hub bearings with low friction moment. Effective piston roll-back system design and friction control technology for calipers and brake linings will facilitate the development of "zero" drag calipers. Innovations in hub bearing sealing technology and breakthroughs in lubricating technology, as well as system optimizations for materials and structures, will further catalyze the development of hub bearings with way lower friction.

For thermal management technology, the technology roadmap for thermal management systems with wide temperature range in NEVs is outlined as follows: (1) Develop a novel heat pump system built with high-energy-efficiency and environment-friendly refrigerant, which applies to low-temperature condition, alongside matching high-efficiency compressor and heat exchanger parts. (2) Detail integrated design of thermal management systems, and devise methods for coordinated control of heat sources, for realizing efficient and comprehensive use of vehicle energy. (3) Implement intelligent regulation of thermal management, and keep adaptive regulation system always optimal, as part of ultimate high-efficiency design of thermal management.

The energy management technology will become more intelligent to consistently optimize vehicle energy consumption. Predictive energy management technology, combined with car networking information, will further increase energy savings to 5–15% in conventional transport scenarios. The coordinated control of systems will further enable integration of energy management and thermal management, as well as intelligent driving systems, elevating energy savings to 7–20%. For vehicle-road-cloud-integrated control, a centralized, standardized and highly compatible infrastructure and control framework established in the industry will help realize large-scale mass application of the vehicle-road-cloud-integrated systems in intelligent & connected vehicles, with energy consumption optimized by 10–14%.

The technology roadmap for vehicle energy conservation is as shown in Fig. 2.11.

		2030	2035	2040
Overarching Goal		Passenger vehicle:A00/A0/A/B/C/D segment EV energy consumption under CLTC with normal-temperature≤8/9.0/10.0/11.0/11.7/12.5kWh/100km A/B/C/D segment HEV/PHEV CS mode fuel consumption under CLTC with normal-temperature ≤3.1/3.4/3.9/4.9L/100km A/B/C segment ICEV fuel consumption under WLTC with normal-temperature≤5.0/5.4/5.8L/100km Commercial vehicle : The reduction in energy consumption for light/medium/heavy-duty trucks and buses under CHTC is higher than (comparison to 2024) ICEV 10%/12%/13%/12%, HEV/PHEV 25%/26%/24%/24%, EV 10%/8.5%/8.5%/10%	Passenger vehicle:A00/A0/A/B/C/D segment EV energy consumption under CLTC with normal-temperature ≤7.7/8.5/9.5/10.5/11.2/12.0kWh/100km A/B/C/D segment HEV/PHEV CS mode fuel consumption under CLTC with normal-temperature ≤2.8/3.1/3.6/4.6L/100km Commercial vehicle : The reduction in energy consumption for light/medium/heavy-duty trucks and buses under CHTC is higher than (comparison to 2024) ICEV 15%/20%/22%/19%, HEV/PHEV 33%/37%/35%/33.5%, EV 18%/14%/13.5%/17%	Passenger vehicle:A00/A0/A/B/C/D segment EV energy consumption under CLTC with normal-temperature ≤7.5/8.2/9.2/10.2/10.9/11.7kWh/100km A/B/C/D segment HEV/PHEV CS mode fuel consumption under CLTC with normal-temperature ≤2.6/2.9/3.4/4.4L/100km Commercial vehicle : The reduction in energy consumption for light/medium/heavy-duty trucks and buses under CHTC is higher than (comparison to 2024) ICEV 20%/25%/27%/23%, HEV/PHEV 38%/44%/41%/39%, EV 25%/19%/17%/21%
Passenger Vehicle	Lightweighting	Vehicle lightweight index is reduced by 15% compared to 2024	Vehicle lightweight index is reduced by 25% compared to 2024	Vehicle lightweight index is reduced by 30% compared to 2024
	Low-resistance	Seden/SUV/MPV EV Cd≤0.18/0.25/0.26 Seden/SUV/MPV HEV/PHEV Cd≤0.23/0.27/0.28 Seden/SUV/MPV ICEV Cd≤0.23/0.29/0.29 Rolling resistance coefficient ≤5.5‰	Seden/SUV/MPV EV Cd ≤0.17/0.24/0.24 Seden/SUV/MPV HEV/PHEV Cd ≤0.22/0.26/0.27 Rolling resistance coefficient ≤5.2‰	Seden/SUV/MPV EV Cd ≤0.17/0.23/0.22 Seden/SUV/MPV HEV/PHEV Cd ≤0.21/0.25/0.26 Rolling resistance coefficient ≤4.9‰
	Low-friction	Drag torque of calipers (single-piston floating caliper / dual-piston floating caliper / fixed caliper) ≤1.5/2.5/3.5 N.m Friction torque of wheel hub bearing ≤2 N.m	Drag torque of calipers (single-piston floating caliper / dual-piston floating caliper / fixed caliper) ≤1/2/2.5 N.m Friction torque of wheel hub bearing ≤1.75 N.m	Drag torque of calipers (single-piston floating caliper / dual-piston floating caliper / fixed caliper) ≤0.5/1.5/2 N.m Friction torque of wheel hub bearing ≤1.5 N.m
	Thermal Management	Average air conditioning power consumption for a typical Class A EV model under CLTC at 35°C/-7 °C/-20 °C ≤650W/ 650W/1800W	Average air conditioning power consumption for a typical Class A EV model under CLTC at 35°C/-7 °C/-20 °C ≤600W/ 600W/1600W	Average air conditioning power consumption for a typical Class A EV model under CLTC at 35°C/-7 °C/-20 °C ≤550W/ 550W/1400W
	Energy Management	Mature application of vehicle control technology based on predictive energy management	Mature application of vehicle control technology based on the coordination of intelligent driving and energy management	Mature application of vehicle control technology based on the integration of vehicle-road-cloud systems
Commercial Vehicle	Lightweighting	Lightweight index for light/medium/heavy-duty trucks is reduced by 10%/10%/5% compared to 2024 Crub Weight for light/medium/heavy-duty trucks is reduced by 100kg/100kg/150kg compared to 2024 Energy consumption by Lightweight for light/medium/heavy-duty trucks is reduced by 1.26%/0.36%/0.19% compared to 2024	Lightweight index for light/medium/heavy-duty trucks is reduced by 18% /10%/ 10% compared to 2024 Crub Weight for light/medium/heavy-duty trucks is reduced by 200kg/200kg/300kg compared to 2024 Energy consumption by Lightweight for light/medium/heavy-duty trucks is reduced by 2.44%/0.73%/0.38% compared to 2024	Lightweight index for light/medium/heavy-duty trucks is reduced by 26% /13%/ 15% compared to 2024 Crub Weight for light/medium/heavy-duty trucks is reduced by 300kg/300kg/500kg compared to 2024 Energy consumption by Lightweight for light/medium/heavy-duty trucks is reduced by 3.70%/1.09%/0.65% compared to 2024
	Low-resistance	ICEV Cd: Heavy-duty trucks:Cab over engine≤0.50; Semi-cowl≤0.46; Cab behind engine≤0.45; Medium-duty trucks:Cab over engine≤0.55; Semi-cowl ≤0.53 Light-duty trucks:Cab over engine≤0.46 ; Semi-cowl ≤0.43 Large and medium-sized buses :≤0.45 NEV Cd: Heavy-duty trucks :Cab over engine≤0.40; Semi-cowl ≤0.36; ; Cab behind engine≤0.35; Medium-duty trucks :Cab over engine≤0.48; Semi-cowl ≤0.45 Light-duty trucks :Cab over engine≤0.39 ; Semi-cowl ≤0.37 Large and medium-sized buses :≤0.45 Rolling resistance coefficient : Heavy-duty trucks(12R22.5):4.5‰, reduced by 10% compared to 2024 Medium-duty trucks (275/80R22.5):5‰ , reduced by 9.1% compared to 2024 Light-duty trucks (7.00R16):5.5‰ , reduced by 11.3% compared to 2024 Buses(295/80R22.5):5‰ , reduced by 9.1% compared to 2024	ICEV Cd: Heavy-duty trucks :Cab over engine≤0.47; Semi-cowl ≤0.43; Cab behind engine≤0.42; Medium-duty trucks :Cab over engine≤0.52; Semi-cowl ≤0.50 Light-duty trucks :Cab over engine≤0.43 ; Semi-cowl ≤0.41 Large and medium-sized buses :≤0.45 NEV Cd : Heavy-duty trucks :Cab over engine≤0.38; Semi-cowl ≤0.34; ; Cab behind engine≤0.33; Medium-duty trucks :Cab over engine≤0.45; Semi-cowl ≤0.43 Light-duty trucks :Cab over engine≤0.37; Semi-cowl ≤0.34 Large and medium-sized buses :≤0.43 Rolling resistance coefficient : Heavy-duty trucks (12R22.5):4‰ , reduced by 20% compared to 2024 Medium-duty trucks (275/80R22.5):4.5‰ , reduced by 18.2% compared to 2024 Light-duty trucks (7.00R16):5‰, reduced by 19.4% compared to 2024 Buses (295/80R22.5):4.5‰, reduced by 18.2% compared to 2024	ICEV Cd: Heavy-duty trucks :Cab over engine≤0.44; Semi-cowl ≤0.41; Cab behind engine≤0.4; Medium-duty trucks :Cab over engine≤0.49; Semi-cowl ≤0.47 Light-duty trucks :Cab over engine≤0.41 ; Semi-cowl ≤0.38 Large and medium-sized buses :≤0.45 NEV Cd : Heavy-duty trucks :Cab over engine≤0.35; Semi-cowl ≤0.32; ; Cab behind engine≤0.31; Medium-duty trucks :Cab over engine≤0.42; Semi-cowl ≤0.40 Light-duty trucks :Cab over engine≤0.35 ; Semi-cowl ≤0.32 Large and medium-sized buses :≤0.40 Rolling resistance coefficient : Heavy-duty trucks (12R22.5):3.8‰, reduced by 24% compared to 2024 Medium-duty trucks (275/80R22.5):4.3‰, reduced by 21.8% compared to 2024 Light-duty trucks (7.00R16):4.8‰, reduced by 22.6% compared to 2024 Buses (295/80R22.5):4.3‰, reduced by 21.8% compared to 2024
	Low-friction	Caliper drag torque for light(hydraulic)/ light(air)/medium/heavy-duty trucks and buses ≤3.5/6/7/7/7N.m Front axle hub bearing friction torque for light/medium/heavy-duty trucks and buses ≤2/3.5/4.5/4.5N.m Rear axle hub bearing friction torque for light/medium/heavy-duty trucks and buses ≤4.5/6/7/7N.m	Caliper drag torque for light(hydraulic)/ light(air)/medium/heavy-duty trucks and buses ≤2.5/5/5/6/6N.m Front axle hub bearing friction torque for light/medium/heavy-duty trucks and buses ≤1.5/2.5/3.5/3.5N.m Rear axle hub bearing friction torque for light/medium/heavy-duty trucks and buses ≤3.5/4.5/5.5/5.5N.m	Caliper drag torque for light(hydraulic)/ light(air)/medium/heavy-duty trucks and buses ≤ 1.5/3.5/3.5/3.5/3.5N.m Front axle hub bearing friction torque for light/medium/heavy-duty trucks and buses ≤ 1/2/2.5/2.5N.m Rear axle hub bearing friction torque for light/medium/heavy-duty trucks and buses ≤ 2.5/3/3.5/3.5N.m
	Thermal Management	Average air conditioning power consumption for EV light/medium/heavy-duty trucks and buses under CHTC at 35°C≤ 2.6kW/18.2kW/18.2kW/6.8kW, at -7 °C ≤ 3.2kW/13.8kW/18.2kW/8.2kW, at -20 °C ≤ 10.5kW/26.3kW/26.3kW/18kW	Average air conditioning power consumption for EV light/medium/heavy-duty trucks and buses under CHTC at 35°C≤ 2.6kW/18.2kW/18.2kW/6.8kW, at -7 °C ≤ 2.9kW/12.4kW/12.4kW/7.4kW, at -20 °C ≤ 9.5kW/23.7kW/23.7kW/16.2kW	Average air conditioning power consumption for EV light/medium/heavy-duty trucks and buses under CHTC at 35°C≤ 2.1kW/14.8kW/14.8kW/5.5kW, at -7 °C ≤ 2.6kW/11.2kW/11.2kW/7.2kW, at -20 °C ≤ 8.5kW/21.3kW/21.3kW/14.6kW
	Energy Management	Fuel-saving rate of predictive energy management has reached 3%-4% Fuel-saving rate of Vehicle-Road-Cloud Energy Management has reached 3.5%-7%	Fuel-saving rate of predictive energy management has reached 3.5%-4.5% Fuel-saving rate of Vehicle-Road-Cloud Energy Management has reached 4%-8.5%	Fuel-saving rate of predictive energy management has reached 4%-4.5% Fuel-saving rate of Vehicle-Road-Cloud Energy Management has reached 4.5%-9.5%

Fig. 2.11 Technology roadmap for vehicle energy conservation

Note 1: The vehicle energy consumption test standards are sourced from the *GB 18386.1 Test Methods for Energy Consumption and Range of Electric Vehicles* (2021) and *GB 18352.6 Limits and Measurement Methods for Emissions from Light-duty Vehicles* (2016).

Note 2: In Roadmap 3.0, all indicators are leading indicators, except for lightweighting coefficient defined as an average indicator.

Chapter 3
New Energy Technology

3.1 NEV Batteries

3.1.1 Domestic and International Technical Status Comparison

3.1.1.1 Critical Materials for Power Battery Cells Present Diversified Iteration

Cathode materials: Layered ternary oxides, olivine-structured lithium iron phosphates and spinel-structured lithium manganese oxides have embraced mass production, and lithium-rich manganese-based materials have come to the introduction phase.

Anode materials: Graphite is the primary material, with synthetic graphite gaining dominance. Silicon-based composites with high specific capacity have reached the commercial mass manufacturing stage, and lithium metal anodes have started trial use.

Separators: Lithium-ion batteries mainly use polyolefin separators, which are made of polypropylene (PP) and polyethylene (PE). Wet-coated separators have become increasingly prevalent in recent years, leading to the extensive use of alumina ceramic and PVDF coating.

Electrolytes: Liquid electrolytes are still dominated by carbonate solvents and lithium hexafluorophosphate ($LiPF_6$), while new high-voltage resistant solvents and lithium bis(fluorosulfonyl)imide (LiFSI) are identified as priorities. In terms of solid-state electrolytes, despite the continuously improving ionic conductivity of polymer, oxide, and sulfide electrolytes, application verification remains necessary.

Technology Roadmap for Energy Saving and New Energy Vehicles 3.0,
https://doi.org/10.1007/978-981-95-2502-7_3

Innovative Cell Design Drives the Development of High-Energy Fast Charging Technology and Next-Generation Batteries

Specific energy in power battery cells is on the rise. Many manufacturers have developed NCM batteries with specific energy of 300Wh/kg, and some have launched 360Wh/kg hybrid solid–liquid batteries. The specific energy of lithium iron phosphate batteries can reach up to 205-210Wh/kg. Another critical metric—lifespan—continues to improve as well. For high-energy-density batteries, regular models have a lifespan of 3,000–3,500 cycles, commercial models 5,000–6,000 cycles, and premium models 2,800–4,000 cycles; energy-power balanced batteries can undergo 4,000–5,000 cycles or more; and high-power batteries last up to 50,000 cycles. Fast charging technology keeps evolving. NCM batteries have reached 4C fast charging and are headed toward 6 and 8C, while LFP batteries have already gone beyond the 4–6C level.

At the moment, businesses, academic institutions, and research organizations have made all-solid-state batteries a top priority, with several technical routes developing concurrently. Chinese enterprises have adopted different technical paths. Leading battery manufacturers like CATL and BYD that are focused on sulfide electrolytes plan to achieve mass production and assembly by 2026–2027. Emerging players like WELION and Qingtao that specialize in solid-state batteries are primarily aimed at oxide and polymer composite electrolytes.

Regarding next-generation batteries, the specific energy of lithium-sulfur battery cells has reached a maximum of 705Wh/kg, but drawbacks such as a short cycle life are impeding their industrialization.

Significant Progress Has Been Made in Technologies Such as Battery System and Structure Design, Safety, and Battery Management

Electrical and structural designs: Battery systems have now reached a new stage of platform-based development. The resulting lightweight, high assembly efficiency, superior protection performance and high mechanical strength have all greatly increased product competitiveness. With the benefit of being lightweight, the aluminum alloy casing with composite material cover has emerged as the preferred design solution. Furthermore, the assembly efficiency of battery systems has been improved through the integrated design of structural components, electrical connectors, and other parts.

Thermal management and thermal safety technology: Rapid heating at low temperatures and phase change cooling technologies have advanced quickly, fostering global competitiveness; nevertheless, all-weather applicability still requires improvements. Progress has been made in thermal runaway mechanism and diffusion-free active safety technology, with key metrics such as warning accuracy and thermal diffusion control being improved. Advances have also been achieved in the development of new thermal insulation materials.

Battery management systems: Remarkable results have been seen in improving the monitoring and early warning capabilities of battery systems as well as promoting intelligent management and adaptive optimization. Technologies like digital twins and artificial intelligence (AI) have enabled cloud management to provide more precise models and intelligent management strategies. Smart battery technology has started to be used, and verified in conjunction with power battery cells.

System integration and application: A key trend in the sector is the continued decline in battery system costs. To save costs and boost efficiency, automakers and battery manufacturers have also placed a high priority on innovation in battery system integration and application. Battery integration technologies such as CTP (Cell to Pack), CTC (Cell to Chassis), and CTB (Cell to Body) offer benefits such as higher energy density, lower costs, and simplified production processes. These technologies are now being used with maturity.

Power Battery Cell Manufacturing Has Benefited from a Larger Scale, Higher Quality and Lower Costs

Significant technological progress has been made for battery manufacturing, with a substantial reduction in production costs. There has been a prominent increase in single-unit production capacity, with single-line capacity standing at 6GWh. The process capability index (Cpk) for critical processes has surpassed 1.33, and the defect rate of battery systems built on protective technology has been lowered to PPB. Further research and improvement are required for the online monitoring and identification technology for manufacturing defects in battery materials, cells, and battery systems, as well as the battery manufacturing safety technology. Hybrid solid–liquid batteries have achieved mass production and assembly, while all-solid-state batteries are in the early stages of transitioning from laboratory samples to mass production.

A Multifaceted Quantitative Testing and Evaluation System for Power Battery Cells is Maturing

The testing and evaluation methodology for power battery cells is steadily moving from qualitative to quantitative assessment, with the gradual application of advanced technologies such as non-destructive testing, online testing, and in-situ testing. Testing technologies tailored to real-world settings are also rapidly developing. CT scanning, ultrasonic scanning, and in-situ XRD have been widely applied to non-destructive battery testing. Battery system testing methods are increasingly adapted to real-world application scenarios and operational conditions. Transitioning from qualitative to quantitative assessment, they make up a quantitative evaluation system for reliability and safety. In light of the complicated thermal runaway circumstances during vehicle driving, new test items such as high-temperature thermal runaway and multi-point thermal runaway that simulate real-world vehicle occupancy status are developed based on the methods specified in mandatory standards. This results in a comprehensive test methodology and evaluation system for vehicle thermal diffusion.

The Recycling Industry Continues Innovation, and a Carbon Footprint Database for Power Battery Cells is to Be Established

Cascade utilization technology has made a significant progress and achieved fruitful commercial application. Varied products with a combined capacity of 20GWh have benefited from the technology in a wide range of commercial scenarios such as backup power in communication base stations, forklifts, AGVs, and small energy storage systems. Several technical routes of cascade utilization now coexist, including dismantling and repurposing, module-level recycling, and whole-pack recycling. With the popularity of power battery cell integration technology, whole-pack cascade utilization, which is more cost-effective and secure, is taking up a greater share.

Recycling refers to the process of dismantling, crushing and metallurgical recovery. The dismantling and recycling process is usually divided into two parts: pre-treatment and metal recovery. Metal recovery may be accomplished in a variety of technological ways using well-established processes. Therefore, developing more convenient and less expensive direct repair and regeneration procedures for the cathode materials of lithium-ion batteries is of great significance.

The industrial chain for power battery cells is intricate. It is challenging to collect primary prospective data from the upstream industry chain in order to establish a battery carbon footprint database. How to quickly and effectively collect and consolidate key industry chain data without compromising privacy and security is a difficult and urgent mission to be completed.

3.1.2 Outlook on Technology Development Trends

3.1.2.1 Higher Specific Capacity and Lower Costs Are Priorities for the Development of Critical Materials

Cathode materials are advancing toward higher specific capacity and lower costs, with diversified materials in layered, olivine, and spinel structures developing in tandem. Ultra-high nickel materials, mid-nickel ultra-high-voltage materials, high-compaction-density lithium iron phosphates, high-voltage spinel lithium nickel manganese oxides, high-specific-capacity lithium-rich manganese-based oxides, high-manganese lithium iron manganese phosphates, among others, are expected to offer better comprehensive electrochemical performance.

In terms of anode materials, graphite is anticipated to progress toward greater specific capacity, higher C-rate, and lower costs. It is also important to improve the cycle life and initial Coulombic efficiency of high-specific-capacity silicon-based, tin-based anode materials and their composites. High-capacity alloy anode materials, such as lithium metal composite anode, are expected to improve the uniformity of lithium deposition through sophisticated alloying design and 3D structuring.

Thinner separators is becoming increasingly popular without compromising safety. Besides separator coating, base material research has focused on developing new separator substrates using synthetic materials like polyimide (PI), polyethylene terephthalate (PET), meta-aramid (PMIA), para-aramid (PPTA), and poly(p-phenylene benzobisoxazole) (PBO) as well as using high-temperature resistant resins as separator substrates in order to increase separator safety.

The development of new products such as novel lithium salts, new additives, and high-voltage electrolytes is a key focus, with emphasis on high-voltage electrolytes, fast-charging electrolytes for lithium iron phosphate batteries, flame-retardant electrolytes, low-temperature electrolytes, and electrolytes for high-nickel NCM batteries.

Higher ionic conductivity is the common goal of solid electrolyte development. Polymer electrolytes require higher oxidation resistance to be suitable for higher-voltage cathodes; sulfide electrolytes and halide electrolytes require improved air stability and lower requirements on humidity control in the production environment; and composite solid electrolytes require comprehensive optimization of ionic conductivity, voltage window, and interface compatibility.

3.1.2.2 Battery Cells Are Evolving Towards Higher Specific Energy, Greater Safety, Faster Charging, and Lower Costs

Liquid lithium-ion battery technology continues to improve in energy density, safety, power, and environmental adaptability. For higher specific energy, high-voltage, high-nickel, and lithium-rich cathode materials are to be developed. High-voltage, wide-temperature range electrolytes, as well as film-forming additives for both the cathode and anode are key areas of development. Silicon-carbon/silicon-oxide anodes with high capacity and high initial Coulombic efficiency should be developed to work with technologies such as pre-lithiation of cathodes and anodes and lightweight auxiliary materials. Fast charging requires the use of technologies such as bulk-phase doping or surface coating of the cathode and amorphous carbon coating of the anode, as well as matching high-conductivity electrolytes, optimizing the conductive agent network, and applying high-porosity separators.

As for hybrid solid–liquid lithium-ion batteries, it is necessary to continuously improve key application indicators such as safety, specific energy, and power while maintaining high energy density. Hybrid solid–liquid electrolytes with low liquid content, in-situ solidification, and high-safety, high-capacity anodes are to be developed for higher safety. Developing lightweight, low-expansion lithium alloy anodes and pairing them with cathode materials with high specific capacity, such as high-nickel and lithium-rich materials, are crucial steps in increasing energy density. For higher power, it is important to continuously optimize electrode materials and microstructures such as electrodes to enhance the compatibility of solid–solid and solid–liquid interfaces, reduce interfacial impedance, construct a 3D conductive network, and achieve efficient conduction of both electrons and ions.

In the field of all-solid-state lithium batteries, cathode materials are focused on high specific capacity, high-nickel NCM systems in the short term; long-term development will shift toward high-capacity, high-voltage materials like lithium-rich manganese-based and nickel manganese lithium oxides. Regarding the anode system, graphite anodes are intended for short-term usage, silicon-based anodes for medium-term use, and lithium metal anodes for long-term use, while stability issues still need to be addressed. It is necessary to develop oxide, sulfide, halide, and polymer solid electrolytes and their composite applications to resolve challenges in solid electrolyte material development, solid electrolyte membrane forming processes, and stable interfacial constructions.

Finally, next-generation batteries are under research along several technical routes. Cathode and anode materials come in a wide range of options and are still being tested. Mature systems are yet to be identified. Lithium-sulfur batteries will be improved in cathode material design, electrolyte system selection, separator modification, and decay mechanism research.

3.1.2.3 System Integration is Developing Towards Lightweight, High Safety, and Maintainability

New high-performance materials are being applied to the electrical and structural design of power battery cells. New low-density lightweight materials are under development, including high-strength aluminum alloys, magnesium alloys, and carbon fiber composites. Leading trends in mechanical protection for power battery cells include material technology, refined structural design, establishment of multi-level security systems, and development of intelligent monitoring and early warning systems.

In terms of thermal management and thermal safety, internal heating and phase-change cooling are gaining momentum. Thermal management systems are becoming increasingly integrated, and AI-based thermal control has emerged as a new trend. The mechanism and theory of battery thermal runaway are maturing, thermal runaway prevention technologies and applications are advancing quickly, and thermoelectric separation has become a widely-accepted approach in battery system design.

Regarding battery management, SOX estimation is embracing high precision, adaptability, and intelligence. With the development of AI and big data, SOX is expected to enable hierarchical processing from the edge to the cloud. Smart batteries capable of real-time monitoring, dynamic regulation, and autonomous repair are an industry-wide demand.

Concerning vehicle application and integration design, battery system integration technologies continue to innovate and merge, alongside a further decline in the number of components and structural parts. Future development will concentrate on long range, fast charging, high safety, and intelligence. Modular CTP technology is aimed at battery swapping, while integrated CTC/CTB technology tends toward fast charging. Priorities in solid-state battery system integration technology include control over a broad operating temperature range for all climatic conditions, efficient gas monitoring and safety protection, controllable high-strength restraint systems, and efficient balancing technology.

3.1.2.4 Larger-Scale, Extreme Battery Manufacturing Seeks a Balance Between Efficiency and Quality, as Well as Safety and Inexpensiveness

Battery materials: The manufacture of cathode materials will place a high priority on material structural stability, surface and interface modification, effective particle morphology control, and new energy-efficient production processes. The future trends in anode material manufacturing are material structure optimization, innovation in synthesis methods, and interface modification. The development of more efficient synthesis methods, improvement of forming processes, and optimization of sintering processes will be the main areas of concentration for the production of solid electrolytes.

Liquid cells: Standardized, high-quality, large-scale, and intelligent manufacturing is the trend. Active and passive measures such as detection and elimination will be utilized to achieve safety control in battery manufacturing. It is also important to establish large models for the battery manufacturing process using data-driven methods. This will enable closed-loop management of incoming materials, processes, and outputs, leading to steady improvement in battery manufacturing quality.

All-solid-state battery cells: Lamination process will be the mainstay, while elastic complementarity is required on the battery structure. Priorities include the comprehensive application of high-speed continuous lamination, laser die-cutting, laser welding, isostatic pressing, ultrasonic and thermal pressing technologies, and the development of online control technologies and equipment for pores and porosity during the manufacturing process.

Battery systems: Battery system manufacturing is aiming for higher energy density, longer service life, lower costs, higher safety, and better environmental compatibility. The standardization of battery interfaces and dimensions will help reduce manufacturing costs and improve the compatibility and replaceability of battery systems.

3.1.2.5 The Testing and Evaluation and Standard System is Internationally Leading, and R&D Tools Need Faster Breakthroughs

In the field of power battery simulation tools, electrical-thermal-mechanical multiphysics and multi-dimensional coupled simulation is expected to help accelerate product development and shorten the R&D cycle. It is necessary to develop simulation technologies at different product levels, including battery cells, modules, and systems, and to make breakthroughs in the integration of multi-physics, multi-dimensional, and multi-level simulation technologies as well as in the development of R&D tools.

In addition, industry-wide standardized, consistent testing methodology should be established for critical materials, and lifecycle rapid evaluation procedures should be developed to establish structure–activity relationship with battery performance. It is also important to make critical material testing more intelligent and digital, achieve quantitative evaluation, build lifecycle simulation models for critical materials, and utilize R&D tools to realize digital upgrading of the battery cell development process. Regarding the development and application of next-generation batteries, efforts are required to assess the reliability of packing technology and the fatigue durability of high-strength modules, and establish a mechanical structure reliability evaluation system under ultra-large constraints.

3.1.2.6 Battery Recycling Efficiency Shows an Increase and the Lifecycle Carbon Footprint Management of Power Battery Cells Becomes a Global Research Focus

In terms of cascade utilization, breakthroughs should be made in key technologies such as the identification of safety hazards in retired batteries and the analytical method based on "white box" historical data should be improved. Extending to the upstream, it is necessary to conduct research on battery design that facilitates cascade utilization, promote standardized and modular battery design to simplify disassembly and recycling, and lower the complexity and expenses of the recycling process.

As for recycling, breakthroughs should be made in critical technologies such as the efficient recovery of materials like electrolytes, and barriers to the high-value usage of battery materials with low residual value should be removed. Low-carbon, compact-process recycling procedures should be developed to reduce energy consumption and carbon footprint; and the integrated technology process that combines recycling, double-salt materials and precursors should be promoted. Additionally, it is essential to develop automated and intelligent equipment, make recycling equipment more automated and intelligent, and optimize the recycling process using AI and IoT technologies for greater efficiency.

In the carbon footprint management system for power battery cells, establishing a battery production database and an industrial reference database is the most crucial step in the consolidation of foundational data. Future efforts should concentrate on building a reliable carbon footprint database for critical battery materials and recycled materials, with comprehensive and accurate data. Also, it is important to develop carbon footprint calculation models applicable to businesses and products to accurately assess the carbon footprint of power battery cells and provide a scientific basis for the subsequent identification and analysis of potential in carbon footprint reduction.

3.1.3 Development Goals and Milestones for 2040

As the automotive industry reaches a new stage of electrification and intelligent transformation, power battery cells are expected to play an increasingly crucial role. It is not only a solution to many outstanding issues with new energy vehicles but also a key to the integration of energy and transportation as well as low-carbon, sustainable development.

By 2030, it is estimated to achieve an energy density of 500 Wh/kg and 1,000 Wh/L, and a cycle life of 1,000 cycles/10 years for the high specific energy route; and an energy density of 250 Wh/kg and 500 Wh/L, and a cycle life of 3,000 cycles/15 years for the high cost performance route. Focuses are on increasing the nickel content in NCM materials, gradually transitioning to low-cobalt/cobalt-free multi-element materials, and enhancing the compaction density of lithium iron phosphate materials; and also improving the performance of silicon-based materials. It is necessary to conduct application verification for materials used in next-generation batteries such as manganese-based cathodes and high-capacity alloy anodes, develop low-liquid-content hybrid solid–liquid electrolyte materials and technologies, and accelerate the system design, engineering process development, and application verification of all-solid-state batteries. Research is required on the efficient heat dissipation technology for fast charging of new energy vehicles, the intelligent design and optimization of battery thermal management systems, the no thermal runaway and diffusion design for power battery systems, and the digital safety protection technology. Efforts should be made to study the efficient manufacturing technology for silicon anodes, research on the mass manufacturing technology for power battery cells and develop related equipment, and develop integrated equipment for slurry preparation, coating, rolling, and slitting. It is also essential to develop an R&D toolchain for power battery cells, establish sound evaluation technologies and standards for critical materials of power battery cells, and build a system of testing standards for next-generation batteries and systems. Research should also be made on the rapid performance evaluation and screening technology and flexible and non-destructive disassembly and reassembly technology for retired power battery cells, as well as eco-friendly, green, low-carbon, and sustainable recycling technologies. Finally, carbon emission management during the battery production phase should be strengthened based on research on the lifecycle carbon footprint of batteries.

By 2035, it is estimated to achieve an energy density of 600 Wh/kg and 1,200 Wh/L, and a cycle life of 1,200 cycles/10 years for the high specific energy route; and an energy density of 300 Wh/kg and 600 Wh/L, and a cycle life of 3,000 cycles/15 years for the high cost performance route. Focuses are on the research, development, and industrial promotion of high-nickel composite cathode materials, spinel lithium nickel manganese oxides, and lithium-rich manganese-based materials for solid-state batteries; and also the research and development of lithium metal composite anode materials, and the enhancement of battery performance and safety through sophisticated alloying design and 3D structuring. It is necessary to further improve key indicators such as energy density, safety, and lifespan of all-solid-state batteries, reduce the costs and manufacturing expenses of battery materials, and accelerate their widespread application. Efforts are required to research on the electrochemical models, battery management technology, thermal management technology, and safety technology of power battery cells, promote the application of new structural materials as well as conductive and thermal management materials, and develop new technologies and processes for the manufacturing of power battery systems. It is also essential to apply process simulation and digital twins to the manufacturing process, study the online monitoring and identification technology for battery manufacturing defects, and develop continuous assembly processes and novel manufacturing equipment for all-solid-state battery cells. Efforts should further be made to construct an AI-based material development platform, gradually achieve the localization of industrial R&D tools, develop high-equivalence, multi-factor coupling accelerated lifespan testing technology and lifecycle dynamic safety evaluation technology, and establish standards for the multi-physical-field, multi-dimensional comprehensive performance simulation and virtual evaluation of batteries. Research is required on direct recycling and repair technologies for raw materials from different sources as well as targeted recycling technologies for new power battery cell technology routes. Finally, it is important to promote the use of recycled battery materials, thus reducing the carbon footprint throughout the lifecycle of power battery cells.

By 2040, it is estimated to achieve an energy density of 700 Wh/kg and 1,400 Wh/L, and a cycle life of 1,500 cycles/10 years for the high specific energy route; and an energy density of 350 Wh/kg and 700 Wh/L, and a cycle life of 3,000 cycles/15 years for the high cost performance route. Focus is on the development and industrialization of multi-electron transfer materials. It is necessary to develop and apply low-lithium-content and anode-free technologies, and promote the development and application of all-solid-state batteries and next-generation batteries with higher specific energy. Efforts are required to research on new power battery system integration technologies and develop technologies that integrate batteries, chassis, and safety based on novel materials. All-solid-state battery manufacturing technologies should be developed, including research on the batch preparation technology for electrolyte materials, the interface modification technology, the lamination process technology, the preparation and assembly technology for solid electrolyte membranes, the dry manufacturing technology, and novel binder applications. Finally, it is essential to develop R&D tools that cover applications at the levels of materials, electrodes, battery cells, and battery systems, develop multi-field coupled simulation evaluation technologies for battery systems and twin technologies for usage safety status, and improve comprehensive battery performance evaluation standards.

3.1.4 Technology Roadmap

In the future, critical battery materials will embrace better performance through ongoing optimization. Cell design technology is expected to keep improving cells' specific energy, cycle life, and cost performance. System integration is divided into four key aspects: electrical structure and design, thermal management and safety, battery management systems, and vehicle application and integration. The battery manufacturing technology roadmap covers three major topics: material manufacturing, battery manufacturing, and battery system manufacturing. The technology roadmap for R&D tools, testing & evaluation, and standard system focuses on R&D toolchain, material testing, lifespan and safety assessment, and standard system building. Performance evaluation of retired batteries, non-destructive dismantling, and green recycling are primary components of the recycling dimension, all with the goal of promoting the battery industry's sustainable development. The thematic technology roadmap is shown in Fig. 3.1.

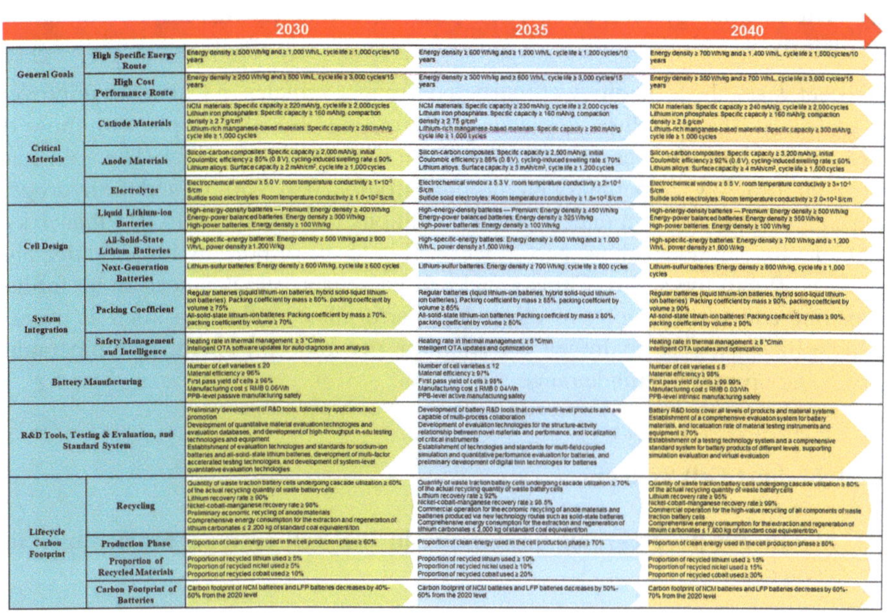

		2030	2035	2040
General Goals	High Specific Energy Route	Energy density ≥ 500 Wh/kg and ≥ 1,000 Wh/L, cycle life ≥ 1,000 cycles/10 years	Energy density ≥ 600 Wh/kg and ≥ 1,200 Wh/L, cycle life ≥ 1,200 cycles/10 years	Energy density ≥ 700 Wh/kg and ≥ 1,400 Wh/L, cycle life ≥ 1,500 cycles/10 years
	High Cost Performance Route	Energy density ≥ 250 Wh/kg and ≥ 500 Wh/L, cycle life ≥ 3,000 cycles/15 years	Energy density ≥ 300 Wh/kg and ≥ 600 Wh/L, cycle life ≥ 3,000 cycles/15 years	Energy density ≥ 350 Wh/kg and ≥ 700 Wh/L, cycle life ≥ 3,000 cycles/15 years
Critical Materials	Cathode Materials	NCM materials: Specific capacity ≥ 220 mAh/g, cycle life ≥ 2,000 cycles Lithium iron phosphates: Specific capacity ≥ 160 mAh/g, compaction density ≥ 2.7 g/cm³ Lithium-rich manganese-based materials: Specific capacity ≥ 280 mAh/g, cycle life ≥ 1,000 cycles	NCM materials: Specific capacity ≥ 230 mAh/g, cycle life ≥ 2,000 cycles Lithium iron phosphates: Specific capacity ≥ 160 mAh/g, compaction density ≥ 2.75 g/cm³ Lithium-rich manganese-based materials: Specific capacity ≥ 290 mAh/g, cycle life ≥ 1,000 cycles	NCM materials: Specific capacity ≥ 240 mAh/g, cycle life ≥ 2,000 cycles Lithium iron phosphates: Specific capacity ≥ 160 mAh/g, compaction density ≥ 2.8 g/cm³ Lithium-rich manganese-based materials: Specific capacity ≥ 300 mAh/g, cycle life ≥ 1,000 cycles
	Anode Materials	Silicon-carbon composites: Specific capacity ≥ 2,000 mAh/g, initial Coulombic efficiency ≥ 85% (0.8 V), cycling-induced swelling rate ≤ 90% Lithium alloys: Surface capacity ≥ 2 mAh/cm², cycle life ≥ 1,000 cycles	Silicon-carbon composites: Specific capacity ≥ 2,500 mAh/g, initial Coulombic efficiency ≥ 88% (0.8 V), cycling-induced swelling rate ≤ 70% Lithium alloys: Surface capacity ≥ 3 mAh/cm², cycle life ≥ 1,200 cycles	Silicon-carbon composites: Specific capacity ≥ 3,200 mAh/g, initial Coulombic efficiency ≥ 92% (0.8 V), cycling-induced swelling rate ≤ 60% Lithium alloys: Surface capacity ≥ 4 mAh/cm², cycle life ≥ 1,500 cycles
	Electrolytes	Electrochemical window ≥ 5.0 V, room temperature conductivity ≥ 1×10^{-3} S/cm Sulfide solid electrolytes: Room temperature conductivity ≥ 1.0×10^{-2} S/cm	Electrochemical window ≥ 5.3 V, room temperature conductivity ≥ 2×10^{-3} S/cm Sulfide solid electrolytes: Room temperature conductivity ≥ 1.5×10^{-2} S/cm	Electrochemical window ≥ 5.5 V, room temperature conductivity ≥ 3×10^{-3} S/cm Sulfide solid electrolytes: Room temperature conductivity ≥ 2.0×10^{-2} S/cm
Cell Design	Liquid Lithium-ion Batteries	High-energy-density batteries — Premium: Energy density ≥ 400 Wh/kg Energy-power balanced batteries: Energy density ≥ 300 Wh/kg High-power batteries: Energy density ≥ 100 Wh/kg	High-energy-density batteries — Premium: Energy density ≥ 450 Wh/kg Energy-power balanced batteries: Energy density ≥ 325 Wh/kg High-power batteries: Energy density ≥ 100 Wh/kg	High-energy-density batteries — Premium: Energy density ≥ 500 Wh/kg Energy-power balanced batteries: Energy density ≥ 350 Wh/kg High-power batteries: Energy density ≥ 100 Wh/kg
	All-Solid-State Lithium Batteries	High-specific-energy batteries: Energy density ≥ 500 Wh/kg and ≥ 900 Wh/L, power density ≥1,200 W/kg	High-specific-energy batteries: Energy density ≥ 600 Wh/kg and ≥ 1,000 Wh/L, power density ≥1,500 W/kg	High-specific-energy batteries: Energy density ≥ 700 Wh/kg and ≥ 1,200 Wh/L, power density ≥1,800 W/kg
	Next-Generation Batteries	Lithium-sulfur batteries: Energy density ≥ 600 Wh/kg, cycle life ≥ 600 cycles	Lithium-sulfur batteries: Energy density ≥ 700 Wh/kg, cycle life ≥ 800 cycles	Lithium-sulfur batteries: Energy density ≥ 800 Wh/kg, cycle life ≥ 1,000 cycles
System Integration	Packing Coefficient	Regular batteries (liquid lithium-ion batteries, hybrid solid-liquid lithium-ion batteries): Packing coefficient by mass ≥ 80%, packing coefficient by volume ≥ 75% All-solid-state lithium-ion batteries: Packing coefficient by mass ≥ 70%, packing coefficient by volume ≥ 70%	Regular batteries (liquid lithium-ion batteries, hybrid solid-liquid lithium-ion batteries): Packing coefficient by mass ≥ 85%, packing coefficient by volume ≥ 85% All-solid-state lithium-ion batteries: Packing coefficient by mass ≥ 80%, packing coefficient by volume ≥ 80%	Regular batteries (liquid lithium-ion batteries, hybrid solid-liquid lithium-ion batteries): Packing coefficient by mass ≥ 90%, packing coefficient by volume ≥ 90% All-solid-state lithium-ion batteries: Packing coefficient by mass ≥ 90%, packing coefficient by volume ≥ 90%
	Safety Management and Intelligence	Heating rate in thermal management: ≥ 3 °C/min Intelligent OTA software updates for auto diagnosis and analysis	Heating rate in thermal management: ≥ 5 °C/min Intelligent OTA updates and optimization	Heating rate in thermal management: ≥ 8 °C/min Intelligent OTA updates and optimization
Battery Manufacturing		Number of cell varieties ≤ 20 Material efficiency ≥ 96% First pass yield of cells ≥ 96% Manufacturing cost ≤ RMB 0.06/Wh PPB-level passive manufacturing safety	Number of cell varieties ≤ 12 Material efficiency ≥ 97% First pass yield of cells ≥ 98% Manufacturing cost ≤ RMB 0.04/Wh PPB-level active manufacturing safety	Number of cell varieties ≤ 8 Material efficiency ≥ 98% First pass yield of cells ≥ 99.99% Manufacturing cost ≤ RMB 0.03/Wh PPB-level intrinsic manufacturing safety
R&D Tools, Testing & Evaluation, and Standard System		Preliminary development of R&D tools, followed by application and promotion Development of quantitative material evaluation technologies and evaluation databases, and development of high-throughput in-situ testing technologies and equipment Establishment of evaluation technologies and standards for sodium-ion batteries and all-solid-state lithium batteries, development of multi-factor accelerated testing technologies, and development of system-level quantitative evaluation technologies	Development of battery R&D tools that cover multi-level products and are capable of multi-process collaboration Development of evaluation technologies for the structure-activity relationship between novel materials and performance, and localization of critical instruments Establishment of technologies and standards for multi-field coupled simulation and quantitative performance evaluation for batteries, and preliminary development of digital twin technologies for batteries	Battery R&D tools cover all levels of products and material systems Establishment of a comprehensive evaluation system for battery materials, and localization rate of material testing instruments and equipment ≥ 70% Establishment of a testing technology system and a comprehensive standard system for battery products of different levels, supporting simulation evaluation and virtual evaluation
Lifecycle Carbon Footprint	Recycling	Quantity of waste traction battery cells undergoing cascade utilization ≥ 60% of the actual recycling quantity of waste battery cells Lithium recovery rate ≥ 90% Nickel-cobalt-manganese recovery rate ≥ 98% Preliminary economic recycling of anode materials Comprehensive energy consumption for the extraction and regeneration of lithium carbonates ≤ 2,200 kg of standard coal equivalent/ton	Quantity of waste traction battery cells undergoing cascade utilization ≥ 70% of the actual recycling quantity of waste battery cells Lithium recovery rate ≥ 92% Nickel-cobalt-manganese recovery rate ≥ 98.5% Commercial operation for the economic recycling of anode materials and batteries produced via new technology routes such as solid-state batteries Comprehensive energy consumption for the extraction and regeneration of lithium carbonates ≤ 2,000 kg of standard coal equivalent/ton	Quantity of waste traction battery cells undergoing cascade utilization ≥ 80% of the actual recycling quantity of waste battery cells Lithium recovery rate ≥ 95% Nickel-cobalt-manganese recovery rate ≥ 99% Commercial operation for the high-value recycling of all components of waste traction battery cells Comprehensive energy consumption for the extraction and regeneration of lithium carbonates ≤ 1,800 kg of standard coal equivalent/ton
	Production Phase	Proportion of clean energy used in the cell production phase ≥ 60%	Proportion of clean energy used in the cell production phase ≥ 70%	Proportion of clean energy used in the cell production phase ≥ 80%
	Proportion of Recycled Materials	Proportion of recycled lithium used ≥ 5% Proportion of recycled nickel used ≥ 5% Proportion of recycled cobalt used ≥ 10%	Proportion of recycled lithium used ≥ 10% Proportion of recycled nickel used ≥ 10% Proportion of recycled cobalt used ≥ 20%	Proportion of recycled lithium used ≥ 15% Proportion of recycled nickel used ≥ 15% Proportion of recycled cobalt used ≥ 30%
	Carbon Footprint of Batteries	Carbon footprint of NCM batteries and LFP batteries decreases by 40%–50% from the 2020 level	Carbon footprint of NCM batteries and LFP batteries decreases by 50%–60% from the 2020 level	Carbon footprint of NCM batteries and LFP batteries decreases by 60%–70% from the 2020 level

Fig. 3.1 Thematic technology roadmap

3.2 Fuel Cell

3.2.1 *Domestic and International Technical Status Comparison*

3.2.1.1 Fuel Cell Vehicle

(1) **Some technical indicators of fuel cell commercial vehicles are internationally leading**

China has the largest number of fuel cell commercial vehicles in the world, and its large-scale verification is relatively rich. At present, the demonstration application is mainly in medium and short-distance scenarios in demonstration urban clusters, while also actively promoting the application in medium and long-distance transportation scenarios. Foreign fuel cell commercial vehicles are mostly in the stage of prototype production or small-scale trial operation. Domestic fuel cell commercial vehicles have a lifespan of about 400,000 km, a pure hydrogen range of about 500 km, a whole vehicle purchase cost of about 1 to 1.5 million yuan (for 12 m buses), and a minimum hydrogen consumption of 5 kg per 100 km (for 12 m buses) in actual road conditions. Although it is still far from the industrialization target, it leads in performance indicators such as cost compared with international counterparts of the same type, and is on par with international counterparts in terms of hydrogen consumption per 100 km and fuel cell power.

(2) **The technology level of fuel cell passenger vehicles has improved significantly**

In recent years, the technology of fuel cell passenger vehicles in China has improved significantly. The overall performance indicators are basically on par with those of foreign products, but there is still a gap from the world's top level. The cold start temperature at low temperatures has dropped from −20 to −30 °C, and the hydrogen consumption per 100 km under typical conditions has decreased to less than 1 kg/100 km. Toyota models have performed well in terms of pure hydrogen range and the best 30-min top speed. China's fuel cell passenger vehicles need to be further improved and verified in terms of product performance indicators such as overall vehicle lifespan, cost, hydrogen consumption per 100 km, operating temperature range, and operating altitude range.

3.2.1.2 Fuel Cell System

(1) **Significant progress has been made in fuel cell systems for commercial vehicles**

In recent years, the domestic level of fuel cell systems and components has improved significantly. Compared with the advanced level abroad, the domestic level has risen from catching up in 2020 to running side by side in 2024. During the 14th Five-Year Plan period, the performance of commercial vehicle fuel cell systems has improved significantly in terms of rated power, maximum efficiency, mass power density, and low-temperature starting temperature.

(2) **Significant progress has been made in fuel cell systems for passenger vehicles**

In recent years, the technical level of fuel cell systems for passenger vehicles in China has improved significantly. The overall performance indicators are basically on par with those of foreign products. The rated power of the system has increased from 60 to 90 kW, and the volumetric specific power of the system has increased from 600 to 800W/L; The peak efficiency of the system has been optimized from 56 to 60%; The low-temperature environment adaptability has been reduced from −20 to −30 °C, and the start-up time has been significantly shortened, basically meeting the usage requirements in most areas of the country. At present, the performance indicators of fuel cell systems for passenger vehicles in China, such as rated power, peak efficiency, volumetric specific power and cold start temperature, are basically on par with international standards. However, the test and evaluation criteria for life remain to be improved, and there is still a gap in the durability test method that combines vibration, temperature and humidity variation, and the influence of pollutants.

(3) **Some technical indicators of BOP for vehicle fuel cells are close to the international advanced level**

The BOP technology for vehicle fuel cells is close to the international advanced level, and the product performance has been greatly improved. China has achieved large-scale production of first-level components for fuel cells by domestic enterprises. The technologies of air compressors, hydrogen circulation systems, humidifiers and electronic water pumps in each component of the BOP industrial chain are relatively mature. The domestic fuel cell air compressor technology for vehicles is close to the international advanced level. The technical indicators such as response time, efficiency and pressure ratio of fuel cell air compressors have been significantly improved and are basically close to the international advanced level, but there is still a certain gap in the maximum speed (limited by the technology itself and the level of the controller) and noise control. New materials, new design concepts and new manufacturing processes have been applied to the hydrogen cycle system, driving significant performance improvement and rapid cost reduction.

3.2.1.3 Fuel Cell Stack

(1) **Stack performance indicators have improved significantly**

Typical indicators of fuel cell stacks include single-stack power, power density, minimum cold start temperature, lifespan and cost, all of which have improved significantly in recent years. At present, fuel cell stacks are still produced in small batches. More than 7,000 stacks were shipped in 2023, with total power rising from 175 MW in 2019 to 931.2 MW. Graphite stacks overtook metal stacks by 54% in 2023. Compared with the leading level abroad, China's commercial vehicle fuel cell stacks have achieved parallel and even leading performance in terms of single-stack power, stack power density and cold start temperature; It lags behind foreign leading levels in terms of cost and lifespan.

(2) **The performance of the plate batch manufacturing process is on par with international standards**

The domestic graphite bipolar plate technology has developed very rapidly in recent years and is on par with that of foreign countries, but to ensure the strength of the plates, the thickness is usually more than 2 mm. To meet the demands of high-power fuel cells, composite film-pressed carbon plates have developed rapidly in China. Metal plate manufacturing technology has broken through the multi-step forming technology of fine-grained microchannels, increasing the depth to width ratio of microchannels from less than 0.4 to more than 0.7, significantly improving the heat and mass transfer efficiency of the plates, reaching the level of metal plates used in two generations of Toyota MIRAI abroad; At the same time, a breakthrough was made in the corrosion-resistant conductive coating technology, which passed the vehicle operation test for more than 10,000 h. Compared with the more mature fuel cell business model abroad, China's metal plate manufacturing is lacking in terms of manufacturing efficiency and cost control. China has made considerable progress in plate technology in terms of manufacturing accuracy and mass production, but there is still room for improvement in efficient manufacturing methods and processing cost control. Toyota Boshok has reduced the manufacturing time of its new production line by 10 times through the development of continuous plate forming technology. The Fraunhofer Institute in Germany has developed roll-to-roll plate manufacturing technology. Ballard has launched the "3 by 3" plan for manufacturing ultra-thin and low-cost graphite plates, aiming to further improve plate manufacturing efficiency and reduce plate manufacturing costs.

3.2.1.4 Membrane Electrode Assembly for Fuel Cell

(1) **Membrane electrode technology has caught up with the international advanced level**

China's domestic fuel cell membrane electrode technology has steadily improved. The membrane electrode power density has improved significantly from 1.1 W/cm^2 in 2021 to 1.6 W/cm^2 in 2024. The lifespan of the membrane electrode also increased from 10,000 h in 2021 to 20,000 h in 2024. The Pt loading of domestic membrane electrode assembly decreased from 0.45 mg/cm^2 in 2021 to 0.25 mg/cm^2 in 2024, while the platinum usage was significantly reduced while maintaining or even improving performance. China's domestic fuel cell membrane electrode technology has caught up with the international advanced level. While ensuring performance and lifespan, the Pt loading is lower than that of foreign products, which is more cost-effective.

(2) **The industrialization capacity of key materials has broken through rapidly, and the gap with foreign countries has narrowed**

China has made significant progress in key materials for fuel cells such as proton exchange membranes, catalysts, carbon paper and bipolar plates, and the gap with foreign countries has narrowed. Further breakthroughs are needed in the high consistency film-forming process of proton exchange membranes over a wide temperature range, the high consistency high yield preparation process of catalysts, the high consistency dispersion process of carbon paper, and the high durability low cost coating process of plates.

3.2.2 *Outlook on Technology Development Trends*

3.2.2.1 Fuel Cell Vehicles

China leads foreign countries in the research and development and demonstration of fuel cell commercial vehicles. Abroad, hundreds of fuel cell buses are still being demonstrated, while fuel cell trucks are mainly in the development and testing stage. In China, the main models for promoting fuel cell commercial vehicles are light trucks, buses and heavy-duty trucks, among which long-distance heavy-duty trucks will be the focus of future promotion. The development of fuel cell power systems with high power, long range, low energy consumption, long life and high safety is the key to promoting them to medium and long-distance logistics and medium and long-distance heavy-duty transportation scenarios.

Passenger vehicles have higher requirements for the comfort and volumetric power density of fuel cell systems. In the future, key technologies such as fuel cell vehicle power matching and control for different scenarios (such as full power type, range extended type, etc.), vehicle energy management and waste heat utilization, intake and exhaust noise control will be focused on to significantly improve various performance indicators. A vehicle power technology platform with high universality and safety will be formed. On this basis, develop multiple application scenarios such as railways, ships, aircraft, hydraulic excavators, forklifts, agricultural tractors, fixed power stations, combined heat and power, etc., to promote the wide application and comprehensive progress of fuel cell technology.

3.2.2.2 Fuel Cell Systems

Fuel cell systems for commercial vehicles: The **power** of fuel cell systems is constantly increasing to better meet the operational needs of medium and heavy commercial vehicles. In the commercial vehicle operation scenario, hydrogen costs account for a high proportion of the total cost of ownership throughout the vehicle's life cycle. Commercial vehicle fuel cell systems need to focus on **improving efficiency**. The durability of the fuel cell system is also an important factor affecting usage and maintenance costs. Both at home and abroad, the durability target for commercial vehicle fuel cell systems has been set at 30,000 h. It is necessary to study the performance degradation characteristics of fuel cell systems under coupled load cycles, vibration conditions, temperature and humidity alternations, and the influence of pollutants, to develop whole machine health management technology, and to establish relevant test and evaluation standards.

For fuel cell systems in passenger vehicles: In addition to the indicators mentioned above, the architecture of fuel cell power systems is constantly evolving, and the structural form is gradually transitioning from modular distributed and integrated in the cabin to integrated fuel cell systems and power systems in the cabin. **High dynamic response characteristics** are important considerations for fuel cell systems in passenger vehicles due to the demand of dynamic variable load conditions. Fast startup and lifespan in low-temperature conditions also need to be improved. In addition, attention needs to be paid to mass production and cost reduction technologies.

For fuel cell system accessory BOP: Two-stage air compressors and centrifugal air compressors with expuders may become the mainstream type of air compressors for fuel cells in the future. The circulating pump + ejector parallel system may become the mainstream option for the current fuel cell hydrogen supply system and has significant potential in future technological developments. As the system power increases, the problem of fuel cell heat dissipation will become more prominent. Improving coolant cooling systems, phase change material cooling, and high thermal conductivity material cooling will become increasingly important. High integration and high efficiency of the electrical control system will help improve efficiency and reduce costs. An electronic control system software and hardware platform that combines functional safety, high real-time computing power, and supports AI algorithms is also a future trend.

3.2.2.3 Fuel Cell Stacks and Membrane Electrode Assembly

The technological development directions for fuel cell stacks include improving stack efficiency, reducing costs, extending lifespan, and optimizing the use of base materials, such as using lighter and stronger bipolar plate materials, and enhancing the performance of membrane electrode assemblies (MEAs). In terms of key technologies for stacks and membrane electrode assembly in our country, the main problem lies in the insufficient product advancement of key materials and the inadequate manufacturing level. Before 2030, the focus should be on technologies such as bipolar plate materials and preparation, membrane electrode assembly, electrolyte materials, catalysts, gas diffusion layers, and seals; Before 2040, focus should be on material technology and evaluation and analysis technology, as well as production and manufacturing technologies such as high-performance coating, membrane electrode and battery packaging, flow channel forming, surface treatment, aging inhibition, impurity and sealing inspection.

3.2.3 Development Goals and Milestones for 2040

By means of national leadership, industry collaboration and enterprise guidance, focus on the pain points and challenges of fuel cell vehicles, build an artificial intelligence-assisted multi-level collaborative design and fabrication system of vehicle—system—stack—membrane electrode, and tackle key core technologies and fabrication processes.

By 2030, the scale of fuel cell vehicles will be more than 500,000 units. The pure hydrogen range of commercial vehicles should be no less than 1,000 km, the hydrogen consumption per 100 km under CHTC conditions should be no more than 8 kg, the overall vehicle life should be no less than 1 million km, and the overall vehicle cost should be no more than 800,000 yuan; Passenger vehicle pure hydrogen range ≥800 km, CLTC hydrogen consumption ≤0.7 kg per 100 km, durability ≥200,000 km@8 years, whole vehicle cost ≤200,000 yuan.

By 2035, the scale of fuel cell vehicles will be more than 1,000,000; Commercial vehicles with a pure hydrogen range of no less than 1,000 km, CHTC hydrogen consumption of no more than 7 kg per 100 km, vehicle life of no less than 1.5 million km, and vehicle cost of no more than 600,000 yuan; Passenger vehicle pure hydrogen range ≥900 km, CLTC hydrogen consumption ≤0.65 kg, durability ≥300,000 km@12 years, whole vehicle cost ≤150,000 yuan.

By 2040, the number of fuel cell vehicles will be more than 4,000,000; The pure hydrogen range of commercial vehicles is no less than 1,000 km, the hydrogen consumption per 100 km under CHTC conditions is no more than 6 kg, the overall vehicle life is no less than 2 million km, and the overall vehicle cost is no more than 500,000 yuan; Passenger vehicle pure hydrogen range ≥1000 km, CLTC hydrogen consumption ≤0.6 kg per 100 km, durability ≥600,000 km@15 years, whole vehicle cost ≤120,000 yuan (Fig. 3.2).

3.2.4 Technology Roadmap

3.2.4.1 Overall Technology Roadmap

3.2.4.2 Fuel Cell Vehicle Technology Roadmap

The development technology route for fuel cell commercial vehicles (with 49t heavy-duty trucks as the typical model) starts demonstration operation and industrial promotion of fuel cell commercial vehicles with three key time points of 2030, 2035 and

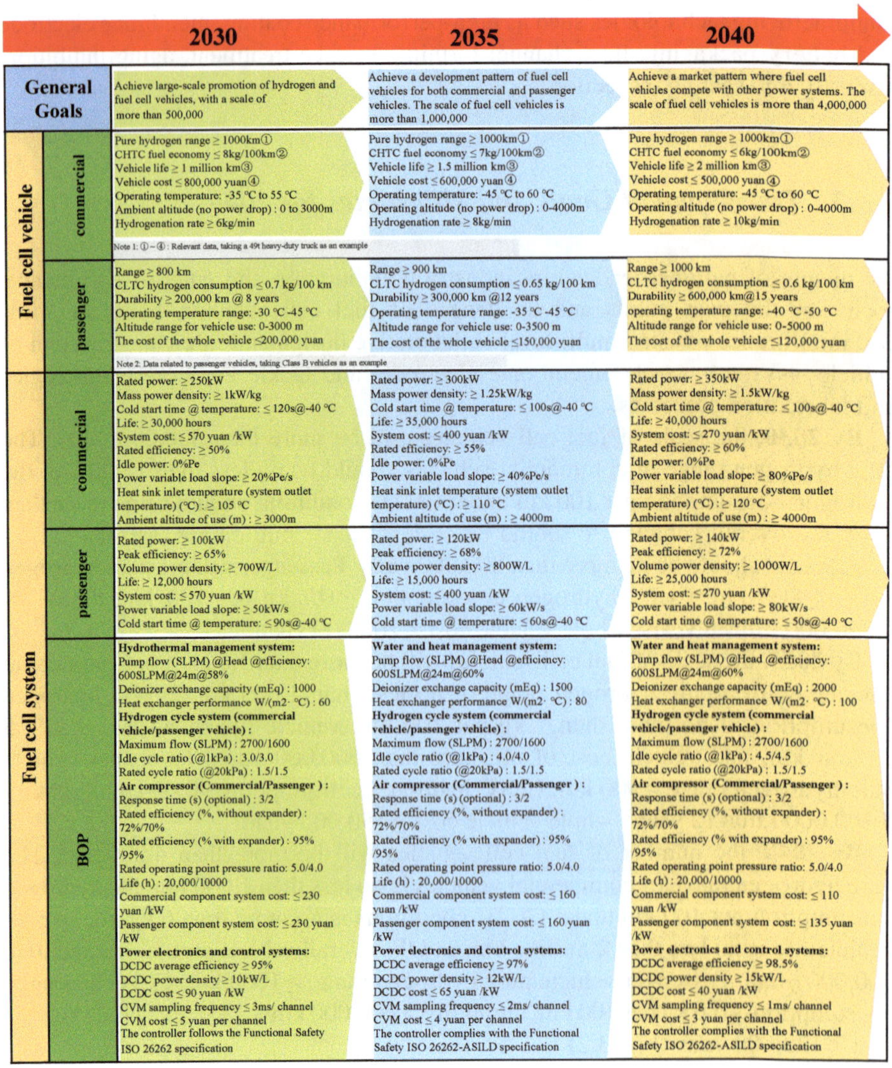

		2030	2035	2040
General Goals		Achieve large-scale promotion of hydrogen and fuel cell vehicles, with a scale of more than 500,000	Achieve a development pattern of fuel cell vehicles for both commercial and passenger vehicles. The scale of fuel cell vehicles is more than 1,000,000	Achieve a market pattern where fuel cell vehicles compete with other power systems. The scale of fuel cell vehicles is more than 4,000,000
Fuel cell vehicle	commercial	Pure hydrogen range ≥ 1000km① CHTC fuel economy ≤ 8kg/100km② Vehicle life ≥ 1 million km③ Vehicle cost ≤ 800,000 yuan④ Operating temperature: -35 °C to 55 °C Ambient altitude (no power drop) : 0 to 3000m Hydrogenation rate ≥ 6kg/min	Pure hydrogen range ≥ 1000km① CHTC fuel economy ≤ 7kg/100km② Vehicle life ≥ 1.5 million km③ Vehicle cost ≤ 600,000 yuan④ Operating temperature: -45 °C to 60 °C Operating altitude (no power drop) : 0-4000m Hydrogenation rate ≥ 8kg/min	Pure hydrogen range ≥ 1000km① CHTC fuel economy ≤ 6kg/100km② Vehicle life ≥ 2 million km③ Vehicle cost ≤ 500,000 yuan④ Operating temperature: -45 °C to 60 °C Operating altitude (no power drop) : 0-4000m Hydrogenation rate ≥ 10kg/min
		Note 1: ①~④: Relevant data, taking a 49t heavy-duty truck as an example		
	passenger	Range ≥ 800 km CLTC hydrogen consumption ≤ 0.7 kg/100 km Durability ≥ 200,000 km @ 8 years Operating temperature range: -30 °C -45 °C Altitude range for vehicle use: 0-3000 m The cost of the whole vehicle ≤200,000 yuan	Range ≥ 900 km CLTC hydrogen consumption ≤ 0.65 kg/100 km Durability ≥ 300,000 km @12 years Operating temperature range: -35 °C -45 °C Altitude range for vehicle use: 0-3500 m The cost of the whole vehicle ≤150,000 yuan	Range ≥ 1000 km CLTC hydrogen consumption ≤ 0.6 kg/100 km Durability ≥ 600,000 km@15 years operating temperature range: -40 °C -50 °C Altitude range for vehicle use: 0-5000 m The cost of the whole vehicle ≤120,000 yuan
		Note 2: Data related to passenger vehicles, taking Class B vehicles as an example		
Fuel cell system	commercial	Rated power: ≥ 250kW Mass power density: ≥ 1kW/kg Cold start time @ temperature: ≤ 120s@-40 °C Life: ≥ 30,000 hours System cost: ≤ 570 yuan /kW Rated efficiency: ≥ 50% Idle power: 0%Pe Power variable load slope: ≥ 20%Pe/s Heat sink inlet temperature (system outlet temperature) (°C) : ≥ 105 °C Ambient altitude of use (m) : ≥ 3000m	Rated power: ≥ 300kW Mass power density: ≥ 1.25kW/kg Cold start time @ temperature: ≤ 100s@-40 °C Life: ≥ 35,000 hours System cost: ≤ 400 yuan /kW Rated efficiency: ≥ 55% Idle power: 0%Pe Power variable load slope: ≥ 40%Pe/s Heat sink inlet temperature (system outlet temperature) (°C) : ≥ 110 °C Ambient altitude of use (m) : ≥ 4000m	Rated power: ≥ 350kW Mass power density: ≥ 1.5kW/kg Cold start time @ temperature: ≤ 100s@-40 °C Life: ≥ 40,000 hours System cost: ≤ 270 yuan /kW Rated efficiency: ≥ 60% Idle power: 0%Pe Power variable load slope: ≥ 80%Pe/s Heat sink inlet temperature (system outlet temperature) (°C) : ≥ 120 °C Ambient altitude of use (m) : ≥ 4000m
	passenger	Rated power: ≥ 100kW Peak efficiency: ≥ 65% Volume power density: ≥ 700W/L Life: ≥ 12,000 hours System cost: ≤ 570 yuan /kW Power variable load slope: ≥ 50kW/s Cold start time @ temperature: ≤ 90s@-40 °C	Rated power: ≥ 120kW Peak efficiency: ≥ 68% Volume power density: ≥ 800W/L Life: ≥ 15,000 hours System cost: ≤ 400 yuan /kW Power variable load slope: ≥ 60kW/s Cold start time @ temperature: ≤ 60s@-40 °C	Rated power: ≥ 140kW Peak efficiency: ≥ 72% Volume power density: ≥ 1000W/L Life: ≥ 25,000 hours System cost: ≤ 270 yuan /kW Power variable load slope: ≥ 80kW/s Cold start time @ temperature: ≤ 50s@-40 °C
	BOP	**Hydrothermal management system:** Pump flow (SLPM) @Head @efficiency: 600SLPM@24m@58% Deionizer exchange capacity (mEq) : 1000 Heat exchanger performance W/(m2· °C) : 60 **Hydrogen cycle system (commercial vehicle/passenger vehicle) :** Maximum flow (SLPM) : 2700/1600 Idle cycle ratio (@1kPa) : 3.0/3.0 Rated cycle ratio (@20kPa) : 1.5/1.5 **Air compressor (Commercial/Passenger) :** Response time (s) (optional) : 3/2 Rated efficiency (%, without expander) : 72%/70% Rated efficiency (% with expander) : 95% /95% Rated operating point pressure ratio: 5.0/4.0 Life (h) : 20,000/10000 Commercial component system cost: ≤ 230 yuan /kW Passenger component system cost: ≤ 230 yuan /kW **Power electronics and control systems:** DCDC average efficiency ≥ 95% DCDC power density ≥ 10kW/L DCDC cost ≤ 90 yuan /kW CVM sampling frequency ≤ 3ms/ channel CVM cost ≤ 5 yuan per channel The controller follows the Functional Safety ISO 26262 specification	**Water and heat management system:** Pump flow (SLPM) @Head @efficiency: 600SLPM@24m@60% Deionizer exchange capacity (mEq) : 1500 Heat exchanger performance W/(m2· °C) : 80 **Hydrogen cycle system (commercial vehicle/passenger vehicle) :** Maximum flow (SLPM) : 2700/1600 Idle cycle ratio (@1kPa) : 4.0/4.0 Rated cycle ratio (@20kPa) : 1.5/1.5 **Air compressor (Commercial/Passenger) :** Response time (s) (optional) : 3/2 Rated efficiency (%, without expander) : 72%/70% Rated efficiency (% with expander) : 95% /95% Rated operating point pressure ratio: 5.0/4.0 Life (h) : 20,000/10000 Commercial component system cost: ≤ 160 yuan /kW Passenger component system cost: ≤ 160 yuan /kW **Power electronics and control systems:** DCDC average efficiency ≥ 97% DCDC power density ≥ 12kW/L DCDC cost ≤ 65 yuan /kW CVM sampling frequency ≤ 2ms/ channel CVM cost ≤ 4 yuan per channel The controller complies with the Functional Safety ISO 26262-ASILD specification	**Water and heat management system:** Pump flow (SLPM) @Head @efficiency: 600SLPM@24m@60% Deionizer exchange capacity (mEq) : 2000 Heat exchanger performance W/(m2· °C) : 100 **Hydrogen cycle system (commercial vehicle/passenger vehicle) :** Maximum flow (SLPM) : 2700/1600 Idle cycle ratio (@1kPa) : 4.5/4.5 Rated cycle ratio (@20kPa) : 1.5/1.5 **Air compressor (Commercial/Passenger) :** Response time (s) (optional) : 3/2 Rated efficiency (%, without expander) : 72%/70% Rated efficiency (% with expander) : 95% /95% Rated operating point pressure ratio: 5.0/4.0 Life (h) : 20,000/10000 Commercial component system cost: ≤ 110 yuan /kW Passenger component system cost: ≤ 135 yuan /kW **Power electronics and control systems:** DCDC average efficiency ≥ 98.5% DCDC power density ≥ 15kW/L DCDC cost ≤ 40 yuan /kW CVM sampling frequency ≤ 1ms/ channel CVM cost ≤ 3 yuan per channel The controller complies with the Functional Safety ISO 26262-ASILD specification

Fig. 3.2 General map of the fuel cell technology route

2040, taking high-power fuel cell heavy-duty trucks as the market entry point. Gradually increase the power of commercial vehicle fuel cell systems, introduce big data and artificial intelligence technologies, break through key technologies such as scene-driven power system platform integration and control, vehicle energy management and thermal management, vehicle lightweighting and environmental adaptability, and improve vehicle efficiency, durability and range. With fuel cell heavy-duty trucks as the pilot, gradually expand the application scope, so that the key indicators of fuel cell commercial vehicles in terms of power, economy, durability, environmental

Fuel cell stack	Commercial	• Stack power ≥ 300kW • Power density ≥ 4.0kW /L@0.7Vcell • Life ≥ 35000 h • Cost ≤ 350 yuan /kW • Cold start temperature: -40 ℃ • Maximum operating temperature: 105℃ • Rated pitch voltage standard deviation ≤ 10mV • Rated point efficiency ≥ 55%	• Peak stack power ≥ 350kW • Peak power density ≥ 5.5kW/L@0.7Vcell • Life ≥ 40,000h • Cost ≤ 260 yuan /kW • Cold start temperature: -40 ° C • Maximum operating temperature: 110℃ • Rated pitch voltage standard deviation ≤ 8mV • Rated point efficiency ≥ 59%	• Peak stack power ≥ 400kW • Peak power density ≥7.5kW/L@0.7Vcell • Life ≥ 45000h • Cost ≤ 160 yuan /kW • Cold start temperature: -40 ℃ • Maximum operating temperature: 120 ℃ • Rated pitch voltage standard deviation ≤ 5mV • Rated point efficiency ≥ 63.5%
	Passenger	• Peak stack power ≥ 120kW • Peak power density ≥ 6.5k /L@0.68Vcell • Life ≥ 12000h • Cost ≤ 350 yuan /kW • Cold start temperature: -40℃ • Maximum operating temperature: 105℃ • Rated pitch voltage standard deviation ≤ 10mV • Rated point efficiency ≥ 55%	• Peak stack power ≥ 140 kW • Peak power density ≥ 7.5kW/L@0.68Vcell • Life ≥ 15000h • Cost ≤ 260 yuan /kW • Cold start temperature: -40 ℃ • Maximum operating temperature: 110℃ • Rated pitch voltage standard deviation ≤ 8mV • Rated point efficiency ≥ 59%	• Peak stack power ≥ 160kW • Peak power density ≥ 9.0kW /L@0.68Vcell • Life ≥ 25000h • Cost ≤ 140 yuan /kW • Cold start temperature: -40 ℃ • Maximum operating temperature: 120 ℃ • Rated pitch voltage standard deviation ≤ 5mV
	Metal bipolar plate	• Applicable current ≥ 3A/cm2 @0.70V • Durability life ≥ 40,000 h • The preparation speed of the plate film layer is ≤1 second per piece • Cost ≤ 50 yuan /kW	• Applicable current ≥ 3.5A/cm2 @0.75V • Durability ≥ 45,000h • Plate film layer preparation speed ≤ 0.5 s/ sheet • Cost ≤ 35 yuan /kW	• Applicable current ≥ 4A/cm2 @0.8V • Durability life ≥ 50,000 hours • Plate film preparation speed ≤0.3s per sheet • Cost ≤ 25 yuan /kW
	Graphite bipolar plate	• Flexural strength ≥50MPa • Thickness ≤1.4mm • Life ≥ 40,000 hours • Cost ≤70 yuan /kW	• Flexural strength ≥60MPa • Thickness ≤1.35mm • Life ≥ 50,000 hours • Cost ≤50 yuan /kW	• Flexural strength ≥75MPa • Thickness ≤1.3mm • Life ≥ 60,000h • Cost ≤30 yuan /kW
	Plate substrate	• Corrosion current ≤ 5.0 × 10^{-7} A/cm ^{2} (≤ 1.0 × 10^{-6}A/cm ^{2} after 40,000 hours of vehicle operation) • Contact resistance ≤ 8.0mΩ.cm ^{2} (≤ 10.0mΩ.cm ^{2} after 40,000 hours of vehicle operation) • Flexural strength ≥ 50MPa	• Corrosion current ≤ 2.5 × 10^{-7} A/cm ^{2} (≤ 5.0 × 10^{-7} A/cm ^{2} after 45,000 hours of vehicle operation) • Contact resistance ≤ 5.0mΩ.cm ^{2} (≤ 8.0mΩ.cm ^{2} after 45,000 hours of vehicle operation) • Flexural strength ≥ 60MPa	• Corrosion current ≤ 1.5 × 10^{-7} A/cm ^{2} (≤ 3.0 × 10^{-7} A/cm ^{2} after 50,000 hours of vehicle operation) • Contact resistance ≤ 2.5mΩ.cm ^{2} (≤ 5.0mΩ.cm ^{2} after 50,000 hours of vehicle operation) • Flexural strength ≥ 80MPa
Membrane electrode assembly	MEA	• Cathode platinum loading ≤ 0.2mg/cm ^{2} • Performance requirement ≥ 1.6W/cm2 @0.7V • Durability ≥ 40,000 h (maximum operating temperature 115 ° C) • Cost ≤ 200 yuan /kW	• Cathode platinum loading ≤ 0.17mg/cm ^{2} • Performance requirement ≥ 1.6W/cm2 @0.75V • Durability ≥ 45,000 h (maximum operating temperature 120 ° C) • Cost ≤ 140 yuan /kW	• Cathode platinum loading ≤ 0.12mg/cm ^{2} • Performance requirement ≥ 1.6W/cm2 @0.8V • Durability ≥ 50,000h (maximum operating temperature 130 ° C) • Cost ≤ 80 yuan /kW
	PEM	• EW: 950 • Glass transition temperature ≥ 120 ° C • Tensile strength ≥ 40 MPa	• EW: 800 • Glass transition temperature ≥ 125 ° C • Tensile strength ≥ 50 MPa	• EW: 700 • Glass transition temperature ≥ 150 ° C • Tensile strength ≥ 60 MPa
	Catalyst	• Mass specific work ≥ 0.8A/mgPt @0.9V: • 0.6V-0.95V 50,000 times, mass specific activity decay rate ≤ 30%	• Mass specific activity ≥ 1.5A/mgPt @0.9V: • 0.6V-0.95V 50,000 times, mass specific activity decay rate ≤ 15%	• Mass specific activity ≥ 10 A/mgPt@0.9V: • 0.6V-0.95V 50,000 times, mass specific activity decay rate ≤ 10%
	GDL	• Horizontal permeability @1.0MPa≥5 μm^2 • Resistivity @1.0MPa≤5m Ω cm^2 • Thickness tolerance @1.0MPa≤±15 μ m	• Horizontal permeability @1.0MPa≥8 μm^2 • Resistivity @1.0MPa≤4m Ω cm^2 • Thickness tolerance @1.0MPa ≤± 10 μ m	• Horizontal permeability @1.0MPa≥12 μm^2 • Resistivity @1.0MPa ≤ 2.5m Ω cm^2 • Thickness tolerance @1.0MPa ≤± 10 μ m
Key breakthrough technology		• Integrated thermal management for FCV • FCV acceleration durability and life prediction Construction of the standard system for testing and evaluation of FCV • FCV lightweighting and environmental adaptability	• All-scenario, all-weather vehicle development technology • All-scenario fuel cell vehicle hydrogen safety design technology	• Intelligent low hydrogen consumption fuel cell vehicle energy management • Artificial intelligence technology for fuel cell control and diagnosis
		• Digital twin technology for fuel cell systems • Ai-based FC state identification and state control technology • Fuel cell efficient heat dissipation technology • Integrated development technology for high-power, high-efficiency,long-range FC systems • Integrated and platform-based development of hydrogen FC systems for different vehicle models • Design and fabrication of key components for high-power long-life fuel cell systems	• High reliability and high safety fuel cell system design technology • Fuel cell system life assessment and rapid prediction technology, life prediction and health management technology • Rapid activation, leak detection and foreign object detection techniques for fuel cell systems	• Efficient intelligent manufacturing technology for fuel cell systems • Intelligent optimization technology for the entire life cycle of fuel cells • Domestic simulation software technology for the entire process of fuel cell systems • Development of low-cost fuel cell system testing equipment
		• Performance improvements: Improved electrode materials and structures, stack assembly matching technology • Life enhancement: Online water management monitoring, rapid life assessment technology for stacks and components • Cost reduction: Development of mass-production processes for nationally produced critical materials, automated assembly lines for battery stacks • Environmental adaptation: multiple low-temperature non-destructive cold start technology, high-temperature long life operation technology • Reliability improvement: High consistency component materials, fabrication process, integrated single-cell structure design	• Performance improvement: New membrane electrode structure design, improved plate flow field and battery stack structure • Life enhancement: Improved durability materials, intelligent condition monitoring and diagnosis • Cost reduction: Development of nationally produced membrane electrodes and nationally produced plates based on domestic materials • Environmental adaptation: High temperature, high pollution, high altitude environmental adaptation technology • Reliability improvement: impact-resistant stack structure design, improved sealing structure design	• Performance improvement: Development of key materials for new membrane electrodes, new plate flow fields and battery stack structures • Life enhancement: New durable materials, long life stack technology with low metering ratio • Cost reduction: High consistency, low cost domestic membrane electrodes/plates, increased volumetric power density of battery stacks • Environmental adaptation: Develop fuel cell stacks suitable for extreme environmental conditions • Reliability improvement: New sealing structures and materials
		• Overall goal: Mass production process of nationally produced materials • Proton exchange membrane: High consistency film-forming process and e-PTFE quantifiable controllable preparation technology • Catalysts: Synthesis and bulk preparation process of highly active, highly durable mesoporous catalysts • Carbon paper: High consistency dispersion and carbonization process • Plates: High durability and low cost composite graphite, metal plate material systems and mass production processes	• Overall objective: High-temperature resistant material batch preparation process • Proton exchange membrane: Synthesis of high-temperature resistant proton exchange membrane and iomeric resin chain structure and molecular weight adjustable • Catalyst: High consistency and high yield preparation process for high-temperature mesoporous catalysts • Carbon paper: A high consistency dispersion process for strong thermal conductivity carbon paper • Plate: High-temperature resistant low-cost metal plate coating process, high-temperature resistant graphite plate material system	• Overall objective: New material mass production process • Proton exchange membrane: New high temperature and low humidity resistant polyelectrolyte structure and its film-forming process • Catalyst: Preparation process of high activity, high durability mesoporous alloy/non-platinum catalyst • Carbon paper: Preparation process of new gas diffusion layer substrate material • Plate: A new material system for high-performance, low-cost plates
		• Initially establish professional databases and AI agents in the fields of materials, membrane electrodes, stacks and systems, and explore AI large models and AI agent technologies	• Form specialized vertical large models in the field of fuel cells, initially realize the application of artificial intelligence throughout the entire industrial chain, and explore new technologies such as autonomous synthesis and research and development of advanced materials based on large models	• Form a relatively complete platform for large models to be applied throughout the entire industrial chain

Fig. 3.2 (continued)

adaptability and cost meet the industrialization requirements for batch promotion, and complete the construction of power system and vehicle batch manufacturing capacity.

The development technology route for fuel cell passenger vehicles (with B-class vehicles as the typical model) is based on three key time points: 2030, 2035, and 2040. Explore full power, plug-in, range extension and other technical routes, introduce big data and artificial intelligence technologies, and carry out continuous technological innovation and industrialization in vehicle energy management, durability optimization, environmental adaptability improvement, hydrogen and electricity safety improvement, intelligent production and manufacturing, testing and verification, and standard system, so that the cost of purchase and use can meet the needs of ordinary customers. Durability covers the entire life cycle, and the vehicle products have the ability to be commercialized on a large scale.

Accelerate the innovative application of artificial intelligence technology in the field of fuel cell vehicles. By 2030, build large artificial intelligence models for vehicle engineering development, quickly analyze the performance indicators of each assembly through machine learning algorithms, shorten the R&D cycle, improve vehicle performance and lifespan, and provide customized solutions for vehicle power matching. By 2035, a large artificial intelligence model for fuel cell vehicle manufacturing will be established to enhance the production efficiency and quality control of fuel cell vehicles through artificial intelligence, reduce production costs and accelerate large-scale application. By 2040, a collaborative ecosystem for fuel cell vehicles will be established. Through the vehicle's artificial intelligence system, users' driving habits will be learned, dynamic power allocation strategies will be optimized, and the interaction between vehicles and transportation infrastructure will be coordinated to further improve the hydrogen consumption, lifespan and user convenience of the vehicle.

3.2.4.3 Technology Roadmap for Fuel Cell Systems

The technical roadmap for the development of fuel cell systems for commercial vehicles is based on the current situation in 2025, with 2030, 2035, and 2040 as key milestones. At present, the power of fuel cell systems on the market has exceeded 200 kW. Heavy-duty commercial vehicles have a high demand for the power of fuel cell systems, especially in scenarios such as trunk logistics transportation and heavy-duty freight transportation on mountainous or non-urban roads, which require further power increase of fuel cell systems. The characteristics of heavy-duty conditions cause the power output of commercial vehicle fuel cell systems to be concentrated in both high-power and low-power areas, thus demanding high efficiency and overall service life for long periods of high-power operation. It is necessary to optimize the system structure and function, introduce big data and artificial intelligence technologies, break through system design and integration for high power, long life and wide temperature range, stack state perception, diagnosis and control technologies, improve system performance, so that the key indicators of the fuel cell system in terms of power density, efficiency, environmental adaptability, life and cost can meet industrialization requirements.

The roadmap for the development of fuel cell systems for passenger vehicles is based on the current situation in 2025, with 2030, 2035, and 2040 as key nodes. For different fuel cell passenger vehicle technology routes such as full power, plug-in, and extended-range, breakthrough technologies such as system design and integration for different attribute requirements (high dynamic response, high volume power density, wide temperature range, long life), stack state awareness, diagnosis and control, and a new generation of software and hardware electronic control platforms that support AI, To achieve optimal matching and control for different passenger vehicle powertrain configurations. The operating conditions of the fuel cell system are complex and changeable, and the electrochemical reaction mechanism inside the stack is complex. It is difficult to directly observe the internal reaction state and effectively regulate the operating state of the stack, resulting in rapid performance degradation of the stack and a short lifespan of the entire machine. It is necessary to study the degradation mechanism of fuel cells in vehicle operating conditions, introduce artificial intelligence methods to achieve rapid assessment and prediction of fuel cell life for actual operating conditions, propose performance recovery and degradation suppression strategies, so as to achieve efficient and long life operation, and ultimately make the key indicators of fuel cell systems meet industrialization requirements in terms of power density, efficiency, environmental adaptability, life and cost.

Promote the innovative application of AI technology in the field of fuel cell systems. By 2030, a professional database and AI agents will be initially established in the field of fuel cell systems, and the application of AI large models and agent technology in the integrated design, control development, performance improvement, process optimization and cost reduction of fuel cell systems will be explored. By 2035, we will gradually improve the professional vertical large models in the field of fuel cell systems and explore the application of large models in system integration, BOP development, intelligent control and online intelligent monitoring and diagnosis of health status. By 2040, a large model platform in the field of fuel cell systems will be established, and the application of large models in system integration, intelligent control and intelligent manufacturing will be explored.

3.2.4.4 Fuel Cell Stack Technology Roadmap

Develop fuel cell stacks that can operate at high temperatures for the efficient heat dissipation requirements of fuel cell vehicles; Increase the production cycle and pass rate of stacks, key components and materials, and reduce manufacturing costs; Further enhance stack performance, power density and durability to meet the requirements for the commercial promotion of millions of fuel cell vehicles; Develop integrated thermal management technology for power systems to meet the multiple low-temperature and non-destructive cold start requirements of fuel cells. In addition, based on the current status of domestic and international technological and industrial development, different requirements are given in terms of power, power density, lifespan and cost according to the different application characteristics of commercial vehicles and passenger vehicles.

The development goals of bipolar plates are mainly to meet the development requirements of high-power, long-life vehicle fuel cells, achieve breakthroughs in the design and manufacturing technology of long durable, thin, and high-performance plates, focus on improving the level and quality of plate batch manufacturing, significantly increase plate manufacturing efficiency and reduce plate manufacturing costs, and lay a solid foundation for the development of fuel cell vehicle industry. It is necessary to break through the design technology of large area strong drainage plate flow field, and improve the uniformity of plate flow field distribution and mass transfer capacity; Develop wide temperature range acid and oxygen corrosion-resistant plates to increase the expected lifespan of the plates in fuel cells under harsh conditions such as high temperature, acid and oxygen; Develop thin plate manufacturing processes to increase the power density of fuel cell stacks; To break through the bottlenecks of plate manufacturing efficiency and cost, such as precision continuous plate forming technology, low-cost coating technology, and high-efficiency fast packaging technology; Research on wide temperature range stable sealing materials and structural design schemes to simplify the water and thermal management of the stack and increase the expected lifespan; Develop and mass-produce national plates based on domestic materials to reduce the cost of plates and stacks.

Accelerate the innovative application of artificial intelligence technology in fuel cell stacks. By 2030, initially establish professional databases and AI agents in the stack field, and explore the application of AI large models and agent technology in fuel cell structure design, output performance improvement, production process optimization, and manufacturing cost reduction. By 2035, professional vertical large models in the field of fuel cell stacks will be formed, and the application of large models in new nationally produced plate flow fields and stack structure design, as well as intelligent monitoring and diagnosis of stack status will be explored. By 2040, a complete platform for large models in the field of fuel cell stacks will be established, and the application of large models in new stack structures and integrated thermal management strategies will be explored.

3.2.4.5 Fuel Cell Membrane Electrode Technology Roadmap

Research low platinum high power density membrane electrode technology, while improving catalyst utilization and catalyst activity, reducing fuel cell costs, and promoting its transition to mass production and market application. Study wide temperature range membrane electrode technology: develop high-temperature resistant proton exchange membrane technology, break through the glass transition temperature limit, expand the maximum operating temperature of membrane electrode assembly, and provide a guarantee for high-temperature adaptability in operating environments. In addition, research mesoporous carbon carriers and local oxygen transport control technology to precisely control pore structure provides a structural basis for efficient oxygen reduction reactions and improves fuel cell output performance. Study advanced membrane electrode encapsulation technology to avoid stress concentration at the junction of the frame and proton membrane through integrated encapsulation, thereby preventing mechanical damage failure of the membrane electrode and extending its lifespan in actual operation.

Promote the innovative application of artificial intelligence technology in the field of fuel cell membrane electrode assembly. By 2030, a professional database and AI agents will be initially established in the field of membrane electrode assembly, and the application of AI large models and agent technology in electrode material and structure improvement, as well as in the batch production of nationally produced materials will be explored. By 2035, professional vertical large models in the field of fuel cell membrane electrode assembly will be formed, and the application of large models in the design of new membrane electrode structures, the development of nationally produced membrane electrode assembly, and the design of key materials and structures that can withstand high temperatures will be explored. By 2040, a complete platform for large models in the field of fuel cell membrane electrode assembly will be established, and the application of large models in the development of key materials for new membrane electrode assembly with high performance, long life and low cost will be explored.

3.3 Electrical Driving Assembly

3.3.1 Domestic and International Technical Status Comparison

(1) Traction Motor: High-power density, high-efficiency, high-speed, low-noise flat wire traction motors are developing rapidly, key performance indicators such as power density, peak efficiency, maximum speed, and NVH quality are the same level in local and overseas. Light rare-earth motors, permanent magnet assisted reluctance motors, electrical exciting synchronous motors, and induction motors develop continuously, and General Motors, Toyota have completed R&D and validation of ferrite permanent magnet motor. Key materials and components such as high-performance silicon steel, low heavy rare earth permanent magnets, high class insulation materials and electromagnetic flat wires and high-speed bearings have sustained progress and applied in electric vehicle.

(2) Motor Controller: Key technology such as high integration, high efficiency, high electromagnetic compatibility, high functional safety and high network security have enhanced the performance and quality of motor controller, and power density, efficiency of motor controller has continually increased. The third-generation wide-bandgap power semiconductor devices such as silicon carbide (SiC) reduce motor controller losses, increase integration and power density

level and achieves series application in electric drive systems for high voltage rates powertrain system. High temperature film materials and film capacitors require continuously research and developing. Software and hardware technologies such as multi-core microprocessor, domain software architecture, operating systems, develop and diagnostic toolchains develop steadily.

(3) Electric Drive Assembly: The electric drive assembly are the mainstream product for new energy vehicles in local and overseas market. Series, standardized, scalable electric drive assembly platform products have been launched, and powertrain integrated with dual motors and reduction/transmission systems, and electric axle systems with planetary gears and coaxial reducers are applied. Beside integrated with motor, inverter and reducer, multi-electric drive assembly integrates electrical components such as DC/DC converter, on-board charger (OBC), power distribution unit (PDU), vehicle control unit (VCU) and thermal management system (TMS), and the muli-integration technology decrease the volume and weight of electric drive assembly, and the electrical integration and domain control level are continuously progress.

(4) Electromechanical Coupling Assembly: The integration level, mechanical and electrical efficiency, NVH of electromechanical coupling powertrains continuously improve. Various configurations of plug-in electromechanical coupling assembly products have been developed with platform-based and wildly applied in market. Technology of range extender assembly significantly reduce the energy consumption of range-extended electric vehicles (REV). For medium and heavy duty electrical trucks, traction motor integrated with multi-speed gearboxes are wildly applied, and high speed motor integrated with reducer are applied in light duty electrical trucks and logistics electrical vehicles. Traction motor with flat wire stator assembly are applied and volume are increasing, and the electric axle which enhance integration and reduce the vehicle weight are applied in commercial vehicle.

(5) In-wheel Motor Assembly: In-wheel motor assembly integrated with steer system, brake unit and suspension system benefit for vehicle layout space saving and enable flexible control, and In-wheel motor system are the core and key powertrain components of distributed electric vehicles. The torque density of In-wheel motors increase continuously and the distributed drive passenger vehicle are testing and application, and there need to advance the research, development, and engineering of In-wheel motor system and vehicle application.

3.3.2 Outlook on Technology Development Trends

(1) **Technology development trends for traction motor include improving the comprehensive performance of motors in mechanical-electrical-thermal-magnetic-acoustic aspects, reducing NVH and cost, and enhancing the technology and product competitiveness of key materials and components.**

Key design and software tooling technology directions for traction motor includes low rare earth (or free rare earth) permanent magnet motors, efficient cooling structure and thermal management, high voltage and high frequency rates stator insulation systems, innovative motor topologies and structures, AI-enabled intelligent multi-field coupling motor simulation software, and NVH analysis software for electric drive system. Technical directions for key materials and components are low iron-loss high-magnetic silicon steel and stator core manufacturing processes, light rare earth permanent magnet materials and grain boundary diffusion and controllable preparation processes, free rare earth permanent magnet materials and manufacture processes, high frequency PDIV electromagnetic and low AC resistance flat winding processes, high temperature and high thermal conductivity insulation impregnation resins and potting compounds, insulation composite paper design and processes, high speed and high wear-resistant and anti-corona bearings precision manufacturing process, as well as new materials such as super copper wires, amorphous alloys and soft magnetic composite materials.

(2) **High power density, high efficiency, high reliability, high safety class and high electromagnetic compatibility levels are the technical directions for motor controller, and technology developing focus on deep integration of power electronic components and high quality control, as well as key electronic components.**

New integration design and thermal management methods, such as wide-bandgap power semiconductor device packaging and power components integration, embedded power semiconductor module packaging and novel power semiconductor device integration with intelligent gate-drive technology, are important technical approaches to enhance the integration level and power density of motor controller. High-grade electromagnetic interference (EMI) filter topology and magnetic core materials, high electromagnetic compatibility (EMC) level design, high function safety and high information security class design and verification, motor control technology and operating health management are the key technology to improve continuously motor controller quality. Key technical directions of electronic components includes wide-bandgap semiconductor device materials and super power semiconductor chip design, power device sintering packaging and processes, efficient cooling structure of power modules and power components integration, high temperature film material and capacitors, high precision current sensor and position sensors, etc.

(3) **Improving continuously system integration, operating cycle efficiency, and NVH quality are the key technical direction for electric drive assembly, and the integration technology focus on electrical integration, chip integration and domain control integration.**

Deep electrical integration and thermal management, on-board chargers (OBC) and DC/DC converters integration, mutual utilization of power module and motor windings, multi-level power electronic topologies, new semiconductor power devices, high class EMI filter are the key technical directions to enhance the integration and power density of power electronics assembly. Developing system microprocessor complying with functional safety, software compilers and toolchains, system domain control software ecosystem are crucial technology for system domain control integration. Develop advanced control algorithms, such as active noise suppression and shaft bearing current reduction, fault diagnosis methods based on big data and artificial intelligence (AI) technologies, and improve operating cycle efficiency and real-time monitoring and evaluation of electric drive assembly. Continuously research on interdisciplinary deep integration and lightweight structures, planetary gear sets and coaxial reducers, multi-speed transmissions and low-viscosity lubricants, as well as innovative clutches, facilitates to reduce the volume and weight of electric drive systems.

(4) **Technical development of electromechanical coupling powertrain for passenger vehicles are product platform and domain control integration, enhancing system integration level and product quality and reducing vehicle energy consumption. Technology direction of powertrain for commercial vehicles focus on deeply integrating of powertrain and chassis, upgrading operational cycle efficiency and NVH performance**.

Key technology such as new configurations of electromechanical coupling powertrains for passenger car, deep integration of traction motor and transmissions, high efficiency heat exchange and thermal management, multi-domain control integration and software tooling enhance the operating cycle efficiency of electromechanical coupling powertrains and reduce energy consumption. Continuously develop key components such as high efficiency traction motor, dedicated reduction and transmission systems and deeply integrated power electronics controllers and promoting the product platform development. Develop new topological configurations for commercial vehicle powertrains, deep integration of powertrains with chassis systems and electric axles, high efficiency and heat exchange cooling structures, efficient lubrication systems as well as NVH suppression technologies and to enhance the integration level and product quality of commercial vehicle powertrains. Carry out the product platform of traction motor and controllers, specialized gearboxes and high load bearings to build the supply chain for commercial vehicle powertrains.

(5) **Deep integration of In-wheel motors with braking systems, breakthrough in specialized basic materials and key components, and manufacturing processes are technical and engineering direction of distributed In-wheel drive assembly. Distributed electric drive powertrains with dual motor and electronic differential systems are technical directions for high performance passenger cars**.

In-wheel motor integrates with driving, braking and steering by wire, suspension systems and suppression of the negative effects of unsprung mass are the necessary conditions for engineering of electric wheel system. New insulation material, thermal conductive materials, high line speed and low friction dynamic sealing components, and high reliability braking systems are the key material and components electric wheel system. High torque density lightweight in-wheel motors, high power density traction motors integrated with reducers, high safety levels and cost effective need to develop continuously. Focuses the integrated design of dual motors and electronic differential systems, multi-field integration design of distributed electric drive assemblies and intelligent chassis, domain control integration and safety control, coordination and redundancy control, and accelerate the engineering of intelligent chassis power systems and distributed electric drive.

(6) **Continuously pushing the interdisciplinary collaboration and technological innovation, increasing the testing and evaluation capabilities, founding the evaluation specifications and standard, and continuously increasing the testing facility and evaluation system for electric drive system.**

Evaluation systems and standards, environmental adaptability series standards, noise quality evaluation, and the impact of electromagnetic radiation on the human body need to dynamic upgrade. Resources will be allocated to advancing the comprehensive evaluation system for operating cycle efficiency, energy consumption of electric drive systems, functional safety and cybersecurity certification systems, and establishing a technical standard system covering key materials and components, as well as electric drive assemblies, along with carbon emission assessment methods. High-dynamic performance dynamometers, high quality and full load NVH testing systems, and high electromagnetic compatibility testing systems are priorities to develop. Based on integrating intelligent and big data analysis technologies, technical platform and service system of electric drive system need to establish to promote the lifecycle evaluation and development of electric drive system products for NEVs.

3.3.3 Development Goals and Milestones for 2040

In 2040, developing targets for electric drive system are:

(1) In terms of technological innovation, consistently intensify the research and development of key materials and components for electric drive systems applicable in electric vehicle with multi-voltage rates, encourage the development of new configurations and products for centralized and distributed electric drive systems, and enhance the innovative design and application of system microprocessors, domain control software architectures and tooling chains, and improve the competitiveness of electric drive products.
(2) In terms of industrial integration, increase collaborative development and application of electric drive systems with automotive microchips, intelligent chassis, and intelligent manufacturing, accelerate the enhancement of dynamometer systems and testing evaluation equipment capabilities, establish low carbon manufacturing and smart factories, develop recyclable production lines, and build a comprehensive low carbon manufacturing and evaluation system to covering key materials and components and electric drive assembly, and to achieve the recycling and remanufacturing rate 70%.

From 2026 to 2040, short-term, medium-term, and long-term milestones of the electric drive system developing target are the follows:

(1) **Short-term developing targets and priorities (Y2026–2030)**

In 2030, continuously improve the performance of traction motor and controller systems, breakthrough in new materials, new devices, and new configurations, achieve high quality power electronics assemblies, engineering validation of system microprocessor and domain control software, deep integration of centralized electric drive system and distributed electric drive system with electronic differential gear, in-wheel motor being integrated within intelligent chassis, and performance improve and configuration innovate of electromechanical coupling assembly. Establish testing and evaluation specifications and standards of electric drive system, form the full lifecycle carbon emission evaluation system, construct green and low carbon manufacture and smart factory with recycling rate 50% of key material and components of electric drive system.

(2) **Medium-term developing targets and priorities (Y2031–2035)**

In 2035, continuously improve the performance of traction motor and controller systems, breakthrough in new materials, new devices, and new configurations, achieve high quality power electronics assemblies, series application of system microprocessor and domain control software, deep integration and quality increasing of centralized electric drive system and distributed electric drive system with electronic differential gear, series application of in-wheel motor and intelligent chassis, performance improving and configuration innovate of electromechanical coupling assembly. Establish testing and evaluation specifications and standards of electric drive system, form the full lifecycle carbon emission evaluation system, construct green and low carbon manufacture and smart factory with recycling rate 60% of key material and components.

(3) **Long-term developing targets and priorities (Y2036–2040)**

In 2040, continuously improve the performance of traction motor and controller systems, breakthrough in new materials, new devices, and new configurations, achieve high quality power electronics assemblies, series application of system microprocessor and domain control software, increase the quality and series application volume of centralized electric drive system and distributed electric drive system with electronic differential gear, series application of in-wheel motor and intelligent chassis, performance improving and configuration innovate of electromechanical coupling assembly. Establish the testing and evaluation specifications and standards of electric drive system, form the full lifecycle carbon emission evaluation system, construct green and low carbon manufacture and smart factory with recycling rate 70% of key material and components.

3.3.4 Technology Roadmap

In 2040, the developing target and key technical indicators of electric drive systems: power density of traction motors for high performance passenger car is 18 kW/kg and power density of motor controller with wide-bandgap semiconductor for passenger car is 120 kW/L, power density of high speed traction motor for commercial vehicles is 8 kW/kg and torque density of high torque traction motor for commercial vehicles is 30 Nm/kg, power density of power electronics assembly for high performance passenger car is 60 kW/L and power density of electrical drive system for passenger car is 5.0 kW/kg, torque density of electric bridge for light commercial vehicle is 90 Nm/kg and torque density of electric bridge for medium and heavy commercial vehicle is 115 Nm/kg, torque density of in-wheel motor assembly for passenger car is 27 Nm/kg and torque density of electromechanical coupling assembly is 32 Nm/kg.

To meet the target and key technical indicators of the electric drive system in 2040, the key technologies and direction are the follows:

(1) Traction Motor: To meet the different request and operating conditions of passenger cars and commercial vehicles, there need to focus on multi-domain integrated design, advanced cooling and thermal management, new stator winding assembly and key processes, low iron loss stator core materials and key processes, and new configuration traction motor design. It is necessary to improve key technical indicators such as power density, torque density, peak efficiency, operating cycle efficiency, and NVH quality. Further research are required on key materials and components such as low iron loss high magnetic silicon steel, free rare earth and light rare earth permanent magnets, high PDIV electromagnetic wire, high insulation class materials, anti-corona high-speed bearings, and high precision position sensors. It is essential to achieve the engineering level enhancement of the industrial chain of traction motor and process of green manufacturing.

(2) Motor Controller: To meet the technological request of motor controllers for high-performance and cost effective passenger car, as well as various categories of commercial vehicles, it demands deep integration of power components in mechanical, electrical, thermal, and magnetic fields, the intelligent integration of power devices and gate drive circuits, high electromagnetic compatibility integration design and control technology, and motor controllers with new power semiconductor devices. It is also vital to enhance the volume power density, peak efficiency and electromagnetic compatibility level of motor controllers. Priorities include high current density power semiconductor device chip design and manufacture process, power module packaging materials and manufacture processes, new power semiconductor devices and innovative packaging processes, high-temperature film materials and packing technology, high-precision current sensor chips, and continuously efforts to improve the technological level of key components such as power semiconductor devices, film capacitors, and current sensors.

(3) Power Electronics Assembly: Key technology need to focus on the power electronics assembly in terms of deep electrical, mechanical, and thermal integration design of motor controllers, DCDC converters, on-board chargers (OBC), and other power electronics components, as well as in cross-domain system control and high electromagnetic compatibility integration design. And there should also need to research and breakthrough in system-level microprocessor chips, domain control architecture, and tooling chains, construct system-level microprocessor software and hardware ecosystem. It is necessary to accelerate the innovation of new configurations and topologies of embedded power electronics assemblies, promote deep integration and control of power electronics assemblies with vehicle powertrain control systems and distributed intelligent chassis in multiple fields integration.

(4) Electric Drive Assembly: According to powertrain of passenger car and commercial vehicle, there are centralized electric drive assembly, distributed electric drive assembly and electromechanical coupling powertrain, and the key technologies and direction are the follows:

① Centralized Electric Drive Assembly: Innovation on integration of electromechanical thermal and domain control architecture, accelerating integration and power density, NVH quality and electromagnetic compatibility levels, high speed bearing with anti-corona, new structures and new configuration research of electric drive assembly. Deep electromechanical coupling integration and multi-speed transmission, with core components platform and universal application of electric powertrain system for new energy commercial vehicle. The electric axle for commercial vehicles focus on integrated with traction motor, reduction and transmission, differential gear and axle, with sharing and lightweighting of cooling and lubrication system components.

② Distributed Electric Drive Assembly: There are still technical gaps in operating cycle efficiency, NVH quality and electric wheel integration of in-wheel motor. Technology breakthroughs are needed in key components such as high load hub bearings, high reliability dynamic seals and lightweight brake system, along with the advancement of engineering levels. Further there should focus on deep integration of electromechanical and thermal systems in distributed electric drive system with dual motors and electronic differentials gear, deep coupling and domain control integration of electric drive assembly and distributed intelligent chassis, and power coordination and safety control.

③ Electromechanical Coupling Powertrain: For the electromechanical coupling powertrain applied in passenger car, sustained efforts should be made in deep electromechanical and thermal integration, multi-speed capabilities, cooling and lubrication media and thermal management, multi-power units management and shifting gear strategies, power electronics integration and control technology. It is necessary to improve key performance indicators such as torque density, operating cycle efficiency, and NVH quality. Engineering of lightweight gears, planetary gear, clutches and shifting mechanisms, along with ongoing research into new structural and configuration electromechanical coupling powertrain systems. It is essential to speed up the development of core

	Y2030	Y2035	Y2040
Overall Target of Electric Drive System	Continuously improve the performance of traction motor and controller systems, breakthrough in new materials, new devices, and new configurations, achieve high quality power electronics assemblies, engineering validation of system microprocessor and domain control software, deep integration of centralized electric drive system and distributed electric drive system with electronic differential gear, in-wheel motor being integrated within intelligent chassis, and performance improve and configuration innovate of electromechanical coupling assembly. Establish testing and evaluation specifications and standards of electric drive system, form the full lifecycle carbon emission evaluation system, construct green and low carbon manufacture and smart factory with recyclable application rate 50% of key material and components of electric drive system..	Continuously improve the performance of traction motor and controller systems, breakthrough in new materials, new devices, and new configurations, achieve high quality power electronics assemblies, series application of system microprocessor and domain control software, deep integration and quality increasing of centralized electric drive system and distributed electric drive system with electronic differential gear, series application of in-wheel motor and intelligent chassis, performance improving and configuration innovate of electromechanical coupling assembly. Establish testing and evaluation specifications and standards of electric drive system, form the full lifecycle carbon emission evaluation system, construct green and low carbon manufacture and smart factory with recyclable application rate 60% of key material and components of electric drive system.	Continuously improve the performance of traction motor and controller systems, breakthrough in new materials, new devices, and new configurations, achieve high quality power electronics assemblies, series application of system microprocessor and domain control software, increase the quality and series application volume of centralized electric drive system and distributed electric drive system with electronic differential gear, series application of in-wheel motor and intelligent chassis, performance improving and configuration innovate of electromechanical coupling assembly. Establish testing and evaluation specifications and standards of electric drive system, form the full lifecycle carbon emission evaluation system, construct green and low carbon manufacture and smart factory with recyclable application rate 70% of key material and components of electric drive system.
Traction motor	Power density of traction motors for high performance passenger car is 14kW/kg, and power density of traction motors for cost effective passenger car is 8kW/kg	Power density of traction motors for high performance passenger car is 16kW/kg, and power density of traction motors for cost effective passenger car is 10kW/kg	Power density of traction motors for high performance passenger car is ≥18kW/kg, and power density of traction motors for cost effective passenger car is ≥12 kW/kg
	Power density of high speed traction motor for commercial vehicles is 6kW/kg, and torque density of high torque traction motor for commercial vehicles is 24Nm/kg	Power density of high speed traction motor for commercial vehicles is 7kW/kg, and torque density of high torque traction motor for commercial vehicles is 27Nm/kg	Power density of high speed traction motor for commercial vehicles is 8kW/kg, and torque density of high torque traction motor for commercial vehicles is 30Nm/kg
	Iron loss of silicon steel sheets P1.0/400 ≤ 11W/kg, Permanent magnets Br ≥ 1.45T and coercivity Hcj ≥ 2,070kA/m, Corona resistance of electromagnetic wires at 30kHz > 200h and PDIV ≥ 1.4kV, Dm·n value of high-speed bearings ≥ 1,200,000 (grease lubrication), Accuracy of position sensors ±20′	Iron loss of silicon steel sheets P1.0/400 ≤ 10W/kg, Permanent magnets Br ≥ 1.47T and coercivity Hcj ≥ 2,030kA/m, Corona resistance of electromagnetic wires at 30kHz > 300h and PDIV ≥ 1.5kV, Dm·n value of high-speed bearings ≥ 1,400,000 (grease lubrication), Accuracy of position sensors ±15′	Iron loss of silicon steel sheets P1.0/400 ≤ 9W/kg, Permanent magnets Br ≥ 1.50T and coercivity Hcj ≥ 1,990kA/m, Corona resistance of electromagnetic wires at 30kHz > 400h and PDIV ≥ 1.8kV, Dm·n value of high-speed bearings ≥ 1,500,000 (grease lubrication), Accuracy of position sensors ±10′
Motor Controller	Power density of motor controller with wide-bandgap semiconductor for passenger car is 80kW/L, and power density of motor controller with silicon semiconductor for passenger car is 50kW/L	Power density of motor controller with wide-bandgap semiconductor for passenger car is 100kW/L, and power density of motor controller with silicon semiconductor for passenger car is 60kW/L	Power density of motor controller with wide-bandgap semiconductor for passenger car is 120kW/L, and power density of motor controller with silicon semiconductor for passenger car is 70kW/L
	Power density of motor controller with wide-bandgap semiconductor for commercial vehicle is 50kW/L, and power density of motor controller with silicon semiconductor for commercial vehicle is 35kW/L	Power density of motor controller with wide-bandgap semiconductor for commercial vehicle is 60kW/L, and power density of motor controller with silicon semiconductor for commercial vehicle is 45kW/L	Power density of motor controller with wide-bandgap semiconductor for commercial vehicle is 80kW/L, and power density of motor controller with silicon semiconductor for commercial vehicle is 55kW/L
	Current density of silicon carbide devices is 700A/cm≤ (1200V), current density of silicon semiconductor is 350A/cm≤(750V), ripple current high-temperature capacitors is 0.50A/μF(150℃), signal detection accuracy of current sensor is ±1.5%	Current density of silicon carbide devices is 750A/cm≤ (1200V), current density of silicon semiconductor is 375A/cm≤(750V), ripple current high-temperature capacitors is 0.60A/μF(150℃), signal detection accuracy of current sensor is ±1.0%	Current density of silicon carbide devices is 800A/cm≤ (1200V), current density of silicon semiconductor is 400A/cm≤(750V), ripple current high-temperature capacitors is 0.70A/μF(150℃), signal detection accuracy of current sensor is ±0.5%
Power Electronics Assembly	Power density of power electronics assembly for passenger car is 50kW/L, and power density of electric control systems for commercial vehicle is 15kW/L	Power density of power electronics assembly for passenger car is 60kW/L, and power density of electric control systems for commercial vehicle is 20kW/L	Power density of power electronics assembly for passenger car is 70kW/L, and power density of electric control systems for commercial vehicle is 25kW/L
	Average efficiency of DCDC ≥ 93.5%, average efficiency of OBC ≥ 94.8% (full load). Computing capacity of MCU is 8KDMIPS compliance with ASIL D, Complete architectures and functionalities of domain control system, support multi-core architectures	Average efficiency of DCDC ≥ 94.0%, average efficiency of OBC ≥ 95.3% (full load). Computing capacity of MCU is 16KDMIPS compliance with ASIL D, Complete architectures and functionalities of domain control system, support multi-core architectures	Average efficiency of DCDC ≥ 94.5%, average efficiency of OBC ≥ 95.8% (full load). Computing capacity of MCU is 32KDMIPS compliance with ASIL D, Complete architectures and functionalities of domain control system, support multi-core architectures
Centralized Electrical Drive Assembly	Power density of electrical drive system for passenger car is 4.2kW/kg, and power density of electrical drive assembly for cost effective car is 2.7kW/kg	Power density of electrical drive system for passenger car is 4.5kW/kg, and power density of electrical drive assembly for cost effective car is 3.0kW/kg	Power density of electrical drive system for passenger car is ≥5.0kW/kg, and power density of electrical drive assembly for cost effective car is 3.3kW/kg
	Torque density of electric bridge for light commercial vehicle is 70Nm/kg, torque density of electrical bridge for medium and heavy commercial vehicle is 95Nm/kg; torque density of electric drive system for medium and heavy vehicle is 65Nm/kg	Torque density of electric bridge for light commercial vehicle is 80Nm/kg, torque density of electric bridge for medium and heavy commercial vehicle is 105Nm/kg, torque density of electric drive system for medium and heavy vehicle is 75Nm/kg	Torque density of electric bridge for light commercial vehicle is 90Nm/kg, torque density of electric bridge for medium and heavy commercial vehicle is 115Nm/kg, torque density of electric drive system for medium and heavy vehicle is 85Nm/kg
Distributed Electrical Drive Assembly	Torque density of motor assembly for passenger car is 22Nm/kg, torque density of in-wheel motor assembly for commercial vehicles is 33Nm/kg, and power density of distributed electrical drive system is 4.5kW/kg	Torque density of in-wheel motor assembly for passenger car is 25Nm/kg, torque density of in-wheel motor assembly for commercial vehicles is 39Nm/kg, and power density of distributed electrical drive system is 4.8kW/kg	Torque density of in-wheel motor assembly for passenger car is 27Nm/kg, torque density of in-wheel motor assembly for commercial vehicles is 45Nm/kg, and power density of distributed electrical drive system is 4.8kW/kg
Electro-mechanical Coupling Assembly	Volume and weight decrease ratio of electromechanical coupling assembly for passenger car is 15% comparing in 2025, and torque density of electromechanical coupling assembly is 24Nm/kg	Volume and weight decrease ratio of electromechanical coupling assembly for passenger car is 25% comparing in 2025, and torque density of electromechanical coupling assembly is 28Nm/kg	Volume and weight decrease ratio of electromechanical coupling assembly for passenger car is 35% comparing in 2025, and torque density of electromechanical coupling assembly is 32Nm/kg
	Torque density of electromechanical coupling assembly for light commercial vehicles is 30Nm/kg, torque density of electromechanical coupling assemblies for medium and heavy commercial vehicles is 48Nm/kg	Torque density of electromechanical coupling assembly for light commercial vehicles is 36Nm/kg, torque density of electromechanical coupling assemblies for medium and heavy commercial vehicles is 56Nm/kg	Torque density of electromechanical coupling assembly for light commercial vehicles is 42Nm/kg, torque density of electromechanical coupling assemblies for medium and heavy commercial vehicles is 65Nm/kg
Low Carbon Manufacture and Recycling	Establishment of lifecycle accounting standards and data system for carbon footprint covering industrial chain of electric drive system, reduction ratio 30% of carbon emissions during manufacturing process comparing 2025, recyclable application rate ≥ 50% of key material and components	Establishment of lifecycle accounting standards and evaluation system for carbon footprint covering industrial chain of electric drive system, reduction ratio 40% of carbon emissions during manufacturing process comparing 2025, recyclable application rate ≥ 60% of key material and components	Establishment of lifecycle accounting standards and limitation value for carbon footprint covering industrial chain of electric drive system, reduction ratio 50% of carbon emissions during manufacturing process comparing 2025, recyclable application rate ≥ 70% of key material and components

Fig. 3.3 Technology roadmap for electric drive systems

components such as efficient hybrid powertrains and configuration designs for commercial vehicles, dedicated transmissions, dedicated engines, and traction motor and controller platform, and enhance the scalability and robustness of the electromechanical coupling powertrain system.

(5) Testing System and Low Carbon Manufacturing: Focuses include strengthening the standardization of testing and verification standard and evaluation systems for electric drive system, establishing low carbon manufacturing and smart factories to achieve the recycling of key materials and components, and developing carbon emission assessment system to cover the full lifecycle of electric drive assembly. Meanwhile, there need development of soft tooling on mechanical, electromagnetic, thermal, NVH, and control algorithm. To improve the comprehensive performance of the electric drive system, the testing equipment and evaluation system as well as the manufacturing equipment for key materials and components are need to be accelerate development. And it is necessary to accelerate the formulation of basic material standards and normative material recycling and reuse standards for low carbon manufacture.

The technology roadmap of electric drive system from 2026 to 2040 is the follows (Fig. 3.3).

3.4 Vehicle-Energy Interaction and Infrastructure

3.4.1 Charging Facilities

3.4.1.1 Domestic and International Technical Status Comparison

High-Power Ultra-Fast Charging Technology Significantly Reduces Charging Duration, While the Global Fast-Charging Network Deployment is Fully Accelerating

Since 2017–2018, European and American automakers have successfully developed and commercialized high-power charging technologies exceeding 350kW. Europe has deployed 400 fast-charging stations with 1,586 charging piles along its highways and intercity highways, covering over twenty countries and regions in Europe. The region plans to install approximately 7,000 high-power charging piles by 2025. Across North America, 800 super charging stations with over 3,500 charging piles have been deployed in the U.S. and Canada, with plans to install an additional 1,800 charging stations and 10,000 super charging piles by 2026. In November 2024, CharIN submitted detailed recommendations to the U.S. Federal Highway Administration (FHWA) for medium- and heavy-duty electric vehicle (EV) charging infrastructure standards, encompassing Megawatt Charging System (MCS) solutions and interface interoperability requirements.

China's high-power ultra-fast charging technology is undergoing revolutionary advancement, with rapid breakthroughs in key technologies including power pooling, full liquid cooling, and DC buses. The high-power charging interface standard has been updated and implemented, increasing the maximum charging current from 250 to 800A and boosting charging power to 800kW. According to the National Energy Administration (NEA), since the start of 2025, the popularization of high-power charging facilities with a single-port charging power exceeding 250kW has accelerated, and the number of such facilities in China has surpassed 37,000 units. In the heavy-duty truck fast-charging sector, Huawei and other manufacturers have developed megawatt-level ultra-fast charging systems, now deployed in mining and port high-duty trucks. Huawei's megawatt-level ultra-fast charging product boasts a maximum charging current of 2,400A and a peak power output of 1.44 MW. With an impressive energy replenishment rate of around 20kWh per minute, it enables a complete energy replenishment within just 15 min. This represents a nearly fourfold increase in energy replenishment efficiency, propelling the heavy-duty truck sector towards a fully electrified future.

The Battery Swapping Technology for Electric Vehicles is Expanding from Passenger Vehicles to Heavy-Duty Trucks, and the Battery Swapping Model Has Been Applied on a Large Scale

Overseas, Better Place, an Israeli holding group corporation, rolled out a three-minute battery swapping service. Nevertheless, owing to the inadequate backing from a broader range of manufacturers, the operational business model of Better Place eventually met with insolvency. Tesla also delved into the battery swapping model. Nevertheless, due to the exorbitant battery swapping service fees, it failed to win the favor of consumers. Consequently, Tesla eventually discarded its battery swapping service.

In China, prior to 2015, the technical approach of battery swapping predominantly centered around lateral compartment battery swapping, with buses serving as the exemplars. As the degree of automation has escalated, battery swapping technology has witnessed substantial progress in the automatic battery swapping of passenger vehicle chassis. It is primarily utilized in battery swapping services for online ride-hailing vehicles and private cars under the auspices of automakers. Since 2023, there has been a meteoric rise in the sectors of short-distance transportation and highway freight heavy-duty trucks. Technologies such as battery swapping locking systems, electrical interfaces of connectors, AGV replacement apparatuses, and station control technologies are trending towards maturity. However, in terms of battery box dimensions, electrical interfaces, and locking mechanisms, there still remain a variety of structural sizes that lack uniformity. China is intensifying its efforts to propel the compatibility and standardization of shared battery swapping protocols. As of the end of 2024, China had amassed over 1,000 battery swapping stations specifically for heavy-duty trucks. It had successively rolled out more than 800 models of battery-swapping heavy-duty trucks, with a cumulative sales volume of 59,000 vehicles. The battery capacity configurations were set within the range of 280 to 500kWh.

The Automatic Charging Approach is Highly Congruent with the Trajectory of Future Development, and Proactive Explorations Have Been Undertaken Worldwide

Machine-assisted automatic charging technology:

Overseas, by the end of 2018, Volkswagen rolled out a mobile charging machine. Researchers from Graz University of Technology crafted a prototype of the "robotically-controlled CCS rapid charging system", making use of a UR10 robotic arm.

In China, Domestic enterprises have successively launched multiple robotic arm-assisted automatic charging devices. Examples include Shanghai Electric's intelligent charging robotic arm C-POD, the mobile charging robot self-developed by NaaS, and the "Xiaohei G60" developed by DHForce, among others. In the upcoming several years, humanoid charging robots are poised to rapidly attain technological breakthroughs. Their operation methods and service efficacy will exhibit even more pronounced advantages.

Wireless automatic charging technology:

Overseas, in 2018, Germany BMW unveiled the industry's inaugural wireless charging model, 530Le. Concurrently, automakers including Daimler, Audi, and Volkswagen also embarked on the development of corresponding products. In March 2024, the Oak Ridge National Laboratory (ORNL) in the United States successfully showcased a 100kW wireless charging technology. In partnership with the Volkswagen AG, it achieved a wireless fast-charging power of 270kW, utilizing the Porsche Taycan electric vehicle as the testing platform. In October 2024, Tesla officially declared that its Robtaxi product, Cybercab, would implement automatic wireless charging. Automakers such as Honda, Volkswagen, FCA, McLaren, and Bentley are actively advancing the mass-production development of related products. Several of them have already finalized their pre-installation plans for wireless charging systems.

In China, the wireless charging approach has garnered widespread acclaim among OEMs for its unparalleled convenience, prompting them to make technical reserve. In 2018, SAIC's passenger vehicle unit pioneered the release of the mass-produced Marvel X model, which featured a 7 kW wireless charging function. In 2022, an 11 kW wireless charging option was integrated into the IM L7 model. FAW commenced its research on wireless charging technology in 2014, developing 3.3 kW and 6.6 kW functional prototypes. By 2022, it had commercialized 11 kW wireless charging technology. In April 2019, China's major mainstream automakers such as BAIC, Dongfeng Voyah, BYD, Geely, GAC, Changan, Great Wall, along with emerging automotive manufacturers like SERES and Xiaomi, actively embarked on research on wireless fast-charging technology.

Vehicle-to-Grid (V2G) Technology Has Entered a Rapid Development Phase, With Multiple Chinese Government Departments Collaborating in Demonstration and Promotion Efforts

Overseas, the V2G technology in Europe and the United States has reached a relatively sophisticated level. The standard frameworks for charging and discharging grid integration, vehicle-to-grid metering, virtual power plants, and communication information authentication are being progressively optimized. Through a multitude of early-stage pilot demonstrations across diverse scenarios, experience in the high-rate absorption of renewable energy sources has been amassed, leading to the establishment of a real-time electricity price modulation mechanism. Large-scale commercial implementations have been achieved in developed countries.

In China, positive progress has been made in the research of V2G technology. Leading enterprises have developed V2G AC-DC charging and discharging apparatus. Integrated with the load scenarios of various stations and buildings within parks, it, in conjunction with the photovoltaic, energy storage, charging, discharging and battery swapping systems, constitutes a comprehensive microgrid system. V2G pilot application demonstrations have been launched in numerous cities, including Beijing, Shanghai, Baoding, Wuxi, Chongqing, and Shenzhen. In 2024, spurred by the enhanced impetus of policies, major charging operators and power grids have deployed virtual power plant platforms in multiple cities, conducting V2G demonstration applications demand response and load regulation. The commercialization process is fully accelerating. The V2G standard system encompasses 92 items, consisting of 47 national standards and 45 industry standards. To date, 35 items have been promulgated, 30 items are currently under formulation and revision, and a total of 27 items are slated for formulation and amendment.

3.4.1.2 Outlook on Technology Development Trends

High-Power Charging is on the Verge of Maturity, and Megawatt-Level Ultra-Fast Charging Has Come into Existence, Jointly Constituting an Extremely Swift Energy Replenishment Approach Alongside the Battery Swapping of Heavy-Duty Trucks

China has made remarkable feats in the domain of high-power charging technology, formulating diverse technical trajectories such as liquid cooling, heat conduction-isolated air cooling, and conventional air cooling. Each of them boasts its unique advantages in terms of scenario adaptability, laying a groundwork for the high-quality development of charging technology. Technologies like the flexible integrated power battery regulation technology grounded in an intelligent matrix, the design of immersion-type gun cables and full-link liquid cooling heat dissipation featuring high reliability and superior protection performance, and the optimized noise suppression technology have all lent impetus to the construction of the high-power charging network. With the breakthrough in the 6C high-rate safe fast-charging performance of power batteries, megawatt-level ultra-large current charging technology has emerged. In the future, the power of a single megawatt charging gun is anticipated to gradually escalate to 3.75 MW/1,250V. Simultaneously, the battery swapping technology for heavy-duty trucks has been steadily maturing and deployed on a large scale in a networked manner, yielding remarkable achievements in enhancing the interactive efficiency between stations and the grid and bolstering safety operation capabilities. In the future, high-power ultra-fast charging, megawatt-level ultra-fast charging, battery swapping for heavy-duty trucks, and integrated comprehensive energy replenishment facilities that incorporate photovoltaics, energy storage, charging, hydrogen refueling, and battery swapping will collectively constitute an extensively distributed and point-line-and-surface extremely swift energy replenishment infrastructure. It is projected that by 2040, these facilities will supply comprehensive energy replenishment electricity, accounting for over 60% of the total for various electric vehicles.

Embodied Robots in Conjunction with the Integration of Communication, Sensing, Computing, and Control Will Emerge as a Preeminent Technological Combination for Automatic Charging, Bestowing Upon Intelligent Driving Vehicles a More Seamless and Amicable Energy Replenishment Experience

With the advancement of intelligent driving vehicles and the widespread adoption of automatic parking technology, the application requirements for intelligent guidance, automatic charging, and automatic discharging are poised to surge rapidly. Notably, public fast-charging stations will evolve into one of the pivotal means for power grid load regulation, enabling the implementation of high-power V2G reservation-based regulation. Leveraging end-to-end automated driving system and reservation commands, vehicles will be able to autonomously park in designated charging and discharging bays. Humanoid robots, distinguished by their exceptional intelligence and flexibility, will assume traditional manual operation functions such as mobile surveillance of stations, grasping and plugging in charging guns, and station cleaning duties. Their locomotion and maneuvering capabilities, as well as operational efficiency, will far surpass those of current fixed robotic arms or mobile robotic arms mounted on small vehicles. Anchored in the projected growth scale of the embodied intelligent robot industry, an automatic charging solution utilizing robots will materialize, offering distinctive advantages in terms of cost and comprehensive service efficacy. Meanwhile, wireless automatic charging and chassis conductive auto-charging will be deployed across different application scenarios. The corresponding common technology involves establishing an integrated communication-sensing integrated network capable of meeting diverse vehicle requirements including all-weather operation, 3D garage coverage and multi-vehicle/multi-space real-time data interaction required for ambient environment sensing, high-precision positioning with communication-guided navigation, and autonomous parking. The communication infrastructure can be implemented through integrated 5G/6G, WiFi 8, NearLink, or

UWB technologies. Initial implementations are anticipated in online ride-hailing charging stations, micro-public fast-charging stations, and commercial center 3D parking systems.

V2X Expedites the Bidirectional Integration of Transportation and Energy Sectors. The High Synergy Among Vehicles, Energy Systems, Road Infrastructure, Buildings, and Cloud-Based Platforms Stands as a Pivotal Avenue for Enhancing Low-Carbon Economic Benefits, Propelled by the Dual-Carbon Initiatives

As policies concerning V2X and V2G continue to be refined, technological innovation surges forward, standards gradually converge, key equipment undergoes continuous upgrading and iteration, demonstration projects are progressively implemented, business models attain increasing maturity, and cross-border cooperation in V2X exhibits a robust development trajectory. Over the next 5–15 years, spurred by the V2X business, the distributed energy network will achieve harmonious and complementary coordination among diverse energy modalities. V2G technology will also aggregate distributed resources via virtual power plants, furnishing the power grid with substantial flexible and adjustable resources. By harnessing AI and big data analysis, it will enable precise predictions, facilitating the regulation and response of V2X loads, optimizing charging and discharging strategies, and elevating both economic viability and user experience. With the widespread application and popularization of integrated photovoltaic, energy storage, charging, and testing station, as well as V2X technology within parks, the regulatory capabilities of charging facilities stations, serving as nodes for electricity exchange, will become increasingly flexible, intelligent, and real-time. These stations will gradually evolve into directly connected and self-governing microgrids in conjunction with surrounding loads, implementing collaborative electricity regulation on the user side. The key technologies of V2X and V2G will persistently break new ground, optimizing load regulation and the consumption capacity of green electricity. This will turn electric vehicles into dual-function instruments, facilitating people's mobility while also enabling their participation in electricity trading. This approach satisfies the needs of electric vehicle users to engage in charging and discharging load regulation and green electricity consumption, positioning electric vehicles as versatile tools for both transportation and electricity market participation. In the future, the extension and expansion of V2X application scenarios to the energy consumption of buildings within parks will effectively drive the formation of an application ecosystem of smart energy involving multiple entities, across multiple tiers, and in various regions. This will catalyze the development of the energy and carbon trading market, fostering the flourishing of the V2X business landscape within the dual-carbon economic framework.

AI Empowers the Innovation of Charging Safety Monitoring Technology, Pioneering a New Trajectory of High-Quality Development for Photovoltaic, Energy Storage, Charging, Hydrogen Refueling, and Battery Swapping Facilities

In the prospective scenario of the convergence between transportation and energy sectors, ultra-fast charging technology throughout the entire lifecycle will gain even wider prevalence. Charging and discharging safety technology has ascended to a pivotal realm propelled by innovation. Real-time monitoring and fault diagnosis technologies are utilized to achieve continuous status surveillance, early fault warning, and control of traction batteries and energy storage system batteries. This requires continuous improvement in battery safety detection accuracy to ensure secure, stable, and reliable system operation. Meanwhile, leveraging the broad application prospects of integrated photovoltaic, energy storage, charging, hydrogen refueling, and battery swapping energy replenishment system, the charging safety monitoring systems will expand their coverage to include photovoltaics, hydrogen-electricity coupling, and high/low voltage ride-through protection for station microgrids, holistically enhancing system-wide early warning, fault tolerance, and failure protection capabilities. By capitalizing on AI models, through multi-modal perception, big data analysis, and the identification of risks associated with battery-related safety characteristic parameters, it becomes feasible to promptly perceive safety-related fluctuating factors and excavate internal laws. This approach can more effectively augment the sensitivity and veracity of early warnings, rectify the inadequacies in detection accuracy and early warning precision inherent in traditional technologies, and bolster the system's adaptability to the operational environment and the influence of high-rate charging and discharging on battery longevity. As the charging safety monitoring technology undergoes continuous innovation, it will catalyze the transformation towards high-quality development of new energy vehicle charging facilities and realize sound and sustainable advancement.

The Synergy Between Big Data and Cloud Networks Has Evolved into a Novel Form of Productive Force, Propelled by the Core Data Elements of V2X Infrastructure

Amidst the rapid progression of V2X technology, the widespread deployment of electric vehicles, distributed energy resources, and cutting-edge energy storage facilities necessitates that charging operators and comprehensive energy service providers harness big data networks and cloud platform technologies. They must forge intimate partnerships with new energy vehicles, charging and energy storage facilities, as well as distribution network facilities. This is essential for ensuring the efficient manageability of energy replenishment infrastructure, optimal electricity allocation, and bidirectional dispatching, all of which cater to the ever-changing energy consumption requirements. Aggregate service providers can achieve flexible dispatching across multiple interconnected parties, balance supply and demand,

and optimize energy utilization efficiency by integrating scattered power resources from diverse origins. Transaction settlement can be accomplished through electricity integration and real-time metering. By leveraging remote monitoring and digital twin technologies, operational management efficiency can be enhanced. Through the perception of scenario conditions and the auxiliary analysis enabled by big data and AI, precise prediction and instantaneous handling of faults and operational statuses, including accurate fault prediction and automated resolution, can be realized. As the scale of distributed network interconnections and operational networking expands, information interoperability and cross-domain collaboration have gained heightened significance. Technologies such as reliable communication authentication and data traceability are essential. These technologies serve as the bedrock for supporting automatic charging guidance, shared charging and battery swapping services, electricity exchange in V2G, energy and carbon trading, and cross-domain collaborative resource allocation, thereby enabling intelligent and automated operations. They also represent a vital technological pathway driven by data elements, indispensable for the operation of future smart energy systems. This pathway embodies a novel form of productive force that elevates overall coordination, safety, and operational efficiency.

3.4.1.3 Development Goals and Milestones for 2040

Over the next 15 years, China will embark on a comprehensive endeavor to construct an integrated 3D charging infrastructure network that is characterized by its green and low-carbon footprint, extensive coverage, intelligent operation, and high efficiency. Leveraging the V2X infrastructure as a pivotal link, it will spearhead the profound integration of the transportation and energy sectors. This will give rise to a multi-energy complementary system encompassing photovoltaics, energy storage, charging, hydrogen refueling, and battery swapping, propelled by big data and AI. Moreover, it will foster continuous innovative breakthroughs in key technologies related to automatic charging and discharging, as well as smart energy solutions, providing all-round support for a substantial leap in the service capabilities of new quality across diverse energy replenishment scenarios. By 2030, China will have essentially established a high-quality charging infrastructure system that boasts extensive coverage, a moderate scale, a rational structure, and comprehensive functionality, offering robust support for the development of the new energy vehicle industry. By 2035, the charging service will, as a general norm, achieve the plug-and-charge and automatic charging/battery swapping modalities. Additionally, it will embrace intelligent charging operations, online safety monitoring, shared charging access, and professional operation services. These advancements will serve to further enhance the quality of charging services, ensuring efficient, secure, and excellent operation services. By 2040, China will have fully established an integrated standard system spanning the domains of transportation, energy, construction, and communication. Simultaneously, a support system for the integration of communication, sensing, and intelligent computing will be put in place. Automatic charging and battery swapping will blanket more than 50% of public fast-charging stations dedicated to energy replenishment. The multi-energy complementary system of "photovoltaic, energy storage, charging, hydrogen refueling, and battery swapping" that integrates transportation and energy will extend along the routes of expressways, contributing to green and low-carbon efficiency enhancements. The coverage rate of comprehensive stations for photovoltaic, energy storage, charging, and battery swapping (including those integrating hydrogen refueling) on expressways will reach 65–80%, marking the initial realization of a safe and ample complementary utilization of multiple energy sources.

3.4.1.4 Technology Roadmap

In the future, the development paths of V2X and charging infrastructure system architecture will be implemented in parallel. Guided by the core principles of green, low-carbon, and high-quality development, the focus will be on enhancing the overall level of "intelligence, bidirectionality, and sharing" of charging facilities. By promoting the collaboration among the vehicle, energy, road, cloud, and building industries, a new situation of efficient linkage, a new ecosystem of transportation-energy integration, and a new format of zero-carbon industries will be formed. Through the construction of a carbon emission accounting and indicator evaluation system, vehicle-charging pile-power grid systems will be guided to participate in power integration and regulation, achieving a high-proportion consumption of comprehensive green electricity and accelerating the process of green transformation. The enhancement of core technological capabilities will be implemented across five key technical domains through a systematic framework. By leveraging insights into global cutting-edge technologies and emerging technological trends, and driven by next-generation embodied AI robotics + automated charging scenarios + universalized core module chipization as pivotal enablers, we will establish a dominant common supporting technology portfolio featuring "integrated communication-management-intelligent computing-control + cross-domain trusted identity authentication + large-model-based precision prediction". This will form the central pillar empowering the V2X industry, accelerating the intelligent end-to-end integration of vehicle-charger-grid-cloud power regulation. Through market guidance via policies and standards, and by taking multiple measures simultaneously, within 10–15 years, a high-quality transformation featuring "excellent user experience, high electricity efficiency, and strong safety redundancy" will be achieved. Meanwhile, the V2X-related photovoltaic, energy storage, charging, and battery swapping facilities will accumulate trillion-level carbon assets, which will stimulate the booming development of green and low-carbon industries worth tens of trillions. This will support the initial realization of China's vision for low-carbon transportation (Fig. 3.4).

Fig. 3.4 Vehicle-energy interaction and charging facilities overall technical roadmap

3.4.2 *Hydrogen Energy Infrastructure*

3.4.2.1 Domestic and International Technical Status Comparison

Overall Design of Hydrogen Refueling Stations: Leading Global in Gas Hydrogen Refueling, no Liquid Hydrogen Refueling Stations

The number and growth rate of hydrogen refueling stations are the highest in the world, and the cost of hydrogen fuel is the lowest in the world. As of December 25, 2023, there were 428 hydrogen refueling stations in operation across the country, an increase of 70 from the end of 2022, the largest number and growth rate in the world, covering 30 provinces, municipalities and autonomous regions, with a cumulative supply capacity of 208,000 kg per day; The retail price of hydrogen at hydrogen refueling stations in China is about 35 yuan/kg (35MPa), with a small number as low as 30 yuan/kg. Hydrogen fuel prices rose in most countries around the world except China in 2023, but declined in China.

The average designed refueling capacity is high, and the investment cost of the station construction equipment is low. As China's hydrogen industry policy encourages high-power, long-range commercial vehicles, the average daily refueling capacity of hydrogen refueling stations in China is generally higher than that of foreign hydrogen refueling stations. More than 80% of hydrogen refueling stations have a capacity of no less than 500 kg/12 h, and the maximum can reach 4800 kg/12 h, but the actual operational efficiency and utilization rate have not yet met the design expectations. At the same time, the equipment of hydrogen refueling stations has been fully domesticated and cost controlled. The domestic equipment investmentcost has been controlled within 8 million yuan per ton of refueling capacity, while the equipment investment cost per ton of refueling capacity at foreign hydrogen refueling stations is generally over 10 million yuan. The cost of equipment for hydrogen refueling stations in China is significantly lower than the global average.

At present, all hydrogen refueling stations in China are high-pressure hydrogen storage stations. The energy consumption for hydrogen refueling is high. On the one hand, the actual utilization rate of hydrogen refueling stations is lower than the designed refueling capacity. On the other hand, the rapid refueling of high-pressure hydrogen increases the energy consumption of the refrigeration machine. The lack of a mature liquid hydrogen supply chain in China means that domestic hydrogen refueling stations can only provide high-pressure hydrogen refueling services and cannot commercialize liquid hydrogen or cryogenic high-pressure hydrogen refueling. The United States, Germany and Japan have commercialized high-pressure hydrogen refueling for liquid hydrogen storage, with obvious advantages in 70 MPa refueling efficiency, and have achieved refueling and demonstration operations for liquid hydrogen heavy-duty trucks. The United States and Germany are conducting research on relevant standards and demonstration operations for cryogenic high- pressure hydrogen.

The overall design of hydrogen refueling stations at home and abroad is shown in Table 3.1

Table 3.1 Technical indicators of the overall design of hydrogen refueling stations at home and abroad

Indicator name	Domestic implementation (2023)	Realization abroad (2023)	Domestic compared with foreign	Completion towards 2025 goals
Number of hydrogen refueling stations (units)	428	362 (US)	Significant advantage	There is still a big gap to 1,000 hydrogen refueling stations by 2025
Fuel costs for hydrogen refueling stations (yuan/kg)	20–40 (North) 35–60 (South)	51 (Korea)-200 (USA)	Significant advantage	Reach 35 yuan/kg after subsidies by 2025
Hydrogen refueling station designed refueling capacity (t/d)	0.5	0.3	Significant advantage	Expected to reach 1
Hydrogen refueling stations can refuel vehicle types	EXcept for liquid hydrogen fuel	All vehicles	Domestic stations only have high-pressure hydrogen storage, while foreign ones have liquid hydrogen storage	All vehicles
Maximum continuous refueling capacity at hydrogen refueling stations (kg/min)	2.7 (High-pressure gas hydrogen)	High-pressure gas hydrogen data is unknown 8–11* (Deep cryogenic high pressure) 10 (Liquid hydrogen)	There is only high-pressure hydrogen storage at domestic stations, while there is liquid hydrogen storage abroad	It isExpected to reach 10
Energy consumption at hydrogen refueling stations (kWh/kgH_2)	2.1@35 MPa 2.6@70 MPa (Diaphragm compressor)	2@35MPa 2.5@70 MPa	Energy consumption is slightly higher than foreign levels	Expected to reach foreign levels 2@35MPa 2.5 @ 70 MPa
Investment cost of hydrogen refueling station (10,000 yuan/t refueling capacity)	800 (National average)	1200	Significant advantage	Expected to reach 600–700
Operating costs of hydrogen refueling stations ($yuan/kgH_2$)	8–10@35 MPa 14–15@70 MPa	15–100	Significant advantage	7–9@35 MPa 10–12@70 MPa

Compared with the leading level abroad, China's hydrogen refueling station technology shows differentiated development characteristics: China's 35/70 MPa hydrogen refueling station technology level is lagging behind, basically on par with the leading level abroad, but there is still a significant gap in the construction scale of 70 MPa stations; Hydrogen refueling station technology for liquid hydrogen storage and transportation has not yet achieved commercial application, and key links still need technological breakthroughs.

In China, liquid hydrogen production has not yet been commercialized, and the development of equipment and key components related to liquid hydrogen, such as liquid hydrogen cylinders, liquid hydrogen pumps, liquid hydrogen valves, and liquid hydrogen refueling guns, has been relatively slow, which has affected the commercial promotion of liquid hydrogen refueling stations.

From the perspective of the key components and technological development trends of hydrogen refueling stations: (1) China has made significant progress in gas-hydrogen conversion systems, while liquid-hydrogen conversion systems are still blank; (2) In-station high-pressure hydrogen storage technology is becoming increasingly mature, and in-station hydrogen storage methods are becoming increasingly diverse; (3) The domestic production process of hydrogen refueling machine systems is accelerating, but there is still a shortage of refueling capacity; (4) Progress has been made in the informatization, digitalization and intelligence of the station control system; (5) The in-station hydrogen production system has moved from exploration to acceleration, and green electricity hydrogen production has potential for development; (6) The hydrogen exchange system technology has the conditions for demonstration operation in China and has the potential for innovation.

High-Pressure Hydrogen Storage and Liquid Hydrogen Systems Are the Main Development Directions of On-Board Hydrogen Storage Systems

China's vehicle-mounted high-pressure type III hydrogen storage cylinder technology has matured, while type IV hydrogen storage cylinders are still in a stage of rapid development. High-pressure hydrogen storage is currently the main technology route for global hydrogen energy. Before 2020, China mainly developed 35 and 70 MPa type III high- pressure hydrogen storage cylinders, while internationally, type IV hydrogen storage cylinders were the main type. China has achieved large-scale production of vehicle-mounted high- pressure type III hydrogen storage cylinders, ranking first in the world in terms of both production capacity and inventory. In 2023, the national production of type III hydrogen storage cylinders was about 30,000. Compared with 2019, a relatively complete volume series of Type III hydrogen storage cylinders has been established, with nominal volumes ranging from 28 to 410L; The mass hydrogen storage density has increased from 4.0 to 5.4%; The cost of hydrogen storage for type III cylinders (without valves) was reduced from 3,200 yuan/kg H_{22} to 2,600 yuan/kg H.

Compared with Type III hydrogen storage cylinders, Type IV hydrogen storage cylinders have the advantages of high hydrogen storage density and good fatigue resistance, and occupy a large proportion in international hydrogen energy vehicles. The research and development of type IV hydrogen storage tanks in China started relatively late. Since 2017, domestic related enterprises have successively carried out research and development work, but it has developed rapidly. Currently, several enterprises have the production capacity of 35 and 70 MPa type IV hydrogen storage tanks, among which 35 MPa type IV hydrogen storage tanks have achieved application demonstration. However, compared with the international level, there is still a gap in the design and manufacturing technology of 70 MPa type IV hydrogen storage cylinders. Problems such as the main reliance on imported plastic liner materials, the need to improve the consistency of batch manufacturing of gas cylinders, and the relatively high manufacturing cost still need to be solved urgently.

Compared with on-board high-pressure hydrogen storage systems, on-board liquid hydrogen cylinders and liquid hydrogen cylinder valves are still in the research and development and application demonstration stage. Due to the incomplete liquid hydrogen supply chain, technologies such as the structure and insulation design of on-board liquid hydrogen cylinders and the optimization of cold and hot energy in the gas supply system need to be broken through. In Europe, America and other countries, the maximum single volume of liquid hydrogen cylinders carried by heavy-duty trucks is 720L, with a single hydrogen storage capacity of 40 kg and a maintenance time of about 72 h. In the field of cryogenic high- pressure technology, Germany has developed a 40 kg cryogenic high-pressure hydrogen storage cylinder from 450L@40 MPa, which is currently in the demonstration stage of application. China's vehicle-mounted liquid hydrogen storage system is in the development stage. The vehicle-mounted liquid hydrogen cylinders under research have a capacity of 650 L per cylinder, a capacity of 38.7 kg per cylinder, and a duration of 76 h. The technical indicators are basically on par with international standards.

There is still a considerable gap between China and foreign countries in terms of the valve of on-board hydrogen storage cylinders. Except for the 35 MPa on-board high-pressure hydrogen storage cylinder valve which has achieved domestic commercial application, the 70 MPa on-board high-pressure hydrogen storage cylinder valve has initially achieved domestic production and has not yet carried out application demonstration. Liquid hydrogen cylinder valves are mainly imported, and the localization of key components such as liquid hydrogen cylinder valves is still in the research and development stage.

Vehicle manufacturers are actively exploring innovations in on-board hydrogen storage technology. Represented by domestic and foreign enterprises such as BMW and Dongfeng Motor, they have developed and applied modular and integrated high-pressure hydrogen storage systems for passenger vehicles to achieve efficient utilization of vehicle space and structural design optimization, promote the co-platform production of multiple types of vehicles such as hydrogen and electricity, and further reduce vehicle manufacturing costs and improve overall performance.

Table 3.2 Technical specifications for vehicle hydrogen storage systems at home and abroad

Product name	Indicator name	Domestic implementation (2023)	Realization abroad (2023)	Comparative analysis at home and abroad	Progress towards the 2025 target
Type III hydrogen storage cylinders	Mass hydrogen storage rate (w.t.%)	5.4	5.4	Basically equivalent	Reach the target
	35 MPa Gas cylinder hydrogen storage cost (yuan/kgH_2)	2600 (Excluding cylinder valves) 3000 (with bottle valve);	3200 (Without bottle valve) 3500 (with bottle valve)	Domestic manufacturing costs are about 20% lower than international ones	Meet the standards
	70 MPa Hydrogen storage cost (yuan/kgH_2)	4500 (Excluding valves, 70 MPa) 8000 (with valves, 70 MPa)	5400 (Without bottle valve) 8400 (with bottle valve)	Domestic manufacturing costs are about 20% lower than international ones	Meet the standards
Type IV hydrogen storage cylinder	Mass hydrogen storage rate (w.t.%)	6.8 (35 MPa, 390 L)	8.0 (35 MPa, 638 L) 5.6 (70 MPa, 64.9 L)	Mass hydrogen storage density is affected by factors such as cylinder	Meet the target
				Pressure and volume; Mass hydrogen storage density needs to be improved;	
	Cost of hydrogen storage (yuan/kgH_2)	It has not yet been commercialized	6850 (Without bottle valve) 11000 (with bottle valve)	The cost of hydrogen storage still needs to be significantly reduced	Unfinished
On-board liquid hydrogen storage cylinders	Mass hydrogen storage rate (w.t.%)	Still in the research and development stage /	9.2%	The application demonstration has not yet been achieved	/

(continued)

Table 3.2 (continued)

Product name	Indicator name	Domestic implementation (2023)	Realization abroad (2023)	Comparative analysis at home and abroad	Progress towards the 2025 target
	Maintenance time (hours)	Still in the development stage /	72		/
	Hydrogen storage cost (yuan/kgH_2)	Still in the research and development stage	Not made public		/

The technical specifications for on-board hydrogen storage systems are shown in Table 3.2.

3.4.2.2 Outlook on Technology Development Trends

Large Flow, Low Energy Consumption and Continuous Refueling of Various Vehicles Are Important Trends in the Development of Hydrogen Refueling Stations

With the commercialization of fuel cell vehicles, the design and operation of hydrogen refueling stations are moving towards high flow, low energy consumption, and continuous refueling, with the aim of providing rapid and continuous refueling for hundreds of vehicles and completing refueling within 5 min with a single gun. There are two technical solutions for hydrogen refueling stations: gas hydrogen compressor boost and liquid hydrogen pump boost (normal temperature high pressure and deep cold high pressure). Among them, the energy consumption optimization of the gas hydrogen intake compressor boost technology solution is the key to improving operational efficiency and economy; The liquid hydrogen inlet pump booster technology solution can use cold energy to reduce the temperature rise of the on-board hydrogen cylinder and thereby improve the single-gun refueling capacity; Deep cryogenic high-pressure liquid hydrogen injection technology can achieve zero-emission high-speed continuous refueling, reduce vaporization loss and safety risks, and is an important direction for the development of hydrogen refueling station technology.

High Flowrate and Low Cost Are the Future Development Trends of Hydrogen Conversion Systems in Hydrogen Refueling Stations

The flowrate of the hydrogen conversion system in a hydrogen refueling station determines the refueling capacity of the station. Currently, the maximum flowrate of 45 MPa compressor has not exceeded 90 kg/h. Under 24-h full-load operation, the theoretical daily refueling capacity can only be slightly above 2 tons, which is an order of magnitude difference from the daily supply capacity of over 100 tons at natural gas stations. Increasing the flowrate to achieve a leap in refueling efficiency has become the core focus of the technological iteration of hydrogen conversion systems. In addition, as the core equipment of a hydrogen refueling station, the hydrogen conversion system has the highest operating energy consumption and maintenance costs within the station, and its economy and reliability directly determine the maintenance costs during the entire station's operation process. Cost is at the core of commercial application. Therefore, extending the maintenance cycle of gas-hydrogen conversion systems, developing more efficient liquid hydrogen conversion systems, and reducing the conversion cost of hydrogen within hydrogen refueling stations are the technical strategies of the hydrogen conversion systems.

High-Pressure Gas Hydrogen and Liquid Hydrogen Are Important Directions for the Development of In-Station Hydrogen Storage Systems

High-pressure hydrogen storage systems are evolving towards structural diversification. On the one hand, the working pressure of hydrogen storage containers for vehicles and hydrogen refueling stations in China has increased, and the pressure of seamless hydrogen storage containers for station spinning has increased significantly. On the other hand, underground hydrogen storage Wells have attracted attention due to their advantages such as occupying less space, and the application of various hydrogen storage equipment has made the high-pressure hydrogen storage system for hydrogen refueling stations more diverse. With the continuous improvement of the hydrogen storage container process and the continuous decline in the cost of key components, high-pressure gas hydrogen storage systems will still be the main type of in-station hydrogen storage systems. Liquid hydrogen is an important development direction for in-station hydrogen storage systems due to its high hydrogen storage density, large hydrogen storage capacity per unit space, and the ability to support various forms of high-flow refueling. In recent years, solid-state hydrogen storage technology has developed rapidly, and domestic application demonstrations of solid-state hydrogen storage in stations have also begun, and its development trend is worthy of attention.

The Development Trend of Hydrogen Refueling Machines is High- Pressure and High-Flow Refueling Technology

The development of global hydrogen refueling technology is becoming more diversified and specialized, with core performance such as refueling speed, status monitoring, and communication stability constantly improving. In particular, the filling of 70 MPa type IV cylinders involves an overall improvement in safety performance. The integration and coordination of hydrogen refueling machines with other equipment in hydrogen refueling stations are also receiving increasing attention.

Station Control Systems Are Evolving from Single-Station Distributed Control to Multi-Station and Upstream and Downstream Integrated Control

Digitalization is an important way to reshape the hydrogen energy industry chain and achieve cost reduction and efficiency improvement throughout the entire industry chain. Based on technologies such as the Internet of Things, cloud computing, big data and artificial intelligence, hydrogen refueling station control systems are gradually moving towards vehicle- station linkage and multi-station integration. Developing high-precision and high-reliability sensing and monitoring technologies, standardizing the public data acquisition protocol for hydrogen refueling stations, and connecting the data link of hydrogen refueling stations are the foundations for promoting the digitalization of hydrogen refueling stations. Building virtual models of hydrogen refueling stations, hydrogen supply end and application end using geometric models, physical models, behavioral models and rule models is the key to achieving digital twins and integrated control of hydrogen refueling stations. Through full data mining and machine learning, low-cost hydrogen supply processes, precise equipment status monitoring and fault diagnosis, as well as dynamic management and control of hydrogen refueling station risks can be achieved.

In-Station Hydrogen Production Technology is Moving Towards Integration, Low-Carbonization and Low Cost

The current in-station hydrogen production technology focuses on the following issues:

(1) Standardization and integration. Reduce floor space by optimizing equipment structure and process design, among which equipment integration is the main technical approach at present;
(2) Low carbon and zero carbon. Hydrogen production from water electrolysis forms a complete green chain by coupling with green electricity (verified by multiple projects at home and abroad), while hydrogen production from methanol/ammonia decomposition ensures green raw materials (supported by future green methanol and green ammonia projects);
(3) Low cost and high efficiency. In the short term, low-cost hydrogen production will be achieved mainly through low-cost and readily available raw materials such as natural gas/methanol. In the long term, better economic efficiency will be achieved through water electrolysis technology—by consuming surplus green electricity in coordination with photovoltaic/wind power, and by optimizing the design of alkaline electrolyzers (for example, in some cases, it has

reached <4kWh/Nm^3 electricity consumption) to continuously reduce hydrogen production costs.

Hydrogen Exchange System Technology May Become a Breakthrough Point for Business Model Innovation

The economic timing for developing hydrogen exchange systems for fuel cell heavy-duty trucks is now ripe. At present, hydrogen refueling stations such as in-station hydrogen production, long-tube trailer hydrogen supply, and pipeline hydrogen transportation and supply are developing rapidly in China. Currently, the market conditions for refined operation and optimization of hydrogen supply and demand for fuel cell vehicles through innovative hydrogen swap business models are in place. The hydrogen swap model can not only reduce the initial purchase cost of vehicles by separating the vehicle from the hydrogen cylinder, but also has the potential to reduce the cost of hydrogen for fuel cell vehicles. Technical feasibility has been achieved. China's battery swapping industry has formed a complete industrial chain, has autonomy in the industrial chain of battery swapping equipment, and has accumulated rich experience in battery swapping technology. The existing battery swapping equipment can be retroactive and upgraded for hydrogen swapping. Although there are no international standards and norms for hydrogen swap systems, Japan and Europe have already applied this model to hydrogen-powered ships, and Japanese automakers such as Toyota have proposed hydrogen swap solutions for heavy trucks. Attention should be paid to the potential of the hydrogen swap model for the promotion and application of fuel cell heavy-duty trucks, and the business model should be explored by taking advantage of the maturity of China's battery swap equipment industry.

On-Board Hydrogen Storage System: High Hydrogen Storage Density and Low Cost Are the Trends of Development

With the continuous optimization of the technical parameters of hydrogen storage cylinders, the hydrogen storage densities of type III and type IV vehicle-mounted hydrogen storage cylinders in China have reached 5.4wt% and 6.8wt% respectively, reaching the same level as the target set by the U.S. DOE. In terms of cylinder volume, China's current maximum capacity is 410 L, which is still a gap from the international advanced level of 800 L. Through technical approaches such as increasing the volume of gas cylinders, enhancing the strength of carbon fiber materials, and optimizing structural design, the hydrogen storage density of high- pressure gas cylinders will be further promoted. At the international forefront, vehicle-mounted liquid hydrogen storage and transportation and deep cryogenic high pressure technologies are developing rapidly. A demonstration application of liquid hydrogen systems carried by heavy trucks has been achieved abroad, with a mass hydrogen storage density of 9.2wt% and the ability to operate for about 72 h. Germany's current development of cryogenic high- pressure hydrogen storage cylinders has formed a technical parameter reserve, while China's in-development vehicle-mounted liquid hydrogen storage cylinders have achieved a hydrogen storage density of 10.0wt%, but the cryogenic high-pressure technology is still at the theoretical research stage. In the field of supporting components, 35 MPa hydrogen storage valves have been fully domestically produced and commercialized, while 70 MPa and liquid hydrogen valves have completed technical development but have not yet been commercialized. In terms of cost control, the unit cost of 35 MPa type III hydrogen storage cylinders in China is about 2,600 yuan/kgH_2, and type IV has not yet achieved commercial mass production. There is still a cost gap compared to the U.S. DOE target, but there is potential for cost reduction through large-scale production and the advancement of the localization process. For the research and application needs of fuel cell commercial and passenger vehicles, the technology of efficient, modular and integrated on-board hydrogen storage systems needs to be continuously explored and innovated, and the supporting system construction such as relevant standards and regulations, testing and certification needs to be strengthened.

3.4.2.3 Development Goals and Milestones for 2040

The overall goal for hydrogen infrastructure and on-board hydrogen storage systems is to provide a safe, fast, and low-cost supply of hydrogen for vehicles, support the commercialization of hydrogen fuel cell vehicles, and drive the building of a hydrogen society. By 2040, a mature, safe, efficient and environmentally friendly hydrogen infrastructure network will be established.

By 2030, there will be 3,000 hydrogen refueling stations, commercial demonstration of liquid hydrogen storage and refueling stations, hydrogen exchange stations and integrated energy stations, with an average daily refueling capacity of 2t/d, and the cost of hydrogen at the nozzle of hydrogen refueling stations will be 25 yuan/kgH_2@35 MPa. In terms of on-board hydrogen storage, the cost of on-board hydrogen storage systems will reach 2,300 yuan/kgH_2 (including cylinder valves), the mass hydrogen storage density of type IV hydrogen storage cylinders will reach 8.0wt %, and on-board liquid hydrogen systems will be industrialized.

By 2035, there will be 5,000 hydrogen refueling stations, liquid hydrogen storage and refueling stations, hydrogen exchange stations and integrated energy stations in operation, with an average daily refueling capacity of 3t/d, and the cost of hydrogen at the nozzle of hydrogen refueling stations will be 20 yuan/kgH_2@35 MPa. Establish a relatively complete market for high-pressure on-board hydrogen storage system hydrogen supply commercial and passenger vehicles, form a basically mature business model for hydrogen fuel cell heavy trucks, and the cost of on-board hydrogen storage system reaches 1,900 yuan/kgH_2 (including cylinder valve).

By 2040, there will be 10,000–20,000 hydrogen refueling stations, large-scale promotion of liquid hydrogen storage and refueling stations, hydrogen exchange stations and integrated energy stations, with an average daily refueling capacity of 4t/d, and the cost of hydrogen at the gun of hydrogen refueling stations will be 20 yuan/kgH_2@35 MPa&70 MPa. On-board hydrogen storage system: The cost of on-board hydrogen storage system reaches 1400 yuan/kgH_2 (including cylinder valve), the mass hydrogen storage density of type IV hydrogen storage cylinder is 9.2wt%, and the volume hydrogen storage density is 29.0v%.

3.4.2.4 Technology Roadmap

The overall design of hydrogen refueling stations is based on indicators such as maximum continuous refueling capacity, hydrogen refueling energy consumption, investment cost, and operating cost; For on-board hydrogen storage systems, the indicators are mass hydrogen storage rate, volume hydrogen storage density, and unit hydrogen storage cost. In addition, key indicators are set for hydrogen conversion systems, in-station hydrogen storage systems, hydrogen refueling machine systems, in-station hydrogen production systems, and hydrogen exchange systems (Fig. 3.5).

	2030	2035	2040
General Goals	Hydrogen refueling station: 3,000 hydrogen refueling stations, liquid hydrogen storage hydrogen refueling station commercial demonstration, average daily refueling capacity 2t/d, hydrogen refueling station gun hydrogen cost 25 yuan /kgH_2@35MPa Vehicle-mounted hydrogen storage system: Mass hydrogen storage density of type IV hydrogen storage cylinder reaches 7.5wt%, industrialization of vehicle-mounted liquid hydrogen system, vehicle-mounted hydrogen storage system cost reaches 2300 yuan /kgH_2 (including cylinder valve)	Hydrogen refueling station: 5,000 hydrogen refueling stations, liquid hydrogen storage and hydrogen refueling station scale operation, average daily refueling capacity 3t/d, hydrogen refueling station nozzle cost 20 yuan /kgH_2@35MPa On-board hydrogen storage system: Establish a relatively complete market for commercial and passenger vehicles supplying hydrogen with high-pressure on-board hydrogen storage systems, and form a basically mature business model for liquid hydrogen heavy-duty trucks.	Hydrogen refueling station: 10,000-20,000 hydrogen refueling stations, liquid hydrogen storage hydrogen refueling station large-scale promotion, average daily refueling capacity 4t/d, hydrogen refueling station gun hydrogen cost 20 yuan /kgH2@35MPa&70MPa On-board hydrogen storage system: Mass hydrogen storage density of type IV hydrogen storage cylinders is 9.2wt%, volume hydrogen storage density is 29.0%, and the cost of on-board hydrogen storage system reaches 1,400 yuan /kgH_2 (including cylinder valve).
Overall design indicators for hydrogen refueling stations	Maximum continuous refueling capacity 7.2kg/min (gas hydrogen intake) 11kg/min (liquid hydrogen intake) Hydrogen refueling energy consumption 3 kWh/kg (gas hydrogen intake) 2.0kWh/kg (liquid hydrogen intake) @70MPa Investment cost :4 million yuan/1000kg refueling capacity; operating cost: 10 yuan /kg H_2@70MPa	Maximum continuous refueling capacity 18kg/min (liquid hydrogen intake), hydrogen refueling energy 2.5 kWh/kg (gas hydrogen intake) 1.8kWh/kg (liquid hydrogen intake) @70MPa Investment cost: 3 million yuan / 1000kg refueling capacity,; operating cost: 8 yuan /kg H_2@70MPa	Maximum continuous refueling capacity 18kg/min (liquid hydrogen intake), hydrogen refueling energy consumption 2 kWh/kg (gas hydrogen intake) 1.5kWh/kg (liquid hydrogen intake) @70MPa Investment cost: 2.5 million yuan / 1000kg refueling capacity; operating cost: 6.5 yuan /kg H_2@70MPa
Hydrogen conversion system indicators	Flow rate: 2000Nm3/h, pressure 90MPa, conversion cost $\leq$ 4.2 yuan /kg (12.5-90MPa), diaphragm/liquid drive maintenance cycle $\geq$ 8000/6000h; Liquid drive leakage rate $\leq$ 0.2%	Flow rate: 4000Nm3/h, pressure 90MPa, conversion cost $\leq$ 3.2 yuan /kg (12.5-90MPa), maintenance cycle $\geq$ 10000h, average leakage rate $\leq$ 0.2%	Flow rate: 400kg/h, working pressure 90MPa, conversion cost $\leq$ 2.5 yuan /kg (0.6-90MPa), maintenance cycle $\geq$ 10,000 h, flash rate $\leq$ 2
In-station hydrogen storage system indicators	45/90MPa high-pressure gas hydrogen, liquid hydrogen storage, with high-pressure gas hydrogen storage as the main. Liquid hydrogen storage systems have been commercialized. The maximum working pressure is 90MPa; The cost of hydrogen storage is within 2800 yuan /kg hydrogen (45MPa) and 10,000 yuan /kg hydrogen (90MPa)	There are various hydrogen storage methods within the station, including 45/90MPa high-pressure gas hydrogen and liquid hydrogen storage. The in-station liquid hydrogen storage system has been industrialized. Maximum working pressure 90MPa; The cost of hydrogen storage is within 2,600 yuan /kg hydrogen (45MPa) and 7,000 yuan /kg hydrogen (90MPa)	The hydrogen storage methods within the station are diversified, including 45/90MPa high-pressure gas hydrogen, liquid hydrogen storage, and cryogenic high-pressure hydrogen storage. Maximum working pressure 90MPa; The cost of hydrogen storage is within 2,500 yuan /kg hydrogen (45MPa) and 5,000 yuan /kg hydrogen (90MPa)
Hydrogen refueling machine system indicators	Achieve the average refueling rate of gas hydrogen: 7.2kg/ min, the average refueling rate of liquid hydrogen and cryogenic high-pressure hydrogen: 11kg/min, the localization rate of components: 80%, achieve the localization of components such as breakaway valves and hydrogen refueling guns, and demonstrate their application	Achieve average filling speed of gas hydrogen: 9kg/ min, average filling speed of liquid hydrogen and cryogenic high-pressure: 18kg/min, 90% localization rate of components, achieve localization of high-pressure high-precision flowmeters, high-pressure hoses and other components, and demonstrate application	Achieve an average hydrogen filling rate of 12kg/ min, liquid hydrogen and cryogenic high-pressure filling rate of over 20kg/min, 100% localization of components, achieve full localization of components and commercial application
Station control system indicators	Build a centralized information collection platform for the entire station and a vehicle-station upstream and downstream collaborative data monitoring and linkage data platform, and form national standard norms for early warning management and intelligent control of hydrogen refueling stations.	Realize digital twins of hydrogen refueling stations and establish a national integrated big data and intelligent control platform for hydrogen refueling stations driven by digital twins.	Based on AI technology, build an intelligent control platform for the upstream and downstream of the entire industrial chain of hydrogen production - transportation - refueling - use, and form an intelligent unmanned fuel cell vehicle hydrogen refueling industrial chain
In-station hydrogen production system	The proportion of integrated hydrogen production and refueling within the station will reach over 15%, the cost of hydrogen production within the station will be 20 to 25 yuan/kg, and the average scale of hydrogen production within the station will be 800kg/day	The proportion of integrated hydrogen production and refueling within the station is over 25%, the cost of hydrogen production within the station is 15-18 yuan /kg, and the average scale of hydrogen production within the station is 1,500kg /d	The proportion of integrated hydrogen production and refueling within the station is over 30%, the cost of hydrogen production within the station is 10 to 12 yuan /kg, and the average scale of hydrogen production within the station is 2,000 kg/d
Hydrogen exchange system indicators	Build a economically viable and feasible business model of hydrogen exchange stations business model. The demonstration operation scale of hydrogen exchange stations should reach 10, and the loading and unloading time of hydrogen exchange should not be longer than the time required for hydrogen refueling under the same conditions	Form a basically mature hydrogen swap business model, with an operational scale of 50 hydrogen swap stations and a single hydrogen swap loading and unloading time of less than 10 minutes	The hydrogen exchange business model has become an important way to replenish hydrogen energy. There are over 100 hydrogen exchange stations in operation, and the loading and unloading time for a single hydrogen exchange is less than 8 minutes
On-board hydrogen storage system	The cost of hydrogen storage reached 2,300 yuan /kgH_2 (with valves), the mass hydrogen storage density of type IV hydrogen storage cylinders reached 7.5 wt %, and 390,000 to 980,000 high-pressure hydrogen storage cylinder trucks were achieved Industrialization of on-board liquid hydrogen systems	Establish a relatively complete high-pressure on-board hydrogen storage system for commercial and passenger vehicles for hydrogen supply, with hydrogen storage costs reaching 1,900 yuan /kgH_2 (with valves), and achieve 700,000 to 180,000 high-pressure hydrogen storage bottled vehicles Form a basically mature business model for liquid hydrogen heavy-duty trucks	The system cost is 1,400 yuan /kgH_2 (including the cylinder valve), the mass hydrogen storage density of type IV hydrogen storage cylinders is 9.2wt%, the volume hydrogen storage density is 29.0%, and 350,000 to 600,000 vehicles will be loaded with high-pressure gas cylinders The liquid hydrogen heavy-duty truck business model became one of the mainstream business models for heavy-duty trucks

Fig. 3.5 Hydrogen infrastructure technology roadmap

Chapter 4
Intelligent Connection Technology

4.1 Intelligent Driving

4.1.1 Domestic and International Technical Status Comparison

4.1.1.1 Current Status and Comparison of Technologies

Real-Time Analysis in Environmental Perception Technologies

Environmental perception technology is a core supporting domain for achieving autonomous driving, and its advancement directly impacts the safety and reliability of such systems. In recent years, major countries around the world have engaged in fierce competition around perception technologies, leading to a technological development landscape focused on visual perception, multi-sensor fusion, 3D modeling, and real-time environmental analysis.

The United States holds a global leading position in environmental perception technologies. Companies such as Tesla, Google Waymo, and NVIDIA have pioneered and implemented perception paradigms like BEV+Transformer architectures and occupancy network-based approaches, capturing a significant share of the global market. Europe emphasizes precision and stability in environmental perception, developing solutions centered on multi-sensor fusion and real-time local map updates. Companies like BMW and Daimler primarily adopt LiDAR-based perception models, focusing on the development of high-reliability technologies for complex traffic environments, while also actively participating in the formulation of international standards such as OpenDRIVE and OpenSCENARIO, laying a foundation for broader technology adoption.

China has made rapid progress in recent years. Companies such as XPeng Motors, Huawei, and NIO have developed multi-sensor fusion solutions combining LiDAR,

Technology Roadmap for Energy Saving and New Energy Vehicles 3.0,
https://doi.org/10.1007/978-981-95-2502-7_4

millimeter-wave radar, and cameras. The gap with international leading companies is gradually narrowing, although limitations remain in areas such as in-vehicle chip performance and sensor in-house development capabilities. As a result, the global competition in intelligent driving perception technologies is expected to continue intensifying.

Transition of Decision-Making and Planning Technologies from Rule-Driven to Data-Driven Approaches

Intelligent decision-making technology is the core component that enables autonomous control in self-driving systems, and its capabilities directly affect vehicle safety and reliability in complex traffic environments. The United States continues to maintain a global leadership position in this field. Tesla's end-to-end autonomous driving decision-making system, FSD V12, is regarded as a milestone breakthrough in the industry, significantly enhancing decision-making capabilities in complex scenarios through large-scale data-driven technologies. Europe adopts a hierarchical decision-making and control architecture to better comply with strict regulatory and safety requirements. Companies like BMW and Daimler focus on modular decision-making systems, achieving high-reliability decisions by optimizing individual planning and control modules. China's intelligent driving decision-making technologies have developed rapidly in recent years. Leading enterprises such as Baidu Apollo and Huawei have achieved a decision-making accuracy of over 90% in typical scenarios. They are also actively exploring intelligent decision-making systems driven by deep learning and reinforcement learning, conducting multi-scenario testing and validation in designated testing areas to provide real-world environmental support for the development of data-driven decision-making technologies.

End-to-End Intelligent Driving Experiences Explosive Growth, Becoming a Mainstream Technology

In recent years, end-to-end intelligent driving has rapidly emerged as a key development direction, aiming to integrate perception, decision-making, planning, and control within a fully neural network-based architecture, directly mapping sensor inputs to control outputs to enhance system real-time performance and decision-making efficiency. Internationally, research commenced earlier: Tesla's FSD V12, trained on video data, achieved open-road deployment in 2024; the Max Planck Institute proposed multimodal, display-free models; and institutions such as Cambridge and Wayve developed models like MILE, excelling in simulation. Waymo recently introduced EMMA, an end-to-end multimodal system leveraging a foundation large language model adapted for autonomous driving to enhance reasoning and interpretability.

In China, end-to-end capabilities are also advancing. Shanghai AI Laboratory proposed UniAD, achieving state-of-the-art performance across multiple tasks, while

Tsinghua University developed China's first three-stage end-to-end system. Companies including Baidu, Huawei, XPeng, and Li Auto have achieved mass production deployments. The R&D paradigm is shifting toward data-driven approaches, increasing the demand for large-scale video data and closed-loop data systems. However, compared to international leaders, challenges remain in building industrial-scale data infrastructures, achieving cross-scenario adaptability, and advancing high-precision map generation and simulation capabilities. Strengthening vehicle-road-cloud collaboration, developing foundation models, integrated data labeling systems, and improving model optimization and computing efficiency are critical for the full-scenario commercialization of end-to-end autonomous driving.

Testing and Evaluation Technologies Are Continuously Improving

In recent years, testing and evaluation technologies for intelligent and connected vehicles (ICVs) have accelerated globally, with significant progress achieved in the development of scenario libraries, testing toolchains, and evaluation frameworks. Institutions such as M-City in the United States and AstaZero in Germany have built large-scale scenario libraries covering diverse urban environments, weather conditions, and traffic situations, while also establishing mature testing toolchains and comprehensive performance evaluation systems. Companies like NI (National Instruments) in the U.S. and dSPACE in Germany hold a prominent advantage in testing toolchain development, offering high-performance, fully functional, and standardized interface products that provide robust support for multidimensional testing of autonomous driving systems. In China, initial progress has been made in building an independent testing toolchain encompassing simulation testing, closed-field testing, and open-road testing. Cities such as Beijing and Shanghai have established intelligent connected vehicle test zones and released technical specifications. Institutions like Baidu and Tsinghua University have developed internationally influential datasets. Organizations such as the China Automotive Technology and Research Center (CATARC) and National Innovation Center of Intelligent and Connected Vehicles (CICV) have constructed typical scenario libraries covering nominal, hazardous, and edge-case scenarios, providing scientific performance assessment references for automotive companies. However, compared with international leaders, China's scenario libraries still lag behind in terms of scale, complexity, and diversity. Core capabilities in the independent development of testing toolchain hardware and software also remain insufficient. It is necessary to accelerate the establishment of a national-level scenario data center to achieve data sharing and resource integration, enhance independent R&D capabilities in testing equipment, and make breakthroughs in key technologies related to testing toolchains, thereby driving innovation in intelligent and connected vehicle testing and evaluation technologies.

4.1.2 *Outlook on Technology Development Trends*

Autonomous driving is rapidly advancing toward a paradigm characterized by closed-loop data systems and intelligent evolution. To address the challenges posed by long-tail scenarios and the high costs of acquiring real-world data, the generation of high-fidelity synthetic data is emerging as a mainstream approach. Meanwhile, the integration of multi-source heterogeneous information and the adoption of new 3D detection paradigms such as occupancy grids have significantly improved perception accuracy and safety redundancy in complex environments. At the decision-making level, the industry is shifting from traditional rule-based approaches to data-driven methods, increasingly incorporating large model capabilities. Technologies such as Tesla's FSD V12, XPeng's XPlanner, and Horizon Robotics' UniAD leverage the combination of deep learning and reinforcement learning to enhance understanding and responsiveness to dynamic traffic situations. End-to-end architectures are developing rapidly, providing streamlined solutions that integrate perception, prediction, and control processes, offering efficient approaches for general autonomous driving across diverse scenarios. Simultaneously, testing and evaluation systems are continuously improving, with multiple regions issuing technical regulations, establishing high-level demonstration zones, and promoting the large-scale development of simulation-based testing. Looking ahead, the industry will focus on large model pre-training, multimodal fusion, collaborative annotation between simulation and real-world data, and the independent development of scenario libraries and testing toolchains. These efforts will comprehensively support the deployment of full-scenario autonomous driving applications.

4.1.3 *Development Goals and Milestones for 2040*

4.1.3.1 Development Vision

The industrial development vision for intelligent driving is centered on people, aiming to meet human demands for comfort, safety, and efficiency in transportation through intelligent upgrades of vehicles, thereby effectively enhancing human well-being. Furthermore, through the continuous application of new technologies, it seeks to promote the integrated development of industries and strengthen the overall level of high-tech advancement.

4.1.3.2 Goals and Milestones

Looking toward 2040, the overarching goal is to fully achieve L5-level autonomous driving across all scenarios and to continuously optimize the product experience at this level. Key technological breakthroughs will be realized in areas such as obstacle detection, intelligent decision-making, and integrated drive-by-wire systems. Based on a vehicle-road-cloud integrated architecture, comprehensive collaborative control will be achieved, and the widespread application of end-to-end algorithms and emerging technologies will be promoted to ensure safe and reliable operation in complex environments. By 2030, China's autonomous driving technology will achieve comprehensive breakthroughs in core areas such as perception, decision-making, and planning, and establish a test and evaluation system for L4-level intelligent connected vehicles, with the overall technological level approaching or reaching the international leading standard. By 2035, autonomous driving technology will undergo leapfrog development, with significant advancements in perception, decision-making, planning, and vehicle-road-cloud collaboration capabilities. An initial test and evaluation system for L5-level intelligent connected vehicles will be established, and the overall technological level will reach a globally leading position, supporting the commercialization of intelligent connected vehicles. By 2040, full realization of vehicle-road-cloud collaborative autonomous driving will be achieved.

4.1.4 Technology Roadmap

4.1.4.1 Overall Technological Roadmap for Key Topics

By 2030, significant advancements in intelligent driving technology are expected across various domains. In urban scenarios, interventions per 10,000 km will drop to under 30, and to fewer than 3 on highways. Environmental perception systems will achieve detection ranges from 0.05 m to 500 m, while computational latency will be limited to 70 ms in urban settings and 50 ms on highways. The accuracy of obstacle recognition, lane detection, and parking line recognition will exceed 97%. In autonomous decision-making, the accuracy of obstacle prediction and key behavioral decisions will exceed 95% and 98%, respectively, with dynamic updates under 80 ms. Breakthroughs in end-to-end technology will bring system performance close to human driving levels, facilitating productization and industrial application. By 2035, interventions per 10,000 km will decrease to under 3 in urban areas and under 0.3 on highways, with environmental perception ranges extending to 1000 m and 0.03 m. Latency will be under 50 ms for urban and 30 ms for highway scenarios. Accuracy rates for obstacle, lane, and parking recognition will surpass 99%, and decision-making accuracy will reach 99%, with dynamic updates within 60 ms. Vehicle intelligence will fully match human capabilities. The industry will establish test and evaluation systems for L5-level vehicles, with test coverage and toolchain adaptation exceeding 95% and 50%, respectively. Real-world testing mileage will surpass 5 billion kilometers, advancing the large-scale commercialization of intelligent driving. By 2040, full vehicle–road-cloud integration will achieve autonomous driving surpassing professional drivers, with collaborative decision-making fully implemented (Fig. 4.1).

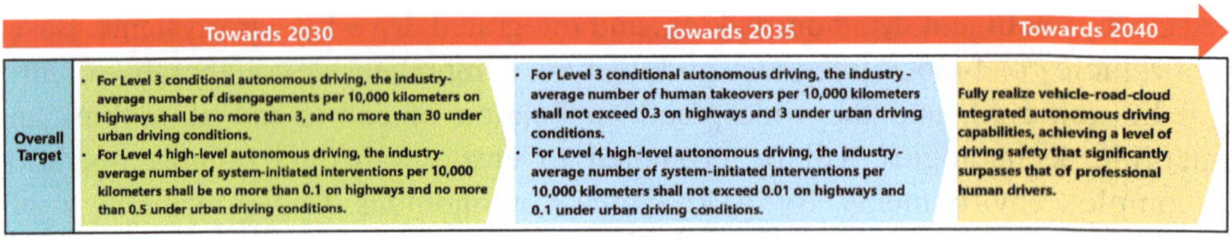

Fig. 4.1 Roadmap for intelligent driving

4.1.4.2 Technological Roadmap for Environmental Perception

Currently, intelligent driving environmental perception technologies are undergoing significant transformations. Environmental perception sensors are primarily composed of cameras, LiDARs, and 4D millimeter-wave radars. Multi-modal data fusion has become the prevailing technological trend; by leveraging the complementary advantages of different sensors, it can effectively enhance the vehicle's overall perception capabilities. Generative AI-based data generation technologies are utilized to create high-fidelity, diverse scene data, thereby reducing data acquisition costs and improving the coverage of long-tail scenarios. Occupancy grid prediction technologies, offering fine-grained environmental representations and robust detection capabilities, enhance perception performance in complex environments. Simultaneously, vehicle-road-cloud integrated perception improves safety redundancy and road utilization efficiency through beyond-line-of-sight sensing and resource optimization.

Nevertheless, the development of environmental perception technologies still faces three major barriers: technical, market, and policy-related. From a technical perspective, cameras and LiDARs experience significant performance degradation under adverse weather conditions. Although 4D millimeter-wave radars offer advantages, their point clouds are sparse and noisy, and there remains a lack of specialized algorithms tailored to them. Multi-sensor fusion algorithms encounter challenges such as time synchronization and spatial alignment, requiring high standards of calibration accuracy and real-time performance. Additionally, achieving efficient fusion under limited computational resources remains a major challenge. From a market perspective, the high cost of sensors and the immaturity of the supply chain limit the performance improvement of perception systems. Homogenization of solutions and limited market demand create supply–demand contradictions. Incidents involving autonomous vehicles further undermine investor confidence and public acceptance. Moreover, insufficient localization of core sensor components increases dependence on foreign suppliers. From a policy standpoint, regulations on data privacy and security impose stringent requirements on information collection and processing, restricting large-scale deployment of perception technologies in real-world scenarios.

In summary, intelligent driving perception technologies are advancing toward multi-source fusion, high performance, and high reliability. However, continuous efforts in critical technology breakthroughs, industrial cost optimization, and compliance assurance are essential for achieving comprehensive progress. Taking into

	Towards 2030	Towards 2035	Towards 2040
Overall environmental perception goals	Meets the requirements of high-level autonomous driving systems, ensures real-time computational latency, and improves detection performance.	Meets the requirements of autonomous driving systems by significantly extending perception range through vehicle-road-cloud integration, further reducing computational latency, and enhancing detection performance.	Meets the requirements of autonomous driving systems by enabling beyond-line-of-sight perception through vehicle-road-cloud integration, with low inference latency.
Detection Performance	≥97% accuracy in obstacle, lane, and parking spot detection.	≥99% accuracy in obstacle, lane, and parking spot detection.	≥99.9% accuracy in obstacle, lane, and parking spot detection.
	≥60% accuracy for occupancy grid	≥75% accuracy for occupancy grid	≥85% accuracy for occupancy grid
	Within 200 meters, the average position error ≤ 8%, and the relative velocity error ≤ 13%.	Within 200 meters, the average position error ≤ 6%, and the relative velocity error ≤ 8%.	Within 200 meters, the average position error ≤ 3%, and the relative velocity error ≤ 5%.
Urban/highway delay	70/50ms	50/30ms	30/20ms

Fig. 4.2 Key environmental perception subdomain roadmap

account the overarching goals of this initiative and the aforementioned analysis, corresponding overall and phased targets are set as follows (Fig. 4.2).

4.1.4.3 Technological Roadmap for Decision-Making and Planning

Intelligent driving decision-making and planning technologies are rapidly advancing toward greater intelligence and human-like behavior. In response to challenges posed by complex road structures, dynamic traffic flows, and the randomness of participants, achieving human-like driving behaviors has become crucial for enhancing driving safety, passenger experience, and operational efficiency. Current methodological frameworks are evolving toward a third-generation intelligent decision-making architecture that organically integrates rule-based frameworks with data-driven models, ultimately achieving deep integration with perception and planning algorithms. In terms of key technologies, supervised learning methods, which imitate expert driving behaviors through offline datasets, demonstrate strong generalization capabilities but still face challenges such as sample distribution imbalance and dependence on data labeling. Brain-inspired learning technologies, which aim to eliminate reliance on labeled data, exhibit the potential to surpass human drivers, with optimization efforts focusing on improving training efficiency and ensuring safety. Moreover, hybrid data- and rule-driven methods combine transparency with safety; future advancements need to further enhance adaptive capabilities and rule-learning efficiency. The continuous breakthroughs in these technologies will propel intelligent driving decision-making systems toward a globally leading position.

Nevertheless, data scarcity and low learning efficiency remain major issues for data-driven decision-making systems. Rare operational scenario data are difficult to obtain, and the learning value and evaluation standards for existing driving behaviors are yet to be clearly defined. Furthermore, the "black-box" nature of current systems reduces decision-making transparency and interpretability. From a market perspective, there is a significant risk of supply–demand mismatch. Autonomous driving systems currently lack personalized decision-making capabilities, making it

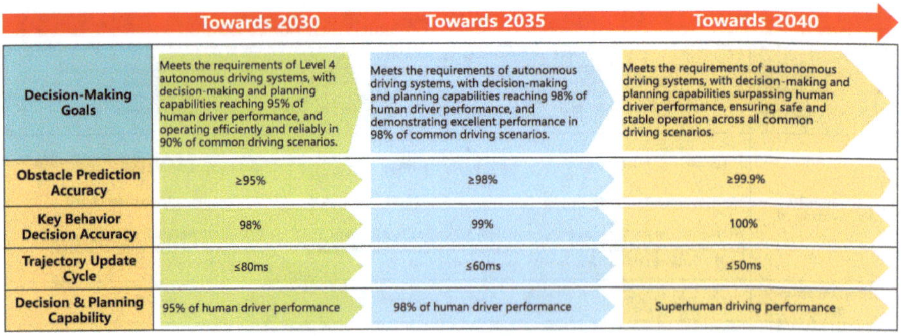

Fig. 4.3 Technical roadmap for critical subdomains in decision and planning systems

difficult to meet the diverse needs of consumers. Inadequacies in safety, comfort, and interaction experience further affect user acceptance and large-scale adoption. At the same time, policy and regulatory frameworks impose constraints on technological development. Issues such as responsibility attribution and ethical considerations for L3-level autonomous driving remain inadequately regulated, legal frameworks for data privacy and security management are incomplete, and cybersecurity oversight remains insufficient.

In summary, intelligent driving decision-making and planning technologies are rapidly evolving toward a fusion of data-driven and rule-based approaches, with large model empowerment trends gradually emerging. By overcoming technological bottlenecks, optimizing user experience, and improving policy and regulatory frameworks, intelligent decision-making systems are expected to achieve a balance between safety and comfort, providing critical support for the comprehensive deployment of autonomous driving industries (Fig. 4.3).

4.1.4.4 Technological Roadmap for End-to-End Driving

End-to-end autonomous driving technology offers significant breakthroughs for intelligent driving in general scenarios. By directly mapping raw sensor data to control outputs, end-to-end models, particularly those using large models for perception, prediction, and decision-making, exhibit structural simplicity and high performance. Current research focuses on integrating multi-source sensor-based perception models, trajectory prediction models, and unified, data-driven decision-control models. Future advancements will rely on three key areas: the intelligent integration of perception and decision systems to improve environmental comprehension, optimization of vehicle-road-cloud collaboration for better system performance, and the deployment of advanced models like Vision-Language and World Models to enhance adaptability and decision-making. Key technological challenges include algorithm

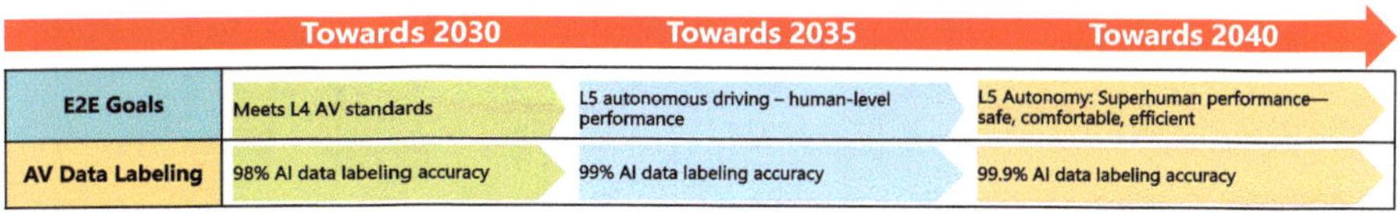

Fig. 4.4 E2E subdomain tech roadmap

optimization, computational capacity, and data utilization. Interdisciplinary advancements in neuroscience and machine learning drive path planning and neural network-based task handling. Breakthroughs in computational resources and deep learning efficiency will support complex scenario processing. Efficient data use aims to balance volume and cost while improving long-tail distribution handling.

Despite progress, integrated perception-decision algorithms still face challenges, including insufficient task-driven modular architecture and poor performance in complex scenarios. Technologically, improvements in sensor precision, data annotation, and algorithm stability are needed, especially for complex urban environments. Market challenges stem from low consumer confidence and traditional driving habits, while policy gaps in responsibility attribution, data security, and privacy protection remain. Overcoming these challenges requires coordinated efforts in technology, market adoption, and policy development to ensure the safe, reliable commercialization of end-to-end autonomous driving (Fig. 4.4).

4.1.4.5 Technical Roadmap for Testing and Evaluation

In 2023, intelligent driving testing and evaluation made significant progress against the backdrop of national support and accelerated commercialization. Achieving independent research and development of intelligent driving testing hardware and software platforms requires breakthroughs across multiple key technological areas. First, high-precision, real-time software platforms must overcome challenges such as physical modeling of complex traffic environments, parallel computing optimization, and AI-driven scenario generation to enhance testing efficiency and accuracy. Second, innovative designs for high-precision, low-latency data acquisition hardware, combined with edge computing capabilities to capture operational data, are essential to provide comprehensive data support for testing and evaluation. Third, the construction of unified, standardized interfaces and communication protocols is needed to improve the interoperability of testing toolchains and promote cross-vendor platform collaboration. Lastly, it is crucial to establish a testing and evaluation system aligned with international trends while reflecting Chinese characteristics, focusing on key dimensions such as functional safety, cybersecurity, and environmental adaptability.

Currently, the development of intelligent driving testing and evaluation technologies faces challenges across technical, market, and regulatory domains. Technologically, there is a lack of high-precision testing platforms and high-coverage scenario

	Towards 2030	Towards 2035	Towards 2040
Testing and Evaluation Framework Objectives	Establish a comprehensive Level 4 autonomous vehicle testing and evaluation system, along with standardized product certification protocols and procedures.	Establish a robust and mature framework for autonomous vehicle testing and evaluation, with well-defined product certification standards and procedures to support the commercialization of intelligent connected vehicles.	Establish a comprehensive autonomous vehicle testing and evaluation system to fully support the testing processes of various types of intelligent connected vehicles.
Comprehensive Test Scenario Coverage	≥90%	≥95%	≥99%
Proportion of Tri-Pillar Simulation Architecture	≥90%	≥95%	≥98%
Test Tool Autarky Rate	≥30%	≥50%	≥80%
Total Road Testing Mileage	1 billion kilometers	5 billion kilometers	10 billion kilometers
Simulation Test Recall Rate	≥50%	≥80%	≥90%

Fig. 4.5 Technical roadmap for testing and evaluation subdomains

generation technologies domestically, with significant shortcomings in multimodal data support and edge-case scenario coverage. From a market perspective, foreign manufacturers dominate due to patent barriers and standards advantages, while domestic equipment struggles to replace foreign products due to technological dependence and ecosystem compatibility issues. On the regulatory front, although there are overarching policy initiatives, detailed standards for testing scenario descriptions and device functionality remain undeveloped, hindering data sharing and consistency of test results. Improving the standardization system, strengthening independent technological innovation, and promoting market adoption are key to overcoming these obstacles (Fig. 4.5).

4.2 Intelligent Cockpit

4.2.1 General Review of Core Areas of Intelligent Cockpits

4.2.1.1 Strategic Significance

As a core domain of technological innovation in the automotive industry, intelligent cockpits are increasingly becoming a pivotal force driving the commercialization of intelligent connected vehicles (ICVs). By integrating multidisciplinary technologies including information and communication technology (ICT), electronics, cognitive science, virtual reality (VR), human–machine interaction (HMI), and artificial intelligence (AI), intelligent cockpits have evolved into an innovation hub combining advanced and cross-disciplinary technologies. These systems not only enhance vehicle hardware electrification and system integration but also optimize cabin environments to become more user-friendly. They serve as a demonstration platform for the application efficacy of intelligent connectivity technologies and represent a critical milestone in the transformation from conventional vehicles to intelligent vehicles.

The development of intelligent cockpits focuses on advancing human–machine interaction and consumer experience, offering greater potential for market penetration compared to autonomous driving technologies. With their extensive technical scope and extensible industrial ecosystem, intelligent cockpits can rapidly assimilate and implement innovations from consumer electronics and internet industries. This positions intelligent cockpits not merely as transportation tools but as intelligent mobile spaces interfacing with ubiquitous connectivity, heralding substantial market potential to propel related industries.

As a key nexus for integrating intelligent vehicles with intelligent transportation systems (ITS) and smart cities, intelligent cockpits are emerging as vital components of next-generation smart terminals. They function not only as human-vehicle interfaces but also as bridges connecting humans, vehicles, and environments. With advancements in HMI, connected services, and scenario expansion, intelligent cockpits will enable ICVs to fully integrate into smart transportation and urban ecosystems.

The innovative trajectory of intelligent cockpits is reshaping global automotive competitiveness. Automakers increasingly prioritize intelligent cockpit development, as it directly impacts product competitiveness and global market dynamics. However, the field faces critical technological challenges, including breakthroughs in foundational technologies, AI convergence, open collaborative ecosystem development, and safety assurance.

To address these challenges, the industry must strengthen innovation in core underlying technologies, deepen integration of AI systems, foster open collaborative industrial ecosystems, and maintain unwavering commitment to safety principles. Through these efforts, intelligent cockpits will deliver safer, smarter, and more comfortable mobility experiences, driving sustained progress in automotive innovation.

4.2.1.2 Technical Architecture and Key Technologies

According to the Intelligent Cockpit Classification and Comprehensive Evaluation White Paper (China Society of Automotive Engineers, 2023), an intelligent cockpit is defined as a mobile space equipped with advanced software/hardware systems that integrate human–machine-environment capabilities through HMI, connected services, and scenario expansion, delivering safe, intelligent, efficient, and enjoyable experiences. The technical architecture encompasses three dimensions: human–machine interaction (HMI), connected services, and scenario expansion, with corresponding intelligence grading criteria as shown in Table 4.1.

In the HMI dimension, grading reflects the execution autonomy of cockpit tasks, categorized into perception agents (environment sensing) and execution agents (task automation), where higher levels indicate stronger proactive interaction capabilities. The connected services dimension classifies service content across four tiers, progressing from cockpit-domain services to cloud-control platform services, with ascending tiers representing enriched service offerings. The

Table 4.1 Classification of automotive intelligent cockpits

Level	Main features	Human–machine interaction	Connected services	Scenario expansion
CL0	Functional cockpit: tasks are executed within the cabin; the cockpit passively responds to the needs of the driver and passengers; vehicle service capabilities are available	Passive interaction	Vehicle service	Part of cabin scenarios
CL1	Perception intelligent cockpit: tasks are executed within the cabin; the cockpit can actively perceive the driver and passengers in some scenarios, task execution requires driver authorization; cabin domain service capabilities are available	Authorized interaction	Cabin domain services	Part of cabin scenarios
CL2	Partial cognitive intelligent cockpit: tasks can be executed in part of both in-cabin and external scenarios; the cockpit can actively perceive passengers in some in-cabin scenarios, tasks can be partially executed; has sustainable and upgradable connected cloud services	Partial active interaction	Upgradable connected Cloud services	Part of in-cabin and External scenarios
CL3	Advanced cognitive intelligent cockpit: tasks can be executed across both in-cabin and external scenarios; the cockpit actively perceives passengers in all in-cabin scenarios, tasks can be partially executed; has open connected cloud service capabilities	Partial active interaction	Open connected cloud services	Full cabin/ partial external scenarios
CL4	Fully cognitive intelligent cockpit: tasks can be executed across all in-cabin and external scenarios, with no driver required inside the cabin; the cockpit actively perceives all passengers in all in-cabin scenarios, tasks can be fully autonomously executed; has cloud control platform service capabilities	Active interaction	Cloud control platform services	Full cabin and external scenarios

scenario expansion dimension differentiates operational scopes between cabin-confined and extended vehicle-environment scenarios, with higher levels denoting broader scenario applicability.

The technical architecture of the Automotive Intelligent Cockpit Technology Roadmap 3.0 encompasses four key domains: Human–Machine Interaction (HMI) key technologies, system and component key technologies, foundational support key technologies, as well as testing and evaluation technologies. The overall technical framework is illustrated in Fig. 4.6.

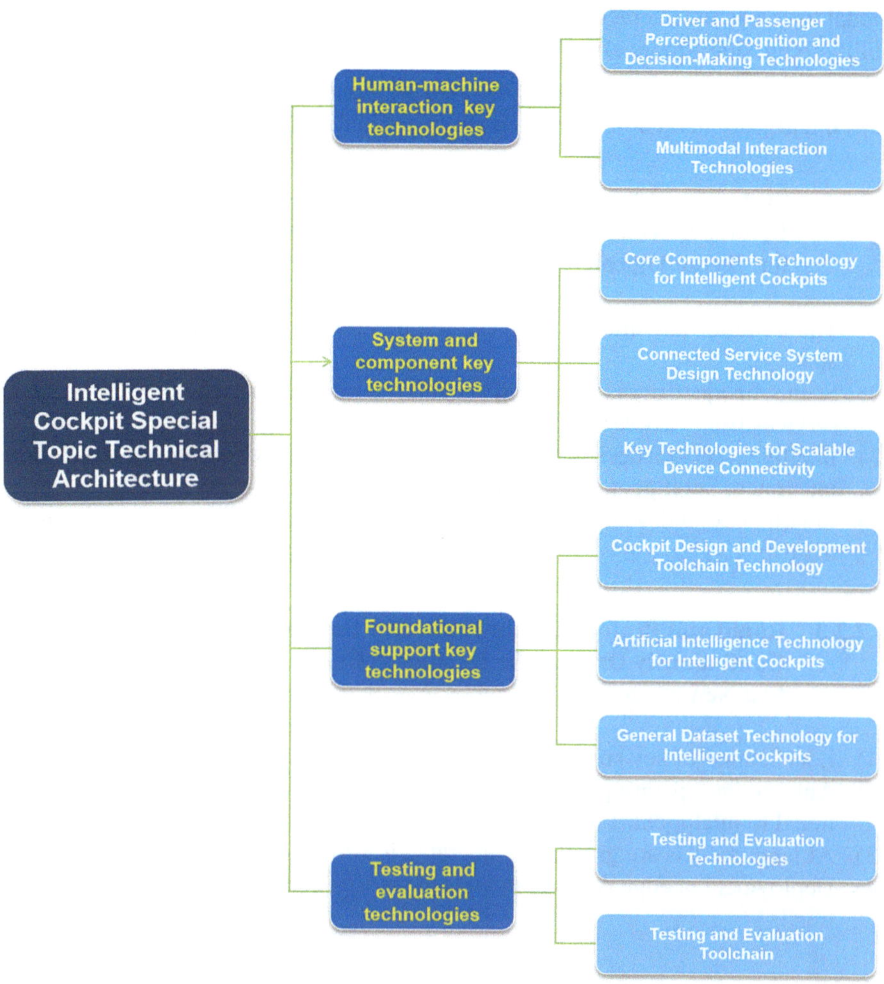

Fig. 4.6 Overall architecture of the automotive intelligent cockpit technology roadmap

4.2.2 *Outlook on Technology Development Trends*

4.2.2.1 Multimodal Fusion Active Interaction Technology Becomes a Key Development Focus

With the rapid advancement of technology and the increasingly diversified demands of consumers, intelligent cockpit human–machine interaction technology is experiencing unprecedented development opportunities and has become an important driving force for innovation in the automotive industry. Against this backdrop, multimodal fusion active interaction technology has gained significant attention due to its ability to provide a more efficient and natural user experience.

(1) Active interaction technology becomes an industry hotspot.
(2) Intelligent interaction moves toward natural interaction.

4.2.2.2 Systems and Components Evolving Toward Smarter and More Diverse Directions to Meet Consumers' Demand for Technologically Advanced and Intelligent Products

(1) The trend toward smart and diversified in-vehicle display technology accelerates.
(2) Scene fusion drives the transformation of intelligent cockpit connectivity services from "active" to "smart".
(3) Intelligent cockpit design and development toolchain technologies are becoming integrated, intelligent, cloud-collaborative, and security-enhanced.
(4) Smartphone and vehicle connectivity applications show a booming industry trend.

4.2.2.3 Rapid and Profound Changes in Key Supporting Technologies, Continuously Driving the Intelligent Cockpit Capabilities to a New Stage

(1) Localization of key supporting technologies accelerates.
(2) Automotive operating systems undergo profound transformation from traditional to intelligent.
(3) AI large models are gradually integrated in vehicles.
(4) Deployment of edge AI large models in intelligent cockpits becomes a growing trend.

4.2.2.4 Improved Intelligent Cockpit Testing and Evaluation System and Standards, Making Evaluation More Efficient

(1) The intelligent cockpit testing and evaluation system will become more comprehensive, significantly improving evaluation quality.

(2) Improving testing efficiency is an inevitable development direction for intelligent cockpit evaluation.

4.2.3 Development Goals and Milestones for 2040

Around 2030, high-level cognitive intelligent cockpits will achieve large-scale market penetration, integrate with open connected cloud services, and realize interconnectivity. These cockpits will possess rich online resources and will initially achieve the integration of virtual and physical spaces in intelligent cockpits. After 2035, the cockpit will reach the stage of fully cognitive intelligent cockpits (CL4), where tasks can be executed in all scenarios both inside and outside the cabin, and there can be no driver inside the cabin. The cockpit has the ability to actively perceive the people inside the cabin in all scenarios, and tasks can be fully executed proactively. After 2040, fully cognitive intelligent cockpits (CL4) will gradually achieve large-scale market development, further integrating into the vehicle-road-cloud unified control platform, as well as other metaverse-related technology platforms. Ultimately, they will form a "third space" that provides a comprehensive experience of safety, intelligence, efficiency, and enjoyment for drivers and passengers.

4.2.4 Technology Roadmap

4.2.4.1 Overall Technical Roadmap for the Topic

The overall roadmap for the intelligent cockpit topic is shown in Fig. 4.7.

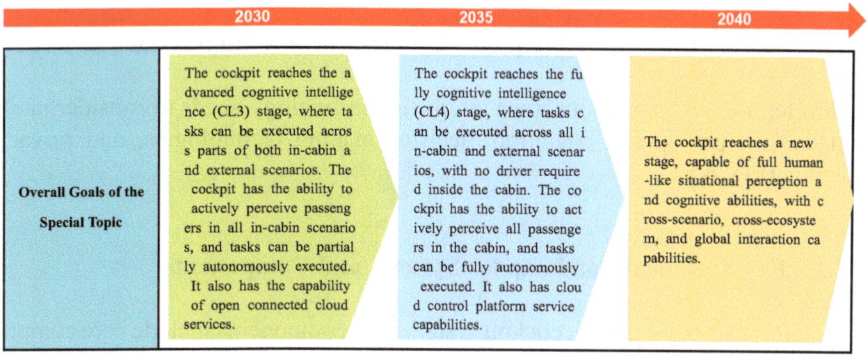

Fig. 4.7 Overall goals of the roadmap 3.0 special topic area

	2030	2035	2040
Human-machine interaction key technologies	For drivers and passengers: Implement partial active interaction for full in-cabin scenarios to reduce the risks associated with assisted driving interaction, providing a safe and efficient in-cabin interaction experience.	For drivers and passengers: Implement partial active interaction for both in-cabin and external scenarios, improving the collaborative driving interaction performance and meeting the personalized and emotional in-cabin and external interaction experience.	For in-cabin occupants: Implement natural interaction for full in-cabin and external scenarios to meet autonomous driving interaction requirements, and enhance service capabilities and user experience across all vehicle scenarios.
Driver and Passenger Perception/Cognition and Decision-Making Technologies	The average accuracy rate of integrated perception for voice, face, posture, and physiological data (heart rate, respiration, pulse, etc.) should not be lower than 85%. The average accuracy rate of comprehensive recognition for the driver and passenger's fatigue, intent, preferences, emotions, and other states should not be lower than 80%. The coverage of active cockpit interaction functionality should not be lower than 30%.	The average accuracy rate of integrated perception for voice, face, posture, and physiological data (heart rate, respiration, pulse, etc.) should not be lower than 90%. The average accuracy rate of comprehensive recognition for the driver and passenger's fatigue, intent, preferences, emotions, and other states should not be lower than 85%. The coverage of active cockpit interaction functionality should not be lower than 50%.	The average accuracy rate of integrated perception for voice, face, posture, and physiological data (heart rate, respiration, pulse, etc.) should not be lower than 95%. The average accuracy rate of comprehensive recognition for in-cabin occupants' fatigue, intent, preferences, emotions, and other states should not be lower than 90%. The coverage of active cockpit interaction functionality should not be lower than 70%.
Multimodal Interaction Technologies	Integrate existing multimodal interaction technologies, optimize the synergy between hardware devices and software algorithms, and provide a safe and efficient in-cabin interaction experience.	Breakthrough in the deep fusion technology of multimodal interaction channels, achieving adaptive matching between driving scenarios and interaction modes to meet the personalized and emotional in-cabin and external interaction experience.	Establish self-learning and evolution technologies for multimodal active interaction, enabling seamless and comprehensive natural interaction for both in-cabin and external scenarios, enhancing service capabilities and user experience across all vehicle scenarios.

Fig. 4.8 Human–machine interaction technology roadmap

4.2.4.2 Key Technical Roadmap for Human–Machine Interaction

The development of human–machine interaction technology needs to consider intelligent cockpit perception, cognition, decision-making technologies, and privacy protection (Fig. 4.8).

4.2.4.3 Key Technical Roadmap for Systems and Components

Key technologies of intelligent cockpit systems and components include core component technologies of intelligent cockpits, design technologies of networked service systems, and key technologies of scalable device interconnection (Fig. 4.9).

	2030	2035	2040
Core Components Technology for Intelligent Cockpits	**Perception Components**: The in-cabin multimodal perception technology based on cameras, microphones, and radar is accelerating its penetration and continuous upgrades to meet the passengers' needs for safe and comfortable interaction. The recognition accuracy rate is ≥85%. In collaborative autonomous driving technology, the adoption rate of this technology in new vehicles is ≥60%. **Display Components**: The quality of in-vehicle displays has significantly improved. Advanced driver assistance systems provide more safety driving information to passengers, with diverse display forms. Flat displays dominate, while projection displays are accelerating their penetration, and spatial displays are becoming a hot topic. The pixel density of the display quality is ≥120. **Execution Components**: Cockpit comfort systems, in-vehicle lighting systems, in-vehicle ventilation systems, in-vehicle audio systems, and other execution components are gradually evolving towards intelligence and scenario-based spatialization. Coordination between components has been largely achieved, with intelligent functions mostly existing independently. The coverage of active perception and autonomous execution is ≥60%.	**Perception Components: In the context of L3-level autonomous** driving design **for** the human-machine interaction system focused on the driver, the functionality and accuracy of in-cabin multimodal perception components are further enhanced. The capabilities of artificial intelligence large models further improve perception and reasoning abilities, while functional safety requirements are also raised. The recognition accuracy rate is ≥90%. In collaborative autonomous driving technology, the adoption rate of this technology in new vehicles is ≥80%. **Display Components**: In-vehicle display quality is further upgraded. Flat displays, projection displays, and spatial displays interact in a coordinated manner. Based on advancements in autonomous driving technology, in-cabin display interactions tend toward multi-member interaction. The pixel density of the display quality is ≥180, and with intelligent driving collaboration, safety display functions are further strengthened. **Execution Components**: Coordination between execution components has been largely achieved. The intelligent functions of the components are gradually moving from isolation to integration, bringing a more coherent intelligent experience for users. The coverage of active perception and autonomous execution based on artificial intelligence is ≥80%.	**Perception Components**: In the context of the L4-level autonomous driving design for the human-machine interaction system focused on passengers, in-cabin multimodal perception technology is further upgraded with enhanced precision. Data fusion and coordination between the various perception components are beginning to be implemented, and the recognition accuracy rate is ≥95%. In collaborative autonomous driving technology, the adoption rate of this technology in new vehicles is ≥95%. **Display Components**: In-vehicle display technology has undergone deep innovation. With the maturity of autonomous driving technology, in-cabin and external displays are no longer treated as independent display units. They are now more seamlessly integrated with external display devices, interior designs, and vehicle body components, allowing for freer interaction and flow. The primary focus is to provide functionality based on safety and scenario-based needs, such as work and entertainment. **Execution Components**: The execution components can fully interact based on passenger status and driving scenarios. The level of vehicle intelligence has significantly improved, creating a full-scenario intelligent driving experience for drivers and passengers. The coverage of active perception and autonomous execution based on artificial intelligence is ≥95%.

Fig. 4.9 Systems and components technology roadmap for intelligent cockpits

Connected Service System Design Technology	**Popularize open connected cloud services**: With the continued penetration of cellular networks and C-V2X, over 50% of vehicles in the PA-level category will be connected to the cloud control platform services. The cockpit will innovate content and services based on the open cloud service platform and continue to upgrade. **Develop intelligent service technologies**: The edge-cloud integrated cockpit large models will be widely used in the cockpit. The accuracy of scenario and intent recognition will see significant improvement. Over 60% of industry applications and ecosystem services will be broken down into atomic functions and integrated into the cockpit intelligent system, completing the service loop with generative AI technology.	**Realize cloud control platform services**: The cockpit will access the vehicle-road-cloud integrated cloud control platform through ultra-low-latency connected technologies, providing real-time interconnectivity with related services and a wealth of online resources, connecting virtual and physical spaces. **Popularize intelligent service technologies**: The cockpit's computing power and algorithm efficiency will continue to improve. With the continuous accumulation of scenario data, there will be a qualitative leap in the perception, planning, and execution capabilities of the intelligent system. Over 95% of industry applications and ecosystem service functions will be integrated into the intelligent system, completing the service loop with generative AI technology.	Further integrate into the vehicle-road-cloud integrated cloud control platform and other metaverse-related technology platforms, ultimately forming a "third space" that provides a comprehensive experience of safety, intelligence, efficiency, and enjoyment for drivers and passengers. The cockpit will achieve de-appification, with the intelligent system automatically selecting a vast array of cloud service resources to meet the scenario needs of passengers and drivers.
Key Technologies for Scalable Device Connectivity	**Achieve service standardization for mobile and vehicle connectivity**: Utilize a comprehensive service software architecture between the mobile phone and the in-vehicle system to enable flexible distribution of traditional mobile app operations, inputs, and outputs on the vehicle's end. **Enable capability sharing and interoperability between mobile phone and in-vehicle system applications**, ultimately achieving connectivity between different mobile phone brands and vehicles.	**Build a multi-device integration instant application and application developer platform**: Through the resource service pool system formed by integration before 2030, developers can easily create lightweight, quick-response service orchestration applications. This will enable an efficient development model of "one-time coding, multi-device deployment," improving development efficiency and broadening profit models. These applications support one-time subscriptions and multi-device deployment, offering an instant-use experience that precisely meets users' specific scenario-based service needs.	Achieve service flow across all endpoints with people: Relying on the advanced technology architecture of developer and application platforms, and through the expansion strategy of an open alliance, the ecosystem will be extended to various devices, including in-vehicle systems, smartphones, and IoT devices. This supports ubiquitous multi-device integration applications, enabling seamless mobility of services with people and providing an all-encompassing application experience.

Fig. 4.9 (continued)

4.2.4.4 Key Technical Roadmap for Fundamental Key Technologies

Fundamental key technologies include artificial intelligence technology for intelligent cockpits, general dataset technology for intelligent cockpits, and design and development toolchain technology for intelligent cockpits (Fig. 4.10).

Fig. 4.10 Cockpit artificial intelligence and general dataset technology roadmap

General Dataset Technology for Intelligent Cockpits	**Rich Type Initial Construction**: Data types include at least 5 major categories such as images, voice, vehicle status, user behavior, etc. **Basic Accuracy Assurance**: Data labeling accuracy reaches 90%, ensuring the reliability of AI model training data. **Initial Accumulation of Massive Data**: Formation of a universal cockpit multimodal dataset architecture, based on industry consensus, covering various sensor data, user interaction data, and more.	**Diverse and Comprehensive Full-Scenario Data**: New data types such as environmental perception and biometric features are added, reaching more than 8 categories, covering more comprehensive scenarios. **Highly Accurate and Reliable**: Data accuracy improves to 95%, with dual protection using advanced algorithms and manual review. **Rapid Expansion in Scale**: The multimodal dataset scale expands further, with broader types and a dataset size exceeding the PB level. A wide range of driving scenarios and user behavior data is collected.	**Omni-Dimensional and Diverse Data with No Blind Spots**: Data types exceed 15, covering frontier fields such as emotion recognition, brainwave data, and more, comprehensively reflecting the cockpit's status. **Extreme Precision with Zero Error**: Data accuracy approaches 100%, utilizing intelligent error correction and multi-round verification mechanisms. **Massive Data Coverage**: Dataset scale further expands, including all types of extreme and regular cockpit usage data from around the world.
Cockpit Design and Development Toolchain Technology	**Product Design**: Design tools integrate VR/AR design, with AI-driven automation design capabilities. **HMI Design**: Integrate multimodal/AR/VR design, with AI-driven automation design capabilities. **Development Tools**: Capable of AI-driven automatic code generation. **Simulation Tools**: Able to simulate cabin performance and complex interaction tests in basic driving environments. **Toolchain Integration**: Gradually integrate tools with design, development, debugging, deployment, and online collaboration capabilities. Design/development tools are initially intelligent, reducing product iteration cycles by over 30%.	**Product Design**: Design tools integrate VR/AR design, with AI-driven automation design capabilities. **HMI Design**: Integrate multimodal/AR/VR design, with AI-driven automation design capabilities. **Development Tools**: Capable of AI-driven automatic code generation. **Simulation Tools**: Able to simulate cabin performance and complex interaction tests in basic driving environments. **Toolchain Integration**: Gradually integrate tools with design, development, debugging, deployment, and online collaboration capabilities. Design/development tools are more intelligent, reducing product iteration cycles by over 40%.	**Product Design**: Fully AI-driven automation design capabilities. **HMI Design**: Fully AI-driven automation design capabilities, meeting the requirements for UI automation design in all user scenarios. **Development Tools**: AI-driven automatic code generation covering all business scenarios. **Simulation Tools**: Capable of simulating cabin performance and interaction tests in all driving scenarios. **Toolchain Integration**: Fully integrated toolchain with design, development, debugging, deployment, and online collaboration capabilities. Design/development tools are fully intelligent, reducing product iteration cycles by over 60%.

Fig. 4.10 (continued)

4.2.4.5 Testing and Evaluation Technical Roadmap

The core of efficient testing and accurate evaluation of intelligent cockpits lies in building a comprehensive testing and evaluation system that is quantifiable and remeasurable, breaking through the key technologies for transforming subjective experience into objective assessment, and developing interactive experience evaluation tools suitable for industrial scale (Fig. 4.11).

	2030	2035	2040
Testing and evaluation technologies	The evaluation system meet s the requirements for simu lating and real-world drivin g scenarios. Testing technol ogy reaches a semi-automat ed level, enabling compreh ensive testing and evaluatio n under offline conditions.	The evaluation system mee ts the requirements for real -world driving scenarios. T esting technology reaches a highly automated level, e nabling comprehensive testi ng and evaluation under p artial real-time online cond itions.	The evaluation system meet s the requirements for natur al driving scenarios. Testing technology reaches an unm anned level, enabling compr ehensive testing, evaluation, and optimization under full y real-time online condition s.
Testing and Evaluation Technologies	Build a quantifiable and r epeatable comprehensive te sting and evaluation syste m for simulated and real-world driving scenarios, o vercoming key technologie s for converting subjective experiences into objective evaluations. Comprehensiv e testing objectivity ≥80%, reaching a semi-automate d level. The cockpit initially achie ves data observability, wit h data collection covering key interaction nodes and the ability to identify abno rmal data in real-time.	Build a quantifiable and r epeatable comprehensive te sting and evaluation syste m for real-world driving s cenarios, overcoming key technologies for converting subjective experiences int o objective evaluations. C omprehensive testing objec tivity ≥90%, reaching a hi ghly automated level. The cockpit fully achieves data observability, with d ata collection covering all interaction nodes and the ability for automated root cause analysis based on diagnostic toolchains.	Build a quantifiable and re peatable comprehensive testi ng and evaluation system f or natural driving scenarios, overcoming key technologi es for converting subjective experiences into objective evaluations. Comprehensive testing objectivity ≥95%, r eaching an unmanned level. The cockpit moves toward full data observability and analysis, supporting data-dri ven design optimization.
Testing and Evaluation Toolchain	The testing and evaluation toolchain partially meets th e semi-automated evaluation needs of edge-cloud integr ation, enabling comprehensi ve testing and evaluation u nder offline conditions.	The testing and evaluation t oolchain fully meets the hig hly automated evaluation ne eds of edge-cloud integratio n, enabling comprehensive t esting and evaluation under partial real-time online con ditions.	The testing and evaluation to olchain meets the unmanned evaluation needs of the inte lligent era, enabling compreh ensive testing and evaluation under fully real-time online conditions.

Fig. 4.11 Testing and evaluation technology roadmap

4.3 Connected and Cooperative

4.3.1 Domestic and International Technical Status Comparison

4.3.1.1 Vehicle and Infrastructure Deployment Accelerates

China has established an innovative development pathway for Intelligent Connected Vehicles (ICVs) based on Vehicle-Road-Cloud Integrated System (VRCIS), supported by developing the world's most advanced and largest-scale Cellular Vehicle-to-Everything (C-V2X) network. As of December 2024, more than 4.1 million 5G base stations and over 11,000 Roadside Units (RSUs) have been deployed nationwide. The pre-installation rates of 5G and LTE-V2X modules are increased annually. Various Original Equipment Manufacturers (OEMs), including FAW,

SAIC, GAC, and NIO, have launched mass production of models equipped with cooperative warning and notification functions.

4.3.1.2 Rapid Progress in Cooperative Interaction Technologies

With the deepening integration of intelligent and connected technologies, cooperative interaction services have expanded from perception to decision-making and control scenarios. The United States Department of Transportation (USDOT) is accelerating C-V2X technology deployment through a national plan and targeted grants. Pilot projects in states such as Arizona, Texas, and Utah cover applications such as emergency vehicle preemption, vulnerable road user (VRU) detection, and other safety alerts. In Europe, the Euro NCAP 2025 protocol awards speed assistance points to vehicles capable of transmitting and receiving local hazards information, with implementation scheduled for January 2026. Republic of Korea has selected C-V2X as its technology of choice with specific spectrum to LTE-V2X for connected mobility, and K-NCAP has introduced C-V2X enabled use cases. In China, large-scale deployment of applications such as traffic signal information dissemination, green light optimal speed advisory (GLOSA) has been achieved in cities including Beijing, Changsha, Wuxi, Xiangyang, and Guangzhou, and is being gradually expanded to 20 VRCIS pilot cities. More than ten automakers have introduced production models equipped with traffic signal notification and local hazard warning functions.

In terms of cooperative decision-making and control functions, testing and deployments are accelerating. In Europe, cooperative automated driving projects funded by the European Union's Horizon 2020 and related EU programs cover functions including cooperative intersections, lane changes, vehicle platooning, cooperative adaptive cruise control (CACC), automated parking, and cooperative routing. In China, multiple OEMs are leveraging production or near-production models to develop and test functions such as cooperative merging, vulnerable road user (VRU) protection, and Cooperative Navigation on Autopilot (C-NOA). Cities like Beijing, Shanghai, Chongqing, and Wuhan have launched routine operations of robo-taxis equipped with cloud-based remote takeover functionality. Such functions are also being promoted in specialized areas such as mines and ports.

4.3.1.3 Advancements in Onboard Communication Systems

Based on the independent R&D capabilities, the Domestic companies have achieved mass production of 4G, 5G, and LTE-V2X communication chips, with some products already adopted in production vehicles. Automotive-grade communication modules have also entered mass production and are widely used in ICV terminals. Internationally, companies such as Qualcomm offer communication chip solutions, while Alps Alpine and LG Innotek provide onboard communication modules.

4.3.2 *Outlook on Technology Development Trends*

4.3.2.1 Convergence of Advanced Communication Technologies

Over 95% of urban roads in China are now covered by 5G networks, and LTE-V2X direct communication has been deployed in key urban areas. A converged communication network integrating 5G, LTE-V2X, and fiber-optic infrastructure has been established, providing wide-area coverage, low latency, high reliability, and large bandwidth services.

As 5G Advanced (5G-A) and sixth-generation (6G) wireless technologies continue to evolve, C-V2X, as a core connectivity enabler, will continue to improve in latency, reliability, system capacity, positioning accuracy, and spectrum utilization. The integration of cellular and direct communications, as well as the convergence of cellular and satellite communications, will enable broader network coverage and seamless connectivity, and is expected to support integrated air-space-ground communications.

4.3.2.2 Commercialization of C-ADAS and C-ADS Scenarios

Although AI-driven vehicle intelligence has made notable progress, it continues to face significant challenges, particularly in addressing long-tail perception blind spots, delayed detection and response, and the complexity of interactions in mixed traffic environments. These limitations impede the realization of seamless, continuous autonomous driving without human intervention. The VRCIS approach offers a promising solution by delivering system-level perception and control information to vehicles. This enables an effective expansion of the vehicle's Operational Design Domain (ODD) and alleviates the computational burden on in-vehicle systems.

Market-oriented assessment programs are accelerating the deployment of vehicle-road-cloud integration technology. The China-New Car Assessment Program (C-NCAP) 2024, the upcoming 2027 version, and the China Intelligent-connected Car Assessment Program (C-ICAP) 2024 all recommend the application of C-V2X in selected use cases. These requirements are prompting OEMs to adopt C-V2X from the design stage to enhance vehicle safety ratings. In parallel, Industry stakeholders are actively validating cooperative decision-making and control functions in scenarios such as smart buses, smart passenger cars, unmanned vehicles, urban logistics, and highway freight. To support scalable deployment, a comprehensive evaluation framework for VRCIS will be established, covering performance, trustworthiness, and both safety and cybersecurity. This framework is expected to facilitate the advancement of Cooperative Advanced Driver Assistance Systems (C-ADAS) and Cooperative Automated Driving Systems (C-ADS).

4.3.2.3 Intelligent and Integrated Development of Onboard Communication

With the transition of electronic and electrical (E/E) architecture toward centralized, cross-domain integration, functions previously distributed across multiple electronic control units (ECUs) are being consolidated into domain controllers. Onboard communication systems are likewise evolving to integrate 5G, C-V2X, GNSS, high-performance processors, and hardware security modules (HSM), greatly enhancing system compactness and efficiency.

With growing demands for connectivity and computing in ICVs, onboard communication systems are becoming core enablers that integrate communication, sensing, positioning, computing, intelligence, and control. They are expected to serve as a core component in ICVs supporting the user experience in smart cockpit and meeting the high functional safety and performance requirements of intelligent driving.

4.3.3 Development Goals and Milestones for 2040

The technology roadmap was formulated to achieve, by 2040, full-scenario Vehicle-Road-Cloud integrated automated driving, cooperative perception, decision-making, and control technologies that satisfy the needs of vehicles with diverse levels of intelligence and connectivity, as well as an Intelligent Transportation System (ITS) that enables swarm intelligence and system-level optimization.

The roadmap summarizes four key performance indicators, including penetration rate and coverage of communication, application scenarios, communication performance, and cooperative interaction (Fig. 4.12).

4.3.4 Technology Roadmap

4.3.4.1 Overall Technical Roadmap

This roadmap considers four major aspects, including the penetration rate and coverage of communication networks, overall communication performance, cooperative interaction capabilities of VRCIS, and the reliability and evolution of communication chips, modules, and intelligent terminals.

The overall connected and cooperative technical roadmap is shown in Fig. 4.13.

4.3.4.2 Communication Network Technology Roadmap

The communication network roadmap serves as the foundation for achieving comprehensive interconnection and efficient information processing among vehicles, roads,

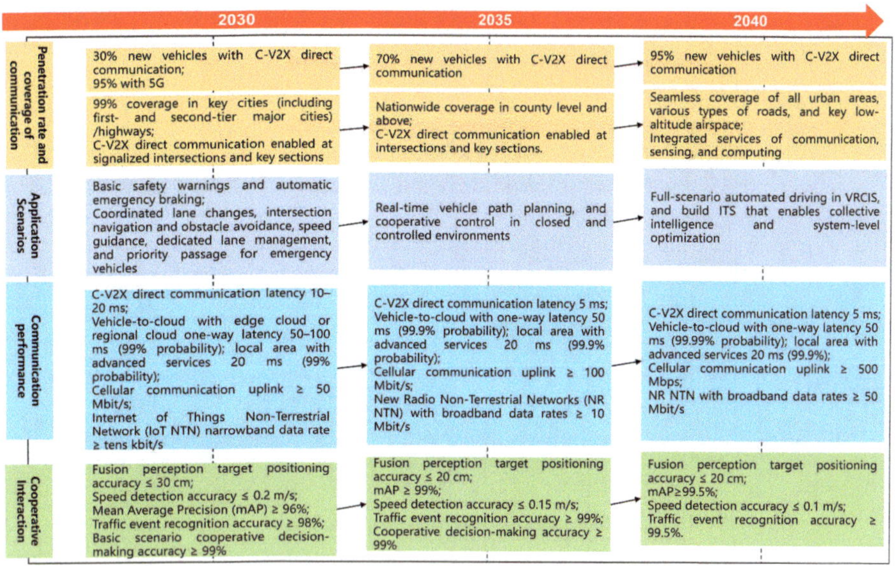

Fig. 4.12 Key indicators of the technology roadmap

	2030	2035	2040
Overall Technology Roadmap	The penetration rate of new vehicles with C-V2X direct communication will be 30%, and the penetration rate of new vehicles with 5G communication will be 95%. The coverage rate of the integrated cellular communication and C-V2X direct communication network on roads in key cities (including first- and second-tier major cities) and on highways will be 99%. Among these, urban signalized intersections, and key sections C-V2X direct communication will be enabled. The latency of C-V2X direct communication will be 10 ms to 20 ms. The vehicle-to-cloud (edge cloud) one-way latency will be 50 ms with 99% probability, and the vehicle-to-cloud (regional cloud) one-way latency will be 100 ms with 99% probability. Within the local area supporting enhanced services, the latency will be 20 ms with 99% probability. The cellular communication will support the uplink bandwidth of 50 Mbit/s or higher per user. The vehicular satellite communication with high-orbit narrowband data rates will be about tens of kbit/s. The VRCIS will achieve at least the following performance: fusion perception target positioning accuracy≤ 30 cm; speed detection accuracy≤ 0.2 m/s; mAP ≥ 96%; traffic event recognition accuracy ≥ 98%; basic scenario cooperative decision-making accuracy≥ 99%. Fully support the realization of cooperative perception and decision-making functions for ICVs. Automotive-grade communication chips and modules meeting reliability requirements will be widely adopted.	The penetration rate of new vehicles with C-V2X direct communication will be 70%. Nationwide coverage of the integrated cellular communication and C-V2X direct communication network in cities will be at the county level and above, as well as on highways and national and provincial trunk roads. Among these, urban signalized intersections, and key sections C-V2X direct communication will be enabled. The latency of C-V2X direct communication will be 5 ms. The vehicle-to-cloud one-way latency will be 50 ms with 99.9% probability. For enhanced services, the latency from the vehicle-to-cloud platform will be 20 ms with 99.9% probability. The cellular communication will support the uplink bandwidth of 100 Mbit/s or higher per user. A preliminary framework will be established for vehicular satellite communication based on NR NTN (New Radio Non-Terrestrial Networks) with broadband data rates ≥10 Mbit/s. The VRCIS will achieve at least the following performance: fusion perception target positioning accuracy≤20 cm; speed detection accuracy≤ 0.15 m/s; mAP≥99%; traffic event recognition accuracy≥ 99%; cooperative decision-making accuracy ≥ 99%. Fully support the cooperative decision-making, and control functions. Fully support the realization of cooperative decision-making and control functions for ICVs. Ensure on-board communication components meet domestic and international reliability certification requirements. On-board intelligent terminal architectures will evolve towards centralized configurations.	The penetration rate of new vehicles with C-V2X direct communication will be 95%. Support seamless coverage of all urban areas, various types of roads, and key low-altitude airspace, as well as integrated services of communication, sensing, and computing. The latency of C-V2X direct communication will be 5 ms. The vehicle-to-cloud one-way latency will be 50 ms with 99.99% probability, and on-demand scalability will be provided to achieve enhanced capability of 20 ms latency with 99.9% probability. The cellular communication will support the uplink bandwidth of 500 Mbit/s or higher per user. Vehicular satellite communication based on NR NTN will achieve broadband data rates ≥ 50 Mbit/s. The VRCIS will achieve at least the following performance: fusion perception target positioning accuracy ≤ 20 cm; speed detection accuracy ≤ 0.1 m/s; mAP≥99.5%; traffic event recognition accuracy ≥ 99.5%. Meeting the requirements of vehicles with different levels of intelligence and connectivity for diverse cooperative perception, decision-making, and control capabilities. The reliability, service life, and stability of key communication components will be further enhanced. On-board terminals will achieve full integration with vehicle E/E architectures, contributing to the efficient collaboration and sustainable development of the ICV industry.

Fig. 4.13 Overall technology roadmap

and clouds. It considers C-V2X, satellite networks, wireless integrated positioning, integrated sensing and communication (ISAC), as well as in-vehicle wireless communication technologies, providing low-latency, high-reliability, high-bandwidth, and wide-coverage connectivity services (Fig. 4.14).

		2030	2035	2040
Communication Network Domain	C-V2X Communication	The penetration rate: New vehicles with C-V2X direct communication will be 30%, and new vehicles with 5G communication will be 95%. The communication performance: The latency of C-V2X direct communication will be 10 ms to 20 ms. The vehicle-to-cloud (edge cloud) one-way latency will be 50 ms with 99% probability, and the vehicle-to-cloud (regional cloud) one-way latency will be 100 ms with 99% probability. Within the local area supporting enhanced services, the latency will be 20 ms with 99% probability. The cellular communication will support the uplink bandwidth of 50 Mbps or higher per user.	The penetration rate: New vehicles with C-V2X direct communication will be 70%. The communication performance: The latency of C-V2X direct communication will be 5 ms with 99.9% probability, and V2V and V2I unicast communication will be supported. The vehicle-to-cloud one-way latency will be 50 ms with 99.9% probability. For enhanced services, the latency from the vehicle-to-cloud platform will be 20 ms with 99.9% probability. The cellular communication will support the uplink bandwidth of 100 Mbps or higher per user.	The penetration rate: New vehicles with C-V2X direct communication will be 95%. The communication technologies and products that meet high-performance and safety requirements will enable vehicles of different intelligence levels to fully realize automated driving. The communication performance: The latency of C-V2X direct communication will be 5 ms. The vehicle-to-cloud one-way latency will be 50 ms with 99.99% probability, and provide on-demand scalability to achieve enhanced service capability of 20 ms latency with 99.9% probability. The cellular communication will support the uplink bandwidth of 500 Mbps or higher per user.
	Vehicular Non-Terrestrial Networks (NTN)	The vehicular satellite communication based on IoT NTN with high-orbit narrowband will achieve data rates of tens of kbit/s. Based on NR NTN will be up to 400 kbit/s. End-to-end latency will be ≤ 300 ms.	A preliminary framework will be established for vehicular satellite communication based on NR NTN with broadband data rates ≥ 10 Mbit/s. Support terminal movement speeds ≤ 0.1 Ma, end-to-end latency ≤200 ms, and handover success rate ≥ 99%.	Vehicular satellite communication based on NR NTN will be broadband data rates ≥50 Mbit/s. Support terminal movement speeds ≤ 0.2 Ma, end-to-end latency ≤200 ms, and handover success rate ≥ 99.9%.
	Integrated C-V2X Networking	Construct required network infrastructure for integrated 5G/5G-Advanced cellular networks and C-V2X direct communication. The coverage rate of the integrated cellular communication and C-V2X direct communication network on roads in key cities (including first- and second-tier major cities) and on highways will be 99%. Among these, urban signalized intersections, and key sections C-V2X direct communication enabled. The preliminarily implemented 5G computing power networks with integrated communication-sensing-computing capabilities, will support vehicle-to-cloud access with 5G or C-V2X direct communication to deliver continuous connected vehicle services.	Comprehensive deployment of integrating 5G/5G-Advanced cellular networks, C-V2X direct communication, and 6G network. Nationwide coverage of the integrated cellular communication and C-V2X direct communication network in cities will be at the county level and above, as well as on highways and national and provincial trunk roads. Among these, urban signalized intersections, and key sections C-V2X direct communication will be enabled. Provide integrated communication, sensing, and computing services, enabling collaborative driving capabilities through coordination. Achieve 6G vehicular network deployment in pilot regions, with gradual adoption of AI-native technologies, significantly enhanced data service security, and ubiquitous coverage via integrated space-air-ground systems. The low-altitude areas and suburban road connectivity will be further supported.	Form a comprehensive space-air-ground-sea vehicular network based on integrated 6G and C-V2X direct communication technologies. Collaborating with 5G/5G-A vehicular networks, this infrastructure will enable seamless coverage across all urban areas, diverse road types, and key low-altitude airspace while delivering integrated communication-sensing-computing services. It will provide ubiquitous connectivity for ground and aerial transportation platforms such as automated driving vehicles and low-altitude aircrafts, fostering synergistic development of automated driving, intelligent transportation systems, and smart cities.
	Wireless Integrated Positioning	The integrated positioning technology will be initially integrated and widely applied in automobiles. The full-scenario positioning latency will be tens of milliseconds. Multi-source positioning technologies (including GNSS, INS, visual sensors, LiDAR, and high-precision maps) will achieve deep integration, significantly enhancing vehicles' positioning accuracy and robustness.	The integrated positioning technology will achieve large-scale application. Full-scenario position latency will be 10 ms. Oriented to the high-level automated driving, the real-time performance, accuracy, and security of positioning systems will be significantly enhanced.	The integrated positioning technology will achieve comprehensively intelligent and personalized services. Full-scenario positioning latency will be less than 10 ms. The integrated positioning technology will holistically support seamless connectivity and collaborative interactions among vehicles, infrastructure, and pedestrians.
	Integrated Sensing and Communication	Leveraging the sensing capabilities of 5G base stations, the system will achieve preliminary city-level integrated communication and sensing coverage in key urban areas through single-frequency deployment. It will support sensing detection, positioning, and tracking based on cellular radio signals. The solution will realize the fused processing of multi-point wireless sensing data and integration with video and radar information. This will provide C-V2X services with integrated communication-sensing-computing capabilities, significantly improving traffic efficiency and reducing accidents. The system will deliver sensing positioning accuracy ≤ 1.5m and ranging resolution ≤ 5m.	By harnessing the 5G-Advanced and 6G integrated communication-sensing base stations combined with multi-mode transceiver capabilities of terminals, the system will utilize a hybrid approach of single-frequency deployment and multi-frequency coordinated deployment. This will expand cellular-based integrated communication-sensing coverage to urban roads, highways, suburban roads, and low-altitude airspace, progressively enabling multi-level coordination between communication and sensing. The system will achieve sensing positioning accuracy ≤ 1 m, ranging resolution ≤ 3 m, with miss detection rate ≤ 5% and false alarm rate ≤ 5%.	Leveraging the multi-mode transceiver of 6G base stations and terminals through a combination of single-frequency deployment and multi-frequency collaborative deployment, this system will achieve comprehensive coverage of integrated communication-sensing across all urban areas, various roadways, and low-altitude airspace. It will further optimize the collaborative capabilities of multi-level communication and sensing, delivering a sensing accuracy of ≤0.5 m and distance resolution of ≤1 m, with further reductions in the miss detection rate and false alarm rate.
	Vehicular Optical Communication	Construct the high-speed vehicular optical communication network with the data rate of 10 Gbit/s or higher, and achieve sub-millisecond vehicular communication links. Support automotive-grade vehicular optical communication technical solutions.	Construct the high-speed vehicular optical communication network with the data rate of 30 Gbit/s or higher, and achieve tens of microseconds vehicular optical communication links.	Construct the high-speed vehicular optical communication network with the data rate of 50 Gbit/s, and achieve microsecond-level vehicular optical communication links.

Fig. 4.14 Communication network technology roadmap

4.3.4.3 Cooperative Interaction Technology Roadmap

The cooperative interaction roadmap involves cooperative perception, decision-making, control, and confidence mechanisms. These enable real-time, high-precision information exchange and vehicle coordination to enhance safety, mobility, and environmental performance on roadways (Fig. 4.15).

4.3.4.4 Core Components Technology Roadmap

The vehicle-side core components roadmap includes automotive communication chips and modules, on-board intelligent terminals, and testing-oriented toolchains, which serve as key enablers for efficient internal and external communication within ICVs and support the validation of system performance and reliability (Fig. 4.16).

		2030	2035	2040
Cooperative Interaction Domain	Cooperative Perception	Establish a foundational cooperative perception system for VRCIS based on integrated C-V2X connectivity and vehicle perception fusion, enabling functions including basic safety warnings and automatic emergency braking to enhance driving safety. The system will achieve fusion perception target positioning accuracy ≤ 30 cm, speed detection accuracy ≤ 0.2 m/s, mAP ≥96% and traffic event recognition accuracy ≥ 98%.	Enhance the cooperative perception system for VRCIS to achieve efficient identification and sharing of dynamic status and intentions including detailed vehicle trajectories. Refine dynamic information exchange mechanisms and customized service strategies to enable cross-domain trajectory tracking and deliver personalized traffic services based on real-time vehicle requirements and routing. The enhanced system will achieve fusion perception target positioning accuracy ≤ 20 cm, speed detection accuracy ≤ 0.15m/s, mAP ≥ 99% and traffic event recognition accuracy ≥ 99%.	Comprehensively establish a cooperative perception system for VRCIS that integrates historical data and real-time information to build trajectory and behavior prediction models for traffic participants, optimizing vehicle routing. Through highly coordinated infrastructure and cloud collaboration, the system will significantly improve cross-domain trajectory tracking accuracy and real-time traffic trend prediction capabilities, enhancing overall traffic safety and efficiency. The system with self-learning optimization capabilities will continuously refine information exchange strategies and achieve fusion perception target positioning accuracy ≤ 20 cm, speed detection accuracy≤ 0.1 m/s, mAP ≥ 99.5%, and traffic event recognition accuracy ≥ 99.5%.
	Cooperative Decision-making	Establish a preliminary cooperative decision-making system for VRCIS that will enable cooperative decision functionality on highways and partial urban roads. The system will support fundamental scenarios including coordinated lane changes, intersection navigation and obstacle avoidance, speed guidance, dedicated lane management, and priority passage for emergency vehicles, with the capability for local optimization of traffic signal timing. The system will achieve basic scenario cooperative decision-making accuracy ≥ 99% .	The cooperative decision-making system for VRCIS will achieve large-scale deployment, deepening the integration of C-V2X connectivity with vehicle decision-making systems to provide precise planning and guidance information on speed, routing, etc. The system will enhance cooperative efficiency, enable efficient coordination and intelligent dispatching within regional domains, and generate regionally optimal traffic management solutions. The system will achieve cooperative decision-making accuracy ≥ 99%.	Comprehensively establish the cooperative decision-making system for VRCIS that will deliver real-time driving guidance based on system-level traffic conditions and vehicle-targeted routing. This system will enhance real-time traffic flow optimization and emergency response capabilities, enabling the realization of the fully optimized ITS solution.
	Cooperative Control	The Technology of cooperative control for VRCIS will be effectively validated, enabling real-time calculation based on the vehicle's historical trajectory, driving intention, and road conditions, generating trajectory planning results in real-time, and sending direct and control information to vehicles to achieve lateral and longitudinal control of the vehicle.	The cooperative control for VRCIS will gradually mature, and based on ensuring stability and robustness, it will further enable the optimization of vehicles, traffic control facilities, and traffic environment, leading to significant improvements in the safety and efficiency of overall traffic.	The cooperative control for VRCIS will achieve large-scale application, enabling vehicles to realize cooperative control applications across all scenarios and possess intelligent dispatching capabilities to respond to emergencies, thereby achieving system-level traffic optimization.
	Cooperative Interaction Confidence Mechanisms	Conduct fundamental research on cooperative interaction confidence mechanism algorithms. Leveraging accumulated VRCIS demonstration data, develop multi-level, quantifiable foundational judgment algorithms for data accuracy, latency, and safety across modules among vehicle, road, and cloud. This will provide reliable support for standardized VRCIS development. Define confidence-level requirements for data in different application scenarios. Achieve phased progress in confidence algorithms and transmission mechanisms at 3 critical stages: data generation/processing, data transmission, and vehicle application. Key performance: overall confidence level of safety warnings information ≥ 99%; overall confidence level of notification information ≥ 95%.	Achieve significant advancements in confidence algorithms, transfer functions, veto mechanism, and vehicle-side cooperative algorithms. The adopted confidence technologies and solutions will fully meet the requirements of VRCIS upon completing extensive testing and validation. Breakthrough progress will be made in vehicle safety and communication latency reduction. The current VRCIS can support C-ADAS and C-ADS features under conditions of computational redundancy on the vehicle side. Key performance: overall confidence level of C-V2X information ≥ 99%; overall confidence level of safety-critical C-V2X information ≥ 99.99%.	Confidence algorithms and cooperative algorithms at the vehicles will continue to mature, with comprehensive verification and optimization across multi-layer functional software and system software. Holistic advancements will be achieved in vehicle safety and communication latency reduction. Low-cost vehicle-side solutions for C-ADAS and C-ADS will be realized by offloading computation burdens to roadside and cloud platforms, driving comprehensive innovation and upgrading throughout the automotive industry chain. Key performance: overall confidence level of C-V2X information ≥99.99%; overall confidence level of safety-critical C-V2X information ≥ 99.999%.

Fig. 4.15 Cooperative interaction technology roadmap

		2030	2035	2040
Core Components Domain	Automotive Communication Chips and Modules	Automotive-grade communication chips and modules meeting reliability requirements will be widely adopted, with increased integration and standardized interfaces to support large-scale deployment and interoperability. 5G chips and modules supporting uRLLC will be widely deployed; 6G chips and modules will enter pilot testing. LTE-V2X direct communication and IoT NTN chips and modules will reach large-scale pre-installation. NR-V2X direct communication chips and modules will reach commercialization.	5G-A chips and modules with uRLLC support will be widely deployed; 6G chips and modules will gradually reach commercialization, offering higher data rates, lower latency, and higher connection density to support complex, data-intensive autonomous driving applications. LTE-V2X direct communication chips and modules will be widely adopted in new vehicles; NR-V2X direct communication chips and modules will reach large-scale pre-installation, promoting the application of cooperative perception, decision-making and control technology. NR NTN chips and modules will be widely commercialized, improving communication quality and coverage.	AI-integrated 6G chips and modules will be widely commercialized, supporting holographic perception, efficient data processing, and improved computational reliability. C-V2X direct communication chips and modules will become standard components in automated vehicles, enabling faster and more advanced intelligent decision-making. The integration of satellite and terrestrial networks will achieve seamless global connectivity, delivering high-speed, low-latency services across all environments.
	On-Board Intelligent Terminals and Toolchains	On-board intelligent terminals will achieve full compatibility with domain-centralized E/E architectures, establishing a mature safety evaluation system. A universal connected scenario database will be established, supporting software/hardware-in-the-loop (SIL/HIL) validation for mass production testing of cooperative perception and initial application of cooperative decision-making functionalities. Field testing tools will be deployed for roadside perception accuracy verification and cooperative perception scenarios validation.	On-board intelligent terminal architectures will evolve towards centralized configurations. The toolchain will support mass-production testing for cooperative decision-making and control functionalities. Vehicle-level simulation test laboratories will be established to verify and certify cooperative perception, decision-making, and control algorithms along with their functional performance at the full-vehicle integration level.	On-board terminals will achieve full integration with vehicle E/E architectures, accompanied by substantial computing power enhancement to support large-scale data transmission and enable cooperative control interactions. The testing toolchain will be developed to service autonomous vehicles.

Fig. 4.16 Core components technology roadmap

4.3.4.5 Fundamental Support Technology Roadmap

The foundational support roadmap covers spectrum planning, policy research, and testing and evaluation, providing essential support for the large-scale deployment of cooperative technologies and ensuring the stability, reliability, and security of vehicle-road-cloud integrated systems across diverse scenarios(Fig. 4.17).

		2030	2035	2040
Fundamental Support Domain	Spectrum Needs and Policy Research	Promote NR-V2X spectrum planning. Conduct NR-V2X studies on spectrum needs, candidate bands, and compatibility; carry out technical trials of wireless devices in new bands; and establish spectrum management measures and device requirements.	Complete 6G vehicular communications studies on spectrum needs, candidate bands, and compatibility; carry out wireless equipment trials in new bands.	Promote spectrum planning for 6G vehicular communication, establish spectrum management frameworks and specify wireless devices technical requirements.
	Testing and Evaluation	Develop comprehensive network testing methods compatible with multiple communication technologies to ensure seamless connectivity for ICVs across various scenarios. Establish a comprehensive functional safety process framework and preliminary certification system for roadside infrastructure, along with operation and maintenance mechanisms. Accumulate reliability verification data to support the development of related hardware and software.	Build a national public scenario data platform for scenarios in VRCIS, promote cross-regional data sharing. Develop data-driven evaluation models for comprehensive vehicle–road–cloud–network–map systems and for evaluating the service quality of VRCIS. Further research the functional safety certification system and intelligent operation and maintenance system. Ensure on-board communication components meet domestic and international reliability certification requirements.	Establish a comprehensive functional safety certification system and intelligent operation and maintenance framework for VRCIS. Significantly enhance the VRCIS data trustworthiness verification capability. Foster the development of multiple independent certification bodies to support testing across various levels of cooperation and connectivity functions.

Fig. 4.17 Fundamental support technology roadmap

4.4 Cloud Control Platform

4.4.1 Domestic and International Technical Status Comparison

4.4.1.1 Cloud Control Platform Architectural Design Remains to Be Explored

Cloud control platform architecture is the overall guideline and framework for implementing the Vehicle-Road-Cloud Integrated System. Europe, the US and Japan have all launched major research projects to advance intelligent vehicles and infrastructure, but have not yet conducted research on the architecture design of a vehicle-road-cloud integratedsystem. Europe, under the Horizon 2020 program, has carried out intelligent connected vehicle research and explored related cloud service technologies; the U.S. Department of Transportation developed and published the Architecture Reference for Cooperative and Intelligent Transportation (ARC-IT); Japan launched the SIP-adus project aiming to build a transportation system integrating vehicles, people and infrastructure. In 2020, China first proposed a vehicle-road-cloud integrated control system and defined its components and operating principles, this work is gaining broad consensus and accelerating advancement.

4.4.1.2 Standardized Component Models for Cloud Control Platform Require Strengthening

In recent years, guided by vehicle-road-cloud integration strategies, China has made significant progress in building cloud control platforms. By the end of 2023, the total length of autonomous driving test exceeded 1,000 km nationwide, including demonstration zones, pilot zones and highway trials. Over 6,000 roadside infrastructure points, and cloud control basic platforms have been completed in Beijing, Shanghai, Chongqing, and other locations. The US "Cloud Smart" federal cloud computing strategy and the EU CCAM roadmap both focus on individual vehicle intelligence and vehicle-road cooperation, with cloud support as secondary, while China has established a complete cloud control platform system. Cloud control basic platforms are key to deploying intelligent connected vehicles. We should leverage our strengths in infrastructure construction and ICT, continuously strengthen collaborative innovation in common foundational technologies, promote cross-industry integration, and promote the development of a new integrated transportation system.

4.4.1.3 Information Infrastructure for the Cloud Control Platform Has Reached a Preliminary Scale

Cloud computing platforms, as the core information infrastructure of cloud control platforms, are an essential engine for driving traffic modernization and informatization. In recent years, cloud control platforms have significantly reduced enterprises' storage-and-compute migration costs, improved efficiency, enhanced cloud support for concurrent endpoints, and been widely applied in AI scenarios, with large-model development and service platforms becoming increasingly mature. Compared with abroad, China is on par with international levels in improving enterprise cloud migration efficiency and reducing costs, keeps pace in concurrency capabilities, intelligent-compute services, and large-model development, and holds experiential advantages in certain areas. However, in intelligent-compute cluster utilization, U.S. firms such as Amazon and Google have reached 40%, while domestic utilization still needs improvement; in computing power, the combined capacity of China's three major telecom operators is only half of Tesla's 100 EFLOPS. To maintain technological parity and local leadership, China must increase investment in high-performance computing storage, AI models, and cloud-native technologies; boost participation in global open-source projects and ecosystem competitiveness; and closely monitor cloud computing trends to flexibly adjust strategic objectives.

4.4.1.4 Maturity of Cloud Control Applications Needs Further Improvement

Cloud control applications, based on service data provided by cloud control basic platforms, empower connected vehicles, traffic management, and industry stakeholders. Currently, applications in China focus primarily on safety, efficiency, and information services outlined by T/CSAE 53-2017 and T/CSAE 53-2020 standards, predominantly in localized trials and demonstrations. Over the past five years, China significantly increased the number of demonstration zones and operational areas, including 17 national-level intelligent connected demonstration zones, 7 national-level vehicle networking pilot zones, 16 dual-intelligence city pilots, and 20 vehicle-road-cloud integration pilot cities. However, cloud control applications have not yet achieved large-scale implementation in terms of vehicles served, service scope, or scenarios, indicating room for improvement.

4.4.1.5 Cloud Control Platform Testing and Evaluation Systems Require Establishment

Testing and evaluation are critical for vehicle-road-cloud integrated systems development and essential for cloud control platform deployment. Currently, inconsistent system function and performance requirements and a lack of standardized testing methods across regions have resulted in uneven quality. Although testing methodologies and tools for cloud platform software and hardware performance are abundant, dedicated methods and tools for integrated vehicle-road-cloud system-level testing remain insufficient. China's 2024 policy for vehicle-road-cloud integration application pilots lists recommended functions for initial 20 pilot cities, offering reference for application classification and testing. In recent years, with the promotion of the vehicle-road-cloud integrated system and cloud control platforms, some enterprises have initiated preliminary explorations into system testing methodologies, procedures, and evaluation metrics.

4.4.2 Outlook on Technology Development Trends

4.4.2.1 Model-Based Systems Engineering Approach as a Key Trend in Top-Level Complex System Design

Vehicle–road-cloud integrated systems require a system engineering approach for comprehensive advancement. Internationally, there is growing support for unified complex system architecture design to foster cross-sector consensus and collaboration. Recent trends focus on employing unified languages, tools, and processes for effective cross-domain, cross-industry coordination.

4.4.2.2 Building Standardized Service Capabilities Via Standardized Components

The cloud control basic platform, as a novel form of infrastructure, is accelerating its deployment and facing ever-growing cross-regional and cross-city service demands. Consequently, a series of targeted R&D efforts on key technologies—sensor fusion, collaborative decision-making, cooperative control, and domain-specific big-data analytics—are underway. Developing domain-specific standard components, standardized data models, and data-sharing service mechanisms represents an important development trend.

4.4.2.3 Developing Fundamental and Industry-Specific Autonomous Large Models

Growing demands for cloud control applications necessitate enhanced information infrastructure capabilities, including capabilities for processing heterogeneous data and supporting high endpoint concurrency. Future domain-specific large models promise greater accuracy in predictive warnings, resource scheduling, and intelligent incident response, supporting adaptability and real-time precision in vehicle-road-cloud scenarios.

4.4.2.4 Cloud Control Applications Becoming Mainstream Based on Pilot Policies

Cloud control applications are services delivered via foundational platforms, designed for representative user scenarios. Such technologies encompass enhancing vehicle perception through vehicle-road-cloud information integration, leveraging cloud computing and connectivity to improve individual vehicle safety, operational efficiency, and energy efficiency within complex vehicle group environments, as well as data empowerment in intelligent transportation, smart cities, and the intelligent connected vehicle industry.

4.4.2.5 Establishing Comprehensive Testing Standards and Evaluation Index Systems

Standardized testing frameworks for cloud control platforms are essential to objectively assess the effectiveness of vehicle-road-cloud integration. With expanding application scales and advancements in artificial intelligence, testing technologies targeting cloud control platforms will increasingly focus on architecture, foundational capabilities, information infrastructure, cloud control applications, and vehicle-road-cloud integrated systems. Establishing comprehensive testing standards and evaluation index systems represents a significant trend in the field.

4.4.3 Development Goals and Milestones for 2040

Building a nationwide or global Big Data Cloud Control Platform by deeply cross domain collaboration is expected to realize intelligent vehicles, digital roads, interacted energy systems, collaborative clouds. By 2030, the goal is to establish standardized Big Data Cloud Control Basic Platforms for intelligent vehicles. These platforms will be featured by logically collaborative yet physically decentralized, deployed with standardized, open-sharing, risk-controllable, secure and reliable software, could basically realize fusion applications of automotive, transportation, energy, and

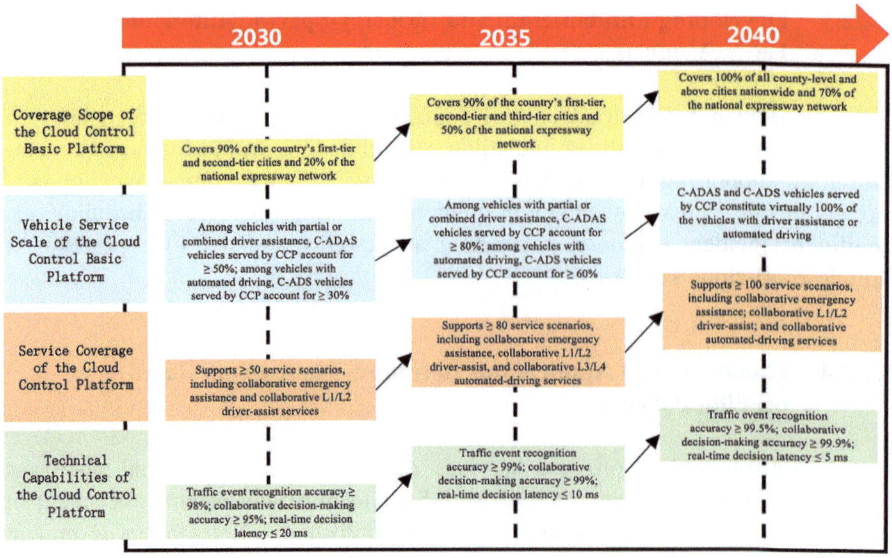

Fig. 4.18 Cloud control platform phased objectives and milestones

communication industries. By 2035, the goal is to establish a national Big Data Cloud Control Basic Platforms for intelligent vehicles. These platforms will be featured by software-defined and hardware-accelerated capabilities, supporting orderly collaboration among vehicles, roads, clouds, and networks. The software will support high-level automated driving, could realize fusion applications of inter domains as above. By 2040, the goal is to establish a global Big Data Cloud Control Basic Platforms for intelligent vehicles. The platform will be featured by integrated software-hardware systems with AI chips and fundamental software systems supporting for fully automated driving, could comprehensively realize fusion applications of inter domain as above (Fig. 4.18).

4.4.4 Technical Roadmap

4.4.4.1 Overall Technical Roadmap

As shown in Fig. 4.19, the overall technical architecture of the cloud control platform is organized into three layers: the top layer corresponds to the five sub-roadmaps; the middle layer contains the key technologies for each sub-roadmap; and the bottom layer comprises the foundational support technologies.

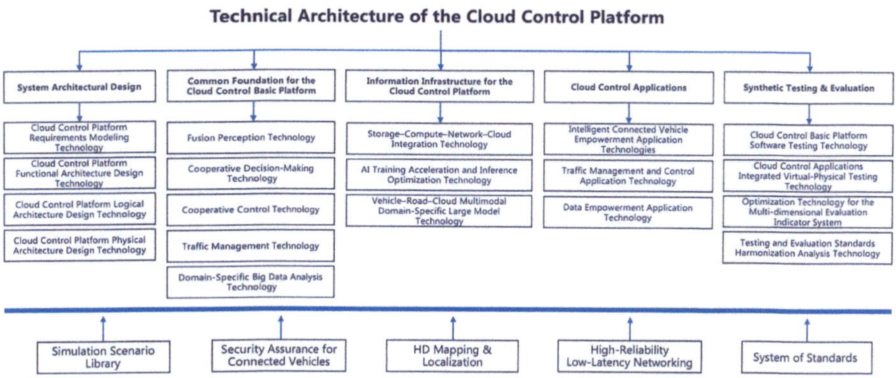

Fig. 4.19 Cloud control platform—overall technical architecture

The technical roadmap for cloud control platforms towards 2040 (see Fig. 4.20) encompasses five key sub-areas: system architectural design, common foundation for the cloud control basic platform, information infrastructure for the cloud control platform, cloud control applications, and synthetic testing & evaluation. To achieve the overarching goals of cloud control platform coverage, vehicle service scale, and service breadth, the roadmap requires establishing unified architectural design capabilities, foundational capabilities including integrated perception, collaborative decision-making and control, and information infrastructure capabilities such as large-scale computational scheduling, AI training acceleration and inference optimization, and multimodal domain-specific large models. These foundations will support diverse cloud control applications and comprehensive testing evaluations, ensuring objectives for each phase are met.

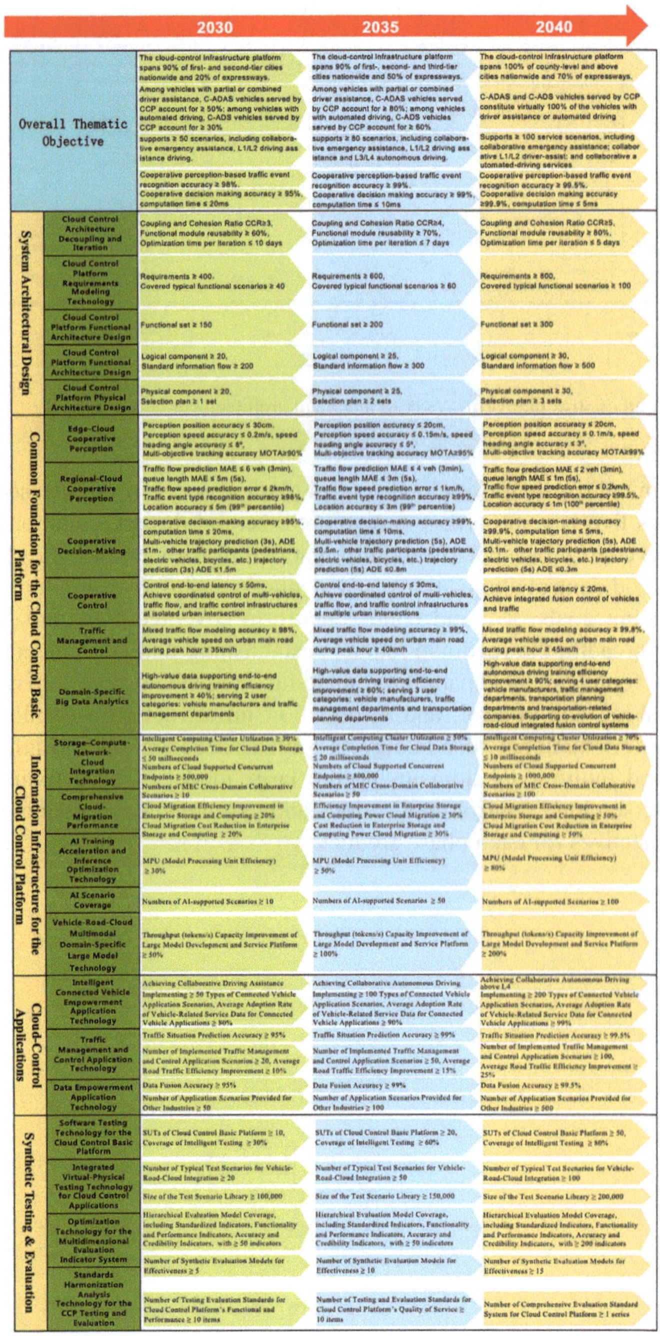

Fig. 4.20 Thematic technology roadmap

4.4.4.2 System Architectural Design

(1) Cloud Control Platform Requirements Modeling Technology

Develop a multidimensional user-requirements model for the cloud control platform, with a focus on advancing its requirements trade-off mechanisms and iterative optimization techniques, to ensure that requirements are clear, rational, and amenable to iteration—and thereby provide guidance for the platform's functional architecture design.

(2) Cloud Control Platform Functional Architecture Design Technology

Establish a macro mapping relationship between the requirements model and system functions; investigate technologies such as model-based architecture description, functional-architecture pre-verification, and configuration-optimization for the cloud control platform; ensure the rationality, flexibility, and efficiency of functional architecture; and support subsequent analysis of the platform's logical components.

(3) Cloud Control Platform Logical Architecture Design Technology

Define layered and decoupled logical components; investigate model-based logical-architecture description and verification techniques for the cloud control platform; focus on breakthroughs in technologies of logical-architecture optimization, configuration selection and iterative refinement; and ensure logical-architecture development of cloud platform is rational, consistent, and readily iterated.

(4) Cloud Control Platform Physical Architecture Design Technology

Establish the unified mapping relationship between logical and physical components; investigate model-based physical-architecture description and verification techniques for the cloud control platform; focus on breakthroughs in physical-architecture configuration optimization technique; and explore iterative and evolutionary methods for the physical architecture to support the platform's real-world deployment.

4.4.4.3 Common Foundation for the Cloud Control Basic Platform

(1) Fusion Perception Technology

Focusing on technologies such as joint filtering techniques for multi-modal cross-domain massive big data, high-precision spatial–temporal alignment techniques for heterogeneous asynchronous perception data, vehicle-cloud collaborative hybrid fusion perception strategies for end-to-end autonomous driving among early-mid-late stages, and fusion perception complementary techniques for perception data discontinuities and failures.

(2) Cooperative Decision-Making Technology

Revealing multi-level collaborative decision-making mechanisms between vehicles and cloud, researching on techniques such as multi-agent cooperative game theory-based multi-objective cross-domain decision-making technologies, decision planning techniques for heterogeneous multi-dimensional vehicles swarm in the mid-to-long-term, and dynamic scheduling techniques for complex heterogeneous multi-task workflows.

(3) Cooperative Control Technology

The main breakthroughs include the distributed control technology for multi-network connected vehicles in high-speed and stable networks, cooperative-game-based optimization control strategy between connected vehicles and traffic management infrastructure under varying penetration rates of connected vehicles, and high-reliability and low-latency cloud-based control technology for autonomous vehicles under complex conditions.

(4) Traffic Management Technology

Researching technologies within vehicle-road-cloud integrated systems, such as traffic flow modeling technology driven by modeling and data fusion, high-precision, cross-domain, and multi-spatiotemporal traffic situation prediction technology, and modeling of cross-domain co-evolution mechanisms and collaborative guidance techniques for micro-meso-macro hybrid traffic flow.

(5) Domain-Specific Big Data Analysis Technology

Researching technologies include automatic labeling technology of massive heterogeneous vehicle-road-cloud data, big data mining technology of high-quality scenarios for high-level autonomous driving, and big data completeness and intelligent analysis technology for vehicle-end applications, and finally establishing fusion data closed-loop for vehicle–road-cloud integrated systems.

4.4.4.4 Information Infrastructure for the Cloud Control Platform

(1) Storage–Computing–Network–Cloud Integration Technology

The object is to support the data-to-cloud requirement of large-scale, high-concurrency, cross-domain vehicle-road-cloud integrated system. The key breakthrough technologies include ultra-large-scale hardware and software computational scheduling technology for high real-time performance, three-layers cloud elastic heterogeneous collaboration, high-bandwidth memory (HBM), parallel file storage, and cache acceleration technologies. Based on above technologies, the evaluation metrics of intelligent computing cluster utilization, the number of concurrent terminal endpoints, and cross-domain collaboration scenarios in Multi-access Edge Computing (MEC) are expected to be increased, the average vehicle-road-cloud data storage latency are expected to be reduced, and the overall enterprise cloud migration performance are expected to be improved (including cloud migration efficiency and cloud migration costs).

(2) AI Training Acceleration and Inference Optimization Technology

The object is to support AI training and inference requirements essential for end-to-end autonomous driving and intelligent cockpits. The key breakthrough technologies include high-precision, lossless elastic distributed AI training optimization and edge-cloud collaborative inference technologies, in order to improve the efficiency of Model Processing Unit (MPU) and develop the innovation of "Cloud + AI" services mode.

(3) Vehicle–Road–Cloud Multimodal Domain-specific Large Model Technology

The object is to support the widespread applications of end-to-end autonomous driving, intelligent cockpits, and intelligent traffic management. Based on the capability enhancement of multimodal domain-specific large model development and service platforms for vehicle-road-cloud scenarios, the platform throughput (tokens/s) are expected to be improved, AI capabilities for cloud control applications are expected to be progressively expanded to enable innovative functions such as multi-intent identification and planning, complex spatial information completion, and traffic incident retrieval and so on.

4.4.4.5 Cloud Control Applications

(1) Intelligent Connected Vehicle Empowerment Application Technology

The technology focuses primarily on three categories of application scenarios: collaborative emergency assistance, collaborative-advanced driver assistance systems (C-ADAS), and collaborative-automated driving system (C-ADS) applications. Collaborative emergency assistance scenarios encompass technologies such as scene identification, and decision prompting triggered by multi-scenario functionalities; C-ADAS scenarios encompass technologies such as cloud-edge converged decision-making triggered by multi-scenarios, and vehicle-cloud converged decision-making considering vehicle operational needs; C-ADS scenarios encompass technologies such as scenario-based connected intelligent driving safety evaluation considering service quality variations, and cloud-supported autonomous parking technologies.

(2) Traffic Management and Control Application Technology

The technology focuses primarily on traffic order management, passenger and freight transportation management control, highway and municipal road supervision, and urban transportation planning. The applications include traffic situation prediction, passenger and freight scheduling, emergency response to road abnormalities, and network capacity analysis and forecasting.

(3) Data Empowerment Application Technology

The technology focuses primarily on data empowerment technologies targeting vehicle manufacturers, component suppliers, and broader industry stakeholders. The applications include new product R&D simulation for vehicle manufacturers, and sensor adaptive calibration for component suppliers. Besides, for industry stakeholders, the technology address R&D collaboration for critical and forward-looking technological breakthroughs, vehicle sales and after-sales services, and dynamic pricing for logistics and vehicle insurance.

4.4.4.6 Synthetic Testing and Evaluation

(1) Cloud Control Basic Platform Software Testing Technology

Research agile and intelligent testing technologies, achieving breakthroughs in intelligent test case generation and data-driven test result analysis, and develop automated testing tools capable of handling large-scale concurrency.

(2) Cloud Control Applications Integrated Virtual-Physical Testing Technology

Research element modeling methods for vehicle-road-cloud integrated systems and simulating complex traffic scenarios and environmental information. Create highly realistic simulation environments and hybrid virtual-real testing methods to support performance and reliability testing of vehicle-road-cloud integrated systems, to reduce the testing costs and time.

(3) Optimization Technology for the Multi-dimensional Evaluation Indicator System

Research methodologies for constructing multi-dimensional evaluation indicator system and conduct comprehensive performance and effectiveness evaluations. Establish a robust evaluation system to validate whether vehicle-road-cloud integrated systems effectively meet diverse user expectations.

(4) Testing and Evaluation Standards Harmonization Analysis Technology

Research methods for standards harmonization analysis. Conduct consistency checks among various technical requirements within testing and evaluation standards, performing quantitative assessments for coordination analysis, and determine the applicability and feasibility of standard implementation.

4.5 Intelligent Connected Safety and Security

4.5.1 Global Technological Progress

4.5.1.1 Functional Safety Develops Rapidly

In terms of functional safety, China has made breakthroughs in standards and regulations, analysis and design, testing and evaluation, certification and supervision, as well as functional safety toolchain and databases, gradually narrowing the gap with the international industry. For standards and regulations, China's functional safety regulatory framework has gradually matured, forming a standard system based on the GB/T 34590 series. Which covers new energy vehicles, power batteries, battery management systems, drive motors, braking, steering, chips, and other key fields. With widespread adoption of functional safety concepts and the introduction of mandatory standards and regulatory policies, domestic OEMs and suppliers have invested substantial resources, yielding notable progress. Regarding testing and evaluation, since 2023, in response to regulatory requirements from overseas export destinations, leading domestic manufacturers have been conducting vehicle functional safety validation activities that go beyond conventional vehicle and related project integration testing, improving the coverage and completeness of test validation. In the area of certification and supervision, China's system and processes are gradually improving. In 2023, a total of 114 functional safety product and process certifications were issued, a significant increase compared to 2022 (approximately 40). At the toolchain level, the development and application of domestic functional safety tools are becoming increasingly systematic and standardized. In 2023, some domestic companies began embedding functional safety development tools and even testing tools into vehicle model project management tools to better align with product development. As for functional safety database, domestic enterprises and research institutions have established extensive databases such as vehicle-level hazard/failure mode libraries, hazard scenario libraries, ESC evaluation model libraries, safety requirement libraries, and test case libraries. They have also developed narrower-scope data resources, such as Safety Libraries for specific chips or operating systems to support their product and technology development. Although domestic functional safety technology has made significant progress, compared with traditional automotive industrial powers (Europe, America, Japan, and Korea), there is still a gap in domestic functional safety technology development. For example, in vehicle-level safety analysis, domestic manufacturers still rely heavily on expert experience. They lack both the foundational databases needed to support quantitative assessment and the supporting equipment and tools, placing the overall industry in a catch-up phase compared to established global leaders.

4.5.1.2 SOTIF is Forming Research Directions with Chinese Characteristics

Since the introduction of the Safety of the Intended Functionality (SOTIF) standard in 2019, China has mainly focused on SOTIF standard development and assessment analysis, while internationally, there has been more emphasis on exploring theoretical methods for SOTIF risk quantification, with significant first-mover advantages in basic research and core technology development. By 2023, China made certain progress in SOTIF assessment methods. Currently, Tsinghua University in China is focusing on real-time monitoring and protection of SOTIF risks, having established a redundant heterogeneous intelligent vehicle SOTIF protection technology architecture, forming a three-layer protection of risk prevention-pre-control-prediction, and implementing real-time SOTIF monitoring and protection through vehicle-road-cloud collaboration, validated in Hongqi vehicles from FAW Group. However, due to factors such as scenario complexity, statistical analysis difficulties, trigger condition dependencies, and AI algorithm uncertainties, current research has not yet clearly and uniformly defined SOTIF risks and their quantitative assessment methods. Additionally, SOTIF real-vehicle closed-field testing requires high-standard field equipment, and currently, China has not established similar test sites with comprehensive closed-test equipment and tools. Furthermore, test scenarios are fundamental elements in the SOTIF testing tool chain, and there is no scenario software in the industry that can comprehensively, faithfully, and efficiently independently reproduce and reconstruct typical known scenarios (with different emphases on perception, decision-making, execution, etc.). The reconstruction of environmental, lighting, road surface, and other factors remains a technical challenge. Although simulation tool chains and technology applications are relatively mature and widespread in the industry, the validation of tool confidence levels remains an unresolved issue.

4.5.1.3 Cybersecurity Standards Still Need Strengthening

In the field of intelligent connected vehicle Cybersecurity, security encryption and authentication technologies, intrusion detection systems, and Cybersecurity operations centers are key components for ensuring vehicle Cybersecurity. Security encryption and authentication technology is the foundation of intelligent connected vehicle Cybersecurity. In recent years, China has made significant progress in vehicle network security, data encryption, and privacy protection, making vehicle networking systems more secure and reliable, and further enhancing user privacy protection. Automotive intrusion detection systems monitor vehicle network data flow in real-time, identify abnormal behavior, and take timely protective measures to prevent attacks from harming vehicles and passengers. In recent years, China's automotive intrusion detection systems have achieved important breakthroughs in algorithm optimization, detection accuracy, and response speed, achieving higher levels of real-time protection. The automotive security operations center is the Cybersecurity hub for intelligent connected vehicles, collecting and analyzing vehicle data, monitoring and managing the security status of the entire vehicle network environment, promptly identifying potential security threats, and taking corresponding protective measures. China has made significant progress in building automotive security operations centers in recent years, enhancing data processing capabilities and real-time monitoring capabilities, while introducing more advanced analytical algorithms and intelligent management tools, greatly improving overall protection capabilities. However, compared to international leading levels, China still has certain gaps in the standardization, interoperability, and large-scale application of vehicle networking technology, with Europe, America, Japan, and Korea performing more maturely and comprehensively in these aspects. Overall, although China has made significant progress in security encryption and authentication technology, intrusion detection systems, and Cybersecurity operations centers, to gain an advantage in global competition, continued investment in research and development is needed, along with strengthening alignment with international standards and regulations. By continuously improving Cybersecurity technology levels, the safe and stable operation of intelligent connected vehicles can be ensured, better promoting industrial development and technological progress.

4.5.1.4 Integrated Safety and Security Needs Further Development

In terms of Integrated Safety and Security, innovative technical research is already underway in areas such as Integrated Safety and Security risk assessment and unified safety and security architecture design. With the development of vehicle-road-cloud integration and the further prominence of the complex cyber-physical system characteristics of intelligent connected vehicles, multi-dimensional safety aspects exhibit coupling, interweaving, and mutual influence. The industry continues to increase its focus on developing Integrated Safety and Security design and development for intelligent connected vehicles. Global research on Integrated Safety and Security is still in its early stages, with basic models initially constructed, and some automobile manufacturers making preliminary attempts at safety and security design process integration in product development. However, there are currently no mature, systematic theories and methods for Integrated Safety and Security analysis and design, product testing, and verification, requiring the industry to concentrate efforts on research and breakthrough. Currently, there are deficiencies in both theory and methodology, and there is a lack of corresponding support for the testing means and tools for Integrated Safety and Security. It is still at the preliminary stage, mainly focusing on the integration of functional safety and SOTIF. Nevertheless, a gradual trend is emerging toward the integration of functional safety, SOTIF, and cybersecurity, and related research on Integrated Safety and Security risk assessment and safety architecture design is already in progress.

4.5.2 Outlook on Technology Development Trends

4.5.2.1 Safety and Security Has Become the Biggest Challenge for Large-Scale Commercial Application of Intelligent Connected Vehicles

Intelligent connected vehicles have being the direction for global automotive industry. With the rapid development of the industry, new safety and security challenges have emerged. Various risks, including driving safety, cybersecurity, and data security, during vehicle operation are intertwined and superimposed, seriously threatening people's lives and property safety. The safety and security of intelligent connected vehicles has the typical characteristics of the "bucket effect," involving upstream and downstream of the industrial chain and the entire lifecycle of vehicle operation. It has become a key factor currently restricting the large-scale commercial implementation and high-quality development of intelligent connected vehicles. Safety and security is also a focus of the global intelligent connected vehicle industry. Major automotive powers around the world have given widespread attention to intelligent connected vehicle safety and security from aspects such as policies and regulations, standards, and technology research and development. The intelligent connected vehicle safety and security field shows the following development trends.

4.5.2.2 Global Acceleration of Safety Standard Implementation and Product Deployment

Standards, as guiding documents that define the safety and security baseline and clarify safety and security requirements for vehicles and key systems, are crucial for ensuring the basic safety and security level of intelligent connected vehicles. In recent years, global industry has accelerated the formulation and implementation of safety and security standards for intelligent connected vehicles. In terms of international regulations, the United Nations World Forum for Harmonization of Vehicle Regulations (WP.29) has incorporated functional safety, SOTIF, and Cybersecurity as core criteria for assessing vehicle safety and security in multiple regulations on autonomous driving and vehicle networking, and included them in type approval management. China is accelerating the development and improvement of a comprehensive standard system for the safety and security development and application of intelligent connected vehicles, key systems, software, and chips. Corresponding practical guidance standards for the safety and security of key systems such as autonomous driving and V2X are also undergoing to meet the needs of industrial development and government management for standardization.

4.5.2.3 Strengthening Product Operational Safety and Security Supervision

As high-level autonomous driving begins to enter the commercial operation phase, the safety and security responsibility during vehicle operation is shifting, bringing enormous challenges to product market access management and product operation supervision. Currently, countries around the world are accelerating research and formulation work on management policies and legal regulations for high-level autonomous driving, especially in terms of product market access and product supervision, putting forward comprehensive and systematic requirements centered on safety and security. With the accelerated evolution of vehicle-road-cloud integration, the safety and security boundaries of automobiles are further expanded. Only by further strengthening product safety and security supervision can the industry be effectively guaranteed. However, the current policies, regulations, standard systems, and key technologies related to intelligent connected vehicle product access and supervision are still unable to support the needs of large-scale safe operation of high-level autonomous driving. Which is urgently needed to conduct systematic and comprehensive research at the industry level to build a multi-level collaborative product market access and operational safety and security supervision system involving government, industry, research, and users.

4.5.2.4 Safety and Security Technologies Develop from "Single-Scattered" to "Multi-Dimensional-Integrated"

Intelligent connected vehicle safety and security encompasses functional safety and security, SOTIF, network security, data security, and more. With the deep development of vehicle-road-cloud integration and the prominence of the complex cyber-physical system characteristics of intelligent connected vehicles, multi-dimensional safety and security aspects increasingly show coupling, interweaving, and mutual influence. The traditional approach of conducting analysis, design, and testing independently for safety and security is increasingly unable to ensure the operational safety and security of intelligent connected vehicles throughout their lifecycle and across all scenarios. There is an urgent need to combine multiple dimensions of safety and security and conduct integrated analysis, design, testing, evaluation, certification, and supervision. Global research on Integrated Safety and Security is still in its early stages. Currently, no mature, systematic theories and methods have been formed for Integrated Safety and Security analysis and design, Integrated Safety and Security product testing, and verification, requiring the industry to concentrate efforts on research and breakthrough.

4.5.3 Development Goals and Milestones for 2040

Looking ahead to 2040, to support the large-scale commercial operation of intelligent connected vehicles, intelligent connected safety and security will evolve toward an integrated vehicle-road-cloud architecture, featuring multidimensional and comprehensive safety and security protection. The ultimate vision is to progressively achieve "zero fatalities" and "zero accidents" for intelligent connected vehicles.

The overall targets by 2030 are as follows:

The industry-average accident interval mileage caused by intelligent connected systems will reach 1 million kilometers per incident on highways and 500,000 km per incident in urban areas.

The compliance rate with cybersecurity protection requirements for vehicle-road-cloud will reach an industry average of $\geq$90%.

Integrated Safety and Security design and development will cover key onboard systems and components related to intelligent driving and internet of vehicles, leading to an Integrated Safety and Security design and development framework.

The overall targets by 2035 are as follows:

The industry-average accident interval mileage caused by intelligent connected systems will reach 2 million kilometers per incident on highways and 1 million kilometers per incident in urban areas.

The compliance rate with cybersecurity protection requirements for vehicle-road-cloud integration will reach an industry average of $\geq$95%.

Integrated Safety and Security design and development will cover key systems and components of the vehicle-road-cloud integration, with the basic establishment of an Integrated Safety and Security design, development, and operational monitoring framework.

The overall targets by 2040 are as follows:

The industry-average accident interval mileage caused by intelligent connected systems will reach 10 million kilometers per incident.

The compliance rate with cybersecurity protection requirements for vehicle-road-cloud integration will reach an industry average of $\geq$99%.

Integrated Safety and Security design and development will achieve full-element coverage of the vehicle-road-cloud integrated system, with the complete establishment of a comprehensive Integrated Safety and Security design, development, and operational monitoring system.

4.5.4 Technology Roadmap

4.5.4.1 Overall Technology Roadmap

The safety of intelligent connected vehicles exhibits a typical "barrel effect," characterized by the interplay among Function Safety, Safety of the Intended Functionality (SOTIF), Cybersecurity, and the compounded challenges of Integrated Safety and Security. These various safety and security aspects involve both upstream and downstream segments of the industrial chain, as well as the entire life cycle of vehicle operation.

Roadmap 3.0 establishes "accident interval mileage caused by intelligent connected systems," "compliance rate with cybersecurity protection requirements," and "Integrated Safety and Security design and development framework" as the overall goals for the intelligent connected vehicles safety and security domain, representing the development targets of overall safety and security performance from different dimensions.

The intelligent connected vehicles safety and security domain is divided into four subdomains: Function Safety, SOTIF, Cybersecurity, and Integrated Safety and Security. Each subdomain consistently structures the key technology mapping and performance indicator setting around three phases: safety development, testing and validation, and operational safety and security (Fig. 4.21).

	2030	2035	2040
Overall Targets	• Accident interval mileage caused by intelligent connected system for industry average level reaches 1 million km/incident for highways, 500,000 km/incident for urban areas*. • Compliance rate with cybersecurity protection requirements for vehicle-road-cloud for industry average level reaches ≥90%. • Integrated Safety and Security design and development covers intelligent driving, networked communication, and other on-board critical systems and components, initially establishing an Integrated Safety and Security design and development system.	• Accident interval mileage caused by intelligent connected system for industry average level reaches 2 million km/incident for highways, 2 million km/incident for urban areas*. • Compliance rate with cybersecurity protection requirements for vehicle-road-cloud for industry average level reaches ≥95%. • Integrated Safety and Security design and development covers vehicle-road-cloud integrated critical systems and components, basically establishing an Integrated Safety and Security design and development and operational monitoring system.	• Accident interval mileage caused by intelligent connected system for industry average level reaches 10 million km/incident*. • Compliance rate with cybersecurity protection requirements for vehicle-road-cloud for industry average level reaches ≥99%. • Integrated Safety and Security design and development achieves full coverage of vehicle-road-cloud integrated system elements, comprehensively establishing an Integrated Safety and Security design and development and operational monitoring system.
Functional Safety	• Intelligent connected vehicle functional safety implementation coverage rate industry average level ≥85%. • Critical system failure prediction coverage rate industry leading level ≥90%.	• Intelligent connected vehicle functional safety implementation coverage rate industry average level ≥90%. • Critical system failure prediction coverage rate industry leading level ≥95%.	• Intelligent connected vehicle functional safety implementation coverage rate industry average level ≥95%. • Critical system failure prediction coverage rate industry leading level ≥99%.
SOTIF	• Residual risk acceptance criteria: Accident interval mileage caused by expected functional safety issues: industry average level reaches 1 million km/incident for highways, 500,000 km/(incident*hundred vehicles) for urban areas. • Hazardous behavior acceptance criteria: Autonomous driving successful response to reasonably foreseeable risk scenario trigger conditions coverage rate industry leading level ≥90%.	• Residual risk acceptance criteria: Accident interval mileage caused by expected functional safety issues: industry average level reaches 2 million km/incident for highways, 1 million km/(incident*hundred vehicles) for urban areas. • Hazardous behavior acceptance criteria: Autonomous driving successful response to reasonably foreseeable risk scenario trigger conditions coverage rate industry leading level ≥95%.	• Residual risk acceptance criteria: Accident interval mileage caused by expected functional safety issues: industry average level reaches ≥10 million km/(incident*hundred vehicles). • Hazardous behavior acceptance criteria: Autonomous driving successful response to reasonably foreseeable risk scenario trigger conditions coverage rate industry leading level ≥98%.
Cyber Security	• Cybersecurity integrated into intelligent connected vehicle design and development, testing and evaluation, operational monitoring full lifecycle, initially constructing a vehicle-road-cloud integrated cybersecurity protection system. • Vehicle-road-cloud cybersecurity protection technical requirement compliance rate industry average level ≥90%.	• Cybersecurity fully integrated into roadside facilities and cloud platform design and development, testing and evaluation, operational monitoring full lifecycle, establishing a vehicle-road-cloud integrated cybersecurity protection system. • Vehicle-road-cloud cybersecurity protection technical requirement compliance rate industry average level ≥95%.	• Comprehensively establishing an cybersecurity protection system meeting the collaborative development of single-vehicle intelligence and network-enabled coordination. • Vehicle-road-cloud cybersecurity protection technical requirement compliance rate industry average level ≥99%.
Integrated Safety and Security	• Integrated Safety and Security design and development covers intelligent driving, networked communication, and other on-board critical systems and components, initially establishing an Integrated Safety and Security design and development system. • Integrated Safety and Security monitoring platform industry leading level achieves ≥70% of intelligent connected vehicle Integrated Safety and Security risk identification and monitoring.	• Integrated Safety and Security design and development covers vehicle-road-cloud integrated critical systems and components, basically establishing an Integrated Safety and Security design and development and operational monitoring system. • Integrated Safety and Security monitoring platform industry leading level achieves ≥80% of vehicle-road-cloud Integrated Safety and Security risk identification and monitoring.	• Integrated Safety and Security design and development achieves full coverage of vehicle-road-cloud integrated system elements, comprehensively establishing an Integrated Safety and Security design and development and operational monitoring system. • Integrated Safety and Security monitoring platform industry leading level achieves ≥90% of vehicle-road-cloud Integrated Safety and Security risk identification and monitoring.

*Triggering EDR event data recording system

Fig. 4.21 Technical roadmap for Safety and Security

4.5.4.2 Technology Roadmap for the Functional Safety

The global automotive industry is accelerating the development and implementation of Functional Safety standards for intelligent connected vehicles.

The World Forum for Harmonization of Vehicle Regulations (WP.29) under the United Nations has designated Functional Safety as a core criterion for evaluating vehicle safety within multiple regulations related to autonomous driving and internet of vehicles, incorporating it into type approval management.

At the same time, product market access and regulatory supervision are being strengthened. Countries around the world are expediting the formulation of laws, regulations, and management policies for high-level autonomous driving, and are proposing comprehensive and systematic requirements regarding Function Safety.

	2030	2035	2040
Functional Safety Overall Goals	• Intelligent connected vehicle functional safety implementation coverage rate industry average level ≥85%. • Critical system failure prediction coverage rate industry leading level ≥90%.	• Intelligent connected vehicle functional safety implementation coverage rate industry average level ≥90%. • Critical system failure prediction coverage rate industry leading level ≥95%.	• Intelligent connected vehicle functional safety implementation coverage rate industry average level ≥95%. • Critical system failure prediction coverage rate industry leading level ≥99%.
Safety Development	• Initially establishing vehicle-road-cloud integrated functional safety architecture. • Intelligent connected vehicle functional safety implementation coverage rate industry average level ≥85%. • Establishing functional safety tool chains with independent intellectual property rights.	• Basically establishing vehicle-road-cloud integrated functional safety architecture. • Intelligent connected vehicle functional safety implementation coverage rate industry average level ≥90%. • Establishing intelligent, independent intellectual property rights functional safety development and management tool chains.	• Comprehensively establishing vehicle-road-cloud integrated functional safety architecture. • Intelligent connected vehicle functional safety implementation coverage rate industry average level ≥95%. • Establishing intelligent, integrated, independently controlled functional safety development, management, and operation tool chains.
Testing and Verification	• Initially establishing a multi-level functional safety testing and evaluation system covering entire vehicles, systems, components, chips, and operating systems. • Testing and evaluation system verification of hazard scenario coverage rate 100%. • Establishing functional safety certification methods and certification systems for new technologies and new products of intelligent connected vehicles.	• Basically establishing a multi-level functional safety testing and evaluation system covering entire vehicles, systems, components, chips, and operating systems. • Testing and evaluation system verification of hazard scenario coverage rate 100%. • Establishing functional safety certification methods and certification systems for roadside facilities and cloud control platforms.	• Comprehensively establishing a multi-level functional safety testing and evaluation system covering entire vehicles, systems, components, chips, and operating systems. • Testing and evaluation system verification of hazard scenario coverage rate 100%. • Comprehensively establishing functional safety certification methods and certification systems covering vehicle-road-cloud integration.
Operational Safety	• Establishing vehicle-road-cloud integrated system failure mode library and safety mechanism library. • Critical system failure prediction coverage rate industry leading level ≥90%.	• Improving vehicle-road-cloud integrated system failure mode library and safety mechanism library. • Critical system failure prediction coverage rate industry leading level ≥95%.	• Continuously improving vehicle-road-cloud integrated system failure mode library and safety mechanism library. • Critical system failure prediction coverage rate industry leading level ≥99%.

Fig. 4.22 Technical roadmap for the Functional Safety

Looking ahead, Functional Safety will be expanded to support the industrial deployment of vehicle-road-cloud integration, while also meeting the requirements for FA-level (Full Automation) intelligent driving. Functional Safety technologies are evolving from a "single and discrete" model toward a "multidimensional and integrated" development pattern (Fig. 4.22).

4.5.4.3 Technology Roadmap for the SOTIF

From a development perspective, addressing SOTIF throughout the life-cycle development process of intelligent connected vehicles has become the primary direction for future advancement.

Current research efforts on SOTIF are mainly focused on breakthroughs in four key areas: hazard recognition, real-time protection, adaptive learning and growth, and testing and validation.

In China, the Ministry of Industry and Information Technology (MIIT) has explicitly stated in the intelligent connected vehicles access requirements that automakers must comply with process assurance requirements for SOTIF. Consequently, major domestic original equipment manufacturers (OEMs) are actively exploring the establishment of internal SOTIF processes and focusing on the deployment of relevant software tools.

Overall, research on SOTIF remains in its early stages, and there is a lack of comprehensive solutions for issues related to risk recognition, real-time protection, adaptive learning, and testing and evaluation. Nevertheless, the development of autonomous driving and the ongoing push for intelligent connected vehicle access are accelerating the industrial application of SOTIF technologies (Fig. 4.23).

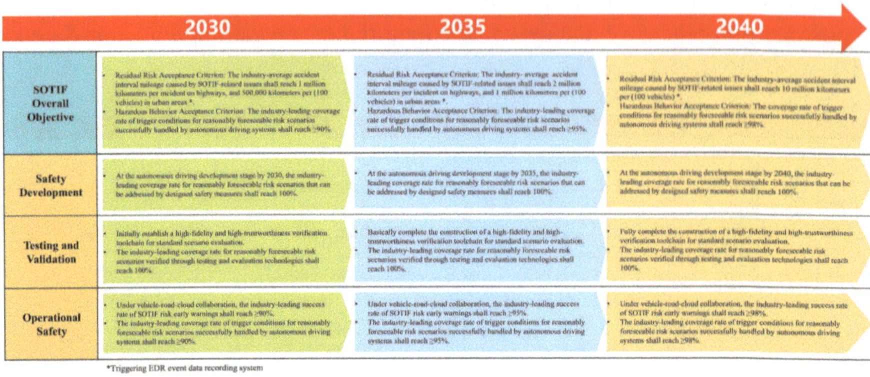

Fig. 4.23 Technical roadmap for the SOTIF

4.5.4.4 Technology Roadmap for the Cybersecurity

With the accelerated development of deep vehicle-road-cloud integration, strengthening cybersecurity for isolated scenarios in intelligent connected vehicles is no longer sufficient to establish an effective overall defense system.

Future development will focus on building an integrated Cybersecurity protection framework across the cloud, network, onboard terminals, and edge nodes, covering diverse security scenarios such as environmental security, data security, and compliance behaviors.

At the same time, an integrated management and control platform combining security management, supervision, detection, and operations will be established.

Supporting Cybersecurity and data security for intelligent connected vehicles through systematic capability building will become a major development trend.

On the other hand, the intelligentization of threat perception and operation is accelerating.

By leveraging AI-based threat detection technologies and integrating data from vehicle operations and road infrastructure, cloud-based intelligent security sensing capabilities will be expanded and applied.

Enhancing situational awareness, intrusion detection, and emergency response capabilities in Cybersecurity is also becoming a key focus area for current industry development (Fig. 4.24).

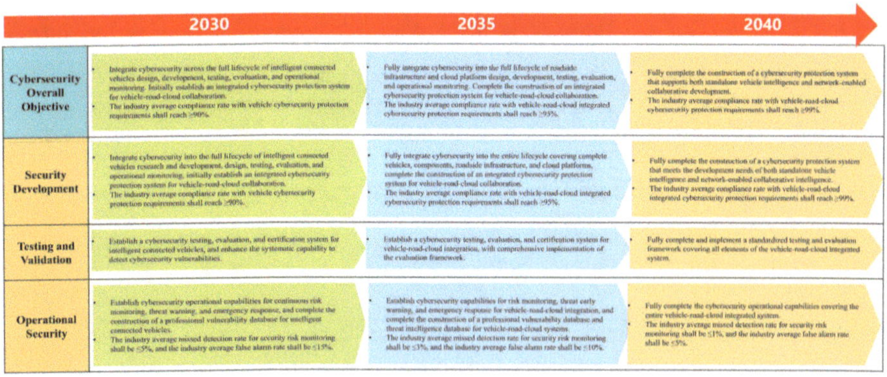

Fig. 4.24 Technical roadmap for the Cybersecurity

4.5.4.5 Technical Development Roadmap for the Integrated Safety and Security

With the widespread and ubiquitous application of intelligent, connected, and digital technologies in intelligent connected vehicles, cybersecurity, functional safety, and SOTIF issues have become increasingly intertwined and difficult to separate. There is an urgent need to effectively address key challenges such as integrated safety and security hazard analysis, risk assessment, and collaborative design across multiple levels—methodology, technology, and practice.

Currently, universities and research institutions worldwide have conducted in-depth studies on integrated safety and security. However, most efforts remain confined to theoretical and methodological research.

It is imperative to accelerate collaborative R&D on critical integrated safety and security technologies with automakers and component suppliers. This includes establishing corresponding integrated safety and security design and development processes, technical standards, and testing/evaluation systems.

Such measures will ensure that functional safety, SOTIF, and cybersecurity requirements are simultaneously addressed throughout the development, testing, manufacturing, and operation of intelligent connected vehicles.

This integrated safety and security architecture will safeguard the high-quality advancement of intelligent connected vehicles(Fig. 4.25).

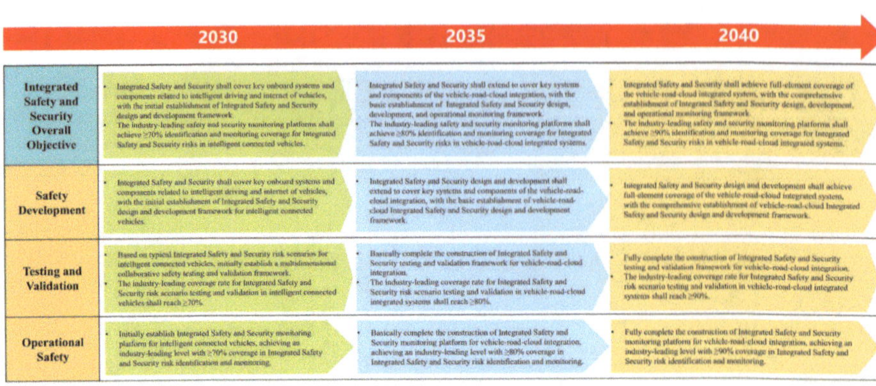

Fig. 4.25 Technical roadmap for the Integrated Safety and Security

4.6 Intelligent Connected Infrastructure (Roads, Maps, and Positioning)

4.6.1 *Maps and Positioning*

4.6.1.1 Domestic and International Technical Status Comparison

Autonomous Driving Mapping Technology

Autonomous driving map generation technology has evolved significantly from reliance on high-cost equipment to intelligent autonomous construction. In early stages, map compilation required specialized collection devices such as LiDAR and cameras, coupled with extensive manual editing, resulting in high costs and long update cycles. Since 2021, SLAM technology based on multi-sensor fusion has enabled real-time local mapping and data feedback at the vehicle end, significantly improving update efficiency. By 2023, Transformer architecture-based end-to-end technology advanced semantic map generation, forming a closed-loop "collection-generation-update-iteration" ecosystem through self-supervised learning. This evolution not only enhanced data update efficiency but also provided economically viable, timely, and safe mapping solutions for autonomous driving via a hierarchical vehicle-cloud collaborative architecture (static topology + dynamic elements).

Amid rapid advancements in autonomous driving, the "perception-heavy, map-light" philosophy has shifted from a simplistic technical dichotomy to scenario-specific differentiation. Whether prioritizing perception or mapping, the core logic hinges on dynamically balancing economic viability and safety. Automakers now employ multidimensional models to evaluate sensor configurations, algorithms, computing platforms, mapping services, and compliance costs—enabling tailored technical stacks for each autonomy level (L2–L5). For instance, L2–L3 systems may rely primarily on vehicle perception with advanced assistant driving maps, while L4–L5 systems demand high-definition maps for safety redundancy, avoiding blanket mandates for high-definition maps across all levels. As illustrated in Table 4.2.

Significant technological disparities exist between domestic and international autonomous driving mapping ecosystems, primarily driven by divergent policy frameworks and market demands. China's regulatory approach emphasizes security compliance through strict qualification requirements and data localization, fostering a "light-map + perception-heavy + regional specialization" model that prioritizes high-definition mapping for complex urban scenarios with compliant multi-source updates in designated zones. In contrast, international markets leverage open policies to achieve comprehensive high-definition coverage through satellite imagery and global crowdsourcing. Key challenges domestically include high compliance costs, underdeveloped data-sharing mechanisms, and urgent technological upgrade needs,

Table 4.2 Comparison of autonomous driving map layer elements and applicable autonomous driving levels

Map type	Classification definition	Main map layers included	Supported autonomous driving levels
Standard navigation electronic map (SD map)	Traditional navigation electronic map Accuracy: 5–10 m Update frequency: quarterly	① Road-level road network layer ② Partial macro traffic information layer	L1/L2/L3 (optional)
Advanced assistant driving map	Add lane-level information, slope, curvature, connection relationships, etc Accuracy: 0.5–1 m Update frequency: monthly/quarterly	① Road-level road network layer ② Macro traffic information layer ③ Road-lane connection layer ④ Lane-level road network layer	L1/L2/L3 (optional); L4 (mandatory)
High-definition map (HD map)	Add ground surface geometry, auxiliary positioning information, provide more detailed roadside traffic facility data, dynamic layers, and decision-making information Accuracy: 0.2 m Update frequency: daily/weekly/monthly	① Road-level road network layer ② Macro traffic information layer ③ Road-lane connection layer ④ Lane-level road network layer ⑤ Map feature information layer ⑥ Dynamic perception container layer ⑦ Intelligent decision support layer	L4/L5 (mandatory)

while international markets face fragmented regulations, geopolitical risks, commercialization uncertainties, and competing technical paradigms between vision-based and multi-sensor fusion solutions.

High-Precision Positioning Technology

The four global satellite navigation system providers announced by the International Committee on Global Navigation Satellite Systems include China's BeiDou Navigation Satellite System (BDS), the United States' Global Positioning System (GPS), Russia's GLONASS, and the European Union's Galileo. The BeiDou Navigation Satellite System (BDS) achieved Asia–Pacific coverage in 2012 and completed its global network deployment and provincial CORS system construction in 2020, enabling worldwide positioning services. Currently, BDS high-precision positioning technology has established a complete "service-algorithm-terminal" ecosystem.

Domestic enterprises have made significant progress in global service coverage, algorithm innovation, and terminal manufacturing, not only meeting the demands of autonomous driving and IoT scenarios but also driving the evolution of high-precision positioning technology toward lower costs and higher efficiency.

The global high-precision positioning service ecosystem demonstrates distinct development patterns between international and domestic markets. Internationally, established players like Trimble (US), Leica Geosystems (Switzerland), and Hexagon (Sweden) have built mature paid augmentation service networks across North America and Europe through proprietary and cooperative base station infrastructure. In China, the market is primarily served by domestic providers including Qianxun SI (operator of the national BeiDou Ground-Based Augmentation System), China Mobile, Dayou Space–Time, and Sixents Technology, which have collectively established comprehensive nationwide high-precision positioning enhancement services. The sector has shown remarkable growth, with over 3 million advanced intelligent driving vehicles in China equipped with high-precision positioning services by the end of 2024, reflecting the rapid adoption of this technology in the domestic automotive industry.

Algorithm innovation has become a key driver of technological breakthroughs. With the commercialization of 5G and the maturation of cloud services, integrated "network-cloud-terminal" high-precision positioning solutions have emerged, offering the potential to provide massive users with convenient, low-cost, all-weather, centimeter-level positioning services. Additionally, the integrated PNT (Positioning, Navigation, and Timing) system, combining GNSS, low-orbit satellites, inertial navigation, vision, LiDAR, and 5G, enables sub-meter-level precision across all autonomous driving scenarios.

The terminal sector shows hierarchical competition and breakthroughs in domestic production. High-precision positioning suppliers are categorized into four layers: application layer (autonomous driving solution providers), platform layer (integrated software-hardware algorithm service providers), hardware layer (multi-sensor integrators), and foundation layer (chip and antenna suppliers). In the hardware layer, domestic manufacturers compete globally by integrating satellite navigation with inertial navigation to develop multi-sensor hardware products, gradually becoming core component suppliers in the high-precision positioning market. In the foundation layer, international leaders like Ublox, Trimble, and Qualcomm dominate the chip sector, while domestic manufacturers strive to close the gap through self-developed high-precision positioning chips.

4.6.1.2 Outlook on Technology Development Trends

Evolution of Autonomous Driving Maps Toward Perception Intelligence and Mapping Services

Amid the global automotive industry's intelligent transformation, autonomous driving maps, as critical infrastructure, are undergoing a paradigm shift from "perception vs. map priority debates" to the deep integration of "perception intelligence" and "map services." This transformation extends beyond optimizing data architectures and real-time update efficiency, fundamentally redefining the role of maps from "auxiliary perception tools" to "intelligent service engines." Through continuous technological iteration and functional restructuring, autonomous driving maps are building service systems tailored to high-level autonomous driving demands, advancing the industry toward self-evolving systems with smarter decision support and enhanced safety assurance.

(1) **Multi-modal AI-Driven Low-Cost Mapping Innovation**

The leapfrog development of artificial intelligence (AI) is reshaping map production. The traditional map data production model, which relies on extensive human labor, inefficiency, and high costs, is being replaced by AI-driven automation. Deep learning algorithms efficiently analyze massive geographic data, automatically identifying terrain, roads, buildings, and other key elements to rapidly generate high-precision maps. For example, neural network models enable automatic parsing of satellite imagery and LiDAR point clouds, improving mapping efficiency by orders of magnitude while enabling real-time updates to reflect road changes. This intelligent production model not only reduces costs but also endows maps with dynamic responsiveness, delivering more reliable and seamless navigation and positioning services for autonomous systems.

(2) **Vehicle-Road-Cloud Integrated Multi-Source Data Real-Time Fusion Updates**

The stringent requirements of autonomous driving for map temporal accuracy have catalyzed the rise of crowdsourced data collection. Onboard sensors (e.g., cameras, LiDAR) and roadside units (e.g., traffic surveillance cameras) have become critical sources for map data updates. Crowdsourced data undergoes storage, processing, and distribution via dedicated map computing service platforms, leveraging edge computing and 5G communication to achieve dynamic map updates. For instance, road construction data collected by vehicles can be transmitted to the cloud within seconds, processed by algorithms, and updated to maps—ensuring autonomous systems access real-time road conditions. This "perception-to-update" mechanism significantly enhances map freshness and coverage.

(3) Static Maps to Dynamic Knowledge Graph-Based Semantic Services

Autonomous driving maps are evolving from static geometric databases to semantic knowledge bases enabling contextual understanding. Traditional maps record only geometric road details, while next-gen semantic maps deeply integrate logical information such as traffic rules (e.g., lane priority) and scenario attributes (e.g., school zones). Through multi-modal data fusion (e.g., visual SLAM with LiDAR point clouds), maps can construct hybrid representations of dynamic scenes, aiding vehicles in interpreting temporary obstacles, weather impacts, and environmental changes. For example, during heavy rainfall, maps can adjust route planning using real-time precipitation data to avoid flooded areas.

(4) Deep Perception-Map Coupling for Enhanced Services

The autonomous driving map and the perception system are moving from "loose coupling" to "deep collaboration". The map guides the perception algorithm through prior information, such as providing lane topology in advance at complex intersections, reducing the scope of visual search and improving the recognition efficiency; the perception system feeds back the map update in real time, uses multi-vehicle data to build local maps, and realizes the dynamic iteration of "perception is mapping". This bi-directional enabling closed-loop system relies on efficient space–time alignment technology to solve the problem of positioning drift, and realizes low latency interaction through standardized interfaces. In the future, with the development of end-to-end autonomous driving architecture, maps may provide seamless support for perceptual decision-making in the form of embedded knowledge engine.

(5) Full-Chain Interpretable Safety Assurance Services

Global emphasis on map data security is driving investments in 5G, V2X, and other communication technologies, alongside stricter legislation and encryption measures. In China, accelerated efforts to establish autonomous driving map standards include technical innovations such as multi-party secure computing for encrypted data processing and digital watermarking for copyright protection, forming an interpretable security chain covering data collection, processing, and distribution. Through rigorous compliance review mechanisms and technological innovation, a dual-layered safeguard effectively supports safety–critical applications in autonomous driving scenarios.

High-Precision Positioning Technology Advances Toward Intelligence and Integration

High-precision positioning technology is advancing toward intelligence and integration, characterized by multi-technology convergence, scenario adaptation, and security assurance.

(1) Integrated Space-Ground-Cloud Augmentation Positioning and Integrity Technology

Globally, space-ground-cloud integrated augmented positioning technology provides vehicles with real-time high-precision spatiotemporal reference. International service providers like Trimble's OmniSTAR and Hexagon's TerraStar already deliver global satellite-based PPP (Precise Point Positioning) services. In China, Qianxun SI has made significant progress in global satellite-based service capabilities, offering fused augmentation services with integrity and functional safety. Future efforts will focus on developing integrated services that combine BeiDou with ground-based and satellite-based high-precision augmentation, alongside high-precision positioning terminals tailored for autonomous driving.

(2) Multi-Sensor Fusion Positioning Technology

Multi-sensor fusion has become critical for enhancing positioning accuracy. Research focuses on calibration and real-time fusion techniques for multi-sensor systems anchored to satellite navigation's absolute positioning framework and relative coordinate frameworks from IMU, vision, and LiDAR. Deep learning solutions enable self-learning capabilities in multi-sensor fusion processing. These advancements will improve the precision and reliability of autonomous vehicles in complex traffic environments, addressing full-domain, full-scenario positioning challenges.

(3) AI-Driven Positioning and Autonomous Driving Map-Assisted Localization

AI is emerging as the core driver of innovation in autonomous vehicle positioning. Key regions such as Japan, the U.S., and the EU prioritize AI-based adaptive positioning algorithms. For example, Japan's autonomous driving projects leverage deep learning to improve urban positioning accuracy, while U.S. companies like Waymo and Tesla develop next-gen autonomous navigation systems for enhanced environmental adaptability. Machine learning-based intelligent positioning algorithms will become mainstream, accelerating the evolution of vehicles into highly intelligent mobile platforms. Concurrently, autonomous driving map-assisted navigation and path planning improve positioning safety and efficiency in complex road environments, serving as a vital complement to AI positioning.

(4) Transition from Onboard Intelligence to Vehicle-Road-Cloud Network Collaboration

The integration of Vehicle-to-Everything (V2X) and Intelligent Transportation Systems (ITS) is shifting positioning technology from standalone onboard intelligence to network-wide collaboration. The EU's C-ITS project optimizes traffic flow and vehicle positioning by integrating the Galileo satellite system. U.S. cities like San Francisco and New York deploy ITS with 5G to enable real-time vehicle-road data exchange, enhancing navigation and positioning accuracy. As autonomous driving faces technical bottlenecks, deep coupling between smart road infrastructure and vehicles becomes pivotal.

(5) **Enhanced Data Security and Privacy Protection**

With growing reliance on vehicle positioning data, global attention to security and privacy has intensified. The EU's GDPR imposes strict guidelines for processing vehicle location data, mandating user consent and driving secure communication protocols and encryption. California's privacy laws require automakers to obtain user consent for data collection and specify usage terms. Japan strengthens data protection frameworks with advanced encryption, anonymization, and real-time threat response systems. These measures collectively elevate global data security standards, providing a robust foundation for automotive technology development.

4.6.1.3 Development Goals and Milestones for 2040

Autonomous driving mapping and high-precision positioning technologies will advance in phases, comprehensively supporting the overarching objectives of autonomous driving through improvements in map update frequency, coverage, security, positioning services, algorithms, and hardware capabilities.

By 2030, autonomous driving maps will provide comprehensive and accurate road information and environmental data for intelligent connected vehicles. Advanced assistant driving map will achieve weekly updates for static data and daily updates for localized static data, while HD maps will enable real-time updates for critical elements and weekly updates for non-critical elements. High-assist maps will cover all publicly accessible roads nationwide, HD maps will cover major first- and second-tier cities, and themed maps will see scaled applications. Concurrently, automated and intelligent data processing technologies will enhance map compliance review efficiency, support rapid online incremental map updates, and establish security frameworks to ensure real-time accuracy. For high-precision positioning, multi-source fusion positioning services centered on BeiDou will be deployed in major Chinese cities, with domestically developed core positioning chips/modules achieving full-chain autonomy. Stable centimeter-level indoor-outdoor integrated positioning will be available in critical scenarios.

By 2035, autonomous driving map update frequency and coverage will further improve. Advanced assistant driving map will achieve daily updates for static data and hourly updates for localized static data, while HD maps will enable real-time updates for critical elements and daily updates for non-critical elements. Advanced assistant driving map will cover all publicly accessible roads, and HD maps will extend to first- and second-tier cities, supporting real-time spatiotemporal data review and lifecycle security monitoring. High-precision positioning services will expand nationwide, delivering seamless indoor-outdoor centimeter-level positioning with software, hardware, and systems meeting functional safety and expected functional safety metrics for high-level autonomous driving.

By 2040, autonomous driving maps will fully transition to HD maps, achieving real-time updates and nationwide coverage of publicly accessible roads. Spatiotemporal data will be secured throughout its lifecycle with real-time supervision and support for data circulation and transactions. High-precision positioning services will achieve global coverage, integrating BeiDou with other satellite positioning and communication systems to deliver real-time, high-precision, high-reliability, high-availability, and high-security positioning solutions.

4.6.1.4 Technology Roadmap

Autonomous Driving Mapping Technology Roadmap

From 2030 to 2040, the autonomous driving mapping technology roadmap will establish clear targets for coverage, update frequency, and security requirements of advanced assistant driving map and high-definition (HD) maps. In alignment with the vehicle-road-cloud integration development strategy and cloud-control infrastructure platform objectives, deployment efforts will concentrate on establishing high-precision dynamic mapping infrastructure platforms, prioritizing implementation in first- and second-tier cities and major highway networks to fulfill the strategic objectives of autonomous driving mapping systems. These technical specifications and implementation details are comprehensively documented in the "Intelligent Connected Vehicle Infrastructure Mapping Technology Roadmap" (Fig. 4.26).

	2030	2035	2040
Map Overall Objective	• Map Update Frequency: Advanced assistant driving map static data achieves weekly updates, local static data achieves daily updates; HD map key elements achieve real-time updates, non-key elements achieve weekly updates; supports incremental updates and rapid online map review. • Map Coverage: Advanced assistant driving map achieves full coverage of all public roads nationwide (excluding enclosed areas and parking lots); HD map covers major first- and second-tier cities; thematic maps achieve large-scale application. • Safety & Compliance: Supports real-time map review, establishes a security prevention and control system, implements mandatory spatiotemporal data standards, achieves safety monitoring for critical processes.	• Map Update Frequency: Advanced assistant driving map static data achieves daily updates, local static data achieves hourly updates; HD map key elements achieve real-time updates, non-key elements achieve daily updates. • Map Coverage: Advanced assistant driving map achieves full coverage of all public roads nationwide; HD map achieves full coverage of first- and second-tier cities. • Safety & Compliance: Supports real-time spatiotemporal data review, achieves full lifecycle security monitoring for spatiotemporal data, and enables safety supervision for critical processes.	• Map Update Frequency: HD map achieves real-time updates. • Map Coverage: HD map achieves full coverage of all public roads nationwide. • Safety & Compliance: Achieves full lifecycle security prevention and supervision for spatiotemporal data, enables data circulation and transactions.
Map Update Frequency	• Advanced assistant driving map static data achieves weekly updates, while local static data achieves daily updates. • HD Map key elements achieve real-time updates, while non-key elements achieve weekly updates.	• Advanced assistant driving map static data achieves daily updates, while local static data achieves hourly updates. • HD map key elements achieve real-time updates, while non-key elements achieve daily updates.	• HD map key elements achieve real-time updates
Map Coverage	• The Advanced Assistant Driving Map achieves full coverage of all public roads nationwide (excluding enclosed areas and parking lots); • The HD Map covers major first- and second-tier cities;Thematic maps have achieved large-scale application.	• The Advanced Assistant Driving Map achieves full coverage of public roads nationwide; • The HD Map achieves full coverage of first- and second-tier cities.	• The HD Map achieves full coverage of all public roads nationwide.
Safety and Compliance	• Fully enables real-time dynamic map review for autonomous driving, allowing map providers to conduct autonomous updates • Establishes a comprehensive security prevention standard system for autonomous driving geographic information, ensuring spatiotemporal data security with mandatory standards fully implemented • Achieves safety monitoring of critical input/output processes for spatiotemporal data	• Fully supports real-time dynamic auditing of spatiotemporal data • Implements a comprehensive security prevention standard system for autonomous driving geographic information • Achieves full lifecycle security monitoring of spatiotemporal data with critical oversight at all data ingress/egress points	• Achieves full lifecycle security protection and real-time monitoring of spatiotemporal data • Enables cross-domain circulation and platform-based transactions of autonomous driving geospatial data

Fig. 4.26 Technical roadmap for thematic mapping

High-Precision Positioning Technology Roadmap

With the mass production and demonstration applications of L3+ autonomous driving and intelligent connected vehicles, differentiated accuracy requirements for high-precision positioning have emerged. Autonomous driving positioning technologies will follow diverse paths, but all implementations rely on the synergy of positioning services, algorithms, and terminals. A comprehensive analysis yields the "Intelligent Connected Infrastructure Positioning Technology Roadmap" as follows (Fig. 4.27).

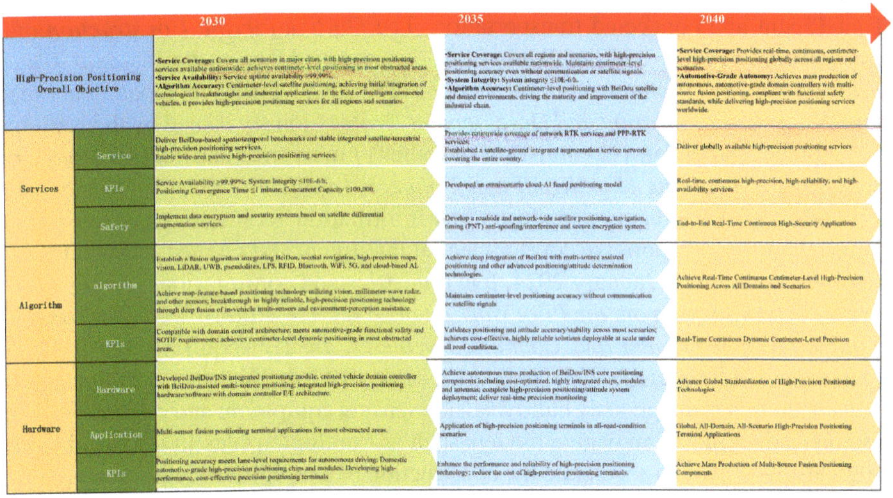

Fig. 4.27 Technology roadmap for positioning topic

4.6.2 *Roads*

4.6.2.1 Domestic and International Technical Status Comparison

Strategic Significance

Developing Intelligent and Connected Road Infrastructure is a Major Task of National Strategies Such as Building a Transportation Power

At the national level, policies continue to be introduced to promote the development of intelligent and connected transportation. The *Outline for the Construction of a Transportation Power* and the *National Comprehensive Three-dimensional Transportation Network Planning Outline* anchor the strategic direction. Documents such as the *Smart Car Innovation and Development Strategy* jointly issued by the National Development and Reform Commission and other 11 ministries and commissions, and the *Vehicle Networking (Intelligent and Connected Vehicle) Industry Development Action Plan* of the Ministry of Industry and Information Technology provide policy guidance for the collaborative development of intelligent and connected vehicles and road infrastructure. In January 2024, five ministries and commissions jointly issued the *Notice on Carrying out the Pilot Work on the "Vehicle–Road-Cloud Integration" Application of Intelligent and Connected Vehicles*, clearly requiring that the pilot areas achieve full coverage of 5G networks, deploy LTE-V2X direct communication roadside units, simultaneously build roadside sensing equipment and edge computing systems, and explore innovative models such as "multiple poles in one" and "multiple sensors in one" to accelerate the construction of a new intelligent transportation ecosystem.

Developing Intelligent and Connected Road Infrastructure is the Main Guarantee for Promoting Intelligent and Connected Vehicles

Intelligent and connected road infrastructure serves as the "extended perception system" for autonomous driving vehicles. Through high-precision radar, cameras, and other sensors deployed on both sides of the road, it breaks through the detection range of vehicle-mounted sensors, pre-senses distant traffic conditions, road construction, and other information, providing key basis for autonomous driving decision-making and significantly improving driving safety and reliability. In terms of traffic efficiency optimization, the collaborative operation of road infrastructure and autonomous driving vehicles has achieved remarkable results. Taking expressways as an example, the vehicle-road-cloud integration technology coordinates the formation driving of multiple autonomous driving vehicles, which not only reduces air resistance and saves energy but also optimizes the collaborative behavior of vehicle groups and greatly improves traffic efficiency.

Developing Intelligent and Connected Road Infrastructure is an Important Means to Improve Traffic Safety and Efficiency

The real-time interactive collaboration between vehicles and road infrastructure is the core mechanism for ensuring safety. At intersections, roadside sensors real-time collect data such as vehicle speed and driving direction, driving vehicles to automatically adjust speed or stop, effectively avoiding traffic accidents caused by driver blind spots, fatigue driving, etc. In the face of sudden road conditions such as vehicle failures and natural disasters, intelligent infrastructure can quickly respond, sense road anomalies through sensors, and immediately notify the traffic management center and surrounding vehicles, realizing the efficient operation of emergency disposal processes. In May 2024, the Infrastructure Digital Transformation and Upgrading Plan jointly issued by the Ministry of Finance and the Ministry of Transport clearly stated that in the next three years, it will support the construction of 30 demonstration areas, promote the digital transformation of national expressways, national highways, and high-grade waterways, with the goal of increasing the traffic efficiency of demonstration corridors by 20% and the emergency response efficiency of sudden incidents by 30%, and comprehensively building a safe and efficient intelligent transportation system.

Research Scope and Revision Notes

Comprehensively considering the business and technical requirements of intelligent and connected vehicles for intelligent and connected road infrastructure, as well as the road network coverage of intelligent and connected road infrastructure, sort out the technical roadmap architecture, highlight the important position of infrastructure in promoting the development of intelligent and connected vehicles, and point out the significance of developing intelligent and connected road infrastructure.

1. **Highlight key points**

This revision further analyzes the supporting role of intelligent and connected road infrastructure for intelligent and connected vehicles, highlights the important position of intelligent and connected road infrastructure in promoting the development of intelligent and connected vehicles, and points out the significance of developing intelligent and connected road infrastructure.

2. **Comprehensively consider the interaction relationship with intelligent and connected vehicles**

Vehicle-infrastructure integrated autonomous driving covers automated driving stages with different integration levels. A mature integrated autonomous driving system must focus on building an information interaction platform with V2X as the core, based on which any vehicle can be interconnected at any time and any place, so as to achieve the collection and integration of full-space–time dynamic traffic information, and realize the true and effective integration of vehicle and road. This type of solution effectively solves the problems of insufficient perception and weak decision-making control of single-vehicle intelligent autonomous driving by building digital and networked new road infrastructure, expands the road environment perception range of single-vehicle intelligence, fills the traffic space–time information gap of single-vehicle intelligence, builds a real-time interactive, extraction, and fusion road-vehicle information domain, improves the independent operation capability of autonomous driving vehicles, and reduces the landing application threshold of vehicle-road-cloud integrated autonomous driving technology.

3. **Reflect the real situation of the road transportation industry**

According to the industry status, actual technical development situation, and development trend, sort out the key technologies of intelligent and connected road infrastructure in the Intelligent and Connected Vehicle Technology Roadmap 3.0, and set core indicators.

4. **Represent the technical development trend and industry development level**

The technical indicators of intelligent and connected road infrastructure proposed should be able to represent the advanced industry level, that is, within the target time, at least one mainstream enterprise in China can meet the corresponding indicators and have the conditions for mass market launch of products.

Technical Architecture and Key Technology Combing

The Intelligent and Connected Road Infrastructure Technology Roadmap 3.0 adopts a three-in-one technical architecture of transportation sensing, transportation control and guidance, and roadside computing. Transportation sensing includes traffic flow sensing, traffic event sensing, infrastructure status sensing, traffic meteorological environment sensing, and traffic participant sensing; transportation control and guidance include traffic signs and markings, traffic information control, traffic information release, and traffic warnings; roadside computing includes data access, data fusion computing, management and control decision computing, roadside computing power collaboration, etc. (Fig. 4.28).

4.6.2.2 Outlook on Technology Development Trends

Domestic and Foreign Technical Status and Comparison

Foreign Technical Progress

Major developed countries and regions such as Japan, the United States, and Europe have attached great importance to the construction of intelligent highways in recent years and carried out a lot of research and practical work.

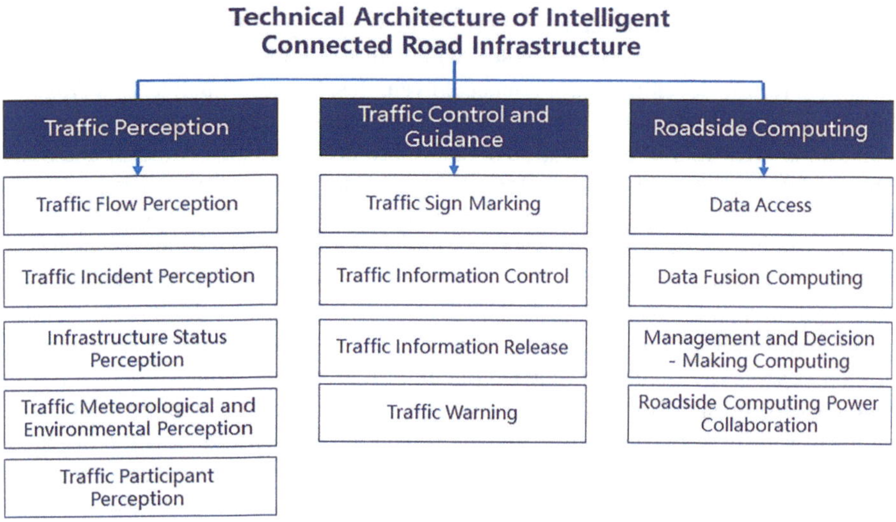

Fig. 4.28 Technical architecture diagram of intelligent and connected road infrastructure

(1) **Japan**

Relying on its mature ETC technology and national networking foundation, Japan has built a Smartway intelligent highway system facing safety, management, and services with vehicle-road interaction technology as the core, entering the ETC 2.0 era. In 2004, Japan launched the Smartway program, which realized interactive services with integrated vehicle terminals with charging, information services, and vehicle-road interaction functions by setting up roadside hotspots (ITS-SPOT) on expressways, and on this basis, carried out an open and shared platform for safety, management, and services. Since October 2014, Japan has started a new service called "ETC2.0". ETC 2.0 is the world's first I2V collaboration system that provides driving support services through high-throughput two-way communication via ITS Spots (antennas) installed beside expressways. The next development focus of Japan's ITS is the research and development of terminal equipment for V2X collaboration systems and market deployment, completing the market-oriented configuration of intelligence level Level 2, and completing the construction of the world's safest roads in 2020, as well as the traffic information open data sharing architecture and application, so as to reduce traffic congestion and provide an operation plan for the 2020 Tokyo Olympics.

(2) **United States**

The United States has carried out highway intelligence in two aspects: one is the construction of Smart Corridor for operation management, and the other is the Connected Vehicle program for vehicle-road cooperation. The main implementation contents of the smart corridor include carrying out Active Traffic Management (ATM) for expressways in regional channels, providing fleet management, vehicle information services, etc. for transport vehicles, which also provides convenient conditions and pilots for the development of connected vehicles. Regions such as Los Angeles, Indianapolis, and Michigan have carried out the construction of smart corridors, such as the 12.3-mile joint operation highway project of the Los Angeles and Santa Monica Expressways, the 35-km-long BRT corridor planned and constructed by Indianapolis to develop autonomous driving technology, and the "Smart Corridor" project established by the Michigan Department of Transportation on Interstates 96 and 696 in Detroit. Connected vehicles use short-range communication technology or other communication technologies to realize vehicle-road and vehicle-vehicle interaction and collaboration, ensure the self-organized efficient and safe driving of vehicles on expressways, and have carried out empirical tests in Ann Arbor, the United States, focusing on demonstrating the safety efficiency of vehicle-vehicle information interaction systems during overtaking, lane changing, and emergency braking in the high-speed operation process of vehicles, as well as the functions of safety auxiliary driving systems in case of line-of-sight blocking, possible rear-end collision, inattention, and other conditions. In 2015, the U.S. Department of Transportation issued the *Intelligent Transportation System Strategic Plan 2015–2019*, which will focus its research on six fields in the next five years: "connected vehicles", "autonomous driving", "emerging functions", "enterprise data", "synergy", and "accelerating industrial expansion". At the same time, it puts forward two strategic priorities of realizing vehicle interconnection and promoting vehicle automation, creating safer vehicles and roads to ease traffic pressure, enhance traffic mobility, protect the environment with the construction of a green intelligent transportation system, comprehensively promote the development and innovation of intelligent transportation technology, and build an advanced vehicle networking system to promote information sharing.

(3) **Europe**

Europe has carried out the Easyway project with the main feature of active traffic management and the Cooperative Intelligent Transportation System (C-ITS) strategy, mainly solving the problems of traffic control, vehicle-road communication, and cross-national collaborative management. The Easyway project takes the information sharing and collaborative dispatching of European transnational expressways as the main goal, and carries out regional traveler information services, active traffic management services, and freight and logistics services. The main goals of EasyWay are to improve safety, reduce congestion, reduce pollution, and promote the continuity of regional and European ITS services. The purpose of the EU C-ITS project is to establish a competitive and resource-effective transportation system. The three countries of the Netherlands, Germany, and Austria have proposed a cooperative ITS corridor project for the C-ITS strategy, aiming to carry out safety early warning demonstrations for driving based on V2X and provide international cooperation and applications for vehicle-road cooperative ITS. In 2019, cooperative intelligent transportation systems were large-scale configured on the roads of EU countries to realize the "intelligent communication" between vehicles and between vehicles and road facilities.

Domestic Technical Progress

(1) **Increasing policy support**

At the national level, a series of policies have been issued to promote the development of intelligent and connected vehicles. For example, in January 2024, seven departments issued the *Implementation Opinions on Promoting the Innovative Development of Future Industries*, proposing to break through super terminals such as high-level intelligent and connected vehicles; in August, the Office of the Ministry of Industry and Information Technology issued a notice to promote the application of mobile Internet of Things in the field of intelligent and connected vehicles; in November, 12 departments issued the *5G Scale Application "Sailing" Action Upgrade Plan* to promote "5G on vehicles"; in December, the two offices issued opinions to promote the collaborative development of smart city infrastructure and intelligent and connected vehicles.

Local governments have also actively responded. Beijing has issued detailed management measures for the access and road operation of intelligent and connected vehicles, clarifying the standards and requirements for using domestic high-precision positioning systems such as Beidou; Shanghai has improved the policy environment for the testing and application of intelligent and connected vehicles and increased the construction of open test roads; Guangzhou plans to support the application of intelligent and connected vehicles in multiple scenarios and participate in the "vehicle-road-cloud integration" application pilot work.

(2) **Gradual improvement of infrastructure construction**

The intelligent transformation of roads has accelerated. According to the data of the Ministry of Industry and Information Technology, the country has cumulatively opened more than 20,000 km of intelligent and connected vehicle test roads, and 17 test demonstration areas, 16 "Double Smart" pilot cities, and 7 national vehicle networking demonstration areas have completed the intelligent upgrading and transformation of more than 7,000 km of roads. Some key cities such as Wuxi have carried out the upgrading and transformation of roadside intelligent facilities for about 700 km of urban roads; Chongqing Yongchuan has carried out intelligent transformation of dozens of intersections and deployed V2X vehicle–road collaboration systems; Wuhan East Lake High-tech Zone will form a full-domain "800+ kilometers" open test road in the next 3 years.

The coverage of communication networks continues to expand. The construction of 5G and LTE-V2X networks continues to advance. It is expected that by 2025, national vehicle networking pilot areas, demonstration areas, and Double Smart pilot cities will basically complete the comprehensive upgrading and transformation of infrastructure at open road intersections in the main urban area and build continuous coverage of 5G and LTE-V2X networks to support the operation and application of C-V2X mass-produced vehicle models. At present, many cities have achieved 5G full coverage and high-precision positioning service full coverage in some areas. For example, the Shenzhen Pingshan open test area has completed the networking infrastructure transformation of roads, and the whole domain has realized the communication foundation of 5G independent networking full coverage.

(3) **Gradual formation of industrial ecology**

Relevant enterprises have gathered for development. A number of intelligent and connected vehicle industrial parks and clusters have been formed in various places. The intelligent and connected vehicle industrial park in Beijing has gathered many high-tech enterprises involving Beidou navigation, vehicle networking, artificial intelligence, and other fields; Suzhou's "Intelligent Driving Avenue" represented by Nantiancheng Road, the main road of Suzhou High-speed Railway New Town, has gathered more than 140 intelligent and connected vehicle enterprises, covering more than 30 subdivided fields.

(4) **Increasingly rich application scenarios**

In terms of urban roads, it has realized the information reminder of vehicle violation handling, municipal road construction, etc., the real-time traffic light status at the front intersection, the real-time information notification of green wave passage, as well as the application of active safety early warning, bus signal priority, etc. In terms of expressways, many expressways such as the Yanchong Expressway and the Chengyi Expressway are carrying out the construction of vehicle networking infrastructure to explore application scenarios such as networking-empowered autonomous driving. In specific areas, such as the Beijing Yizhuang core area, a city-level engineering verification platform has been built to realize the application of scenarios such as intelligent public transportation, autonomous driving taxis, autonomous parking, and expressway trunk logistics; in some closed and semi-closed scenarios in cities, intelligent and connected vehicles such as autonomous driving logistics and cleaning have been deployed.

Development Trends

The Scene Coverage and Perception Accuracy of Intelligent and Connected Transportation Sensing Facilities Continue to Improve

Relying on advanced transportation sensing facilities such as millimeter-wave radar, laser radar, and AI cameras, the sensing capabilities of key information such as road traffic flow, traffic events, and traffic environment have been significantly enhanced. At present, the coverage rate of sensing facilities in the road network of trunk highways in some provinces and cities has reached 60%, and the coverage rates of expressway video monitoring facilities in the eastern, central, and western regions have achieved 100%, 90%, and 80% respectively, building a three-dimensional sensing network. The multi-source fusion sensing technology has made a major breakthrough, with the positioning accuracy reaching 0.2 m and the event recognition accuracy as high as 95%, strongly supporting the landing of innovative functions such as accompanying information services and ultra-line-of-sight sensing, and building a data foundation for intelligent traffic management.

The Response Time and Information Update Frequency of Transportation Control and Guidance Technology Continue to Shorten

At home and abroad, continuous efforts have been made in the field of transportation control and guidance technology. Although there are differences in the development process, both are accelerating innovation around the intelligent direction. Globally, the intelligent transportation management system has become the construction focus. The deep integration of Internet of Things, artificial intelligence, and big data technology has realized the real-time monitoring and analysis of traffic flow and vehicle status, promoting the optimization and upgrading of traffic control. In terms of intelligent traffic light technology, developed countries have widely deployed dynamic regulation systems, and China is also piloting adaptive traffic lights in many places, flexibly adjusting the timing scheme through real-time perception of traffic flow. Transportation navigation and map applications continue to iterate. Foreign platforms such as Google Maps and Waze occupy an advantage with mature real-time traffic update and route planning capabilities, while domestic Baidu Maps and Gaode Maps continue to enhance their competitiveness through the integration of local life services, AR navigation, and other characteristic functions. Intelligent parking systems also receive much attention. Foreign cities have formed a perfect parking space reservation and intelligent guidance system, and China is accelerating the promotion of technologies such as ground magnetic induction and video recognition to improve the utilization efficiency of parking resources.

The Collaborative Perception and Decision-Making Capabilities of Roadside Traffic Computing Continue to Increase

Intelligent and connected road infrastructure reshapes the transportation computing system through the innovation of cloud-edge collaboration architecture. Edge computing focuses on real-time needs and undertakes local processing tasks such as immediate optimization of traffic signals and vehicle collision early warning; cloud computing relies on strong storage and analysis capabilities to tap the deep value of traffic data and provide a scientific basis for urban traffic planning. The multi-sensor data fusion technology continues to break through. The radar-vision fusion scheme complements the advantages of radar's accurate ranging and camera's high-definition imaging, realizing the full-dimensional perception of road targets and effectively improving the target recognition accuracy in complex scenarios. The popularization of 5G networks injects strong power into roadside computing, and the high-bandwidth and low-latency characteristics ensure the real-time interaction of massive vehicle-road data. The intelligent decision-making system based on deep learning algorithms can real-time predict traffic flow changes, assess accident risks, and automatically optimize traffic light timing and issue precise guidance commands. In the field of autonomous driving, the deep collaboration between the roadside computing system and vehicles provides autonomous driving vehicles with rich environmental perception information, helping them cope with complex scenarios such as extreme weather and road construction, and accelerating the autonomous driving technology towards the new stage of full automation.

4.6.2.3 Development Goals and Milestones for 2040

Development Vision

In the next 15 years, new generation information technologies such as artificial intelligence, cloud computing, and big data will be deeply integrated with road infrastructure, and intelligent and connected road infrastructure will develop rapidly. The coverage of intelligent intersections in urban roads and intelligent highways will continue to increase, which can empower the development needs of intelligent and connected vehicles and support the landing application of high-level autonomous driving in the transportation industry.

(1) Transportation sensing technologies and products are more mature, and the sensing accuracy continues to improve to meet the needs of high-level autonomous driving development;
(2) The information update frequency and traffic response time of transportation control and guidance continue to shorten to meet the needs of high-level autonomous driving development;
(3) The roadside computing capability continues to improve, and the collaborative perception target accuracy, event perception accuracy, and collaborative decision-making accuracy meet the needs of high-level autonomous driving development.

Goals and Milestones

By 2040, the intelligence of intelligent and connected road infrastructure will fully meet the functions of networked collaborative decision-making and control, and the intelligence level of intelligent and connected road infrastructure will reach the highest level. It is specifically divided into three stages: 2030, 2035, and 2040.

Short-Term Goals and Key Tasks (2026–2030)

By 2030, the coverage rate of intelligent intersections in key cities such as first and second-tier cities across the country will reach 90%, and intelligent expressways will cover 20% of the expressways across the country. The traffic flow recognition accuracy is ≥95%, the traffic event type recognition accuracy is ≥95%, the fusion sensing target position accuracy is ≤50 cm, the roadside collaborative decision-making accuracy is ≥95%, and the real-time decision-making time is ≤100 ms.

Medium-Term Goals and Key Tasks (2031–2035)

By 2035, the coverage rate of smart road intersections in key cities such as first-tier, second-tier, and third-tier cities across the country will reach 90%, and smart expressways will cover 50% of the nation's expressways. The accuracy rate of traffic flow identification will be ≥97%, the accuracy rate of traffic incident type identification will be ≥97%, the accuracy of fused perception targets will be ≤20 cm, the correctness rate of roadside cooperative decision-making will be ≥99%, and the real-time decision-making time will be ≤50 ms.

Long-Term Goals and Key Tasks (2036–2040)

By 2040, the coverage rate of intelligent intersections in cities at or above the county level across the country will reach 100%, and intelligent expressways will cover 70% of the expressways across the country. The traffic flow recognition accuracy is ≥99%, the traffic event type recognition accuracy is ≥99%, the fusion sensing target accuracy is ≤20 cm, the roadside collaborative decision-making accuracy is ≥99%, and the real-time decision-making time is ≤20 ms.

4.6.2.4 Technology Roadmap

Overall Technical Roadmap for the Special Topic

The intelligent and connected road infrastructure specified in this roadmap includes three technical categories: transportation sensing, transportation control and guidance, and roadside computing.

(1) In terms of transportation sensing, focus on the research of traffic flow sensing, traffic event sensing, and traffic environment sensing technologies, and key consider the traffic flow sensing accuracy, traffic event sensing accuracy, traffic environment sensing accuracy, and the coverage of transportation sensing equipment in cities and expressways;
(2) In terms of transportation control and guidance, focus on the research of traffic signal control technology, transportation navigation, and intelligent parking technology, and key consider the intelligence level of traffic signal control technology, the update frequency and accuracy of navigation and map applications, the search success rate and coverage of intelligent parking systems, as well

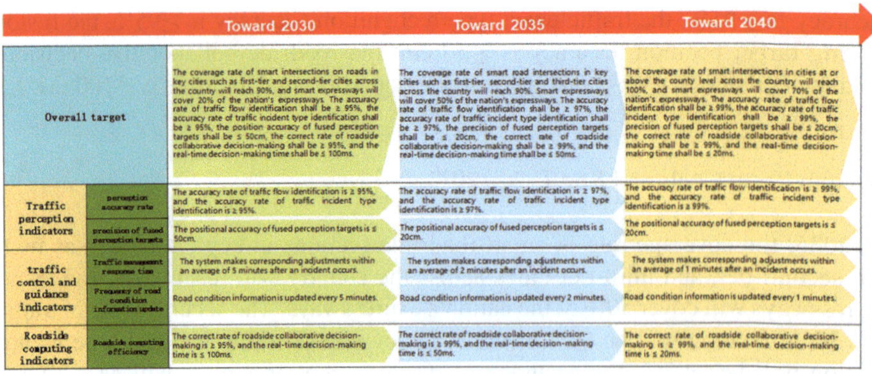

Fig. 4.29 Special topic technical roadmap

as the coverage of transportation control and guidance systems in cities and expressways;

(3) In terms of roadside technology, focus on the research of roadside collaborative perception and roadside collaborative decision-making technologies, and key consider the collaborative perception target accuracy, event perception accuracy, collaborative decision-making accuracy, as well as the coverage of roadside computing equipment in cities and expressways (Fig. 4.29).

Technical Roadmap for Transportation Sensing

At present, the scene coverage and perception accuracy of China's intelligent and connected transportation sensing facilities continue to improve. Relying on transportation sensing facilities such as millimeter-wave radar, laser radar, and AI cameras, it supports the sensing of information such as road traffic flow, traffic events, and traffic time. Some advanced foreign sensors have advantages in ranging accuracy, resolution, and angular resolution, while Chinese sensors, although their performance is continuously improving, still have a certain gap with the top foreign levels in terms of overall accuracy and stability, especially in the performance under some extreme environmental conditions. In terms of cost, some Chinese sensors already have a certain price advantage, such as some domestic millimeter-wave radars and video cameras, which are relatively low in cost and help promote applications in the market. However, in the high-end sensor market, foreign brands still occupy a large share. Foreign countries are relatively leading in the types and innovation of sensors, and can continuously launch new sensor products and technologies to meet the needs of different traffic scenarios. China's innovation capability in sensor research and development is also continuously increasing, but it is relatively lagging in the research and development and application of some new sensors, and needs to increase research and development investment and innovation efforts (Fig. 4.30).

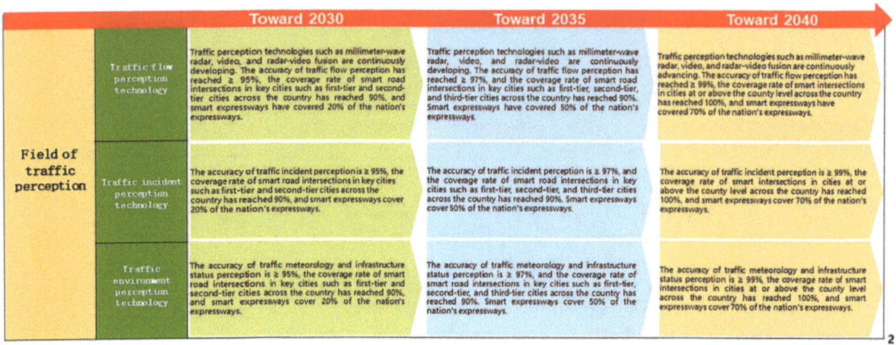

Fig. 4.30 Transportation sensing technical roadmap

Technical Roadmap for Transportation Control and Guidance

At the present stage, the transportation control and guidance technology worldwide is constantly innovating, introducing new technologies such as the Internet of Things, artificial intelligence, and big data, which have improved the intelligence and efficiency of the system. These technologies have been widely applied in many cities, providing intelligent solutions for urban traffic management and travel. Governments in many countries and regions have continuously improved their attention to traffic management, and supported the development of transportation control and guidance technology through policy guidance and capital investment. However, developed countries are relatively leading in the application and maturity of transportation control and guidance technology, while some emerging market countries still have a large gap in the technical application level. At the same time, the traffic data quality and update speed in some regions are relatively low, affecting the actual effect of transportation control and guidance technology. At the same time, the present stage is faced with two bottlenecks. First, there is a problem of insufficient infrastructure construction in some regions, such as the insufficient coverage of monitoring equipment such as sensors and cameras, which affects the collection and analysis of traffic data. Second, there are differences in technical standards and interoperability between different manufacturers and systems, which limits the information sharing and interaction between different systems. This reveals two shortcomings at the present stage, that is, with the popularization of transportation control and guidance technology, information security and personal privacy protection have become important issues, which need to strengthen relevant technologies and policy guarantees. In addition, the user experience and satisfaction of some transportation control and guidance technologies still have room for improvement, and need to be closer to user needs and provide more convenient and practical services. To sum up, the transportation control and guidance technology is constantly progressing worldwide, but it still faces some challenges and problems. In the future, it is necessary to further strengthen technological innovation, policy support, and international cooperation, and jointly promote

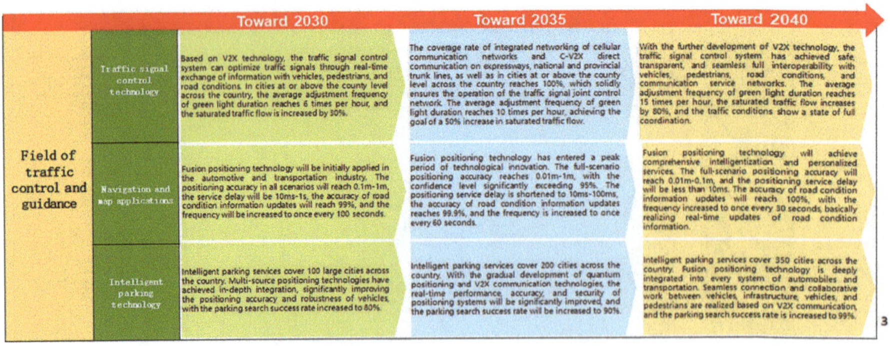

Fig. 4.31 Technical roadmap for transportation control and guidance

the continuous development of transportation control and guidance technology to improve the level of urban traffic management and travel experience (Fig. 4.31).

Technical Roadmap for Roadside Computing

Developed countries such as Europe and the United States started early in vehicle-road-cloud collaboration and roadside computing technology, with 30 years of practical experience. In the early stage, the government took the lead in providing legal protection and policy support, and in the past decade, enterprises have gradually become the dominant, comprehensively increasing investment, and having a certain accumulation in the depth and breadth of technical research and development. For example, some technology giants and automobile enterprises in the United States have long invested a lot of funds in the research and development of roadside computing-related technologies, and are in a leading position in basic theoretical research, key technological innovation, and other aspects. China attaches great importance to the development of intelligent transportation, including roadside computing technology, and has issued a series of policies to promote the development of this field. Enterprises have also actively responded, and the investment in technological research and development has continued to increase. Some domestic enterprises such as Mushroom Car Union and Black Sesame Intelligence have achieved outstanding results in roadside computing technology, with self-developed roadside edge computing systems and high-computing power chips, etc., but overall, there is still a certain gap with foreign countries in the stability and continuity of research and development investment, and the research and development of some underlying technologies and key components still need to be strengthened (Fig. 4.32).

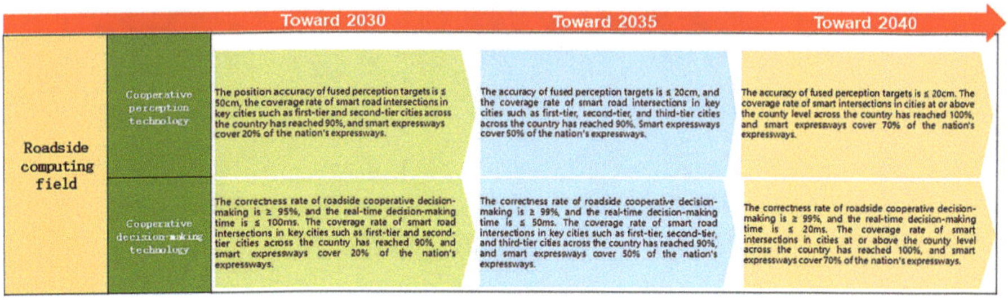

Fig. 4.32 Technical roadmap for roadside computing

Chapter 5
Common Supporting Technology

5.1 Intelligent Chassis

5.1.1 Domestic and International Technical Status Comparison

Amid the electrification and intelligent transition of vehicles, conventional chassis has undergone technological changes and advanced to electric chassis, and intelligent chassis. Intelligent chassis is a platform that encompasses the autonomous driving system, cockpit system, and powertrain system. It is a new topological structure comprised of electric drive, power battery, and X-by-wire systems. It is able to perceive, predict, and control the interaction between wheels and the ground, manage its own operation, and complete intelligent driving tasks. Intelligent chassis serves as the foundation for the actualization of autonomous driving. The combination of intelligent chassis and autonomous driving is critical to sustaining our first-mover advantage in vehicle electrification. While facilitating the safe, reliable driving, energy saving and carbon reduction of intelligent vehicles, intelligent chassis also fuels the electrification and intelligent transformation of the automobile industry as well as cross-over technological innovation. It has now emerged as a strategic growth sector and competitive focus for intelligent vehicle technologies following sensing and decision-making.

5.1.1.1 Intelligent Chassis Makes Initial Progress—Chassis Fusion Control

Since 2020, Chinese automobile manufacturers have stepped up their efforts in the electrical/electronic architecture (E/E architecture), resulting in its greater integration and fusion. In particular, the integration of powertrain and chassis domain controllers

Technology Roadmap for Energy Saving and New Energy Vehicles 3.0,
https://doi.org/10.1007/978-981-95-2502-7_5

has become an industry consensus. In the new generation E/E architecture driven by the central computing unit, the powertrain-chassis domain controller will play a crucial role.

International companies such as Bosch, Continental and ZF have developed mature solutions for E/E architecture. ZF's vehicle motion control system gathers sensor information from the entire vehicle and environment, and prepares it for an optimized, integrated control of active systems in the chassis, steering, braking and propulsion. Bosch's newly introduced Vehicle Dynamics Management allows for collaborative control of braking, rear wheel steering, powertrain and other systems in specific conditions using the feedforward control algorithm of vehicle dynamics modeling. It has also developed integrated brakeslip control, integrated traction control, integrated vehicle dynamics control and other functions to optimize the vehicle's performance.

In China, the intelligent chassis is making rapid progress in the fusion control of powertrain chassis domains. BYD's DiSus Intelligent Body Control System (DiSus System) is a vertically integrated holistic control solution. Its revolutionary binocular camera preview technology employs stereoscopic matching and computation to precisely portray the 3D properties and elevation of the road surface, addressing monocular vision's inability to detect non-standard objects. Huawei has combined the high control precision and rapid reaction of E drive motors with brake systems to enable comprehensive motion controls including traction control, braking pitch angle control, emergency obstacle avoidance, smart parking, drifting and turning around. NIO's full-stack proprietary intelligent chassis controller, launched in June 2022, integrates more than 100 controllers of the core components of the traditional chassis, including suspension, shock absorber and EBP, into a single domain controller at the perception and decision-making levels, and performs intelligent allocation and control through software algorithms.

5.1.1.2 Integrated Chassis and Distributed Drive System Begins Mass Production

The Cell to Chassis (CTC) technology has advanced from conception to mass production, and the multi-motor distributed drive system undergoes accelerated industrialization. China's CTC technology is comparable to that of other nations. Distributed drive becomes a widely recognized idea for both passenger vehicles and commercial vehicles. A variety of configurations have been developed to foster innovation in chassis topology. One key area of future research for new energy vehicles is highly integrated distributed multi-motor drive. Despite their increasing usage in urban buses and passenger vehicles, wheel hub motor and its control system require better integration both in China and overseas. Reliability, durability, electromagnetic compatibility, and environmental adaptability still need to be improved in order to reach mass manufacturing (Fig. 5.1).

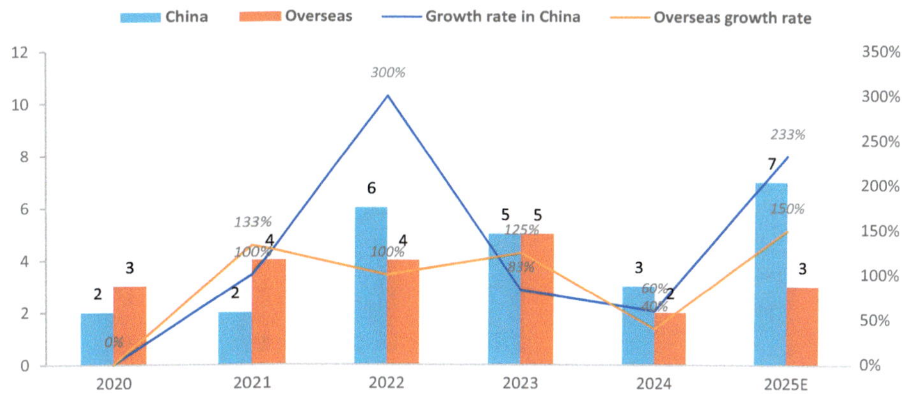

Fig. 5.1 Application of distributed drive technology to passenger vehicles at home and abroad

5.1.1.3 Chassis-by-Wire Takes Shape

With the progress of E/E architecture, sensors and in-vehicle networks, electronic chassis control has developed rapidly. As new all-by-wire electric drive gradually replaces mechanical/hydraulic control and centralized drive, all-electronic chassis control is gaining momentum. To meet the demands of intelligent driving, actuators are progressing towards intra-system functional redundancy, hardware heterogeneous redundancy, and inter-system heterogeneous redundancy. In addition, the kingpin technology suitable for highly integrated new drive units has also emerged as a research hotspot and is anticipated to redefine chassis configuration in the future.

In terms of industrialization, the installation rate of brake-by-wire systems in new energy vehicles is steadily rising in China, and indigenous EHB has achieved mass production and widespread use. Electric power steering has emerged as the mainstream configuration of passenger vehicles. China's EMB and steer-by-wire, which are approaching mass production, are developing in tandem with foreign countries. Semi-active suspension is undergoing faster localization, with a gradual decrease in costs. Also, it is more widely used in entry-level luxury models (Fig. 5.2).

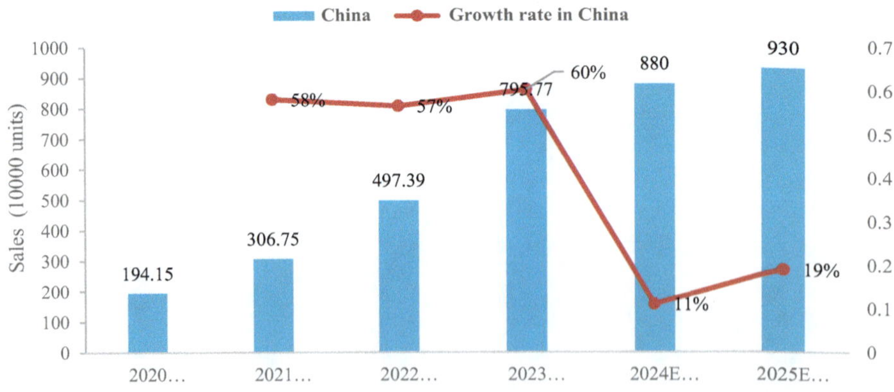

Fig. 5.2 EHB (Brake-by-Wire) market in China

5.1.1.4 Digitalized and intelligentized chassis testing technology is in the early application stage

Since 2020, with intensified domestic automotive market competition and higher consumer quality requirements, the market demand for chassis testing technology has gradually increased. Driver-in-the-loop testing platforms can significantly shorten development cycles and reduce risks. At the same time, vehicle-road-cloud testing and evaluation methods have become research hotspots. Automotive manufacturers and research institutions have increased investment in chassis testing equipment to enhance testing accuracy and efficiency, ensuring product quality and competitiveness. With the rapid development of new energy vehicles and intelligent driving technologies, the demand for chassis testing technology has further increased. OEMs need to more comprehensively and accurately test chassis performance to ensure vehicle safety and stability in various complex scenarios.

5.1.2 Outlook on Technology Development Trends

More flexible forms and more diverse functions to meet more demands. With the rapid development of intelligent driving and electrification technologies, the intelligent chassis is expected to have more flexible forms and functionalities. Functional modules like powertrain, braking, steering, and suspension may be combined into different new drive units. Coupled with the new generation chassis control technology, multi-wheel chassis—such as three-wheel/four-wheel chassis—or irregularly-shaped chassis will become possible, giving birth to custom-made intelligent chassis with unique features.

The chassis components are undergoing comprehensive by-wire, high-voltage, and intelligent transformation. At present, the fully decoupled hydraulic brake-by-wire system has reached mass production and been applied to mid-to-high-end models. Meanwhile, the distributed electromechanical braking system (EMB) is experiencing rapid development. Laterally, the steer-by-wire system that completely eliminates mechanical connections has been produced in mass quantities. Vertically, different types of semi-active suspensions remain the mainstream. The electro-hydraulic split slow-active suspension with a frequency range below 5 Hz has been mass-produced. The present industrial hotspot is full active suspensions with a wide frequency range, such as electro-hydraulic centralized suspensions, electromechanical suspensions, and linear motor suspensions, which are currently in the advanced research stage. The new generation intelligent tire technology allows for both real-time wheel monitoring and, accurate feedback of road conditions through the integration of internal sensors, wireless communication and intelligent chips. This addresses the inefficient sensing of traditional tires and enhances vehicle safety, stability, and comfort while offering a fresh approach to the development of intelligent chassis components. Furthermore, in response to the ongoing rise in the voltage of vehicle electrical platforms, the low-voltage power supply system is shifting toward high-voltage alternatives, represented by the 48 V electrical system.

Multi-level, cross-system domain control integration of powertrain, chassis, cockpit and intelligent driving. With the increasing complexity of varied domain control systems of intelligent vehicles, efficient domain control fusion across levels and systems helps overcome single module limitations and resolve conflicts. This is important for maximizing the potential of available components and improving the comprehensive performance of vehicles. First, vehicle dynamics fusion control is transitioning from one-dimensional fusion (such as coordinated regenerative braking by drive motors and hydraulic brakes), two-dimensional fusion (such as active control for yaw stability by torque vector control and electric power steering) to three-dimensional fusion (motion posture control that fuses drive motors, active steering and semi-active suspension). As the operation zones of the powertrain domain and the chassis domain gradually overlap and merge into one, concurrent collaborative control of actuators will be enabled, and a partial function reuse and redundant safety mechanism will be established to achieve high-level domain control fusion, further improving the driving performance of intelligent vehicles. Second, the cross-system domain control fusion of intelligent driving and intelligent cockpit is also gaining traction. The "cockpit-driving integration" and end-to-end technology are under intensive development and getting close to mass production. This will further reshape the technical route and industrial ecosystem of the cross-system integration between the intelligent chassis and other domains, which will undoubtedly become a major priority for the ecological integration of intellige, electric vehicles.

Intelligent chassis simulation and virtual testing powered by large AI models. Intelligent chassis simulation: The deep learning and reinforcement learning algorithms based on large AI models keep improving simulation accuracy and R&D efficiency. In addition, the scenario generation capacity of large AI models provides a rich set of test environments as well as traffic participants and their simulated behavior patterns for the fusion control of intelligent chassis and autonomous driving. It helps test the implementation of intelligent chassis and how it works with autonomous driving in various settings. Virtual testing of intelligent chassis: Large AI models may be employed for the end-to-end testing of intelligent vehicles from perception to decision-making and execution control, and the comprehensive evaluation of the performance and safety of intelligent chassis and even intelligent vehicles. Furthermore, the cost of testing may be greatly decreased by using virtual testing, which does not need real vehicles or chassis systems. In addition, by anticipating and modeling possible safety threats and failure modes, large AI models may also detect and solve problems in advance, preventing severe safety issues during actual testing.

5.1.3 Development Goals and Milestones for 2040

The concerted development between intelligent chassis and comprehensive electric, autonomous driving is expected to build a foundational platform for new energy vehicles in the intelligent era, reshape the definition paradigm and development methodology of the vehicle platform architecture, and contribute to the vision of low-carbon, efficient and zero casualty mobility.

5.1.3.1 Goals and Milestones

The vehicle chassis is advancing rapidly in electrification, intelligence integration, and motion stereoscopic. The overall goals by 2040,the intelligent chassis technology cluster has been revolutionized, deeply integrated with autonomous driving, achieved full functional unit servitization, and supports unmanned driving in multi—dimensional space. The scale of applying intelligent chassis to passenger and commercial vehicles keeps increasing. The R&D and testing system for intelligent chassis has achieved deep—seated intelligence. Advanced technologies like AI—driven chassis simulation and virtual testing are adopted. They help build new intelligent chassis toolchains in various aspects, including simulation scenario creation, complex dynamics parameter simulation, and data—in—the—loop processes.

5.1.3.2 Short-Term Goals and Priorities (2026–2030)

By 2030, 30% of passenger cars (EMB, steer-by-wire, active suspension) and 60% of commercial vehicles will have intelligent chassis installed. Goals related to key technological innovations: Overcoming technical challenges in the longitudinally, laterally, and vertically integrated, collaborative control and configuration innovation of intelligent chassis based on the deep fusion control of wire-controlled actuators and electric drive systems; the accuracy of vehicle condition estimation ≥90%; improvement in the key performance of intelligent chassis; the driving speed in moose test ≥85 km/h (typical B-segment passenger vehicles); the maximum deceleration capacity of drive motors in braking ≥0.8 g; key systems at ASIL D in all scenarios; the cross-system redundancy switching time $\leq$100 ms; high-precision and high-dynamic simulation by chassis driving simulators in all scenarios; support the L4 driving automation; and the initial establishment of a lifecycle industrial technological innovation system for intelligent chassis spanning R&D, testing and production.

5.1.3.3 Medium-Term Goals and Priorities (2031–2035)

By 2035, 60% of passenger cars (EMB, steer-by-wire, active suspension) and 70% of commercial vehicles will have intelligent chassis installed, and new forms of products will be developed through innovation and evolution. Goals pertaining to technological innovations: New drive units with powertrain, braking, steering and suspension offering a maximum speed of $\geq$150 km/h; the multi-level, cross-system domain control fusion of powertrain, chassis, cockpit and intelligent driving; the maximum deceleration capacity of drive motors in braking $\geq$1.0 g; continuously promoting the deep integration as well as coordinated control of intelligent chassis and autonomous system through the electrical architecture and the multi-domain sharing and fusion of sensing parameters and state parameters; the accuracy of vehicle condition estimation $\geq$95%; the driving speed in moose test $\geq$90 km/h (typical B-segment passenger vehicles); key systems at ASIL D in all scenarios; the cross-system redundancy switching time $\leq$80 ms; cybersecurity assurance level of CAL4, in a bid to provide users with a safer, smarter, more comfortable and convenient driving experience; support the L5 driving automation; and the establishment of a lifecycle industrial technological innovation system for intelligent chassis spanning R&D, testing and production.

5.1.3.4 Long-Term Goals and Priorities (2036–2040)

By 2040, 80% of passenger cars (EMB, steer-by-wire, active suspension) and commercial vehicles will have intelligent chassis installed, and the development scale of intelligent chassis will continue expanding. The intelligent chassis will be reconfigurable, modular and self-evolutionary to suit the new generation E/E architecture, and it will have fully service-oriented functional units. To facilitate the future integration with the three-dimensional transportation industry, a new chassis configuration supporting three-dimensional transportation and unmanned driving in multi-dimensional space will be developed. The intelligent vehicle simulation and virtual testing technology powered by AI models will be applied to help build a new R&D toolchain in all stages of simulation scene construction, complex dynamic parameter simulation and closed-loop measurement in the field of intelligent chassis, and ensure the comprehensive safety of intelligent chassis in all scenarios.

5.1.4 *Technology Roadmap*

This section outlines roadmaps for passenger vehicles and commercial vehicles, the common sub-areas include chassis system technology, component technology and control technology. The chassis system technology primarily involves the mechanical architecture, the E/E architecture, comprehensive security and the generic support technology for testing; the chassis component technology includes the new drive unit, the braking system, the steering system and the suspension system; and the chassis control technology consists of longitudinal, lateral and vertical fusion control, fail-safe redundancy control and chassis health management technology (Fig. 5.3).

5.1.4.1 Intelligent Chassis for Passenger Vehicles

This roadmap specifies the intelligent chassis for passenger vehicles, including chassis system technology, chassis component technology and chassis control technology.

At the level of mechanical architecture, the focus is on the topological configuration of new drive units with high-level integration of powertrain, braking, steering, and suspension at the wheel side, and overcoming challenges in multi-domain integration design such as "quality-topology-synergy" and "heat resistance-compactness-durability." In terms of the E/E architecture, priorities include ensuring the high bandwidth, low latency communication and real-time control of the chassis network, promoting the standardization of communication protocols and interfaces

		2030	2035	2040
Intelligent Chassis		• Comprehensive breakthroughs in critical technologies and functionalities of intelligent chassis; • Representative product: Distributed intelligent chassis with integrated drive and brake; • 30% assembly rate of intelligent chassis (EMB, steer-by-wire, active suspension) in passenger vehicles, and 60% assembly rate of intelligent chassis in commercial vehicles; • Longitudinal, horizontal and vertical coordinated control, significant enhancement the key performance of the intelligent chassis ; • Integration the intelligent chassis and autonomous vehicle industries to support level 4 autonomous ; • Establishment technology innovation system for the intelligent chassis R&D ,testing to production .	• Development of intelligent chassis products in new forms, and substantial upgrade of the intelligent chassis innovation technology cluster; • Representative product: Distributed intelligent chassis based on new drive units; • 60% assembly rate of intelligent chassis (EMB, steer-by-wire, active suspension) in passenger vehicles, and 70% assembly rate of intelligent chassis in commercial vehicles; • Mass production of new drive units with powertrain, braking, steering and suspension; • Integration the intelligent chassis and autonomous vehicle industries to support level 5 autonomous ; • Establishment a comprehensive technology innovation system for the intelligent chassis R&D , testing to production .	• Significant transition of intelligent chassis towards new modes of unmanned driving and air-ground coordinated operation; • Representative product: Split, reconfigurable intelligent chassis; • 80% assembly rate of intelligent chassis (EMB, steer-by-wire, active suspension) in passenger vehicles, and 80% assembly rate of intelligent chassis in commercial vehicles; • Deep fusion of intelligent chassis and autonomous driving, and fully service-oriented functional units; • New chassis configurations that support three-dimensional transportation. • Establish a new R&D toolchain for intelligent chassis based on digital twins and AI.
General Goals on Intelligent Chassis for Passenger Vehicles		• Mass production and application of distributed intelligent chassis with integrated drive and brake design. • 30% assembly rate of intelligent chassis (EMB, steer-by-wire, active suspension) in passenger vehicles; • Longitudinal, horizontal and vertical coordinated control, accuracy of vehicle condition estimation ≥ 90%, and driving speed in moose test ≥ 85km/h (typical segment-B passenger vehicles); • Maximum deceleration capacity of e-motors in braking is ≥ 0.8g; • Driving automation supported: L4.	• Intelligent chassis for passenger vehicles emerging new forms ; • Mass production and application of distributed intelligent chassis with integrated drive and brake design. • 60% assembly rate of intelligent chassis (EMB, steer-by-wire, active suspension) in passenger vehicles; • Information security protection system has been fully implemented; • Longitudinal, horizontal and vertical coordinated control, accuracy of vehicle condition estimation ≥ 95%, and driving speed in moose test ≥ 90km/h (typical segment-B passenger vehicles); • Maximum deceleration capacity of e-motors in braking is ≥ 1.0g; • Driving automation supported: L5.	• New chassis configurations that support three-dimensional transportation; • 80% assembly rate of intelligent chassis (EMB, steer-by-wire, active suspension) in passenger vehicles; • Deep fusion of intelligent chassis and autonomous driving, and fully service-oriented functional units; • Driving automation supported: L5; • Possessing stereoscopic maneuverability and are in mass production.
General Goals on Intelligent Chassis for Commercial Vehicles		• Preliminary promotion of modular and platform-based hardware design and application; • Application of X-by-wire systems: 100%, and penetration rate of chassis domain controllers: 50%; • Further improvement in collaborative development procedures for vehicle functional safety; • Integrated electric drive axle, EMB and SBW are applied on a large scale; semi - active suspension has achieved mass production. • Driving automation supported: L4.	• Share of modular and platform-based production and assembly: 70%; • Penetration rate of chassis domain controllers: 70%; • Improvement in collaborative development procedures for vehicle functional safety, and gradual improvement in design procedures for safety of the intended functionality and information security ; • Integrated development and comprehensive control of distributed in - wheel motor drive systems with electronic braking and suspension systems have been achieved; • Driving automation supported: L5.	• Share of modular and platform-based production and assembly: over 90%; • Penetration rate of centralized chassis domain controllers: over 90%; • Gradual improvement in the self-diagnosis, self-evolutionary and self-learning capabilities of chassis, and greatly enhanced safety; • Mass production of new drive units with powertrain, braking, steering and suspension; • Driving automation supported: L5.
Critical Technologies	Integration	• Integrated design and manufacturing technology for high-level integration of powertrain, battery cells and chassis • Chassis Lightweight	• Integrated design technology for new chassis drive units of powertrain/braking/steering/suspension • Intelligent wheel.	• Self-reconfigurable chassis integration technology .
	Component	• Key Technologies of Distributed Drive, EMB and Composite Brake-by-Wire Systems, Steer-by-Wire and Multi-Mode Steering Systems, High-Performance Active Suspension.	• Integrated design technology for new chassis drive units of powertrain/braking/steering/suspension • Intelligent wheel.	• Standardized and reconfigurable intelligent driving units..
	Safety	• Intelligent chassis functional safety and cross-system redundancy technologies.	• Intelligent chassis functional safety and information security protection system.	• All new motion safety ,functional safety and information security protection system.
	Control	• Multi-source information fusion-based chassis state estimation • Integrated intelligent chassis control with coordinated control across longitudinal, lateral, and vertical dynamics.	• Fusion control technology for intelligent chassis and autonomous driving systems.	• Three-dimensional maneuvering technology and spatial stability system based on a split-type reconfigurable intelligent chassis.
	Testing	• High-precision chassis dynamometers and high-performance driving simulators technologies.	• High-fidelity simulation technology for realistic driving experience.	• Virtual testing and simulation of intelligent chassis systems enabled by foundation model AI technologies.

Fig. 5.3 Overall technology roadmap of intelligent chassis

of electrical architectures from different OEMs, conducting the integration design of 12 V/48 V/high-voltage heterogeneous power supply systems and developing energy management systems, and incubating an industry chain ecosystem for high-voltage actuators and critical chips. Concerning comprehensive security, efforts should concentrate on completing the system architecture design of cross-system redundancy control schemes for intelligent chassis and improving the diagnosis, fault-tolerant control and fault prediction of complicated systems; and standards for the safety of the intended functionality, information security, software upgrade safety will be gradually promoted and applied in the intelligent chassis segment. With regard to testing technology, it is necessary to apply high-fidelity driving simulators, employ high-order and high-complexity controlled object models, apply large models to scene generation and automatic calibration of electronic control system parameters, and implement multi-system and multi-function collaborative simulation and automated testing technologies involving chassis and autonomous driving.

At components level, focuses include addressing the high-level integration of distributed wheel-side/hub drive, braking, steering and suspension, making breakthroughs in the deep integration of hub motors and brake systems within the effective space of the wheel rim and thermal management technology. It is necessary to optimize EMB clamping force control and vehicle integrated control technology; improve the stability, reliability, durability and cost control of steer-by-wire systems and optimize their failure-safe and core algorithms, as well as fault diagnosis and fault-tolerant control algorithms; and develop technical products for fully active suspensions, such as active shock absorbers, high-voltage four-quadrant electrohydraulic pumps, and wire-controlled actuators of motors, including full-link control algorithms, develop energy recovery functions, and improve the dynamic performance, stability and energy-saving features of products.

In response to software-defined vehicles and new centralized control architectures, the role of electric drive systems in longitudinal and lateral chassis motion control is becoming increasingly significant during the process of functional domain integration. By fully leveraging the advantages of electric motors—including fast response time, wide adjustment frequency range, high torque control precision, and distributed architecture—it is possible to optimize longitudinal force distribution across all four wheels, implement multi-level cross-system redundancy for braking and steering functions, and achieve deep integration of longitudinal and lateral control functions across all driving scenarios. Looking ahead, to support the rigorous path toward end-to-end control for intelligent driving, chassis subsystems must adopt an architecture that enables upward integration into the central domain controller. This architecture should support cross-domain functional integration, accurately interpret the driver's true intent, and seamlessly interact with autonomous driving systems to execute motion control. Additionally, it must ensure functional redundancy and backup between human driving, intelligent driving, and the chassis domain under various failure conditions, enabling cooperative control between human and machine (Fig. 5.4).

		2030	2035	2040
General Goals on Intelligent Chassis for Passenger Vehicles		Widespread application of highly integrated chassis; Further improvement in standards for functional safety and safety of the intended functionality; Functional safety at ASIL D in all scenarios; Realize comprehensive, high-fidelity dynamic simulation for chassis driving simulators across diverse driving scenarios; Mass production of EMB\SBW and semi-active suspension; Maximum deceleration delivered by regenerative braking (motor braking): 0.8g; Mass production of longitudinal, lateral and vertical fusion control, and globally leading key technical indicators; Application of collaborative control of chassis and intelligent driving, covering the entire working area of tires; Vehicle-cloud health management technology equipped with components.	Mass production and application of new chassis architectures with high-level integration of distributed wheel-side drive + EMB + wheel-side steering + active suspension + next-generation battery + lower body; Perfection of standards for functional safety and safety of the intended functionality, and the comprehensive implementation of an information security protection system; Highly integrated driving-braking-steering-suspension unit with a maximum vehicle speed ≥150 km/h. Mass production of fast active suspension; Maximum deceleration delivered by regenerative braking (motor braking):1.0g; Mass production of self-learning, self-adaptive and self-calibration chassis fusion control; Mass production of chassis and intelligent driving fusion control; Cloud health prediction and management based on digital twins.	New chassis configurations that support three-dimensional transportation; Comprehensive security of intelligent chassis in all scenarios; New chassis configurations that support three-dimensional transportation; Chassis dynamics control embedded in end-to-end automatic driving to ensure safety; Mass production of three-dimensional maneuverability; Autonomous, maintenance-free health management.
Key technologies of System Integration Sub-area	Mechanical Architecture	CTC packing rate ≥ 80%; Body torsional rigidity: 45,000Nm (typical B-segment vehicles).	Emergence of integration technology for distributed, embedded next-generation batteries; Body torsional rigidity: 50,000Nm (typical B-segment vehicles).	Mass production and application of upper-lower separated chassis architectures; Wide use of integration technology for distributed, embedded next-generation batteries; Body torsional rigidity: 55,000Nm (typical B-segment vehicles).
	E/E Architecture	Communication delay of high-reliability in-vehicle networks ≤ 10ms; Maximum data transmission rate of chassis controllers ≥ 100Mbps; Cross-system redundancy switching time ≤ 100ms; Preliminary application of 48V low-voltage power supply configuration for electronic chassis actuators, and emergence of high-voltage actuators.	Communication delay of high-reliability in-vehicle networks ≤ 5ms; Maximum data transmission rate of chassis controllers ≥ 1,000Mbps; Cross-system redundancy switching time ≤ 80ms; Wide application of 48V low-voltage power supply configuration for electronic chassis actuators, and preliminary application of high-voltage actuators.	Communication delay of high-reliability in-vehicle networks ≤ 2ms; Cross-system redundancy switching time ≤ 50ms; Maximum data transmission rate of chassis controllers ≥ 1,000Mbps; Wide use of 48V low-voltage and high-voltage power supply configurations for electronic chassis actuators.
	Comprehensive Security	Technical maturity and comprehensive promotion of normal-fault-failure operation switching control solutions; Troubleshooting accuracy ≥ 80%; Troubleshooting latency ≤ 80ms; Functional safety at ASIL D in all scenarios; Information security level of CAL3.	Troubleshooting accuracy ≥ 90%; Troubleshooting latency ≤ 30ms; Functional safety at ASIL D in all scenarios; Information security level of CAL4.	Troubleshooting accuracy ≥ 95%; Troubleshooting latency ≤ 10ms; Functional safety at ASIL D in all scenarios; Information security level of CAL4.
	Testing Technology	Further improvement in testing technologies and equipment for functional safety and safety of the intended functionality; Coverage of scenario types by intelligent chassis simulators: 80%; Accuracy of controlled object models under all working conditions: 90%; Automation rate of test and calibration procedures ≥ 70%.	Technical maturity of testing technologies and equipment for functional safety and safety of the intended functionality; Coverage of scenario types by intelligent chassis simulators: 90%; Accuracy of controlled object models under all working conditions: 95%; Automation rate of test and calibration procedures ≥ 85%.	Technical maturity and comprehensive promotion of testing technologies and equipment for functional safety and safety of the intended functionality; Coverage of scenario types by intelligent chassis simulators: 100%; Accuracy of controlled object models under all working conditions: 97%; Automation rate of test and calibration procedures ≥ 90%.
Key technologies of Components Sub-area	New Drive Unit/Powertrain	Maximum deceleration delivered by regenerative braking (motor braking): 0.8g, and energy recovery efficiency ≥ 80%; Equivalent wheel rotation angle delivered by differential drive ≥ 3°@100 km/h;	Maximum deceleration delivered by regenerative braking (motor braking): 1g, and energy recovery efficiency ≥ 90%; Distributed drive motors allowing for horizontal/longitudinal vehicle stability control; Equivalent wheel rotation angle delivered by differential drive ≥ 5°@100 km/h;	Distributed drive motors allowing for full-scenario braking.
	Brake System	Mass production and application of EMB systems, with an assembly rate of 10%; Response time of hydraulic brake-by-wire systems ≤ 140ms@0-10MPa, and response delay ≤ 90ms; Response time of EMB systems ≤ 120ms@0-maximum braking force Braking force control accuracy of braking-by-wire system: 0.2m/s² Equivalent wheel rotation angle delivered by differential braking ≥ 3°@60km/h;	Mass production and application of EMB systems, with an assembly rate of 20%; Response time of EMB systems ≤ 110ms@0–maximum braking force, and response delay ≤ 50ms; Braking force control accuracy of braking-by-wire system: 0.1m/s² Equivalent wheel rotation angle delivered by differential braking ≥ 5°@60km/h;	Mass production and application of EMB systems, with an assembly rate of 40%; Response time of EMB systems ≤ 80ms@0–maximum braking force, and response delay ≤ 20ms;
	Steering System	Mass production and application of steer-by-wire systems, with an assembly rate of 20%; Error of equivalent wheel rotation angle delivered by steady-state response of steer-by-wire/redundant EPS systems: 0.5°; Takeover response delay of redundant systems ≤ 20ms;	Mass production and application of independent steering; Error of equivalent wheel rotation angle delivered by steady-state response of steer-by-wire/redundant EPS systems: 0.3°; Takeover response delay of redundant systems ≤ 15ms;	Full-scenario application of independent steering; Error of equivalent wheel rotation angle delivered by steady-state response of steer-by-wire/redundant EPS systems: 0.1°; Takeover response delay of redundant systems ≤ 10ms;
	Active Suspension System	Industrialization of all Chinese-produced active suspension systems including CDC, air springs, active stabilizer bars, active suspensions and other categories; Response bandwidth of active suspension ≥ 5Hz; Development of regenerative suspension systems, with energy recovery ≥ 0.15kWh/100km@long wave road surface; Adaptive adjustment of active force, stiffness and damping in combination with road preview and vehicle conditions.	Peak force of active suspension actuators ≥ 10KN; Response time of peak driving force of active suspensions ≤ 100ms, and response bandwidth ≥ 10Hz; Development of regenerative suspension systems, with energy recovery ≥ 0.2kWh/100km@long wave road surface; Central integrated control of active suspension and L5 automated driving.	Peak force of active suspension actuators ≥ 15KN; Response time of peak driving force of active suspensions ≤ 50ms, and response bandwidth ≥ 20Hz; Development of regenerative suspension systems, with energy recovery ≥ 0.25kWh/100km@long wave road surface; All-scenario collaborative control of active suspension and L5 automated driving.
Key technologies of Control Sub-area	Longitudinal, Lateral and Vertical Fusion Control	Accuracy of vehicle state estimation: 90%; Longitudinal, lateral and vertical fusion control: Controllable motion boundary increases by 5% (powertrain, braking, differential drive and steering fusion control) Maximum lateral acceleration of steady static circular driving increases by ≥ 1.05g Maximum speed in high-adhesion, half-load moose test ≥ 85km/h (B-segment vehicles) Maximum wheel slip of static acceleration on ice at full throttle ≤ 20km/h, and basic stability of full throttle/emergency braking on surfaces with split coefficient of friction (reduced frequency of ESC triggering)	Accuracy of vehicle state estimation: 95%; Longitudinal, lateral and vertical fusion control – Controllable motion boundary increases by 10% (redefinition of XYZ three-axis control) Maximum lateral acceleration of steady static circular driving increases by ≥ 1.1g Maximum speed in high-adhesion, half-load moose test ≥ 90km/h (B-segment vehicles) Basic stability of full throttle driving/emergency braking on surfaces with split coefficient of friction (basic replacement of ESC)	Accuracy of vehicle state estimation: 98%; Three-dimensional maneuvering; Establishment of a new stability system in three-dimensional space.
	Fail-safe Redundancy Control	Driving automation supported: L4; Cross-system redundancy switching time ≤ 100ms; Fail-safe control: braking at 0.5g; Degraded steering at 60km/h; Single-point failure diagnosis coverage ≥ 99%; Dual-point failure diagnosis coverage ≥ 90%.	Driving automation supported: L5; Cross-system redundancy switching time ≤ 80ms; Fail-safe control: braking at 1.0g; Steering not degraded; Single-point failure diagnosis coverage ≥ 99.5%; Dual-point failure diagnosis coverage ≥ 95%.	Comprehensive security in three-dimensional space; Single-point failure diagnosis coverage ≥ 99.9%; Dual-point failure diagnosis coverage ≥ 99%.
	Health Management Technology	Coverage of critical system components monitoring ≥ 70%; Tire life and looseness detection; Vehicle-cloud health observation.	Coverage of critical system components monitoring ≥ 80%; Life and performance prediction of critical components Cloud health prediction and management	Coverage of critical system components monitoring ≥ 90%; Vehicle-cloud-X health prediction and management; Maintenance-free.

Fig. 5.4 Technology roadmap of intelligent chassis for passenger vehicles

5.1.4.2 Intelligent Chassis for Commercial Vehicles

The development of intelligent chassis for commercial vehicles differs from that of passenger vehicles, as does the technology roadmap for key chassis components. Technically, commercial vehicle chassis now have a much stronger load—bearing capacity. Their electronically controlled chassis components need further development. The intelligent control and functional integration of chassis systems lag behind those of passenger vehicles. In terms of performance, the focus is on health management, low—energy consumption, and high—energy—storage tech. Regulatory upgrades and the demand for intelligent features have set new requirements for commercial vehicle intelligence. Since it's easier to apply high—level autonomous driving to commercial vehicles in closed or trunk line scenarios, their intelligent chassis development emphasizes development with autonomous driving.

In terms of system integration, the mechanical architecture of commercial vehicles is inherently decoupled between the upper body and chassis, makes it easier to integrate powertrain and chassis. Some foreign models have already applied CTC technology, while its market application in China is still in its infancy. Besides further promotion and verification, the lightweight forward design capability should be developed. In the field of E/E architecture, commercial vehicles in China are in the functional domain integration phase. It is necessary to further accelerate the iteration of the integrated control technology characterized by multi-system collaborative control strategy and hierarchical control architecture, the intelligent chassis integration technology that supports the independent development, iteration and rapid upgrade of the upper and lower vehicle bodies, and the technology for integrating the intelligent chassis with upper application systems such as automatic driving, and the Internet of Vehicles. Regarding development and testing, it is essential to improve the multi-physical-domain design software and toolchain for the intelligent chassis used in commercial vehicles, develop digital twin-based intelligent chassis step by step, accomplish the standardization and normalization of MIL, SIL and HIL simulation test procedures, and expand the coverage of real-world testing conditions for unmanned vehicles.

On the dimension of critical components, EBS and EMB are identified as the principal technical routes for braking systems. In the development of electric power steering systems, it is necessary to explore solutions and development technologies for large-load, high-reliability steering gear assemblies. The requirements on the design of functional safety and safety of the intended functionality for commercial vehicles are similar to those for passenger vehicles, i.e., to further strengthen whole-procedure understanding, and improve fault diagnosis, active fault-tolerant control technology and so on. The development of the suspension system for commercial vehicles differs significantly from that of passenger vehicles. In the Chinese commercial vehicle segment, independent suspension configuration, electronically controlled damper/shock absorber design, semi-active suspension, active suspension and longitudinally, laterally and vertically coordinated vehicle control technology have not produced mature applications. Efforts are required to research on designing multi-cavity air springs/hydraulically interconnected springs and magnetorheological shock absorbers, and develop the high durability, low hysteresis, small ratio of dynamic to static stiffness, and multi-stage variable stiffness technology for air springs and regenerative electronically controlled damper/shock absorber/ independently controllable compression damping technology, to enable the global coordination between the suspension and lateral and longitudinal control.

With regard to the control of intelligent chassis, the key is to study the modeling and computation technology of longitudinally, laterally and vertically integrated, multi-degree-of-freedom vehicle dynamics, improve the accuracy of dynamic and static load estimation, build a high-speed communication network, develop high-computing-power hardware control chips, enable the co-calibration of all actuators in the chassis domain, and develop functions such as vehicle weight estimation based on the integration of powertrain, braking and suspension, as well as steering assistance technology based on the integration of powertrain or braking and steering and body stability control based on the integration of steering or suspension and braking. It is also necessary to improve the energy recovery rate, study the response arbitration between longitudinally, laterally and vertically integrated control systems, and reduce the response time of system redundancy switching—all without compromising safety. Chassis health management is an integral part of the new energy vehicle industry's transition to predictive maintenance and intelligent services. In this regard, efforts should be made to improve the wheel thermodynamics modeling and computation technology, oil status modeling and computation technology, and wear parts lifespan modeling and computation technology, enable wheel looseness monitoring, enhance the precision of chassis oil temperature monitoring and wear parts lifespan prediction, and realize comprehensive chassis health management following unmanned driving (Fig. 5.5).

		2030	2035	2040
General Goals on Intelligent Chassis for Commercial Vehicles		Preliminary promotion of modular and platform-based hardware design and application; Application of X-by-wire systems: 100%, and penetration rate of chassis domain controllers: 50%; Further improvement in collaborative development procedures for vehicle functional safety.	Share of modular and platform-based production and assembly: 70%; Penetration rate of chassis domain controllers: 70%; Improvement in collaborative development procedures for vehicle functional safety, and gradual improvement in design procedures for safety of the intended functionality and information security.	Share of modular and platform-based production and assembly: over 90%; Penetration rate of centralized chassis domain controllers: over 90%; Gradual improvement in the self-diagnosis, self-evolutionary and self-learning capabilities of chassis, and greatly enhanced safety.
		Mass production of EMB,EPS Mass production of semi-active suspension;	Realize the integrated development and coordinated control of distributed in-wheel motor drive systems with brake-by-wire and suspension-by-wire systems.	Mass production new driving-braking-steering-suspension unit
		Improvement in control performance of existing longitudinal, lateral and vertical control systems, and independent R&D of partial motion controllers; Local comprehensive control over longitudinal, lateral and vertical systems for different chassis configurations, preliminary lateral and longitudinal integrated control, expansion of vehicle motion control boundaries, and improvement in vehicle driving safety under extreme conditions; Preliminary lateral and vertical integrated control, and comprehensive improvement in anti-roll and driving comfort. Preliminary integrated control of vehicles and trailers, and improvement in braking safety.	Independent R&D and mass production of core controllers of longitudinal, lateral and vertical control systems, and initial development of precise self-awareness capacity for key state of intelligent chassis; Basic perfection and industrialization of multi-degree-of-freedom dynamic control theory, and further improvement in margin of safety and comfort through multi-axis/vehicle-trailer control and other aspects in combination with self-awareness technology for key state.	Comprehensive R&D and mass production of core controllers of longitudinal, lateral and vertical control systems; intelligent perception and learning capacity for key state variables of chassis and key road traffic information; Joint calibration of all components in the chassis domain. Comprehensive longitudinal, lateral and vertical dynamic control of chassis-by-wire in commercial vehicles; Interaction between chassis domain and intelligent driving domain, and expansion of intelligent chassis functions.
Indicators of System Integration Sub-area	Mechanical Architecture	Customization of differentiated battery pack solutions according to vehicle usage scenarios; Further promotion of distributed drive corner modules in light commercial vehicles, with a share of 30% in light commercial vehicles and 15% in heavy commercial vehicles;	Share of bottom-mounted battery packs in commercial vehicles: 70%; Continuously growing share of distributed drive corner modules integrated with wheel hub motors, EMB, independent steering and active suspension in light commercial vehicles;	Application of skateboard chassis to light and heavy commercial vehicles; Complete popularization of bottom-mounted, charging-swapping integrated, large-module battery packs in trucks; Explosive rise in the assembly rate of by-wire corner modules;
	E/E Architecture	Comprehensive promotion of the three-domain fusion architecture, with maximum data transmission rate of chassis domain controllers ≥ 5Mbps and comprehensive computing power of master controllers ≥ 200Tops; Chassis domain of light commercial vehicles dominated by CAN FD and supplemented by Ethernet, and that of heavy commercial vehicles gradually transitioning to Ethernet; Ethernet communication between chassis domain, intelligent driving domain and cockpit domain.	Batched application of the E/E architecture centered on centralized chassis domain controllers, with maximum data transmission rate of chassis domain controllers ≥ 8Mbps; and comprehensive computing power of master controllers ≥ 220Tops; Ethernet becoming a crucial means of communication between components, with communication delay < 2ms.	Comprehensive promotion of the central computing platform of intelligent chassis, and sharing of intelligent sensing fusion information and resources, with maximum data transmission rate of chassis domain controllers ≥ 10Mbps; and comprehensive computing power of master controllers ≥ 250Tops; High-reliability, low-delay Ethernet communication, with delay < 1ms; Cloud-vehicle interaction and remote control emerging as a new vehicle control method.
	Comprehensive Security	Further improvement in chassis intelligence, health diagnosis of critical components of braking, steering and more, and scenario-based development of basic health management systems; Further improvement in functional safety design procedures for chassis products, and completion of demo certification of design procedures for safety of the intended functionality; Application of information security and software upgrade security to intelligent chassis products.	Components coverage of chassis health diagnosis: 70%, and scenario-based development of advanced health management systems. Completion of functional safety certification of centralized chassis domain controllers; Gradual promotion and application of standards for safety of the intended functionality, information security, and software upgrade security to intelligent chassis.	Components coverage of chassis health diagnosis: over 80%; Comprehensive promotion and application of functional safety, safety of the intended functionality, information security and software upgrade security to intelligent chassis, and higher security level of intelligent chassis.
	Testing Technology	Establishment of comprehensive multi-dimensional dynamic response, integrated simulation test platforms for intelligent chassis, and standardization and normalization of MIL, SIL and HIL simulation test procedures; Comprehensive component and vehicle testing capabilities, and coverage of real-world testing conditions for unmanned vehicles on actual roads or in simulated environments: 5% (the proportion of automated test scenarios on actual roads or in simulated environments).	Establishment of a new all-scenario chassis-in-the-loop test technology system; Vehicle dynamics performance simulation and testing under laboratory conditions; Breakthroughs in technology for reproducing bench-level lateral-longitudinal-vertical coupling dynamic characteristics of chassis; Coverage of real-world testing conditions for unmanned vehicles: 20%.	High-performance, high-fidelity driving simulators based on Digital Twin technology; Comprehensive vehicle testing capabilities, and advanced man-machine experience synchronization capabilities; Coverage of real-world testing conditions for unmanned vehicles: 40%.
Indicators of Components Sub-area	Powertrain System	Integrated development and design, software and hardware integration and comprehensive control of integrated electric drive axle systems together with brake-by-wire systems and suspension-by-wire systems, and functional safety at ASIL D; Maximum deceleration capacity of e-motors in braking is ≥ 0.8g.	Enhanced performance of integrated e-drive axles enables mass production and deployment in intelligent chassis applications. Maximum deceleration capacity of e-motors in braking is ≥ 1g.	Continuous improvement in the performance of intelligent chassis in which distributed wheel hub motor drive systems are integrated with brake-by-wire systems and suspension-by-wire systems, and batched installation thereof.
	Brake System	Braking response time of EBS ≤ 400ms; Braking response time of EMB ≤ 220ms; Deceleration control error of EBS ≤ 15%; Deceleration control error of EMB ≤ 10%; Functional safety of EBS: ASIL D; Clamping force of EMB systems ≥ 100kN.	Braking response time of EBS ≤ 300ms; Braking response time of EMB ≤ 200ms; Deceleration control error of EBS ≤ 10%; Deceleration control error of EMB ≤ 7%; Functional safety of EMB: ASIL D; Clamping force of EMB systems ≥ 160kN.	Braking response time of EBS ≤ 200ms; Braking response time of EMB ≤ 160ms; Deceleration control error of EBS ≤ 8%; Deceleration control error of EMB ≤ 5%; Clamping force of EMB systems ≥ 180kN.
	Steering System	Output torque of electric steering gears ≥ 7000Nm, and response delay ≤ 90ms; Mass production of autonomous steer-by-wire systems Compatible with L4+ driving automation	Output torque of electric steering gears ≥ 8500Nm, and response delay ≤ 50ms; Mass production of autonomous steer-by-wire Compatible with L5 driving automation	Output torque of electric steering gears ≥ 8500Nm, and response delay ≤ 30ms; Mass production of autonomous steer-by-wire Compatible with L5 driving automation
	Suspension System	Roll angle during emergency lane change ≤ 5°; Height control error ≤ 7mm; Response time of solenoid valves ≤ 20ms.	Roll angle during emergency lane change ≤ 3.7°; Height control error ≤ 6mm; Response time of solenoid valves ≤ 15ms.	Roll angle during emergency lane change ≤ 2°; Height control error ≤ 5mm; Response time of solenoid valves ≤ 10ms.
Indicators of Control Sub-area	Longitudinal, Lateral and Vertical Fusion Control	Accuracy of dynamic load estimation based on powertrain domain: 90%; Realization of EBD functions based on drive and brake fusion and regenerative braking; Maximum wheel rotation angle of steering assist based on braking ≥ 10°; Accuracy of vehicle condition estimation based on longitudinal, lateral and vertical fusion ≥90%.	Accuracy of dynamic load estimation based on drive and brake fusion: 95%; Realization of ABS functions based on drive and brake fusion and regenerative braking; Cycle of anti-skid control based on powertrain loop ≤ 15ms; Maximum wheel rotation angle of steering assist based on longitudinal and lateral fusion ≥ 45°; Accuracy of vehicle condition estimation based on longitudinal, lateral and vertical fusion ≥95%.	Accuracy of dynamic load estimation based on longitudinal, lateral and vertical fusion: 98%; Maximum wheel rotation angle of steering assist based on longitudinal and lateral fusion ≥ 90°; Accuracy of vehicle condition estimation based on longitudinal, lateral and vertical fusion ≥98%.
	Fail-safe Redundancy Control	System functional safety at ASIL D; Master-redundancy switching time ≤ 10ms; Cross-system redundancy switching time ≤ 100ms; Coverage of system fault diagnosis: 95%; Deceleration of redundant braking ≥ 0.6g, with at least two levels of redundancy and redundant ABS; Residual steering capacity of redundant steering ≥ 50%.	Master-redundancy switching time ≤ 8ms; Cross-system redundancy switching time ≤ 80ms; Coverage of system fault diagnosis: 97%; Deceleration of redundant braking ≥ 0.7g; Residual steering capacity of redundant steering ≥ 60%.	Master-redundancy switching time ≤ 5ms; Cross-system redundancy switching time ≤ 50ms; Coverage of system fault diagnosis: 98%; Redundant braking not degraded; Redundant steering not degraded.
	Health Management Technology	Wheel-side thermodynamic monitoring, with scenario coverage ≥ 90% and monitoring accuracy ≥ 80%; Chassis oil temperature monitoring with accuracy ≥ 95%; Accuracy of life prediction of chassis wear parts ≥ 80%.	Wheel-side thermodynamic monitoring, with scenario coverage ≥ 95% and monitoring accuracy ≥ 90%; Chassis oil temperature monitoring with accuracy ≥ 97%; Accuracy of life prediction of chassis wear parts ≥ 90%.	Wheel-side thermodynamic monitoring, with scenario coverage ≥ 98% and monitoring accuracy ≥ 95%; Chassis oil temperature monitoring with accuracy ≥ 98%; Accuracy of life prediction of chassis wear parts ≥ 95%.

Fig. 5.5 Technology roadmap of intelligent chassis for commercial vehicles

5.2 Electronic and Electrical Information Architecture

5.2.1 Comparison of Domestic and International Technology Status

(1) Comparison of Architecture System Technology: With the development of automotive "new four modernizations," traditional distributed electrical architectures suffer from low communication bandwidth, insufficient computing power, and poor platform compatibility, leading to redundant R&D investments and poor user experience. To enhance vehicle type competitiveness and support continuous user experience upgrades, OEMs have identified electronic and electrical information architecture as a key enabler for smart transformation. Among foreign companies, Tesla upgraded the gateway-distributed architecture to a central computing + zonal architecture in the Model 3 vehicle type, further improving the integration of vehicle controllers. Volkswagen developed the domain-integrated architecture E3 1.0 based on the gateway-distributed architecture, introducing a SoC in the vehicle control domain for the first time. Among domestic companies, large-scale automakers such as NIO, Li Auto, XPENG, Geely, CHANGAN, FAW, and DFMC have gradually transitioned to domain-centralized and zonal architectures. Leveraging model-based systems engineering (MBSE) model databases, the development cycle of vehicle EEI Architecture has been shortened from five years to 18 months, significantly accelerating iteration speed and improving architecture reusability. Independent forward-looking architecture design systems and MBSE-based agile development are mainstream trends among global automakers. With technological advancements and accumulated experience, future architecture design systems combined with agile development and highly integrated architectures will become a major driving force for automotive industry upgrades.

(2) Comparison of Hardware Architecture Technology: In terms of hardware architecture forms, both domestic and international automakers generally exhibit high functional centralization in their central computing platforms and domain controllers, while adopting regionalization in physical architectures. In smart electricity distribution technology, Tesla replaced low-voltage relays and fuses with E-Fuse in the Model 3 vehicle type among foreign automakers. Most domestic automakers have not yet implemented E-Fuse, but it is expected to be adopted in next-generation leading smart vehicle types. Regarding 48 V systems, among international automakers, Mercedes-Benz's Mild Hybrid achieved true mass-production of 48 V systems, while Audi implemented 48 V across its entire A8L lineup with its MHEV (Mild Hybrid Electric Vehicle) drive system. Domestically, at least 16 automakers, including Geely, CHANGAN, and BYD Auto, have deployed 48 V mild hybrid systems. In the coming years, 48 V will see large-scale adoption in vehicles, leading to significant growth. In harness

lightweight technology, automakers worldwide are optimizing electrical architectures by using zonal controllers for localized connections to reduce harness length, with new connectors and lightweight materials considered key enablers.

(3) Comparison of Software Architecture Technology: In service-oriented software architecture technology, many foreign automakers and tech companies have adopted service-based architectures for onboard software systems. The China Automotive Basic Software Ecosystem Committee has released multiple standards and white papers to regulate service-oriented architecture (SOA) applications in the automotive industry. Domestic automakers such as Huawei, Z-ONE (Zero One), BYD Auto, and Geely have begun service-oriented construction of basic functions and interfaces while also providing service-based solutions for developers and end-users in the automotive sector. In automotive middleware technology, AUTOSAR software stack suppliers like Vector, EB, ETAS, Neusoft Reach, and HiRain Technologies have expanded the commercialization of AUTOSAR, further enhancing and enriching its functionality. In software virtualization development technology, major suppliers and cloud service providers have introduced products and standards for virtualized development, such as ETAS's VECU-BUILDER, Continental's CAEdge framework, and Vector's vVIRTUALtarget. With the mature application of these technologies and platforms, the software-defined vehicle (SDV) development model will accelerate, becoming a key driver for automakers to achieve technological breakthroughs and competitive advantages.

(4) Comparison of Communication Architecture Technical Indicators: In communication network technology, traditional vehicle owners primarily use point-to-point or bus-based communication architectures, exchanging information through direct or serial connections, mainly employing bus standards such as CAN, LIN, MOST, FlexRay, and LVDS. As communication bandwidth demands increase, automakers worldwide are also adopting Ethernet for in-vehicle infotainment systems. In Time-Sensitive Networking (TSN) technology, the IEEE 802.1 TSN working group is developing the IEEE P802.1 DG standard for automotive networks, while the OMG has released version 1.0 of the DDS-TSN standard. TSN applications in vehicles primarily use the IEEE 802.1AS clock synchronization protocol, followed by series of protocols such as 802.1Qbv, 802.1Qbu, 802.1CB, and 802.1QCi to meet onboard network traffic dispatching demand. Currently, TSN standardization is led by IEEE with participation from automakers and chip manufacturers, where foreign chipmakers still hold a technological advantage.

(5) Comparison of Architecture Testing and Evaluation Technology: In virtualized simulation testing technology for architectures, foreign research institutions and companies have proposed EEI Architecture simulation tools such as PREEVision, Capital Systems Architect, and Enterprise Architect. Meanwhile, major suppliers and cloud service providers have introduced products and standards for virtualized development. For example, dSPACE's VEOS is a simulation platform for ECU software verification, and dSPACE collaborates with AWS to promote cloud-based simulation for accelerating the verification and validation

of centralized vehicle architectures. In multi-dimensional intelligent evaluation technology for architectures, German automaker Volkswagen Group employs comprehensive multi-dimensional simulation and assessment techniques to model and evaluate vehicle body structures, engine performance, and suspension systems during automotive design. Similarly, the Aviation Industry Corporation of China applies multi-dimensional integrated simulation and evaluation technologies for aircraft simulation and assessment in aircraft design. Both domestic and international architecture evaluations primarily rely on subjective expert assessments for appraisal. A unified, quantifiable architecture evaluation methodology and tool set has yet to be established. Furthermore, current evaluations mainly occur during the architecture development phase and do not cover the entire software life-cycle.

5.2.2 Outlook on Technology Development Trends

(1) Development Trends in Architecture System Technology: Architecture integration is increasing, and the overall industry architecture form is gradually converging. In the short term, a hybrid model combining "central computing + zonal control" will be adopted. In the long term, vehicle-to-cloud collaborative architectures will further integrate functions and reduce overall costs. MBSE combined with agile development has become an industry consensus for forward architecture development methods and tool chains, supporting the entire process from requirements analysis to delivery. The time from new demand proposal to implementation in vehicles will be significantly shortened. AI-driven automated design and personalized customization will dominate most low-level design and implementation processes, drastically reducing development cycles and enabling customer-tailored solutions.

(2) Development Trends in Hardware Architecture Technology: Consumer-grade chips are penetrating the automotive industry, with computing power increasing and chip iteration cycles accelerating. Consumer and server ICs are being adopted in the onboard industry, driving advancements in automotive chip technology. Intelligent power distribution technologies, such as E-Fuse, will see widespread adoption, shortening wiring harness length, reducing vehicle weight, and enabling intelligent power distribution. "Aluminum replacing copper" is becoming the primary direction for wiring harness lightweight, while topology optimization and new connectors also contribute to weight reduction.

(3) Development Trends in Software Architecture Technology: SOA in software will continue to evolve, supporting more cloud-based services and in-vehicle microservices. Software will enable efficient vehicle-cloud collaboration and data closed loops, with companies increasingly adopting hybrid and multi-cloud strategies. Architectures will shift toward cloud-native and containerized platforms. Supporting deeper vehicle-road-cloud integration, SOA and microservices will facilitate rapid development and deployment of new services, ensuring

efficient inter-service communication. Enhanced edge computing integration will further reduce latency and improve data processing efficiency.

(4) Development Trends in Communication Architecture Technology: Communication architectures are moving toward Ethernet, with reduced cable weight and higher data rates as key evolution goals. Real-time communication will be achieved through upper communication protocols like SOME/IP and DDS, enabling functional service-oriented architectures and real-time communication. Partial TSN protocols will be implemented in vehicles. Communication architectures will also extend to vehicle-road-cloud interactions, forming a cloud-centric framework with in-vehicle switching as the foundation and external cooperative connectivity.

(5) Development Trends in Architecture Testing and Evaluation Technology: Evaluation technologies are becoming more automated, intelligent, sustainable, and collaborative. Machine learning and data analytics will enable automated architecture assessment and optimization, improving efficiency and accuracy. Evaluation scenarios will become more comprehensive and realistic. To meet the rapid development demand of intelligent connected vehicles, future software architecture evaluations will emphasize security, reliability, maintainability, portability, and ecosystem compatibility.

5.2.3 Vision, Objectives, and Milestones for 2040

Over the next 15 years, intelligent connected vehicles (ICVs) will inevitably become the development direction of the automotive industry within the integrated "vehicle-road-cloud-network" system. As the core technology of ICV system design, EEI Architecture will have a decisive impact on vehicle hardware-software system integration, functional implementation, development costs, and overall vehicle performance. By 2030, key technologies and performance metrics of EEI Architecture will reach world-leading levels; Domain-centralized architectures will evolve into central computing + zonal architectures, with in-vehicle computing supporting mixed-criticality scheduling; Development time for new architectures will be reduced to 4 months. By 2035, EEI Architecture-related products will achieve global leadership; Centralized architectures will enable efficient vehicle-to-cloud coordination, with preliminary realization of elastic computing resource allocation; Development time for new architectures will be shortened to 2 months. By 2040, the EEI Architecture industry will attain global leadership: Fully centralized vehicle-cloud architectures will be established, with large-scale computations performed in the cloud and comprehensive support for elastic computing resource allocation. Development time for new architectures will be compressed to 1 month.

5.2.4 Technology Roadmap

This Roadmap defines the evolution of EEI Architecture through tight coupling of system technologies, hardware technologies, software technologies, communication technologies, and testing/evaluation technologies. The architecture will progress from domain-centralized to centralized architectures, establish efficient vehicle-to-cloud and vehicle-to-road integration, and ultimately achieve a fully centralized vehicle-cloud architecture by 2040. By then, the EEI Architecture industry will attain global leadership, with development time for new vehicle type EEI Architecture significantly reduced. This will support China's transportation power strategy, ensure full industrial chain security, promote industrial upgrading and transformation, accelerate collaborative innovation, and enhance automotive product competitiveness. The architectural form will transition from distributed to centralized, gradually realizing vehicle-road-cloud integration. It will support decoupled computing and control, information sharing, and cross-device collaboration, enabling coordinated control of vehicles, road segments, and cloud platforms in connected environments. With system architecture design, MBSE and agile development will be widely adopted, supporting the full process from requirements analysis to controller delivery. With hardware architecture, integrated, modular, and lightweight designs will be achieved. Computing power will increase while energy consumption decreases, interfaces will gradually be standardized, wiring harnesses will become lighter, and scalability and security will significantly improve. With software architecture, service-oriented and intelligent designs will be realized. Through modular software design, microservice architecture, containerization and automated deployment, deeply integrated AI, comprehensive security and privacy protection, seamless connectivity, and an open collaborative ecosystem, innovation will be fostered, and rich user experiences delivered. With communication architecture, evolution toward higher speed and reliability will continue. High-speed onboard Ethernet will provide enhanced reliability and security to meet internal/external vehicle-to-cloud high-speed data transmission needs. Standardized vehicle communication interface definitions will support unified software interface design across the vehicle. With architecture testing & evaluation, technologies will adapt to diverse scenarios such as single-vehicle autonomous driving and integrated air-space-ground systems, meeting demands across R&D, validation, and post-sales software updates. Covering the entire vehicle life-cycle, EEI Architecture testing will improve efficiency, accuracy, and reliability, forming a quantifiable and sustainable testing ecosystem (Fig. 5.6).

2026–2030 Period: In architecture system technology, mature domestic industrial design software will emerge to fundamentally support agile development, enabling automakers to efficiently implement MBSE. Sensors and actuators will achieve cross-OEM reusability, reducing redundant R&D investments across the industry chain. Preliminary AI models will be developed for architecture design and evaluation. Hardware architecture technology, based on domain fusion, reduces core controllers to 2–3, meeting requirements for autonomous driving, intelligent cockpit, and vehicle control functions. Smart electricity distribution technology and wiring

	2030	2035	2040
Special Topic Overall Objectives	Key technologies and performance metrics of the architecture will reach world-leading levels; Domain-centralized architectures will evolve into central computing + zonal architectures, with in-vehicle computing supporting mixed-criticality scheduling; Development time for new architectures will be reduced to 4 months.	The EEI Architecture-related products will achieve global leadership; Centralized architectures will enable efficient vehicle-to-cloud coordination, with preliminary realization of elastic computing resource allocation; Development time for new architectures will be shortened to 2 months.	The EEI Architecture industry will attain global leadership: Fully centralized vehicle-cloud architectures will be established, with large-scale computations performed in the cloud and comprehensive support for elastic computing resource allocation. Development time for new architectures will be compressed to 1 month.
Architecture System Technology	The architectural form is converging toward a unified standard, adopting a centralized computing + zonal control approach. New requirements can be implemented in vehicles within 3 months from proposal. Cloud-based large models achieve a vehicle issue detection rate of >80%. A combined development model of Agile + V-Model is adopted, with Agile development accounting for >30% of the process.	Central + Zonal integration degree improved, with tight cloud connection. New requirements can be implemented in vehicles within 1 month from proposal. Cloud-based large models achieve a vehicle issue detection rate of >95%. Agile development is widely promoted, with Agile development accounting for >90% of the process.	Vehicle-cloud integrated architecture with cloud computing empowering vehicle systems. New requirements can be implemented in vehicles within 1 week from proposal. Cloud-based large models achieve a vehicle issue detection rate of >99%. AI + Agile development is widely promoted, with Agile development accounting for >95% of the process.
Hardware Architecture Technology	Hardware architecture technology, based on domain fusion, reduces core controllers to 2-3, meeting requirements for autonomous driving, intelligent cockpit, and vehicle control functions. Smart electricity distribution technology and wiring harness lightweight technology achieve world-leading levels in key technical indicators.	Chips will no longer have strictly defined functional purposes - 2-3 high-performance heterogeneous chips will achieve computing resource allocation through resource pooling to meet diverse functional requirements. Smart electricity distribution technology and wiring harness lightweight technology products will achieve mass-production.	1-2 core chips will achieve full-domain computing function integration, combining with cloud computing power to support complex calculations for high-level autonomous driving. Smart electricity distribution technology and wiring harness lightweight technology will form complete domestic industry chains.
Software Architecture Technology	Software architecture service-oriented interface standardization rate will reach above 80%. High-performance middleware solutions will cover all SoCs. Cloud-based or local virtualized containerized technology will begin application in software development and testing processes.	Service-oriented interface standardization will exceed 90%; middleware platforms will support L4 autonomy; cross-platform middleware will support all mainstream operating systems and hardware platforms. 50% of software development testing will be completed in cloud-based or local virtualized containers.	Service-oriented software will develop extensive developer communities and partner networks. Unified middleware forms will emerge, integrating vehicle-road-cloud resources. 80% of software development testing will be completed in cloud-based or local virtualized containers.
Communication Architecture Technology	It will achieve 1Gbit/s-10Gbit/s vehicle-wide communication applications, with Ethernet technology entering mass-production phase. High-performance physical layer technologies will be implemented, while TSN and DDS technology research verification will be completed	It will achieve 10Gbit/s-30Gbit/s vehicle-wide communication applications, with vehicle optical communication technology reaching large-scale application phase. Wireless technologies, like SparkLink, will be implemented in passenger vehicles, supporting satellite direct connectivity	It will achieve 30Gbit/s-50Gbit/s vehicle-wide communication applications, with all-optical communication expanding from in-vehicle to vehicle-road-cloud infrastructure, realizing vehicle-road-cloud integration communication architecture
Architecture Testing and Evaluation Technology	Architecture testing and evaluation will establish an assessment environment with EEI Architecture virtualization rate reaching 90%, where the fully standardized evaluation environment meets chip computing power of 1KTOPS, communication speed reaching 10Gbps, and autonomous driving virtualization covering L2 to L4 scenarios.	Architecture testing and evaluation will establish an assessment environment with EEI Architecture virtualization rate reaching 95%, where the fully standardized evaluation environment meets chip computing power of 1.5KTOPS, communication speed reaching 30Gbps, and autonomous driving virtualization covering L2 to L5 scenarios.	Architecture testing and evaluation will establish an assessment environment with EEI Architecture virtualization rate reaching 99%, where the fully standardized evaluation environment meets chip computing power of 2KTOPS, communication speed reaching 50Gbps, and autonomous driving virtualization covering L2 to L5 scenarios.

Fig. 5.6 Overall roadmap for electronic and electrical information architecture

harness lightweight technology achieve world-leading levels in key technical indicators. Software architecture service-oriented interface standardization rate will reach above 80%. High-performance middleware solutions will cover all SoCs. Cloud-based or local virtualized containerized technology will begin application in software development and testing processes. Communication architecture technology will achieve 1–10Gbit/s vehicle-wide communication applications, with Ethernet technology entering mass-production phase. High-performance physical layer technologies will be implemented, while TSN and DDS technology research verification will be completed. Architecture testing and evaluation will establish assessment environments with 90% virtualization rate for single-vehicle EEI Architecture, initially building vehicle-road-cloud integration architecture scenario virtualization capabilities covering L2-L4 autonomous driving, enabling definable architecture test scenarios. AI technology will be applied to automated architecture testing, increasing test case coverage by 60% and automation rate by 70%.

2031–2035 Period: Architecture system design tool chains will gradually mature, empowering the entire design process with over 80% functional coverage improvement and forming data closed loops. Meanwhile, AI large models will comprehensively learn mature functional business logic, mastering design rules and methodologies. In hardware architecture technology, chips will no longer have strictly defined functional purposes, 2–3 high-performance heterogeneous chips will achieve computing resource allocation through resource pooling to meet diverse functional requirements. Smart electricity distribution technology and wiring harness lightweight technology products will achieve mass-production. Software architecture service-oriented interface standardization will exceed 90%; middleware platforms will support L4 autonomy; cross-platform middleware will support all mainstream operating systems and hardware platforms. 50% of software development testing will be completed in cloud-based or local virtualized containers. Communication architecture technology will achieve 10Gbit/s-30Gbit/s vehicle-wide communication applications, with vehicle optical communication technology reaching large-scale application phase. Wireless technologies will be implemented in passenger vehicles, supporting satellite direct connectivity. Architecture testing and evaluation will establish assessment environments with 95% single-vehicle EEI Architecture virtualization rate; basic vehicle-road-cloud integration EEI Architecture testing and simulation environments will form, achieving 70% scenario virtualization rate covering L2–L5 autonomous driving. AI technology will be applied to automated architecture testing, increasing test case coverage by 70% and automation rate by 80%.

2036–2040 Period: In architecture system technology, design tool chains will become fully mature with 100% functional coverage improvement. Large model-supported functional design will become more efficient, capable of automatically completing rapid product prototyping. In hardware architecture technology, 1–2 core chips will achieve full-domain computing function integration, combining with cloud computing power to support complex calculations for high-level autonomous driving. Smart electricity distribution technology and wiring harness lightweight technology will form complete domestic industry chains. Service-oriented software will develop extensive developer communities and partner networks. Unified middle ware forms covering vehicle, cloud and multiple heterogeneous platforms will emerge, integrating vehicle-road-cloud resources to achieve dynamic computing power pool allocation and invocation. 80% of software development testing will be completed in cloud-based or local virtualized containers. Communication architecture technology will achieve 30Gbit/s-50Gbit/s vehicle-wide communication applications, with all-optical communication expanding from in-vehicle to vehicle-road-cloud infrastructure, realizing vehicle-road-cloud integration communication architecture. Architecture testing and evaluation will establish assessment environments with 99% single-vehicle EEI Architecture virtualization rate; building upon vehicle-road-cloud integration testing environments, satellite internet-enabled scenario simulation capabilities will be incorporated, achieving 90% scenario virtualization rate covering L2–L5 autonomous driving. AI technology will be applied to automated architecture testing, increasing test case coverage by 80% and automation rate by 90%, forming an integrated space-air-ground architecture evaluation ecosystem.

5.3 Automotive Chip

5.3.1 Domestic and International Technical Status Comparison

5.3.1.1 Control Chips: Market Penetration in Low- to Mid-End Segments, Multiple Barriers Remain in High-End

Automotive-grade MCUs face multidimensional entry barriers, including technological maturity, certification requirements, ecosystem completeness, and OEM acceptance. Historically, overseas suppliers have dominated both R&D capabilities and supply chains, resulting in a relatively stable market structure. With the rapid rise of China's automotive industry and strong policy support, low-end MCU technologies have matured, achieving continuous improvements in performance, stability, and reliability. Nevertheless, significant gaps remain in mid- to high-end MCUs when compared with global leaders, particularly in process node maturity, core IP self-sufficiency, long-term reliability, and the availability of complete product portfolios supporting high functional safety (FuSa) levels.

5.3.1.2 Computing Chips: Notable Progress Made, but Gaps Remain in High-Performance, High-Compute SoCs

In recent years, China has achieved remarkable advancements in automotive SoC technologies, with steady improvements in chip performance, reliability, and stability. Nevertheless, notable gaps persist relative to global leaders in high-performance, high-compute automotive SoCs, industrial ecosystems, and advanced fabrication processes. These gaps are primarily manifested in the following aspects.

First, compute performance: performance disparities stem from architectural design, chip process node limitations, IP core licensing, and cost constraints. Owing to extended development cycles and a relatively late start in large-scale automotive SoC R&D, current domestic solutions continue to lag behind leading international counterparts.

Second, ecosystem: overseas players like NVIDIA and Tesla lead in end-to-end hardware (cloud/edge chips) and corresponding base software/toolchain deployment. Most domestic suppliers still lack full-stack platforms capable of supporting closed-loop autonomous driving data systems.

5.3.1.3 Memory Chips: Generational Gaps Narrowing, but Key Component Supply Chain Vulnerabilities Persist

Significant progress has been achieved in memory chip development, with domestic suppliers progressively narrowing the generational technology gap with leading international manufacturers.

DRAM: China's manufacturers are advancing process nodes from 1x (19–20nm) to 1y (17–18nm), accelerating catch-up with global leaders. Products are compliant with JEDEC standards, enabling both R&D and mass production of LPDDR5/5X solutions for mainstream and selected niche markets, alongside significant achievements in industrial technology research and innovation.

NAND Flash: rapid progress in small-capacity products, with core parameters (performance, interfaces, power consumption) nearing international levels, though reliability, stability, and compatibility gaps remain. Large-capacity, high-performance products still have deficiencies in core parameters, and core components (storage controllers, flash memory chips) still need to be purchased externally.

NOR FLASH: High-FuSa products demonstrate reliability and performance on par with or exceeding global benchmarks in some areas. China's players dominate small-capacity markets, with process nodes advancing to 45nm (vs. international 4xnm).

EEPROM: process nodes have evolved from 130 to 90nm, aligning with global mainstream standards. Cost, capacity, and read/write speeds now compete internationally.

5.3.1.4 Communication Chips: Partial Technical Metrics Reach Advanced Levels, Yet Products Await Market Validation

In wired communication chips, CAN transceiver chips demonstrate performance comparable to international solutions in terms of communication speed and power consumption, with the core technology gap in automotive CAN XL gradually narrowing. LIN chip technology has reached global maturity. For Ethernet (ETH) chips, gaps remain in communication rates and TSN protocol stack support, while PHY functional integration is undergoing rapid development. In terms of raw data-rate metrics, certain domestic SerDes solutions demonstrate competitive, and in some cases leading, performance relative to international counterparts, with relatively mature proprietary protocols. However, the industry lacks unified standards, and public protocol development requires further refinement.

In wireless communication chips, cellular direct connect chips achieve equivalent communication capabilities, with relatively mature large-scale applications in China. Short-range wireless chips exhibit standardization gaps—technologies like Bluetooth, WIFI, UWB, and NFC adhere to mature international standards, while NearLink currently only has association standards, with national standardization in progress. NearLink is expected to coexist with Bluetooth and WIFI technologies long-term. Satellite navigation chips lead in system frequency points while maintaining comparable positioning accuracy.

5.3.1.5 Power Devices: IGBT Achieves Mass Adoption While SiC Product Reliability Requires Improvement

China possesses the world's largest power semiconductor market, with rapid development of automotive power devices based on silicon and third-generation semiconductor materials. Silicon-based IGBT devices have established a relatively complete domestic industrial chain, with product performance approaching internationally advanced levels, and mature products have achieved mass vehicle integration. Driven by the adoption of 800V high-voltage platforms and fast-charging high-voltage DC charging piles, silicon carbide (SiC) MOSFET applications in vehicles are accelerating. The industrial chain has largely matured, with home-made power modules achieving mass production and vehicle integration.

However, gaps persist in R&D innovation capabilities when compared with leading international suppliers. In core technologies, China's manufacturers are still catching up with the latest-generation technologies from overseas suppliers. While chip performance metrics approach international levels, deficiencies persist in parameter balancing (e.g., conduction loss versus switching loss). Particularly for high-voltage/high-current modules, domestically developed products continue to trail international competitors in parameter consistency, long-term reliability, and automotive-grade quality control standards. SiC products also show gaps in heat dissipation, lifespan, and reliability compared to international counterparts.

Additionally, in gallium nitride (GaN) devices, GaN power devices for onboard chargers (OBC) have been released in China. The industry is exploring GaN applications in new energy vehicle traction inverter systems. Currently, 6-inch GaN substrates and epitaxial wafers for traction applications exist as samples, but wafer production maturity will require 2–3 more years. GaN adoption in traction systems further depends on technological innovations in device voltage endurance and electric drive topologies. Small-scale vehicle validation is projected around 2030.

5.3.1.6 LED/Display/Mid-to-Low-End Power Driver Chips Show Positive Progress, While High-Power Drivers Remain Lacking

China's automotive driver chip sector has experienced rapid development in recent years, with sustained market growth, particularly excelling in motor drivers, power management, and LED lighting control applications. For relatively low-power-density products, China's companies have reached internationally competitive levels, even leading in certain aspects. For instance, externally MOSFET-based EFUSE products demonstrate higher bypass current capabilities with capacitive load charging support, while external MOSFET pre-drivers offer more PWM channels and a wider selection of VDS thresholds.

However, the China's market currently focuses primarily on mid-to-low-end segments, showing gaps in high-power-density, highly integrated, and cutting-edge products compared to international standards. In high-power-density products, China's solutions lack high-side drivers with on-resistance below 4mΩ, whereas international counterparts have achieved approximately 0.6mΩ. For built-in MOSFET EFUSE products, constrained by China's process capabilities, most lack high-power solutions with RON_LS+RON_HS better than 30mΩ. Regarding integration, China's alternatives for SPI-controlled multi-channel HSDs remain unavailable, and display-and-touch combo driver chips are still in their infancy. For advanced applications, while Micro LED lighting solutions have reached mass production internationally, China's equivalents are generally unavailable.

5.3.1.7 Power Management Chips: Mid-to-Low-End Needs Largely Met, While High-Integration Products Remain Immature

Driven by new energy vehicle and autonomous driving technologies, China's automotive power management chip industry has achieved significant progress in recent years. First, basic chips now largely meet application requirements. By 2024, compared to 2020, China's solutions have essentially covered 36V/1A-6A DC-DC converters, 5V/1A-6A DC-DC converters, and LDOs below 1A, with development gradually progressing toward higher-current solutions. Second, high-end products remain underdeveloped. Due to their technical complexity, extended R&D and validation cycles, and late market entry, SBC and PMIC products are currently transitioning from pilot deployment to early-stage mass production. As China's chip companies mature their technologies and systems, functionally safe SBC/PMICs and multi-phase controllers are expected to emerge around 2026. Third, synergistic development between chip technologies requires improvement. SBC/PMIC advancement typically follows MCU/SOC progress to provide complementary solutions. China's manufacturers need to strengthen R&D investment and coordinated development in these two fields to gradually achieve fully autonomous, comprehensive solutions.

5.3.1.8 General Analog Technologies Mature, AFE Performance Reaches Advanced Levels, Audio Gaps Remain

In recent years, China's automotive-grade analog chip technology has rapidly advanced, with an increasingly diverse product portfolio. China's general-purpose automotive-grade operational amplifiers and comparators can essentially meet mid-to-low-end application requirements. However, gaps persist in high-performance products such as precision operational amplifiers, wide common-mode voltage current-sensing operational amplifiers, and multi-channel high-power audio amplifiers compared to international leaders. The offset voltage of precision operational amplifiers and the common-mode input voltage range of current-sensing amplifiers still lag significantly behind global benchmarks. While domestic AFE chips have achieved sufficient accuracy and single-chip sampling channels for current applications, they still trail international counterparts. The performance gap in audio power amplifiers and audio transmission chips is narrowing rapidly.

5.3.1.9 Sensor Chips: China's Progress with Strengths in Image Sensors and LiDAR

Over the past five years, China has made substantial progress in sensor chip design and applications. CMOS image sensors and LiDAR modules now match world-class performance in key metrics. CMOS millimeter-wave radar chips have largely caught up with global leaders. Ultrasonic sensors have achieved breakthroughs from scratch, while magnetic and MEMS sensor categories are gradually expanding with improving performance. However, home-made sensors still face significant challenges. Critical components like LiDAR transceiver chips and ultrasonic sensor probes lag behind international standards. Performance gaps remain notable in ultrasonic, magnetic, and MEMS sensors compared to foreign counterparts.

5.3.1.10 RISC-V Development Active but Still Nascent in China

RISC-V has attracted increasing attention in China, particularly in the context of autonomous and secure computing architectures. As an open-standard instruction set architecture (ISA), RISC-V holds strategic importance for China. RISC-V core research has gained initial traction domestically, primarily addressing basic to mid-range IP requirements. In applications, dozens of RISC-V chip models have entered mass production, primarily for IoT scenarios. In automotive, China's companies have begun introducing RISC-V-based products. For automotive ecosystem development, major automakers are collaborating with or investing in chip design firms for automotive-grade chip R&D. In computing scenarios like edge computing, desktops, and data centers, RISC-V chips remain in early development in China. Only a few chips have been unveiled, and their performance and software ecosystems still trail mainstream architectures. RISC-V firms are focusing on data center applications in China. With improvements in RISC-V software ecosystems and breakthroughs in high-performance cores, Chinese RISC-V chips are poised to advance in high-performance domains.

5.3.2 *Outlook on Technology Development Trends*

5.3.2.1 Rapid Performance Advancements in Automotive Chips to Support Expanding Functional Requirements

With increasing complexity in automotive electronic systems and growing functional demands, automotive chips are required to deliver higher computing performance, expanded memory capacity, faster communication bandwidth, and enhanced sensing precision to process greater data volumes and execute more complex algorithms. In control chips, high-frequency, large-memory MCUs have become mainstream. Computing chips require "enhanced computing power + hardware-software decoupled architectures + domain controllers" to meet demands for massive data processing and continuous OTA updates. Memory chip capacities are transitioning from GB to TB levels. Communication chips prioritize high-speed, low-latency, and long-range performance. Power devices evolve toward higher voltage tolerance, lower conduction losses, and faster switching speeds. Driver chips demand higher processing speeds and power density. Power management chips must maintain high energy conversion efficiency across varying load conditions. Analog chips are optimized for higher sampling accuracy, speed, multi-channel capability, and reduced latency. Sensor chips are advancing toward higher precision across all categories.

5.3.2.2 Increasing Integration of Automotive Chips to Adapt to E/E Architecture Evolution

Automotive chips leverage integrated solutions and advanced packaging technologies to consolidate multiple modules and functions, aligning with centralized E/E architectures and software-defined vehicle needs while reducing cost, size, and weight. For control chips, key industry trends include: domain controller MCUs integrating AI-capable coprocessors, edge MCUs incorporating power management, communication, and safety monitoring modules, and enhanced hardware virtualization capabilities. Computing SoC architectures are evolving toward heterogeneous multi-core designs ("CPU + GPU + ISP + NPU + DSP") to address intelligentization requirements. Communication chips are developing toward multi-protocol integration and multi-source convergence technologies. Power devices now integrate on-chip temperature/current sensors and gate driver resistors for status monitoring. Driver, power, and analog ICs are increasing channel counts and digital interfaces. Sensor chips are trending toward greater functional integration and expanded sensing options. RISC-V-based large chips are shifting from GPU/DSA divergence to DPU/super-terminal reintegration.

5.3.2.3 Automotive Chips Require Balancing High Performance with Low Power Consumption

With increasingly complex functional definitions, automotive chips must optimize for specific scenarios through: process node shrinkage, manufacturing process refinement, layout optimization, and hardware-software partitioning strategies to achieve better energy efficiency and power performance. Current mainstream MCUs employ 40nm+ mature nodes, while advanced products have adopted 28nm and below. Computing chips will progress toward 3nm advanced nodes. The NOR Flash market is transitioning from 90 to 40nm processes. Power devices utilize novel processes/technologies to reduce conduction losses. Driver, power, and analog chips minimize non-ideal energy losses through circuit topology optimization, higher switching frequencies, and concurrent EMI performance enhancements.

5.3.2.4 Adoption of New Technologies to Meet High-Safety and High-Reliability Requirements for Automotive Chips

Automotive chips achieve high functional safety, information security, and reliability requirements through optimized hardware-software design, new materials, and advanced manufacturing processes. Memory chips are striving toward zero-defect targets while employing encryption algorithms and secure data erasure techniques to prevent unauthorized access and tampering of stored data. For power devices, automotive-grade RC-IGBT technology significantly reduces chip footprint while enhancing reliability. SiC MOSFETs improve performance and reliability through smaller cell sizes, lower specific on-resistance, reduced switching losses, and enhanced gate oxide protection. Driver chips focus on improving process reliability, integrating more diagnostic functions, and refining protection mechanisms to boost efficiency and reduce EMI. Power management chips place greater emphasis on safety protection and fault detection mechanisms in their design.

5.3.3 Development Goals and Milestones for 2040

The automotive chip industry aims to break through core chip technologies and establish a comprehensive product portfolio covering all automotive application scenarios.

By 2030, home-made chip products will achieve performance enhancements, with intelligent connected vehicle (ICV) chips supporting L4 autonomous driving capabilities and highly integrated, multi-modal interactive cockpit functionalities. Onechip technology will gradually become the mainstream solution for multi-domain fusion chips. Low-carbon powertrain chips will fully support 800–1000 V vehicle voltage platforms, while general-purpose chips will offer a comprehensive product portfolio to meet the application requirements of highly integrated zonal control and central computing platforms. A complete industrial chain encompassing high-reliability and high-security design, manufacturing, packaging & testing, and IP cores will be established.

By 2035, chip integration will advance further, with ICV chips supporting L5 autonomous driving and enabling full-scenario fusion, deeply integrating AI large-model algorithms with multi-modal cockpit interactions. Low-carbon powertrain chips will extend their support to 1200–1500V vehicle voltage platforms. General-purpose chips will integrate AI capabilities, facilitating edge-side AI computing tasks. Home-made 22nm automotive-grade manufacturing processes will be commercialized, and independent chip architectures will be realized. A self-sufficient hardware-software ecosystem will be established, achieving full supply chain autonomy.

By 2040, chip performance will reach world-leading levels. ICV chips will support the transition from general artificial intelligence to super artificial intelligence, enabling safe, autonomous, and sustainable intelligent driving. Low-carbon powertrain chips will continuously improve power density, achieving higher integration and conversion efficiency while reducing power losses. General-purpose chips will meet automotive requirements for high reliability, safety, and low power consumption, further enhancing integration and computing power with embedded AI capabilities, self-learning functionalities, and greater intelligence. Breakthroughs and innovations in key technologies such as chip design, manufacturing, and packaging & testing will be realized. The industry will establish automotive-grade IP and EDA toolchain capabilities, forming a comprehensive automotive chip ecosystem.

5.3.4 Technology Roadmap

The rapid advancement of ICV and new energy technologies is driving the evolution of E/E architectures toward greater centralization and efficiency. This transformation is propelling automotive chip development toward higher performance, greater integration, lower power consumption, and enhanced safety and reliability. Over the next 5–15 years, computing chips are projected to achieve processing power exceeding 3000 TOPS, while control chips are expected to surpass 40K DMIPS in computational performance. Wired communication speeds will exceed 112Gbps, and power chips such as IGBT and SiC devices will continue to improve in power density to support new energy and low-carbon propulsion systems. Memory chips will evolve toward higher capacity and bandwidth, while driver chips and power management chips will see continuous improvements in integration density and power density. Sensor chips will demonstrate significant performance enhancements. The overall technology roadmap is illustrated in Fig. 5.7.

		2030	2035	2040
General Goals		ICV chips will support L4 autonomous driving capabilities and enable highly integrated, multi-modal interactive cockpit systems, with Onechip technology becoming the mainstream solution for multi-domain fusion chips.	ICV chips will support L5 autonomous driving and enable full-scenario integration with deep fusion of AI large-model algorithms and multi-modal cockpit interactions.	ICV chips will support the transition from general artificial intelligence to super artificial intelligence, enabling secure, autonomous and sustainable intelligent driving.
		Low-carbon powertrain chips will fully support 800-1000V vehicle voltage platforms	Low-carbon powertrain chips will support 1,200-1,500V vehicle voltage platforms.	Low-carbon powertrain chips will continuously improve power density, achieving higher integration and conversion efficiency.
		General-purpose chips will offer a comprehensive product portfolio to meet the application requirements of highly integrated zonal control and central computing platforms.	General-purpose chips will integrate AI capabilities, facilitating edge-side AI computing tasks.	General-purpose chips will meet automotive requirements for high reliability, safety, and low power consumption, with further enhanced integration density and intelligence.
		A complete industrial chain encompassing high-reliability and high-security design, manufacturing, packaging & testing, and IP cores will be established.	Home-made 22nm automotive-grade manufacturing processes will be commercialized, Independent chip architectures will be realized. A self-sufficient hardware-software ecosystem will be established, achieving full supply chain autonomy.	Breakthroughs and innovations in key technologies such as chip design, manufacturing, and packaging & testing will be realized. The industry will establish automotive-grade IP and EDA toolchain capabilities, forming a comprehensive automotive chip ecosystem.
Control Chips	CPU	CPU computing power up to 10KDMIPS	CPU computing power up to 20KDMIPS	CPU computing power up to 40KDMIPS
	eNVM	ENVM up to 24 MB	ENVM up to 48 MB	ENVM up to 96 MB
	SRAM	SRAM up to 8 MB	SRAM up to 16 MB	SRAM up to 32 MB
Computing Chips	Cockpit SoC	GPU Computing Power >6TFLOPS	GPU Computing Power >8TFLOPS	GPU Computing Power >10TFLOPS
	Intelligent Driving SoC	AI Computing Power >1,000TOPS	AI Computing Power >2,000TOPS	AI Computing Power >3,000TOPS
	Multi-domain Fusion SoC	CPU computing power >600KDMIPS; GPU Computing Power >6TFLOPS; AI Computing Power >1,000TOPS	CPU computing power >900KDMIPS; GPU Computing Power >8TFLOPS; AI Computing Power >2,000TOPS	CPU computing power >1,200KDMIPS; GPU Computing Power >10TFLOPS; AI Computing Power >3,000TOPS
Memory Chips	Capacity	Automotive-grade memory chips: FLASH capacity up to 4TB; DRAM communication rate up to 12800Mbps	Automotive-grade memory chips: FLASH capacity up to 8TB; DRAM communication rate up to 15Gbps+	Automotive-grade memory chips reach higher capacities and faster rates
	Functional Safety	Functional safety level achieves ASIL B compliance	Functional safety level achieves ASIL D compliance	Functional safety level achieves ASIL D compliance
	Controller & Particles	Achieve independent design, development, simulation and verification of memory chip controllers and dies	Achieve independent design, development, simulation and verification of next-generation storage controllers and particles	Achieve design, development, simulation and verification of next-generation storage controllers and particles
Communication Chips	Wired Communication	Maximum wired in-vehicle communication speed reaches 36Gbps	Maximum wired in-vehicle communication speed reaches 56Gbps	Maximum wired in-vehicle communication speed reaches 112Gbps
	Wireless Communication	Maximum wireless in-vehicle communication speed reaches 500Mbps	Maximum wireless in-vehicle communication speed reaches 1Gbps	Maximum wireless in-vehicle communication speed reaches 2Gbps
	Protocol	Industry establishes and implements public protocols	Public protocols become dominant in the industry	Full adoption of public protocols across the industry
Power Devices	Supported Applications	Power devices fully support the adoption of 800V-1,000V vehicle voltage platforms	Power devices fully support the adoption of 1,200V vehicle voltage platforms	Power devices achieve high integration, supporting adoption of higher voltage platforms
	Current Density	Chip current density (A/cm2): IGBT: 400 (750V), 275 (1,200V) SiC: 800 (750V), 700 (1,200V), 550A (1,700V)	Chip current density (A/cm2): IGBT: 450 (750V), 300 (1,200V) SiC: 850 (750V), 750 (1,200V), 575A(1,700V)	Chip current density (A/cm2): IGBT: 480 (750V), 325 (1,200V) SiC: 900 (750V), 800 (1,200V), 600A (1,700V)
	Test Certification	Preliminary establishment of automotive-grade certification and testing standards for SiC MOSFETs	Refinement and improvement of automotive-grade certification and testing standards for SiC MOSFETs	Establishment of complete automotive-grade certification and testing standards for SiC IGBTs
Driver Chips	On-Resistance	Vertical BCD process achieves 6mΩ high-side on-resistance	Vertical BCD process breaks through 4mΩ high-side on-resistance	Driver chips lead industry development
	Supported Systems	Driver chips support 12V/24V/48V systems with 12V as mainstream	Driver chips support 12V/24V/48V systems with 48V as mainstream	Driver chips achieve full 48V system support
Power Management Chips	48V System Primary Power Supply	Withstand voltage reaches 80V for input; Built-in MOS provides 10A output current capability.	Withstand voltage reaches 100V for input; Built-in MOS provides 20A output current capability.	Withstand voltage exceeds 100V for input; Built-in MOS provides 20A output current capability.
	DrMOS	Current capability: 70-90A; Current density: 90A/100mm2.	Current capability: 90-100A; Current density: 100A/100mm2.	Current capability: 90-100A; Current density: 100A/100mm2
	PMIC/SBC	PMIC/SBC supports ASIL-D functional safety level.	PMIC/SBC supports ASIL-D functional safety level.	PMIC/SBC supports ASIL-D functional safety level.
Analog Chips	Operational Amplifier	Precision operational amplifier achieves ≤±7.5μV offset voltage	Precision operational amplifier achieves ≤±5μV offset voltage	Precision operational amplifier achieves ≤±1μV offset voltage
	AFE	AFE chip achieves ≤±2mV voltage sampling accuracy across full temperature range and lifetime	AFE chip achieves ≤±1mV voltage sampling accuracy across full temperature range and lifetime	AFE chip achieves further improved voltage sampling accuracy
	Audio Power Amplifier	Audio power amplifier delivers ≥150W×4 output power	Audio power amplifier delivers ≥200W×4 output power	Audio power amplifier achieves further increased output power
Sensors	Detection Range	Maximum detection range: 300m	Maximum detection range: 400m	Maximum detection range: 500m
	Detection Accuracy	Maximum detection accuracy: 1cm	Maximum detection accuracy: 0.5cm	Maximum detection accuracy: <0.5cm
RISC-V Chips	Performance	Covers mid-to-low-end chip IP with dual assurance of functional safety and information security	Covers high-end chip IP with dual assurance of functional safety and information security	IP performance reaches advanced level, meeting future smart transportation requirements for functional safety and information security
	Ecosystem	Preliminary establishment of RISC-V ecosystem and applications	Development of mature automotive chip ecosystem applications based on RISC-V	RISC-V becomes one of the mainstream chip architecture choices for automotive

Fig. 5.7 Overall technology roadmap

5.4 Automotive Operating Systems

5.4.1 Domestic and International Technical Status Comparison

Overall, foreign countries started developing automotive operating systems earlier and have certain leading advantages in terms of technology and ecosystem. Domestically, the agile development approach has been adopted, and significant progress has been made recently, with the gap gradually narrowing. However, the functionality, performance, and ecosystem of automotive operating systems still need to be improved.

5.4.1.1 Both Domestic and International Entities Are Actively Exploring the Architecture of Automotive Operating Systems

Currently, the vehicle control operating system and the in-vehicle operating system are two separate systems.

Internationally, there are mainly two technical routes for automotive operating systems oriented towards Assisted Driving. One is based on in-depth customization of Linux, and the other is based on customization of safety–critical real-time operating systems and the AUTOSAR AP platform.

In China, the China Automotive Technology Innovation Alliance (or similar organization) has organized industry entities to research and release the "Reference Architecture for In-Vehicle Intelligent Computing Basic Platform 2.0", which presents a consideration and judgment on the technical architecture of vehicle control operating system products for the next 3–5 years. Companies such as Huawei, ZTE, BanMa, and ZhonglingZhixing have proposed their own product solutions.

Automotive operating systems oriented towards intelligent cockpits are mainly customized based on underlying operating systems such as QNX, Linux, Android, and HarmonyOS. There are also some automotive operating system architectures that support multiple operating system instances through a hypervisor, running separate systems for the instrument cluster and the infotainment system. For example, the typical architecture of "QNX + Android + application-level integration middleware" is widely used.

5.4.1.2 The Core Technologies of System Software Are Mainly Controlled by Foreign Entities

The key technologies of system software include kernel technology, virtualization technology, cross-kernel and cross-hardware technology, and middleware technology. Kernel technology is still dominated by foreign companies, with QNX, Linux, and Android occupying the major market share. Domestic companies such as Huawei,

ZTE, and Banmazhixing have developed corresponding products, but there are still significant gaps in product maturity, application scope, and ecosystem construction. Virtualization technology, which has a longer development history and broader application range in foreign countries, has advantages in functionality and tool support. Middleware technology, which was started earlier in foreign countries with a more complete standard system, faces challenges in China, such as market weaknesses and the need to strengthen toolchains. The "Reference Architecture for In-Vehicle Intelligent Computing Basic Platform 2.0" (2023) proposed the concept of a cross-kernel driver framework, but it is still necessary to absorb advanced technologies from both domestic and foreign sources and promote their implementation.

5.4.1.3 Application Support Technologies Are More Mature in Foreign Countries

In the field of vehicle control function software, foreign countries have a higher level of technological maturity in terms of real-time performance, safety, and stability, with leading companies such as Waymo, Tesla, Mobileye, NVIDIA, and TTTech. Domestic leading companies, including Huawei, Baidu, Horizon Robotics, GuoqiZhikong, and ReachAuto, are increasing their R&D investment to gradually close the gap.

In the field of in-vehicle application frameworks, Google's open-source system Android, with its mature and thriving application ecosystem, holds a leading position in the intelligent cockpit market. China started research relatively late, with representative companies including Huawei and BanmaZhixing, but there is still a significant gap in the prosperity of the ecosystem.

5.4.1.4 Foreign Countries Lead in Common Key Technologies, While China is Accelerating R&D

Common key technologies include intelligent technologies, safety technologies and standards, testing and evaluation technologies, and toolchain technologies. In the field of intelligent technologies, foreign countries have reached a highly mature level. China has made significant progress in areas such as Assisted Driving and voice interaction, but there is still room for improvement in the independent development of core algorithms and components. Safety technologies are mostly dominated by foreign companies, and China is still in the stage of catching up. In the field of standards, testing and evaluation, and toolchain technologies, China started late but has developed rapidly in recent years.

5.4.2 *Outlook on Technology Development Trends*

5.4.2.1 AI Technology is Playing an Increasingly Important Role in the R&D and Application of Operating Systems

High-level autonomous driving is gradually being permitted on roads under certain conditions, intelligent cabin perception and interaction applications are emerging endlessly, and smart connected vehicle technologies are rapidly integrating into society and daily life. To keep pace with AI advancements, higher demands are placed on automotive operating systems in terms of technical architecture, efficient operation, and performance security.

AI can assist in the development of automotive operating systems—for example, by aiding in programming and automatically generating kernel module code (such as device drivers and memory management segments), thereby reducing repetitive tasks. It can also support intelligent resource scheduling and management, improving operational efficiency. Additionally, AI can optimize high-concurrency data processing, V2X communication, and OTA upgrade enhancements in automotive operating systems, better supporting upper-layer intelligent connectivity and applications.

5.4.2.2 Must Support the Development Trends of Intelligent Connectivity and the New Energy Revolution

In the future, the intelligent connected vehicles need to address more complex scenarios, better understand traffic behaviors, and make reasonable decisions and interactions, which require Automotive OS to provide support in areas such as large models, multimodal interaction, and V2X. Automotive OS needs to align with the trends of new energy transformations by optimizing energy consumption management to reduce their proportion in the overall energy consumption of vehicles. Automotive OS should also realize support for energy-saving technologies and applications to improve energy usage efficiency.

5.4.2.3 Will Evolve Toward a Vehicle-Wide Operating System Based on an SOA (Service-Oriented Architecture)

As the E/E architecture shifts towards centralization and software systems evolve towards SOA architecture, OS is beginning to transform into the Vehicle OS. The Vehicle OS is based on the SOA architecture and communication networks, integrating functionalities of Intelligent Cockpit OS, Autonomous Driving OS, and Safety Vehicle Control OS through a central computing platform. It provides a vehicle-level platform with a unified set of programming interfaces. Its characteristics include layered decoupling and unified architecture, enabling dynamic configurability and seamless redundancy through the provision of a unified interface and centralized scheduling of hardware resources and computational power.

5.4.2.4 Smart Connected Applications Impose Higher Performance Requirements on Operating Systems

As the hardware and upper-layer applications of intelligent connected vehicles become richer and more complex, higher demands are placed on Automotive OS in terms of high security, high performance, and stability. Hypervisors will evolve towards a stronger combination of advanced hardware virtualization and flexible software-defined capabilities, high functional safety and information security, to efficient and flexible share on hardware resources. The kernel will optimize for high security, high determinism, and high compatibility, achieving efficient scheduling, reliable services, and ubiquitous deployment. Middleware will develop towards service-oriented, intelligence, and cross-domain integration.

5.4.2.5 Cross-Kernel and Cross-Hardware Technologies Enable Better Adaptation to Heterogeneous Computing Platforms

Currently, Automotive OS consist of multiple kernel types. The porting and adaptation of kernel drivers face issues such as long development cycles, low development efficiency, significant upgrade challenges, and high maintenance costs.

The industry urgently needs a cross-kernel driver framework, by a unified architectural design and the development of hardware abstraction, core interfaces and driver models, which can realize one-time driver development and compatibility with multiple operating system kernels and multiple virtualization managers, significantly enhancing the portability of driver programs.

5.4.2.6 The Security Risks Faced by Automotive OS Are Expanding, Prompting a Transformation in Security Technologies

As cloud computing, big data, and large models integrate more deeply with the automotive industry, intelligent connected vehicles face risks of unknown network attacks and unpredictable coupling risks of "function × network."

First, security approaches are shifting from separate developments in "functional safety" and "network security" following the dual V-model to an integrated approach encompassing "functional safety, network security and data security", forming multiple layers of security resilience mechanisms. Second, there is a transition from "external add-ons from the user side" to "inherent vulnerabilities from the manufacturing side", with more and more clear demands for "upstream" of vulnerability detections and "resilience" of defense strategies. Third, there is a strong emphasis on comprehensive security monitoring and protection throughout the vehicle's lifecycle, ensuring safety in all stages of plan, design, production, operation, and maintenance.

5.4.2.7 Open-Source and Open Collaboration Have Become the Consensus for Building the Automotive OS Ecosystem

Currently, there are significant differences in the development approaches of Automotive OS, with diverse product forms and scattered technical routes, which is not conducive to industry development. By guiding with standards to promote the open progress of Automotive OS, establish standard open interfaces, supporting application development interface standards above, while adapting to chip, sensor, and actuator interface standards below. Through open-source efforts, a unified common foundational platform can be created, promoting software maturity and ecosystem development.

5.4.3 Development Goals and Milestones for 2040

In the future, a comprehensive R&D and industrial application system for vehicle operating systems will be fully established, fostering a thriving development and application ecosystem. An intelligent, adaptive, and vehicle-road-cloud collaborative integrated vehicle operating system will emerge, meeting the technical requirements of high-level autonomous driving and smart cockpit application scenarios. It will serve as a bridge and "intelligent brain" connecting vehicles with the external world, driving the development of smart transportation toward greater intelligence, efficiency, and low-carbon sustainability.

By 2030, the vehicle control operating system and in-vehicle operating system will be integrated to form a unified automotive operating system. The cockpit and autonomous driving systems will be seamlessly integrated into an interactive platform, achieving cross-domain sharing, functional consolidation, and data interoperability. It will support mainstream AI algorithms, frameworks, and large AI models for vehicle deployment; meet the technical requirements of L2–L4 autonomous driving and L1–L2 smart cockpit application scenarios; and ensure extremely high stability, with a 0% vehicle breakdown rate attributable to the operating system. Through component-based modular combinations of a unified architecture, the system will adapt to diverse operational needs. Core products will comply with functional safety and cybersecurity requirements, with expected functional safety processes fully meeting regulatory standards.

By 2035, an integrated vehicle operating system supporting intelligent and adaptive vehicle-road-cloud convergence will be established. Through centralized computing platforms, it will achieve functional integration of in-vehicle OS, autonomous driving OS, and safety–critical vehicle control OS, meeting technical requirements for cockpit HMI, high-performance autonomous driving computing, and highly reliable vehicle control. The system will satisfy technical specifications for L3–L4 autonomous driving and L2–L3 intelligent cockpit application scenarios, support advanced AI reasoning capabilities, equipped with certain native AI capabilities, and comply with multi-layered integrated safety assurance standards. A preliminary global open-source ecosystem will take shape, with development and application ecosystems reaching considerable scale.

By 2040, the integrated intelligent vehicle operating system will achieve deep convergence with cloud services, enabling comprehensive vehicle intelligence and seamless connectivity with smart transportation, smart homes, and smart cities. The system will meet technical requirements for L5 autonomous driving (fully autonomous operation) and L4 intelligent cockpit (comprehensive cognitive cockpit) application scenarios; possess native AI capabilities; the industry collaboratively builds a complete automotive OS standard system with testing evaluation and toolchain support; and develop a thriving global open-source ecosystem with a robust development and application environment.

5.4.4 Technology Roadmap

The vehicle operating system roadmap encompasses three core systems: autonomous driving OS, safety–critical vehicle control OS, and in-vehicle OS. This document presents a multidimensional analysis covering: strategic objectives, OS integration level, cross-hardware architecture compatibility, comprehensive system functionality and performance, intelligent features, connectivity solutions, carbon-reduction capabilities, security protocols, ecosystem development, standardization/testing frameworks and toolchains, market analysis, and application ecosystem development (refer to Fig. 5.8).

		By 2030	By 2035	By 2040
Overall Objectives		◆ Establish preliminary but relatively complete technical capabilities for vehicle operating systems, mastering core system software technologies. ◆ Develop an integrated vehicle OS that meets the technical requirements for L2-L4 autonomous driving and L1-L2 intelligent cockpit. ◆ Support efficient coordination of vehicle-road-cloud data and applications; and initially foster a healthy, open-source, and open industrial ecosystem.	◆ Achieve full technical development capabilities with comprehensive breakthroughs in key core technologies, ensuring functional software technology reaches globally leading levels. ◆ Develop a vehicle-road-cloud collaborative, adaptive, and intelligent vehicle OS that meets the requirements for L3-L4 autonomous driving and L2-L3 intelligent cockpit. ◆ Enable seamless, full-scenario coordination between vehicles, roads, and cloud systems.	◆ Possess full-stack technological capabilities for vehicle operating systems, with a fully developed R&D and industrial application framework. ◆ Support whole-vehicle intelligence and seamless connectivity with smart transportation, smart homes, and smart cities; meet the technical requirements for L5 autonomous driving and L4 intelligent cockpit. ◆ Build a globally open-source and open industrial ecosystem.
Key Technologies	Integration of Vehicle OS	◆ Develop a functionally integrated vehicle OS, where the cockpit and autonomous driving systems seamlessly merge into an interactive platform. ◆ Enabling cross-domain sharing, functional consolidation, and data interoperability.	Achieve OS functional convergence through a centralized computing platform, forming a whole-vehicle OS that compatibly supports: ◆ Cockpit HMI (Human-Machine Interaction) ◆ High-performance computing for autonomous driving ◆ High-reliability vehicle control ◆ with intelligent self-adaptive capabilities.	◆ Establish a standardized, collaborative, and adaptive vehicle OS with: Unified coordination across vehicle, road, and cloud; Flexible functional allocation; Intelligent, personalized adaptation. ◆ Enabling seamless interaction with cloud platforms, roadside infrastructure, and other smart devices/systems.

		By 2030	By 2035	By 2040
Key Technologies	Compatibility and Scalability Across Hardware Architectures and Devices	◆ Establish a cross-kernel, cross-hardware framework design, supporting mainstream automotive-grade chip architectures, sensors, and peripheral devices. ◆ Enabling fusion of heterogeneous computing resources spanning edge (vehicle) and cloud.	◆ Enhance the cross-kernel driver framework design with significant improvements in interface usability, performance, functional safety, and cybersecurity. ◆ Support most automotive-grade chip architectures, sensors, and peripheral devices, while enabling multi-OS aggregation.	◆ Deliver a mature, comprehensive cross-kernel and cross-hardware framework, supporting multi-core heterogeneous hardware architectures and widely compatible with diverse automotive-grade chip platforms and sensor devices. ◆ Enable a ubiquitous OS architecture that integrates multi-cloud and multi-edge computing.
	System Performance and Functionality	◆ Kernel Performance: Autonomous driving scenarios, Interrupt response latency ≤ 10 μs, Task switching time ≤ 50 μs; Safety-critical vehicle control scenarios, Interrupt response latency ≤ 5 μs, Task switching time ≤ 5 μs. ◆ Converged Kernel: Critical scenario boot time within seconds. ◆ Virtualization Efficiency: Software performance overhead $\leq 5\%$, Peripheral performance overhead $\leq 10\%$. ◆ Middleware: Response time controlled at millisecond level. ◆ Architecture: Modular component design enables adaptable OS for diverse service models. ◆ Reliability: Zero vehicle breakdowns caused by OS failures.	◆ Enhanced Kernel Performance: Autonomous driving, Interrupt latency ≤ 5 μs, Task switching ≤ 25 μs; Safety control, Interrupt/task switching ≤ 2 μs. ◆ Boot Time: Converged kernel <1 second. ◆ Virtualization: Software overhead $\leq 3\%$; Peripheral overhead $\leq 5\%$. ◆ AI Integration: AI-driven resource scheduling for optimized subsystem coordination.	◆ Ultra-Fast Initialization: Converged kernel boot <1 second. ◆ Maximized Throughput: Filesystem and network communication throughput reach hardware limits. ◆ Distributed Virtualization: Near-native performance for shared GPU/NPU/storage resources. ◆ Autonomous Management: AI-guided resource allocation strategies govern entire OS operations.

		By 2030	By 2035	By 2040
Key Technologies	Intelligence Level (Autonomous Driving / Smart Cockpit)	◆ Deep integration of AI technologies (machine learning, computer vision, large models) into the autonomous driving OS. ◆ Enhanced compatibility and convergence capabilities of the in-vehicle OS application framework, supporting multiple UI frameworks and cross-platform application ecosystems.	◆ Significant improvement in autonomous driving decision-making and adaptability, enabling end-to-end autonomous operation without human intervention. ◆ In-vehicle OS supports 3D, VR/AR, and advanced HMI technologies, capable of understanding and responding to occupant intentions.	◆ Scalable system architecture with AI data foundation for model deployment and optimization. Comprehensive understanding of occupant intentions and support for omnidirectional interaction capabilities. ◆ Full support for next-generation intelligent vehicle applications and services.
	Intelligence Level (AI Capabilities)	◆ The system supports in-vehicle natural language processing, image recognition, and complex voice command interpretation. It enables AI-based real-time decision-making to enhance driving safety and comfort. ◆ Applying AI technology to assist in the architecture design, functionality, and safety testing of automotive operating systems	◆ The system delivers advanced in-vehicle reasoning capabilities, equipped with certain native AI capabilities;allowing vehicles to continuously self-optimize based on environmental and driving data while dynamically predicting and adapting to complex road and traffic conditions. ◆ AI technology is effectively utilized in the design, development, and testing of automotive operating systems	◆ With native AI capabilities, the system supports self-evolution and continuous learning, endowing vehicles with fully autonomous learning and decision-making intelligence.
	Connectivity	◆ The system incorporates low-latency PCIe technology, Ethernet, and Time-Sensitive Networking (TSN) communication technologies. ◆ It enables real-time data acquisition and exchange between vehicles and the cloud, achieving seamless connectivity and interoperability with cloud platforms, terminal devices, and services.	◆ The system integrates 5G/6G communication technologies on a broader scale. ◆ Advanced low-latency and high-bandwidth technologies mature with hardware protocol conversion capabilities, supporting unified scheduling for vehicle-infrastructure coordination.	◆ The system achieves ultra-low-latency, high-throughput interconnection capabilities. ◆ It natively supports high-speed network protocols and fully integrates cutting-edge technologies like quantum communication, enabling comprehensive and seamless vehicle-road-cloud collaboration.

Fig. 5.8 Technology roadmap for vehicle operating systems

Fig. 5.8 (continued)

Chapter 6
Automotive Intelligent Manufacturing Technology

6.1 Introduction

6.1.1 Background and Positioning

Currently, China's automotive industry has entered a new phase of high-quality development: its industrial foundation continues to strengthen, electrification and intelligent technologies have gained first-mover advantages, and product competitiveness as well as market share have significantly increased. Behind the periodic and partial competitive edge achieved by China's intelligent electric vehicles in the global market lies in the innovative exploration and continuous advancement of the production system and intelligent manufacturing technologies. If product technologies can propel enterprises to short-term leadership, then the underlying manufacturing systems and technologies that enable these products can sustain their dominance. Precisely for this reason, systematically summarizing intelligent manufacturing technologies in parallel with automotive product development is both vitally important and opportune.

In fact, intelligent manufacturing itself carries profound strategic significance—serving both as the ultimate goal of digital transformation in manufacturing and as a new industrial paradigm shaped by new quality productive forces. It must be clearly recognized that **intelligent manufacturing is not merely the improvement of isolated production processes, but rather a comprehensive transformation of the integrated R&D-production-supply-sales-service system empowered by digitally-based intelligent technologies such as artificial intelligence (AI). This transformation exhibits distinctive characteristics of comprehensiveness, systematicity, and complexity**. In its development trajectory, intelligent manufacturing requires prioritized breakthroughs in leading industries to catalyze sector-wide advancement. The automotive sector, as a pivotal strategic emerging industry,

Technology Roadmap for Energy Saving and New Energy Vehicles 3.0,
https://doi.org/10.1007/978-981-95-2502-7_6

presents both the greatest challenges and highest complexity for implementing intelligent manufacturing, while simultaneously offering the most extensive value realization, operational impact and industrial influence. Consequently, the practical implementation of automotive intelligent manufacturing holds far-reaching implications that extend well beyond the sector itself.

Currently, automotive enterprises worldwide—particularly in China—have pioneered cutting-edge innovations across R&D, production, supply chain, marketing, and service operations. These advancements not only effectively enable next-generation vehicle development but are fundamentally redefining automotive manufacturing systems, distinct from traditional paradigms. However, the industry still faces conceptual and practical misunderstandings in implementing intelligent manufacturing, notably: insufficient grasp of its holistic integration, conflating smart manufacturing with mere smart production, and undervaluing cross-functional synergies. Given these challenges, there's an urgent need for an automotive intelligent manufacturing technology roadmap—to consolidate best practices, rectify misconceptions, build industry consensus, chart development pathways, and ultimately drive sustainable advancement of the automotive sector.

Furthermore, the relationship between the automotive intelligent manufacturing system and automotive products and services determines the importance and strategic position of the automotive intelligent manufacturing technology roadmap. First and foremost, the automotive intelligent manufacturing system serves as the "industrial mother machine" for creating automotive products and services. Ultimately, it enables mass production with personalized customization of automobiles while continuously facilitating iterative upgrades for both products and services, as shown in Fig. 6.1. With the support of the intelligent manufacturing system, automotive products and services fully unleash the potential value of data, providing users with intelligent and personalized driving experiences. At the same time, automotive products and services are no longer merely passive "manufactured goods" in the traditional sense. Instead, they actively feed real-time usage data back into the intelligent manufacturing system, driving continuous optimization of both the manufacturing framework and its underlying technologies. This creates a self-reinforcing closed loop where vehicles and their production systems mutually enhance one another. Ultimately, this closed-loop operation is enabled by the circulation and utilization of diverse big data streams, representing the practical implementation of digital transformation in the automotive sector. These relationships demonstrate that automotive intelligent manufacturing serves as the foundational, comprehensive, and systemic framework for product creation. Accordingly, the *Energy-Saving and New Energy Vehicle Technology Roadmap 3.0* has dedicated an independent volume specifically to the automotive intelligent manufacturing technology roadmap. Published as a stand-alone companion to the product technology roadmap, this volume comprehensively outlines the developmental trajectory for the manufacturing systems, industrial frameworks, and technological innovations that shape future vehicles and their production.

The evolution of automotive products has introduced new requirements and driving forces for automotive intelligent manufacturing in the industry. Therefore,

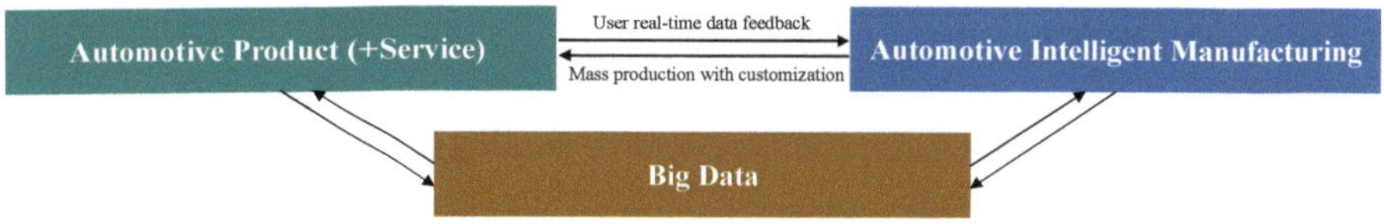

Fig. 6.1 The relationship between automotive intelligent manufacturing and products

the formulation of the automotive intelligent manufacturing technology roadmap should be based on an in-depth analysis of the very products and technologies it aims to advance. Today, automotive products and technologies are undergoing fundamental transformations, leading to entirely new conceptual frameworks and distinctive attributes that fundamentally differ from traditional vehicles. With broad industry consensus, the roadmap defines these next-generation vehicles as the "New Auto" concept—a reimagined category characterized by data-driven intelligence, self-evolutionary capabilities, and the role of an intelligent mobile space.

To address the developmental needs of the "New Auto," **the positioning of the automotive intelligent manufacturing technology roadmap is defined as: a strategic blueprint for establishing the innovative systems, associated technologies, and methodologies to realize the "New Auto"**—in other words, a methodology focused on high-quality industrial development and groundbreaking product creation. Unlike the manufacturing-related sections in the *Energy-Saving and New Energy Vehicle Technology Roadmap 2.0*, which primarily emphasized production processes, this automotive intelligent manufacturing technology roadmap **marks the first comprehensive integration of design, production, and services across the entire automotive manufacturing system**. It features broader boundaries and more diverse elements, encompassing nearly every operational aspect of automotive enterprises. In this sense, the automotive intelligent manufacturing technology roadmap essentially serves as a roadmap for the entire automotive industry's evolution.

On the other hand, the "technology" in the automotive intelligent manufacturing technology roadmap is broad and conceptual in nature—encompassing not only technical elements but also tools, processes, organizational structures, and operational models. Consequently, **this roadmap represents a methodology-driven evolutionary path toward establishing the complex systems engineering framework for the end-to-end development of the "New Auto"—a distinctive and pivotal feature of this technology roadmap**.

In essence, the automotive intelligent manufacturing technology roadmap seeks to serve three purposes: providing automotive enterprises with guidelines for innovation and transformation of their product development systems, charting the course for China's automotive industry to accelerate the establishment of a world-leading intelligent manufacturing ecosystem, and supporting the transition of automotive manufacturing into a new paradigm of production—empowered by new quality productive forces.

6.1.2 Principles

The roadmap's focus on establishing automotive intelligent manufacturing methodologies determines its immense value to both the industry and enterprises, while also presenting numerous challenges in its formulation. To ensure the roadmap's scientific rigor, rationality and feasibility—while addressing the distinctive characteristics of automotive intelligent manufacturing—its development adheres to four fundamental principles.

Firstly, automotive intelligent manufacturing constitutes an integrated macro-system spanning R&D, production, supply chain, sales and services—a vast, interconnected ecosystem featuring numerous interdependent elements. While these components possess distinct characteristics, they maintain intricate interconnections, and are controlled by diverse stakeholders. To clearly demonstrate the multi-element, multi-stakeholder relationships within automotive intelligent manufacturing, we established **core principles for element mapping. First, data flow must permeate all processes**, reflecting both cross-stage integration within manufacturing and circulation across internal and external enterprise boundaries. **Second, adopting a problem-driven approach**, where specialized domains consolidate consensus from cutting-edge practices, identify critical challenges represented by typical scenarios, then conduct systematic analysis through technological, procedural, systemic and ecosystem lenses.

Secondly, automotive intelligent manufacturing is highly complex and constantly evolving, with technological pathways yet to converge and numerous issues awaiting resolution. There remains a lack of unified understanding, inconsistent strategies, and divergent methodologies among stakeholders. To address this, the roadmap establishes the key **scope-defining principles. First, the Macro-Meso Focus**. As a pioneering initiative, the automotive intelligent manufacturing technology roadmap prioritizes clarifying overarching frameworks and strategic trajectories—articulating the megatrends at the strategic level and critical directions for implementation. **Second, the Incremental-Transformative Emphasis (The δ + v Principle)**. The roadmap specifically highlights delta (δ) developments—newly emerging element—and variables (v)—fundamentally transformed aspects—in the process of creating the "New Auto." Traditional or minimally altered conventional content falls outside its scope, captured by the guiding **"δ + v" principle**.

Thirdly, the metrics for the automotive intelligent manufacturing technology roadmap present unique complexities, seldom achieving the consensus-based, quantifiable indicators commonly found in product technology roadmaps. This stems from intelligent manufacturing being as much an organizational challenge as a technical one—encompassing tools, processes, structures, and business models. Even the technological components themselves exist in hybridized forms, where effectiveness emerges only through optimal combinations of multiple technologies integrated with non-technological factors. Addressing these characteristics, **the principle for metric selection** follows two dimensions. **First, while prioritizing technology** (particularly product-enabling, application-oriented, and tool-based technologies), **the roadmap**

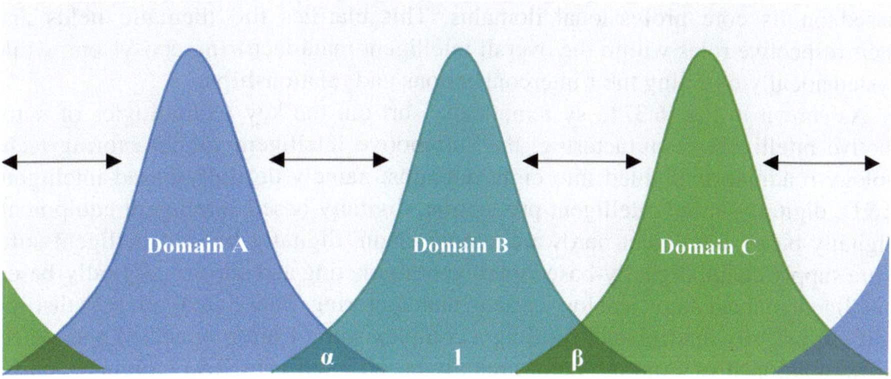

Fig. 6.2 The principles for boundary demarcation of each domain in the automotive intelligent manufacturing technology roadmap

deliberately transcends pure technical parameters by elucidating methodological frameworks through mapping multi-element, multi-stakeholder interdependencies. **Second, adopting a hybrid qualitative-quantitative approach**, where genuinely unquantifiable aspects are addressed through indicator systems blending qualitative analysis of critical elements with measurable parameters where feasible.

Finally, the automotive intelligent manufacturing technology roadmap encompasses eight key domains: R&D, production, equipment, hardware supply chain, software supply chain, marketing & service, management, and low-carbon manufacturing. These domains are highly interrelated, with significant overlaps and interdependencies, necessitating clear delineation of each thematic scope. Accordingly, we established **boundary demarcation principles** for each domain (see Fig. 6.2). **The first is Gaussian Distribution Principle.** Each domain focuses primarily on its core content while appropriately addressing related topics beyond, with research scope expansion guided by normal distribution. **The second is "1 + α + β" Principle.** To be specific, "1" represents the main focus—the core activities of the domain, corresponding to the central part of the distribution. "α" (upstream business) and "β" (downstream business) denote interactions with other domains, corresponding to overlapping regions of normal distributions and illustrating either demand inputs ("α") or support outputs ("β") between domains. During roadmap development, each domian elaborates comprehensively on its primary "1" to ensure emphasis on core priorities while appropriately addressing "α" and "β" to maintain cross-domain synergy, ensuring a cohesive and integrated whole.

6.1.3 *Framework*

Building upon the aforementioned principles, the research scope and logical framework of automotive intelligent manufacturing technology clusters have been defined based on its core professional domains. This clarifies the thematic fields and their respective roles within the overall intelligent manufacturing ecosystem, while systematically outlining their interconnections and relationships.

As shown in Fig. 6.3, to systematically sort out the key technologies of automotive intelligent manufacturing, the automotive intelligent manufacturing technology roadmap is divided into eight domains, namely digitally-based intelligent R&D, digitally-based intelligent production, digitally-based intelligent equipment, digitally-based intelligent hardware supply chain, digitally-based intelligent software supply chain, digitally-based intelligent marketing and service, digitally-based intelligent management, and low-carbon manufacturing. These areas are both distinct and intrinsically interrelated, forming a complex web of interconnected and synergistic relationships. Among them, digitally-based intelligent R&D, digitally-based intelligent production, digitally-based intelligent hardware supply chain, digitally-based intelligent software supply chain, and digitally-based intelligent marketing and service constitute the core operational links of enterprises, collectively forming the application layer of automotive intelligent manufacturing. Digitally-based intelligent equipment (closely integrated with digitally-based intelligent production) and digitally-based intelligent management represent the hard and soft enablers, respectively, jointly comprising the supporting layer. Furthermore, low-carbon manufacturing serves both as a guiding principle and a binding condition for the automotive intelligent manufacturing system. As such, it permeates both the application and support layers, deeply integrating with every operational link to ensure the sustainable development of the automotive manufacturing industry.

It should be further clarified that "digitally-based intelligentization" here refers to an ongoing process of deepening integration between digitalization and intelligentization, driving systematic transformation in business models and organizational management. More specifically, it represents an evolutionary engineering approach that builds upon digitalization (data as the foundation), incorporates various digital and intelligent technologies, and ultimately progresses toward achieving intelligentization (objective)—essentially, digitally-based intelligentization. Precisely because

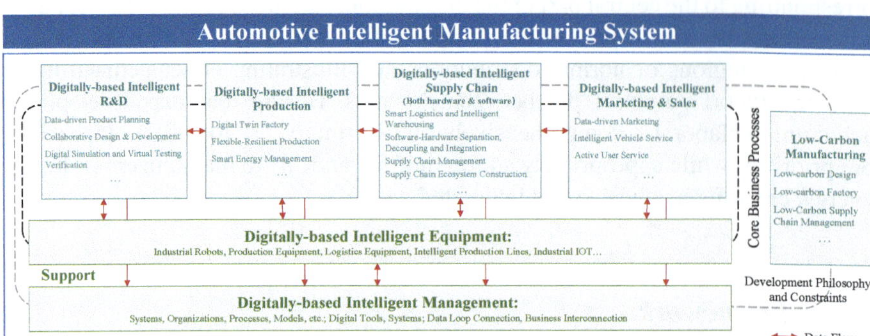

Fig. 6.3 The overall framework of the automotive intelligent manufacturing technology roadmap

of this intrinsic nature, using "Digitally-based Intelligent" to define each specialized professional domain aligns perfectly with the essence of intelligent manufacturing.

6.2 Connotations and Strategic Values

6.2.1 Connotations

6.2.1.1 Basic Concepts of Automotive Intelligent Manufacturing

Accurately comprehending the concept and essence of automotive intelligent manufacturing serves as the foundational prerequisite for the scientific formulation of the automotive intelligent manufacturing technology roadmap. Based on fundamental conditions, core drivers, intrinsic characteristics, and ultimate objectives, **automotive intelligent manufacturing is defined as a New Auto manufacturing system built upon the interconnection of everything, driven by data, endowed with intelligent capabilities, and ultimately capable of self-evolution**. As illustrated in Fig. 6.4, automotive intelligent manufacturing comprehensively encompasses the entire value chain, including R&D, production, supply, marketing, and service. Data permeates and integrates all segments, forming a closed loop, while cutting-edge digital and intelligent technologies—epitomized by AI—enable multi-agent systems to achieve convergent innovation across R&D, production, supply, sales, and service domains. Consequently, the entire value chain of automotive intelligent manufacturing achieves interconnectivity, interoperability, interactivity, and intelligence. In essence, automotive intelligent manufacturing represents a new type of automotive manufacturing system that integrates R&D, production, supply, sales, and service into a unified whole.

The above concepts reveal that intelligent manufacturing and digitalization are inherently interconnected and mutually reinforcing, with their relationship illustrated in Fig. 6.5. At its core, intelligent manufacturing realizes the value of data, positioning it as the ultimate goal of digital transformation and the guiding direction for the future of manufacturing. Conversely, digitalization—the process of managing and applying data—serves as a critical enabler of intelligent manufacturing. Leveraging digital technologies such as IoT, cloud computing, AI, and blockchain, it facilitates

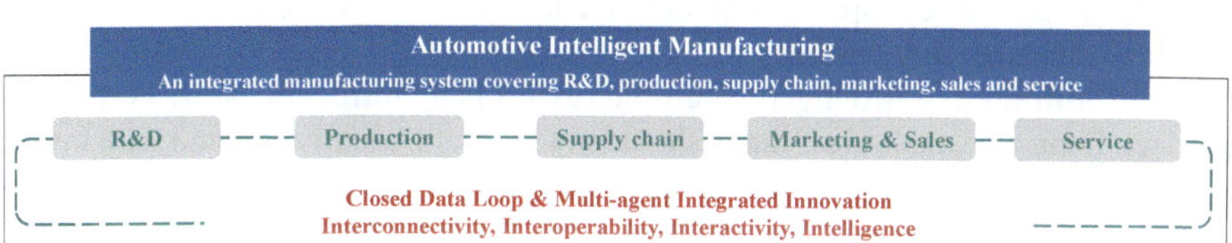

Fig. 6.4 Basic concepts of automotive intelligent manufacturing

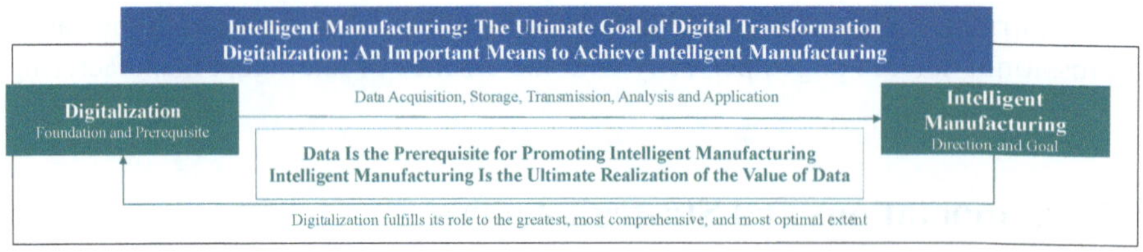

Fig. 6.5 The relationship between intelligent manufacturing and digitalization

the collection, processing, and utilization of massive datasets. This empowers intelligent manufacturing systems to achieve data-driven self-awareness, self-learning, self-optimization, autonomous decision-making, and self-execution. In essence, data bridges intelligent manufacturing and digitalization. Data acts as the prerequisite for advancing intelligent manufacturing. Intelligent manufacturing represents the ultimate realization of data's value. Ultimately, through data acquisition, storage, transmission, analysis, and application, digitalization fulfills its role to the greatest, most comprehensive, and most optimal extent.

It is important to emphasize that automotive intelligent manufacturing targets not just one or a few companies, but the entire industrial ecosystem. This represents not only a macro-level conceptual framework but also a concrete implementation platform. The realization of automotive intelligent manufacturing can never be achieved independently by a single enterprise—it requires collaborative efforts among vehicle manufacturers, software and hardware suppliers, ICT firms, and various service providers, who must share information and integrate resources to ultimately succeed. Throughout this process, next-generation digital technologies and intelligent technologies must be deeply integrated with the entire product lifecycle and manufacturing chain of automobiles. This convergence will forge a highly efficient, multi-stakeholder ecosystem where resources are seamlessly coordinated and value chains systematically interconnected.

6.2.1.2 Key Insights on Automotive Intelligent Manufacturing

Currently, the industry has not yet reached a broad consensus on the definition, characteristics, value, and implementation paths of automotive intelligent manufacturing—a situation that significantly hampers its orderly development. Therefore, clarifying the key aspects of automotive intelligent manufacturing and aligning industry understanding has become an urgent priority.

First, automotive intelligent manufacturing is a comprehensive, systematic project. It must be made clear that it should not be simplistically equated with intelligent production. While intelligent production is indeed a critical aspect of intelligent manufacturing, the concept of automotive intelligent manufacturing encompasses far more—spanning the entire industrial chain including R&D, production, supply, sales, and services, as well as all stages of the automotive product lifecycle. Moreover, it relies on digitally-based intelligent technologies to enable seamless integration and coordinated operations across every phase and process.

Second, automotive intelligent manufacturing represents a comprehensive transformation encompassing technology, organizational structure, and business models. Technologically, it demands proactive adoption of cutting-edge digital solutions—IoT, cloud platforms, AI (particularly large models), and blockchain—to enhance data collection, analysis, and processing capabilities. Simultaneously, modernization of conventional manufacturing technologies remains indispensable. Organizationally, existing industrial division models are increasingly inadequate for the demands of intelligent manufacturing. This necessitates a fundamental reshaping of resource allocation strategies and innovative business models to facilitate seamless resource integration and capability sharing both within and across enterprises. This multidimensional transformation involves redefining technical standards, optimizing and reinventing business processes, restructuring organizational frameworks, and continuously evolving management philosophies and operating models.

Furthermore, automotive intelligent manufacturing represents a new ecosystem co-created, co-shared and co-governed by automakers and suppliers. The automotive intelligent manufacturing system encompasses numerous entities and elements, essentially involving the entire automotive industrial ecosystem, requiring OEMs, software/hardware suppliers and other participants to integrate resources and collaborate synergistically. It should be emphasized that while large enterprises play crucial roles in establishing platforms and consolidating collaborative efforts within this ecosystem, automotive intelligent manufacturing is not exclusively their domain. Small and medium-sized suppliers, with their rapid response capabilities and operational agility, provide irreplaceable value in meeting personal customer demands. Consequently, they constitute indispensable components of the automotive intelligent manufacturing ecosystem.

Lastly, the development of automotive intelligent manufacturing demands both urgent action and sustained investment. As a highly complex, long-term system engineering initiative, achieving its full implementation is projected to take at least two decades. This prolonged timeline means automotive intelligent manufacturing cannot be realized overnight; it requires phased, methodical advancement. However, the extended duration must not become justification for reduced investment or stagnation. The present moment is precisely the optimal time to act—every step forward yields tangible benefits, whereas hesitation risks exclusion. Companies that delay implementation may find themselves unable to integrate when the intelligent manufacturing ecosystem matures, leaving them at a severe competitive disadvantage or even facing obsolescence. Thus, proactive and continuous commitment is imperative.

6.2.2 *Strategic Values*

6.2.2.1 Automotive Intelligent Manufacturing Helps Enterprises Achieve Quality Improvement, Efficiency Increase, Cost Reduction and Low Carbon Emissions

The strategic value of automotive intelligent manufacturing predominantly lies in empowering enterprises to enhance quality, improve efficiency, reduce costs, and achieve low-carbon development. In essence, quality improvement, efficiency enhancement, and cost reduction represent the perpetual pursuit of the manufacturing sector. From this perspective, the fundamental nature of automotive intelligent manufacturing resides in progressively approaching these enduring objectives through digital technologies like AI—specifically, satisfying diverse customer needs with superior quality, faster delivery, and lower costs, thereby generating corporate profits while creating value for end-users.

Indeed, the aforementioned value of automotive intelligent manufacturing has been comprehensively demonstrated through a series of pioneering practices by automakers. The following elaborates on typical scenarios and their significant roles in optimizing R&D, production, supply chain, marketing, and service aspects—examined through the lenses of quality improvement, efficiency enhancement, cost reduction, and low-carbon development.

In terms of quality improvement, introducing virtual testing of hardware and software enables early detection of design flaws, preventing product quality issues at their source. Automated production lines significantly improve manufacturing stability and product consistency. In the supply chain, digital technologies such as blockchain facilitate end-to-end traceability and real-time quality monitoring across the supply network. In the marketing sector, VR/AR-powered immersive purchasing environments elevate the customer buying experience. The service section ensures that the "New Auto" remains fresh and better with each use through continuous self-iteration and evolution of the product.

In terms of efficiency improvement, applying automated hardware/software development and testing technologies with data-driven iterative mechanisms significantly shortens development cycles. In the production process, implementing adaptive collaborative manufacturing modes markedly improve production efficiency; In the supply sector, utilizing digital technologies for OEM-supplier synchronization improves responsiveness to market fluctuations and delivery efficiency. In terms of marketing, data-driven customer insights boost lead conversion rates. In the service segment, user and vehicle data analytics enable predictive maintenance personalization and rapid demand response.

In terms of cost reduction, virtual simulation replacing bench and vehicle testing significantly reduces development costs. In the production process, real-time monitoring and precision control of elements such as personnel, equipment, materials, processes, and environment minimizes resource waste. In the supply chain, smart logistics and smart warehousing maintain lean inventory levels while cutting carrying costs. In the marketing sector, digital optimization through customer profiling enables precision marketing with improved return on investment. In the service sector, AI-powered customer service solutions partially replace manual operations to reduce after-sales service costs.

In terms of low-carbon development, lightweight, modular and recyclable structural designs lay the foundation for low-carbon product operation in the R&D process. Automated manufacturing processes can reduce energy consumption and carbon emissions. In the supply chain, logistics simulation and intelligent scheduling minimize transportation-related carbon footprint. For marketing, expanded online sales channels reduce energy consumption and emissions from physical operations. In the service segment, battery and key material recycling programs substantially reduce lifecycle emissions in battery production.

The aforementioned applications represent only a fraction of how automotive intelligent manufacturing optimizes automotive enterprise performance, yet they convincingly demonstrate that the deep integration of digital technologies with automotive production systems can substantially enhance product quality, service excellence, and overall operational standards, dramatically shorten product development cycles, significantly improve workforce productivity across all levels, effectively reduce comprehensive costs throughout the entire value chain, and achieve carbon reduction and low-carbon development across both product lifecycles and enterprise operations. Looking ahead, as automotive intelligent manufacturing continues to advance, its tremendous potential to generate corporate profits and create user value will be realized across broader domains, in more scenarios, and to greater extents than ever before.

6.2.2.2 Automotive Intelligent Manufacturing Leads to Fundamental Changes in the Automotive Manufacturing Modes

Zooming out to examine from a broader manufacturing perspective, automotive intelligent manufacturing will likely catalyze fundamental changes in production paradigms, thereby possessing unparalleled strategic significance. Historically, as the pinnacle of advanced manufacturing, the automotive industry has spearheaded every major revolution in production methodologies. The current automotive intelligent manufacturing transformation is likewise expected to establish new paradigms and chart the course for manufacturing evolution.

Looking back at the development of the automotive industry, there have been three major and far-reaching changes in manufacturing models, as shown in Fig. 6.6.

The first phase, Manufacturing 1.0, marks the era of mass production, epitomized by Ford's Model T. This revolution standardized product design, implemented assembly line production, and replaced manual labor with machinery, achieving unprecedented economies of scale. The transformation dramatically boosted production efficiency while slashing costs, simultaneously giving rise to the modern supply chain system where automakers collaborate with tiered suppliers—an organizational model that has endured as the manufacturing industry's dominant paradigm.

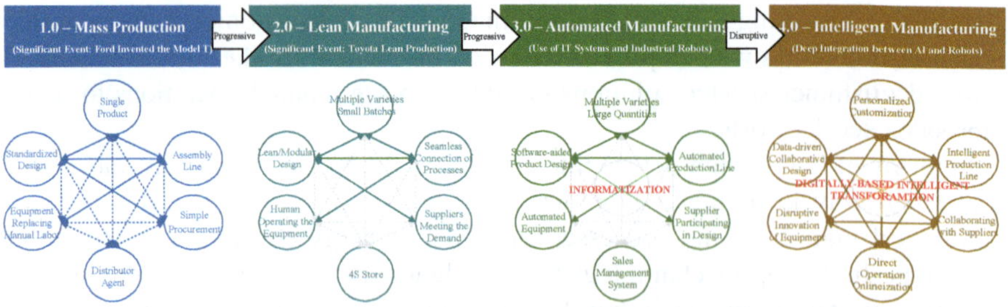

Fig. 6.6 Four stages of fundamental changes in the automotive manufacturing mode

The industry then entered Manufacturing 2.0—the era of lean production, heralded by Toyota's revolutionary approach. This transformation introduced modular design principles in R&D and implemented comprehensive lean manufacturing techniques, including seamless process integration, just-in-time production (JIT), Kanban management, and continuous improvement. These innovations successfully enabled diversified, small-batch manufacturing that could accommodate dynamic market demands. Concurrently, the automotive retail landscape evolved with the establishment of 4S dealership systems. These integrated facilities combined vehicle sales, spare parts, service, and survey capabilities—creating unified platforms that served consumers while providing manufacturers with valuable insights into user needs and vehicle usage patterns. Throughout this phase, automakers maintained their central position in the value chain, with suppliers operating in a strictly hierarchical relationship to execute predefined tasks assigned by OEMs.

Then is Automotive Manufacturing 3.0—The Era of Automated Production. This phase is characterized by the widespread adoption of information systems, industrial robotics, and other advanced technologies. In product development, computer-aided design became standard practice, substantially enhancing both efficiency and quality. On the factory floor, automated equipment and robotic assembly lines were extensively deployed, dramatically improving production consistency and reliability. The supply chain evolved as well, with component manufacturers engaging more deeply in co-design processes, fostering unprecedented collaboration with automakers. The sales ecosystem transformed through comprehensive sales management information systems, delivering measurable gains in distribution efficiency. These cumulative advancements enabled automakers to achieve large-scale production of diverse models, positioning them to efficiently address both the expanding and rapidly evolving consumer demands.

Today, the automotive industry embraces Automotive Manufacturing 4.0—the dawn of digitally-based intelligent manufacturing, distinctly characterized by the deep integration between and widespread application of AI and industrial robotics. While its paradigms continue evolving, this phase differs fundamentally from previous transitional stages that focused on isolated improvements. Digitally-based intelligent manufacturing represents not incremental progress, but a comprehensive, system-wide transformation across every operational dimension. "Digitally-based

Intelligent" serves as the critical enabler of this revolution, with intelligent manufacturing emerging as its ultimate objective. In this new era, R&D undergoes paradigm shifts through novel development methodologies driven by evolving hardware-software architectures, unlocking unprecedented innovation potential. Production achieves self-adaptive manufacturing via intelligent equipment and lines, while breakthrough innovations in processes and machinery redefine traditional automotive manufacturing. Supply Chains evolve into collaborative ecosystems where automakers and suppliers co-create through deep integrated innovation, significantly enhancing systemic competitiveness. Sales & Service witness disruptive models including direct-to-consumer channels, digital marketing, and service ecosystems that fundamentally transform customer purchase and ownership experiences. This convergence enables automakers to achieve the previously impossible: mass production with personal customization that harmonizes scale with personalization. The result is an unprecedented ability to deliver higher-quality products faster, at lower cost, while continuously refreshing offerings to meet dynamic user needs.

In summary, this fundamental transformation in automotive manufacturing is far more complex and far-reaching than previous changes, involving numerous interconnected industries, domains, and elements. Every aspect—from product strategy formulation, design and development, supply chain management, and production line and plant design, to manufacturing processes and equipment upgrades, marketing and service innovations, and enterprise operations management—is undergoing profound changes. In essence, this shift in the entire manufacturing system signifies the increasing prominence of new production factors, with data taking center stage. Advanced productivity enablers like large AI models—which maximize data value—are accelerating development, urgently demanding and giving rise to a new matching production paradigm.

6.3 Current Status and Trends

6.3.1 Current Status Analysis of Automotive Intelligent Manufacturing

6.3.1.1 The Latest Trends and Advancements in Automotive Intelligent Manufacturing

Automakers are actively pioneering new frameworks, technologies, and paradigms for automotive intelligent manufacturing. Across the entire value chain—spanning R&D, production, supply networks, marketing and services—numerous innovative practices have emerged. The following outlines the most representative cutting-edge advancements:

In the realm of R&D, technologies such as VR/AR, AI, and digital twins are reshaping development paradigms, steering **automotive research toward**

virtualization and automation. Leading enterprises have implemented virtual design reviews, simulated testing, and agile software development, significantly compressing product development cycles. Concurrently, **data-driven continuous R&D** is gaining traction—companies now leverage user and vehicle operation data analytics to refine new product development while enabling post-launch product enhancements, ultimately delivering superior user-centric solutions.

In the production domain, **the concept of digital twin factories is materializing**. By establishing digital twin models at the equipment, production line, and entire factory levels, manufacturers can monitor the entire production process and its associated elements in real-time while conducting predictive simulations. This advancement robustly supports adaptive and automated manufacturing while significantly enhancing production efficiency and product quality. **The automotive production landscape is undergoing transformative changes**, exemplified by innovations like integrated mega-casting and the unboxed assembly process. Integrated mega-casting replaces traditional stamping and welding operations, simplifying production workflows while reducing costs and improving product quality. Meanwhile, the unboxed assembly process—through modular production, parallel assembly, and innovative painting techniques—transcends the spatial and temporal efficiency limitations of conventional automotive manufacturing while dramatically reducing labor requirements and operational costs.

In the equipment sector, **demand-driven customized development has become the prevailing trend**. To accommodate evolving automotive production models, manufacturing lines are evolving toward greater flexibility, modularity, and automation. For instance, integrated mega-casting production lines require bespoke high-tonnage die-casting machines specifically engineered for this purpose. Concurrently, **comprehensive networking of intelligent equipment represents another major development**. Through integration with industrial IoT systems, these advanced machines—empowered by data analytics and AI foundation models—are achieving intelligent perception, decision-making, execution and predictive maintenance. This digital transformation significantly enhances resource utilization efficiency across production, logistics, and warehousing operations.

In the hardware supply sector, **intelligent upgrades in logistics and warehousing are becoming a reality**. The adoption of autonomous tow tractors, automated guided vehicles (AGVs), radio-frequency identification (RFID), and IoT technologies has ushered in smarter warehouse management and more precise distribution systems. **Both flexibility and resilience in supply systems continue to strengthen significantly**. From achieving supply chain visibility to establishing collaborative platforms powered by real-time data sharing, an integrated supply chain ecosystem is taking shape. This development significantly enhances automakers' capability to coordinate effectively with suppliers and respond to market fluctuations with agility and efficiency.

In the realm of software supply, the concept of "software-defined vehicles" has gradually emerged as an industry consensus, giving rise to a new development model **where software takes precedence**. Leading enterprises have incorporated agile development and integrated product development (IPD) methodologies into automotive product development processes. Concurrently, industry leaders are **placing significant emphasis on building robust software supply ecosystems**. Many have established open software development platforms equipped with capabilities such as simulation verification and big data analytics. These platforms aggregate relevant development resources and, leveraging service-oriented architecture (SOA) with layered decoupling, enable flexible software development for standardized, atomic hardware components.

In the marketing and service domain, **data-driven precision marketing and personalized intelligent services are being progressively implemented**. The former manifests as enterprises leveraging digital technologies to innovate marketing channels and processes. Emerging practices, such as virtual product launches and user communities, seamlessly integrate online and offline channels, enabling automakers to establish direct consumer connections while precisely conveying product features with targeted impact. The latter refers to enterprises harnessing big data and foundation models to gain profound insights into user needs, proactively delivering customized services while constructing comprehensive service ecosystems spanning multiple scenarios.

In the field of management, enterprises are increasingly recognizing **the necessity of data sharing** and taking measures such as standardizing data protocols and establishing data centers to enhance their governance capabilities, facilitating data exchange both internally and externally. Meanwhile, industry leaders are proactively exploring **cross-sector resource integration and allocation**. By developing open digital platforms that connect diverse enterprises, they are pooling multi-party resources to jointly advance innovation, product development, and user services through collaborative efforts.

In the realm of low-carbon manufacturing, **digital technologies provide robust support for achieving decarbonization goals**. Through advanced sensors, big data, and artificial intelligence, enterprises can monitor carbon emissions in production processes in real time, analyze influencing factors, and implement optimizations. Leading companies are implementing low-carbon materials, clean energy solutions, and emissions-reduction technologies across the entire value chain from R&D to after-sales services. Some pioneers have even established demonstration "zero-carbon factories," setting benchmarks for sustainable development in the automotive industry.

Overall, automotive intelligent manufacturing has made notable progress across various specialized domains. However, substantial development potential remains before achieving full implementation and maximizing its transformative impact.

6.3.1.2 Current Challenges Facing Automotive Intelligent Manufacturing

Based on the practice of automotive enterprises in promoting intelligent manufacturing, we identify three areas where enterprises generally have room for improvement and summarize them into three challenges (Fig. 6.7). **The first challenge is that "individual process has not been upgraded effectively"**, mainly manifested as incomplete production factors and insufficient productivity. **The second challenge is that "the processes have not been fully connected"**, which is mainly reflected in the mismatch of production relations. **The third challenge is that "innovation capability and product competitiveness lack integration"**, which is mainly reflected in the unbalanced emphasis of enterprises on product power and creativity, as well as the insufficient interaction between the manufacturing system and the product.

To address these challenges, enterprises must not only transform traditional capabilities but also cultivate entirely new competencies. Regarding production factors, the key lies in fully unlocking the immense value of data as a new production element.

In terms of productivity, the priority involves both upgrading conventional "legacy" technologies and deploying cutting-edge solutions, such as AI foundation models, cloud computing, blockchain, and intelligent robotics, representing the latest digital and intelligent technologies. Concerning production relations, the critical focus is restructuring multi-factor, multi-entity relationships to enable cross-industry and cross-domain resource integration and optimal allocation.

In other words, the full implementation of automotive intelligent manufacturing requires addressing challenges across singular process enhancements, multi-process integration, and the dynamic interplay between production factors, productivity, and production relations within the manufacturing system and products. Each level and segment involve numerous variables and increments that mutually influence one another. Thus, automotive intelligent manufacturing represents a highly complex undertaking that cannot be achieved overnight. It demands comprehensive planning, sustained and substantial investment from all stakeholders. Only through the progressive accumulation of each incremental advancement can the ultimate objectives of quality improvement, efficiency enhancement, cost reduction, and low-carbon transformation be realized.

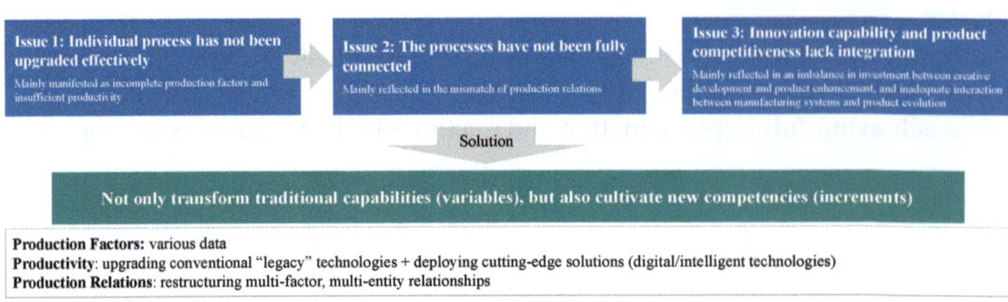

Fig. 6.7 The challenges facing automotive enterprises when promoting intelligent manufacturing

The following will elaborate on the three types of challenges existing in the automotive industry in promoting intelligent manufacturing and analyze the solutions.

- **Challenge One: Individual Process Has Not Been Upgraded Effectively**

Currently, automotive enterprises face obstacles in advancing the intelligentization of individual segments such as R&D, production, supply chain, sales, and services. These challenges primarily manifest in incomplete production factors and insufficient productivity.

As is widely known, production factors constitute fundamental elements in the manufacturing process, mainly including production materials and tools. For automotive intelligent manufacturing, data has become the most critical production factor. However, none of the current stages in automotive intelligent manufacturing have fully realized the value of data. Various issues persist—incomplete data categories, suboptimal quality, inadequate real-time capabilities, and weak usability, which severely constrain each segment of the automotive manufacturing system from achieving data-driven capability enhancement.

Corresponding to data as a new production factor is the emergence of digital technologies for processing data, which have become one of the most vital productive forces. In reality, the underutilization of data stems largely from insufficient advancement in digital technologies. Deficiencies exist across all aspects, including data generation/acquisition (e.g., sensor instrumentation), processing (e.g., data processing software), transmission/storage (e.g., communication networks, cloud platforms), and application (e.g., industrial software, smart equipment).

Therefore, to address challenges in enhancing individual processes, we must implement comprehensive strategies targeting both production factors and productive forces. The specific approaches include:

On one hand, it is essential to heighten awareness regarding the strategic value of data elements while accelerating the adoption and implementation of digital technologies. This involves progressively refining data generation, collection, transmission, storage, processing, and utilization across R&D, production, supply chain, marketing, and service functions, thereby establishing a data-powered framework that drives continuous optimization in the automotive intelligent manufacturing system and facilitates iterative enhancements for intelligent automotive products.

On the other hand, active adoption of AI large models to empower automotive intelligent manufacturing is particularly crucial. As a key component of new productive forces, AI large models are poised to play an unprecedented role in leveraging data production factors, providing an efficient pathway to realize data value. Judging from AI development trends, large models are driving the evolution from ANI (Artificial Narrow Intelligence) to AGI (Artificial General Intelligence) and even ASI (Artificial Super Intelligence), marking a qualitative leap in AI capabilities that will profoundly impact not only the automotive industry and broader manufacturing sector, but virtually every industry and human society as a whole. Given the complexity, representativeness, and integrative nature of the automotive industry, large models hold immense potential yet face extraordinary challenges in their application. In their implementation, companies should construct specialized professional models for each phase—R&D, production, supply chain, marketing, and service—layered atop foundational large models, leveraging their powerful capabilities to fundamentally enhance the performance of these domain-specific models throughout the automotive value chain.

- **Challenge Two: The Processes Have Not Been Fully Connected**

Currently, the various segments of automotive intelligent manufacturing—R&D, production, supply chain, sales, and services, along with their corresponding stakeholders remain inadequately interconnected. The core bottleneck lies in the absence of production relations capable of effectively supporting value chain integration. In other words, the existing internal business processes, organizational structures, inter-enterprise collaborations, and business models (i.e., production relations) fail to align with the developmental demands of digital technologies (i.e., productive forces). This misalignment prevents data from flowing smoothly and being shared in real-time across different segments and stakeholders.

The failure of data to flow and be shared stems from multiple factors, including but not limited to: inadequate safeguards for information security and privacy protection; insufficient advancement in digital technologies for data collection, transmission, processing, and analysis; lack of unified industry-wide data standards and interfaces; techical architecture limitations that hinder system interoperability. At its core, this is not merely an issue of data or digital technologies, but rather one of restructuring industrial division of labor—specifically, how data owners, processors, and users collaborate under revised production relations. This means that, to fully integrate R&D, production, supply chain, sales, and service operations, it is imperative to fundamentally restructure organizational architectures, business processes, collaborative partnerships, and business models. Only by establishing new modes of cooperation, as well as mechanisms for defining and distributing rights and benefits, can seamless interconnection be achieved.

Accordingly, the following strategies should be adopted to address integration challenges:

First, **all relevant stakeholders must elevate their prioritization and align their understanding** to collectively facilitate data circulation and sharing. For governments, it is imperative to refine data openness regulations while ensuring information security and personal privacy, placing greater emphasis on fostering innovation. Industry associations, with government support, should actively coordinate resources to establish public data platforms while advancing data valuation and rights clarification initiatives. Enterprises should participate proactively in constructing and integrating digital data-sharing platforms—aligned with digital transformation and ecosystem development goals—to achieve efficient collaboration with partners.

Second, **innovate production relations to achieve competition through collaboration and mutual gain through sharing**. Data, algorithms, and computing power are the three fundamental pillars supporting intelligent capabilities—none can be omitted. Without data, computing power and algorithms become castles in the air; without computing power and algorithms, data cannot fulfill its potential. However, these key elements—data, algorithms, and computing power—are controlled by different entities. This necessitates automotive enterprises and ICT companies each playing their distinctive roles while jointly innovating mechanisms for resource sharing. By opening data access and integrating resources, we can realize a quantum leap in the overall capabilities of automotive manufacturing systems.

Third, **leveraging the "1 + N + X" large model application framework to interconnect specialized models across domains.** "1" represents the foundational large model. In the future, foundational large models will serve as vital infrastructure for society. The automotive industry must build its own domain-specific foundational model based on general-purpose foundational models. "N" denotes vertical domain-specific large models. These are specialized, high-precision models tailored to common needs in specific fields/scenarios. "X" signifies specialized models. These models correspond to diverse scenarios in various aspects/domains of automotive intelligent manufacturing and integrate with relevant enterprises' data assets to address specific professional challenges, forming the foundational support for competitive advantage. Previously, different specialized models operated in silos, akin to "potted plants" with no interconnection. Now, these models will be built upon the same foundational large model, which functions like "fertile soil"—enabling all specialized models to share "water and nutrients," thereby achieving interconnectivity and mutual reinforcement. This integration will elevate the capabilities of specialized models to unprecedented levels. To facilitate this, specialized models should adopt standardized interfaces and underlying architectures to support effective multi-agent collaboration. This enables seamless connectivity across R&D, production, supply chain, sales, and service, driving end-to-end integration.

- **Challenge Three: Innovation Capability and Product Competitiveness Lack Integration**

Beyond the constraints of individual process improvements and insufficient cross-process integration, automotive intelligent manufacturing faces yet another bottleneck—the disconnect between its creative capacity and product competitiveness. This manifests in two key aspects: an imbalance in investment between creative development and product enhancement; inadequate interaction between manufacturing systems and product evolution.

On one hand, enterprises tend to prioritize applying digital technologies to enhance product competitiveness while comparatively neglecting the cultivation of creativity within manufacturing systems. Taking large models as an example, most cutting-edge applications currently focus on product-side solutions, such as autonomous driving and smart cockpits. Meanwhile, there remains a lack of broad and intensive exploration into leveraging large models to empower various segments including R&D, production, supply chain, sales, and services. Nor have mature implementation paradigms emerged in these areas. On the other hand, inadequate connectivity and mutual reinforcement exist between manufacturing systems and products. Manufacturing systems still cannot effectively support large-scale product customization or sustained self-evolution through iterative upgrades. Concurrently, data generated and acquired at the product side fails to fully cycle back into the manufacturing system to drive its optimization. In essence, manufacturing systems and products continue to develop in isolation, failing to form a synergistic dynamic of mutual enhancement.

To address the interplay between innovation capacity and product competitiveness, we must first fully recognize their intrinsic value. In fact, enhancing innovation capacity across R&D, production, supply chain, marketing, and service functions serves as the fundamental prerequisite for elevating product performance, where improved product capabilities naturally emerge as the inevitable outcome of heightened creativity. Take large models as an illustrative case. Compared with solely focusing on product enhancement, enterprises should prioritize deploying large models to amplify creative potential. This approach not only unlocks the latent value within individual operational links but also generates synergistic effects through cross-process integration, thereby creating expansive opportunities for product optimization. More profoundly, establishing interconnectivity between innovation capacity and product competitiveness yields exponentially greater value. The automotive intelligent manufacturing system and intelligent automotive products were never meant to exist in isolation—they must mutually reinforce each other to achieve optimal states. Simply put: only an intelligent manufacturing ecosystem can produce truly intelligent products while supporting their continuous iteration and refinement. Conversely, only intelligent products can provide clear developmental demands and directional guidance for manufacturing systems, as well as rich data feedback to fuel ongoing system upgrades.

Guided by this understanding, targeted measures should be implemented across the following dimensions.

First, it is imperative to enhance the empowerment of innovation capacity through cutting-edge technologies like large models. These models possess tremendous potential to comprehensively elevate the automotive industry's creative capabilities, driving profound transformation across the entire R&D-production-supply chain-marketing-service value chain. This will require enterprises to fundamentally reimagine their business processes, organizational structures, collaborative partnerships, and commercial models. Such transformation will necessarily entail a radical departure from conventional management and operational paradigms.

Second, it is imperative to foster deep integration between automotive intelligent manufacturing systems and intelligent automotive products. These two elements must function as mutually reinforcing components—each supporting and stimulating the other's development to achieve sustained optimization. Enterprises should adopt a holistic strategy that leverages enhanced manufacturing creativity to elevate product excellence and simultaneously utilizes growing product sophistication to drive innovation within production systems. This dual approach creates a virtuous cycle where manufacturing capabilities and product advancement continuously propel each other forward.

Third, it is imperative to establish a collective intelligence ecosystem characterized by multi-agent convergent innovation. Empowered by advancing digital technologies like large models, "new auto" will progressively evolve into self-evolving intelligent agents. Concurrently, multiple intelligent agents will emerge throughout the automotive intelligent manufacturing value chain—spanning R&D, production, supply, sales, and service. To this end, enterprises should facilitate seamless interoperability and collaborative synergy among product-side and manufacturing-side intelligent agents through shared foundational large models. This integration will enable autonomous generation, processing, exchange, updating, and evolution across both automotive intelligent manufacturing systems and intelligent automotive products. Ultimately, to achieve genuine interoperability between innovation capacity and product competitiveness, industry players must collectively construct a high-efficiency, collaborative ecosystem of multi-agent collective intelligence.

6.3.2 Development Trends

Based on the cutting-edge advancements across R&D, production, supply chain, sales, and service in the automotive industry, we have identified three major development trends for automotive intelligent manufacturing moving forward.

First, automotive intelligent manufacturing will evolve toward an integrated R&D-production-supply-sales-service system built on seamless data connectivity. Current industry practices reveal that enterprises are vigorously advancing data standardization and governance across the entire manufacturing value chain, accelerating data flow and sharing both internally among business units and externally between different entities. This suggests that in the future, fully interconnected data streams will continuously drive the intelligent integration and upgrading of all value-chain segments—leveraging real-time feedback data to guide continuous optimization of automotive products throughout their entire lifecycle. For instance, various types of real-time transmitted data will be harnessed to optimize vehicles across both their complete value chain and lifespan.

Second, automotive intelligent manufacturing will evolve toward an industrial ecosystem characterized by multi-stakeholder collaboration and convergent innovation. Current industry practices demonstrate that enterprises widely recognize the importance and urgency of ecosystem development, actively innovating business models, expanding ecosystem partnerships, and integrating cross-sector resources. Through digital platforms, they are connecting diverse entities across industries and domains to jointly explore and advance ecosystem construction. We anticipate that future automotive intelligent manufacturing ecosystems will feature increasingly diverse participants and progressively refined operational mechanisms. The collaborative synergy among multiple stakeholders—based on specialized division of labor—will continue to strengthen, providing robust support for the steady growth and expansion of the overall automotive intelligent manufacturing ecosystem.

Finally, automotive intelligent manufacturing will advance toward a next-generation manufacturing system that enables self-iterating and self-evolving "New Auto". Current industry implementations demonstrate how enterprises are deploying digital twins, agile software development, and other technologies to dramatically accelerate product updates and user responsiveness. Concurrently, big data and foundation models are progressively endowing vehicles with self-learning capabilities. This evolution indicates that future automotive intelligent manufacturing systems will be deeply empowered by cutting-edge technologies like large models, achieving multi-agent fusion. Through data-driven collaboration between human operators and AI-enhanced machinery, comprehensive self-optimization of "new auto" products and services will be realized, enabling continuous, autonomous evolution.

Looking ahead, as large models and other digital/intelligent technologies achieve comprehensive integration with manufacturing, the automotive intelligent manufacturing system will undergo transformative changes across all dimensions. This revolution will fundamentally reshape inter-enterprise collaboration models. A paradigm shift may emerge where manufacturing platform operators assume complete production responsibility under an OEM model—automotive companies would focus exclusively on product design and digital blueprints, while manufacturing platforms leverage their advanced processes and self-evolving equipment/production lines to bring these designs to physical reality.

6.3.3 Evaluation of "Technology Roadmap 2.0"

Since 2020, the application of digital and intelligent technologies in automotive intelligent manufacturing and critical equipment has deepened significantly. Continuous advancements are being made across three key dimensions: enterprise/workshop-level information systems, physical factory/workshop equipment technologies, and virtual factory/workshop technologies. The industry is accelerating toward the goals outlined in the *Energy-Saving and New Energy Vehicle Technology Roadmap 2.0*—namely generalization, adaptability, transparency, and intelligentization—with encouraging achievements. Currently, China's overall automotive manufacturing technology ranks among the world's leading players, with complementary advantages in certain key technical areas compared to international counterparts. In advanced ICT applications like artificial intelligence and industrial internet, China has taken a global leadership position. Nevertheless, structural gaps remain evident, manifesting as "three highs and three lows": high hardware automation rates but low software localization; high data collection rates but low value extraction; high individual technological breakthroughs (e.g., AI-based quality inspection) but low system-level coordination (weak R&D-production-supply-chain-service integration) (Table 6.1).

In conclusion, the development targets outlined in the *Energy-Saving and New Energy Vehicle Technology Roadmap 2.0* for automotive intelligent manufacturing and key equipment remain largely aligned with recent cutting-edge industry practices. Thanks to the rapid advancement and application of advanced technologies such as artificial intelligence, progress on certain indicators has even slightly exceeded expectations.

Table 6.1 Assessment on "Intelligent Manufacturing and Key Equipment" from the *Energy-Saving and New Energy Vehicle Technology Roadmap 2.0*

Indicator		Targets to be fulfilled by 2025	Progress achieved as of the end of 2024
The overall goal is to achieve four disruptions	Generalization	Achieve production flexibility where diverse products can be manufactured simultaneously on the same line, responding to customer orders without requiring any retooling or production preparation modifications to existing equipment	Nearly half of automotive manufacturers have achieved multi-model co-production with flexible, customized manufacturing. Some enterprises still require partial production line modifications for new model integration. Leading domestic manufacturers have established and upgraded universalized plants for body welding, painting, and final assembly, capable of supporting cross-platform mixed-line production for any vehicle model
	Adaptability	Achieve automated control of production logistics, processes, equipment and assembly lines, enabling self-adaptive JIS (Just-In-Sequence) production matching and zero-risk manufacturing	Production is driven by planning across logistics, operations, and assembly line control, essentially realizing an adaptive JIS production model. Leading enterprises leverage digital planning systems to establish constraint-based matching between long-term forecasts and short-term orders, enabling precise coordination with partners from inventory to production. Critical components are directly delivered from suppliers to assembly stations via automated logistics chains, achieving adaptive JIS matching through system integration

(continued)

Table 6.1 (continued)

Indicator		Targets to be fulfilled by 2025	Progress achieved as of the end of 2024
	Transparency	Enable real-time dynamic monitoring, analysis, and interactive decision-making for products, processes, quality, and equipment operations	Overall, real-time dynamic monitoring and analysis of product quality, processes, and equipment operations have been achieved. Leading enterprises leverage data acquisition systems to transmit real-time equipment, process, and product data to information systems, enabling dynamic monitoring and immediate data interaction
	Intelligentization	Enable predictive analysis and adaptive control of production equipment, process optimization, and product quality, while achieving intelligent production management decisions, analytical insights, and knowledge accumulation to optimize efficiency, costs, and quality	Basic predictive analysis of production equipment, process control, and product quality has been achieved. Certain enterprises have implemented predictive analysis with adaptive control for production equipment, process optimization, and product quality specifically in welding, painting, and other targeted manufacturing stages
Overall and commonality basis		The application of production process equipment, logistics, tooling separation, and "plug-and-play" integrated technologies	Technologies such as offline programming, tooling separation, and "plug-and-play" integration have been broadly implemented in workshops including stamping and welding. Leading enterprises have further applied these advancements to the construction and operation of versatile paint and assembly shops

(continued)

Table 6.1 (continued)

Indicator	Targets to be fulfilled by 2025	Progress achieved as of the end of 2024
	Integrated technology applications connecting user demand endpoints with factory production endpoints	Most OEMs have implemented demand-driven planning through an end-to-end OTD solution, where planning drives logistics, quality control, and production, achieving adaptive end-to-end factory operations
	Connectivity and convergence technologies for heterogeneous industrial big data across manpower, machines, materials, methods, environment, and measurement in production processes	Some companies have established multi-source, heterogeneous industrial big data collection covering personnel, machines, materials, methods, environmental conditions, and measurement—with data fusion applications already in place
	The deployment of AI technologies across production equipment, process control systems, production units, and various management layers	AI application scenarios in production equipment, process control systems, and key stations of production process units have been clearly defined, with related application software still in rapid development

(continued)

Table 6.1 (continued)

Indicator	Targets to be fulfilled by 2025	Progress achieved as of the end of 2024
	Improve the development of process databases/ knowledge bases, smart factory standard libraries, and scenario solution repositories to clarify the interconnections among personnel, equipment, materials, and process workflows—preparing the foundation for AI-driven data applications	Enterprises have preliminarily built domain-specific knowledge bases—such as equipment management, process design, and production operation strategies—to provide foundational knowledge for AI-driven applications. Leading manufacturers have established digital process management systems, completing the construction of 100+ equipment libraries and 40+ standard process libraries, while some workshops have achieved full digital twin modeling via simulation
Enterprise/workshop-level information systems	Accelerate the migration of traditional ERP and other information systems to cloud platforms while developing applications to meet multi-scenario cloud-based demands	Leading companies, in collaboration with suppliers, have migrated enterprise-wide and workshop-level information systems (e.g., ERP, SRM, LES, MES, QMS) to cloud platforms and developed industrial apps for standardized scenarios, significantly improving production efficiency and product quality

(continued)

Table 6.1 (continued)

Indicator	Targets to be fulfilled by 2025	Progress achieved as of the end of 2024
Physical factory/workshop equipment technology	Enable intelligent single-unit or modular equipment that leverages big data analytics to analyze and model problem-generation processes—transitioning from resolving visible issues to preventing them. The intelligent adoption rate in key processes exceeds 40%, with overall equipment effectiveness (OEE) improving by over 5% compared to 2020 and labor productivity rising by more than 20%	Companies have widely achieved operational data collection from individual machines and modular equipment, accumulating substantial datasets to enable process analysis, as well as big-data diagnostics and root-cause investigation for incidents. Leading enterprises have implemented full-scale data acquisition and analytics for robotic systems and select motor-driven equipment, realizing predictive maintenance. Among these industry exemplars, the intelligent adoption rate in critical processes exceeds 90%, with overall equipment effectiveness (OEE) rising by 8% and labor productivity improving by 23% relative to 2020 baselines
Virtual factory/workshop technology	Seek localized optimization through the modeling and simulation of single-unit equipment, specific process stages, and individual operational scenarios	Leading manufacturers have standardized the management of virtual simulation resources—spanning single machines, individual processes, specific scenarios, and factory modeling—to create a digital twin environment for new vehicle launches, achieving "ready-to-operate upon power-on."

It should be noted that the "intelligent manufacturing" framework and objectives outlined in *Roadmap 2.0* primarily focused on production and equipment domains. However, with the rapid evolution of "New Auto" paradigms, continuous breakthroughs in foundational models, emerging disruptive production technologies, and unprecedented demands for supply chain flexibility/resilience, *Roadmap 3.0* will significantly expand this scope, evolving into a comprehensive system spanning the entire R&D-production-supply-sales-service value chain and encompassing eight specialized technical clusters. This transformation will consequently establish more ambitious intelligent manufacturing development visions and targets with broader hierarchical levels, wider application fields, and more extensive technological coverage.

6.4 Grading System and Definitions of Automotive Intelligent Manufacturing

6.4.1 Evolution Paradigm of Automotive Manufacturing

Through research on digitalization, intelligentization, and their interrelationships, combined with an analysis of the current state and future trends of automotive intelligent manufacturing, we propose an evolutionary paradigm for automotive intelligent manufacturing. This framework clearly outlines its progression (measured by digital-intelligent capabilities) through four distinct phases: **digitalization, networking, intelligentization, and self-evolution**, as illustrated in Fig. 6.8.

The first stage is digitalization, the fundamental prerequisite, as it transforms diverse information into digital signals (i.e., data). Enterprises must fully leverage digitalization to enable the complete data lifecycle: generation, transmission, analysis, and utilization. Only by adopting and widely applying digital technologies across the industry can companies cultivate data as a new production factor.

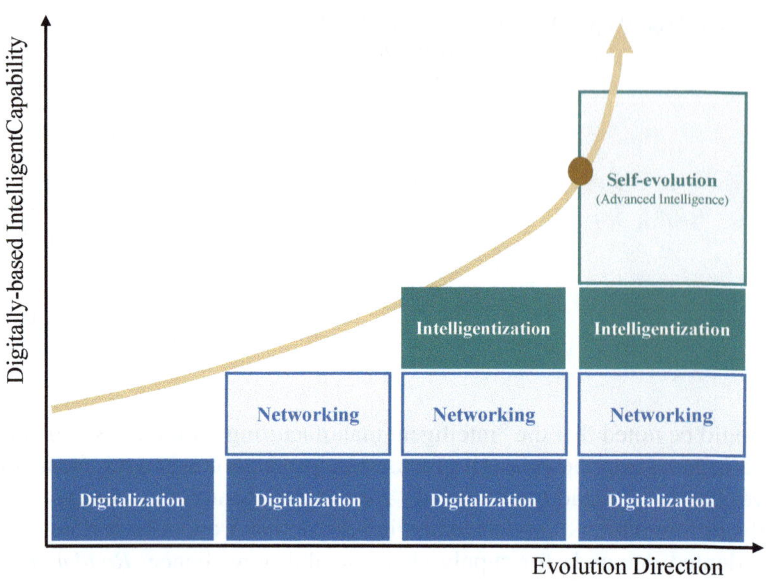

Fig. 6.8 Evolution paradigm of automotive intelligent manufacturing

The second stage is networking, enabling resource integration and allocation. Building upon the technological capabilities and diversified data accumulated during the digitalization phase, the automotive manufacturing system leverages IoT, cloud platforms, and 5G/6G communications to achieve information sharing and collaborative operations. Through a unified manufacturing platform, it integrates and optimizes resource allocation while facilitating seamless data flow across business systems. Networking strengthens connectivity between processes and stakeholders in automotive manufacturing, unlocking data's potential across broader scopes and significantly enhancing system-wide coordination. Only when industry players achieve full networking can they effectively interconnect fragmented manufacturing resources and establish the critical infrastructure for comprehensive data sharing within the production ecosystem.

The third stage is intelligentization, both a technological means and an ultimate objective. With the advancement of networking, the automotive industry's cross-linked ecosystem has begun taking shape. By leveraging big data and large models, the manufacturing system can thus achieve data-driven scientific decision-making, establishing ANI-level foundational intelligence while enabling the realization of "software-defined vehicles." This ANI-level foundational intelligence signifies that both automotive intelligent manufacturing systems and intelligent automotive products possess localized iterative optimization capabilities. In other words, they achieve self-evolution within specific components or modules.

The fourth stage is self-evolution, an intelligent agent's autonomous iteration. This represents the ultimate phase of manufacturing system development, built upon digitalization, networking, and intelligentization. At this stage, the automotive intelligent manufacturing system dynamically integrates diverse data streams to achieve self-enhancement and self-optimization capabilities. In essence, self-evolution constitutes advanced intelligentization, progressing from ANI toward AGI or even ASI-level intelligence, thereby fully enabling "AI-defined vehicles." The transition from intelligentization to self-evolution marks a critical inflection point where digital capabilities undergo qualitative transformation. Consequently, "new auto" products and their related equipment evolve into self-evolving intelligent agents that collaborate efficiently, collectively forming a swarm intelligence ecosystem that advances automotive intelligent manufacturing to unprecedented levels.

It should be emphasized that these four stages do not represent abrupt transitions, but rather a progressive evolution with fluid boundaries, each phase deeply interconnected with and gradually emerging from the previous one. For upgrading automotive intelligent manufacturing systems: digitalization serves as the fundamental prerequisite, networking builds upon digitalization to connect disparate resources, intelligentization functions as both technical means and developmental objective, while self-evolution represents intelligentization's advanced culmination. It is precisely through analyzing these four evolutionary dimensions that the automotive intelligent manufacturing technology roadmap introduces the overarching concept of "digitally-based intelligent". This synthetic term, intentionally incorporated into each thematic section's title, effectively captures the essential trajectory and fundamental characteristics of automotive manufacturing system advancement.

6.4.2 Grading and Definitions of Automotive Intelligent Manufacturing

6.4.2.1 Grading System and Connotation

The development of the automotive intelligent manufacturing technology roadmap requires clearly defining its objectives, evolutionary pathways, and key milestones. To achieve this effectively, establishing a scientifically grounded classification system for assessing different development levels of automotive intelligent manufacturing is essential. To accurately position the progression of automotive intelligent manufacturing, we have **adopted a forward-looking approach that combines "Begin with the End in Mind", "Holistic System Characterization" with "Best-Practices Benchmarking", aligned with China's national intelligent manufacturing framework, and have pioneered an industry-specific classification system for automotive intelligent manufacturing, a first-of-its-kind initiative globally**. This grading framework encompasses both the overall evaluation of automotive intelligent manufacturing capabilities and the assessment of specialized domains. Specifically, it classifies the general maturity level on a scale of iM-n (where "iM" stands for intelligent manufacturing, and "n" represents distinct tiers), spanning four progressive levels from iM-1 to iM-4.

Among these principles: "Begin with the End in Mind" establishes the highest maturity level (iM-4) by defining the ultimate vision of automotive intelligent manufacturing, then systematically derives the preceding three levels (iM-1 to iM-3) based on current industry realities to create a backward-justified progression framework. "Holistic System Characterization" entails comprehensive analysis of intelligent manufacturing's evolving priorities, operational scope, critical processes, and enabling technologies to systematically define stage-specific capabilities across multiple evaluation dimensions at each maturity level. "Best-Practices Benchmarking" involves synthesizing cutting-edge implementations from leading automakers to identify consensus-driven, phase-specific exemplars—providing calibrated development targets and implementation strategies for each evolutionary stage.

This technology roadmap aligns its four-tiered classification of automotive intelligent manufacturing maturity with the previously proposed "four-stage evolution paradigm," with their conceptual correspondence illustrated in Fig. 6.9. Specifically: iM-1 corresponds to the digitalization stage, requiring deployment of data generation, collection, processing, and application infrastructure to ensure all information become digitally processable. iM-2 mirrors the networking stage, demanding cross-process and multi-stakeholder data flows to enable effective manufacturing resource orchestration. iM-3 represents the intelligentization stage, leveraging advanced data processing to iteratively optimize vehicle components/modules through algorithmic solution refinement. iM-4 embodies the self-evolution stage, achieving comprehensive AI-driven data integration that transforms both products and manufacturing entities into adaptive intelligent agents capable of autonomous iteration.

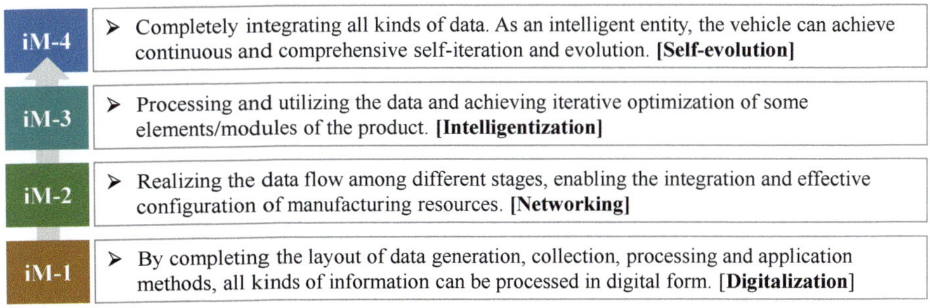

Fig. 6.9 The grading system of automotive intelligent manufacturing

The progression from iM-1 to iM-4 fundamentally represents two transformative dimensions: the horizontal expansion of data applications from isolated functions to enterprise-wide systems; the vertical escalation of capabilities from intra-departmental coordination to cross-ecosystem collaboration. Conversely, this systemic integration generates virtuous cycles where enterprise-wide digital threading amplifies local process efficiency and ecosystem synergies elevate internal capabilities. Ultimately creating compound momentum for industry-wide intelligent manufacturing advancement.

To provide a more intuitive, clear, and detailed representation of the relationship between automotive intelligent manufacturing maturity levels and enterprise operations, we have refined the system into a three-dimensional architecture (Fig. 6.10). This framework consists of: Z-axis, which defines the four progressive levels of intelligent manufacturing (iM-1 to iM-4); X-axis, which encompasses both core business areas (R&D, production, hardware/software supply chains, marketing & services) and supporting functions (equipment, management, low-carbon manufacturing), corresponding to specialized teams in the roadmap; Y-axis, which includes five key factors—scenarios, technologies, processes, systems, and ecosystems–that collectively enable systematic description of business evolution across all maturity stages. This architecture demonstrates how advancements in individual domains collectively determine the overall maturity of automotive intelligent manufacturing.

The hierarchical classification system and implementation methodology for automotive intelligent manufacturing proposed in this roadmap adopt a forward-looking approach that innovates while complying with China's national intelligent manufacturing framework and standards. By thoroughly incorporating the distinctive characteristics of the automotive industry, this framework enables comprehensive, objective and precise classification, analysis and implementation guidance—both for assessing the overall advancement level of smart automobile production and for evaluating progress across specific domains.

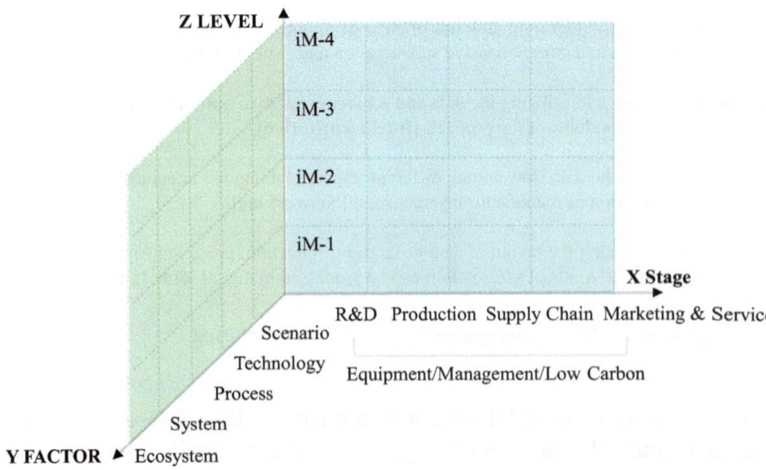

Fig. 6.10 The three-dimensional framework of automotive intelligent manufacturing

6.4.2.2 Overall Level Grading and Definition

Building on the identified future trends of automotive intelligent manufacturing, we define the hierarchical classification of its overall development level across three dimensions: integrated R&D, production, supply, sales and service; automotive intelligent manufacturing ecosystem development; product & service iteration and evolution. The detailed classification criteria are presented in Table 6.2.

6.4.2.3 Specific Levels and Definition Across Fields

Following the same principle ("Begin with the End in Mind", "Holistic System Characterization" with "Best-Practices Benchmarking"), each field of automotive intelligent manufacturing has established its own classification system $\mathbf{iM_X}$-n (X stands for specific field): iM_R-n (R stands for Research and Development), iM_P-n (P stands for Production), iM_E-n (E stands for Equipment), iM_{SH}-n (SH standards for Supply chain Hardware), i iM_{SS}-n (SS stands for Supply chain Software), iM_{MS}-n (MS standards for Marketing & Sales and Users Operation), iM_M-n (M stands for Management), and iM_{LC}-n (LC stands for Low Carbon).

Additionally, each specialized working group elaborates on the evolutionary directions and critical issues within their respective domains from five key dimensions: application scenarios, technologies, processes, systems, and ecosystems. This structured approach effectively presents their cutting-edge practices, development trends, and strategic initiatives, as illustrated in Fig. 6.11.

First, scenarios serve as the core, representing the pivotal challenges of automotive intelligent manufacturing, the significant transformations that "New Auto" brings to

Table 6.2 Classification of the overall development level of automotive intelligent manufacturing

	iM-1	iM-2	iM-3	iM-4
Integrated research, production, supply, sales and service	Deploy key digital technologies to meet business needs, enabling **initial data flow** and utilization **within processes** to achieve digitalization of each business segment	Establish corporate data standards and interfaces to **facilitate internal sharing of design, production, and service data**, realizing interconnectivity across all internal operations	Develop cross-industry unified data standards and interfaces to enable seamless data flow and effective utilization between enterprises, achieving interconnectivity among different business functions	Fully integrate the entire ecosystem with complete data synchronization, dynamically consolidating internal and external data for global optimization, ultimately realizing full integration of R&D, production, supply chain, sales, and service integration
Automotive intelligent manufacturing ecosystem construction	Strengthen collaboration with partners as core enterprises establish **digital platforms with foundational capabilities** to enable basic business cooperation	Form multiple tightly coordinated **intelligent manufacturing micro-ecosystems**, developing open platforms led by core enterprises to expand partnerships and deepen connections	Build a large, highly competitive **intelligent manufacturing macro-ecosystem** by continuously diversifying and expanding its participants, achieving cross-platform integration among micro-ecosystems	Establish **a complete and structurally stable intelligent manufacturing macro-ecosystem** with seamless interoperability across digital platforms, featuring self-refining operational mechanisms and rules
Products and services evolution and iteration	Leverage **digital technologies** to enable user demand analysis and agile software development, providing **initial support for product and service iteration**	Leverage **connectivity technologies** to enable data collection and feedback from users/vehicles, driving product iteration while **providing solid support for continuous service improvement**	Utilize **intelligent technologies** to process and apply data, enabling **partial elements/modules of products to self-evolve, thereby facilitating initial autonomous product iteration**	Multiple intelligent agents in automotive manufacturing achieve self-coordination and self-evolution, collectively shaping an “New Auto” entity that enables continuous, comprehensive, and rapid self-iteration and self-improvement

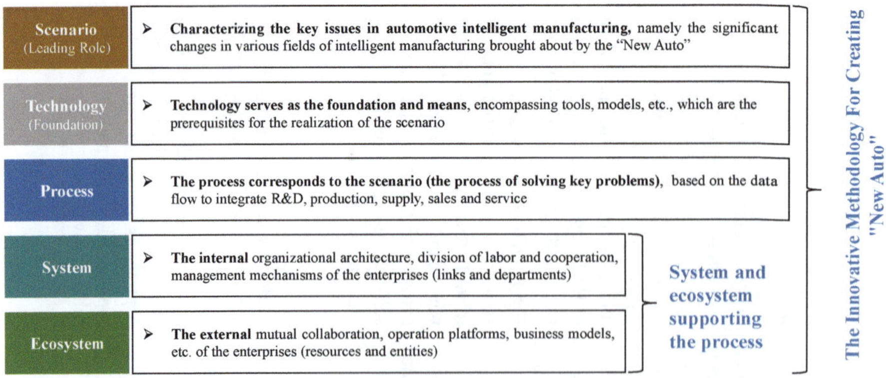

Fig. 6.11 The basic elements for conducting research in each specialized domain of automotive intelligent manufacturing

various domains of smart production. Each working group has identified a comparable number of scenarios with consistent granularity, all interconnected through logical relationships. The other four elements revolve around these scenarios, functioning as different dimensions to articulate key challenges. Second, technology is the foundation and enabler, encompassing tools, models, and methodologies. Technological capabilities determine whether scenarios can be realized, with their evolution directly influencing the speed and extent of implementation. Third, processes correspond to scenarios, essentially constituting the workflow to address critical issues. Enterprises must establish new, data-driven business processes that integrate R&D, production, supply chain, sales, and service, enabling resource sharing and capability convergence. Fourth, systems pertain to internal enterprise structures, including organizational frameworks, division of labor, collaboration models, and management mechanisms. Fifth, ecosystems operate at the external level, defining interactions between enterprises, operational platforms, and business models that support large-scale collaboration.

In reality, these five elements form an organic and interconnected framework. To be specific, scenarios serve as the breakthrough point and focal area for realizing value in automotive intelligent manufacturing. Technology acts as both the prerequisite for scenarios to emerge and the foundation for their implementation. Processes, systems, and ecosystems collectively provide the necessary conditions and action paths for effectively applying technology and unlocking scenario value—with systems and ecosystems jointly reinforcing processes. Thus, the automotive intelligent manufacturing system encompasses a wide range of stakeholders and elements. In summary, scenario defines the transformative shifts across domains, technology provides the foundational support, process ensures seamless data-driven integration across all stages, while system and ecosystem enable internal and external coordination. By thoroughly articulating these five elements, we establish an innovative methodology for shaping the future of "New Auto."

6.5 Development Vision and Overall Goals

6.5.1 Development Vision

Looking ahead, Internet of Everything (IOT) and carbon neutrality stand as two unparalleled driving forces poised to transform industries and human society at large. The automotive intelligent manufacturing system will inevitably be built upon these twin foundations. By fully unleashing the value of data as a new production factor and harnessing digital/intelligent technologies as transformative productive forces, this system will innovatively reshape processes, organizational structures, and business models, establishing modern production relations that align with emerging productive forces. This framework will enable sustained, comprehensive self-evolution of the "New Auto" ecosystem while forging fundamentally new modes of production and living. As illustrated in Fig. 6.12, this represents the ultimate developmental vision for automotive intelligent manufacturing, where technological advancement catalyzes both industrial transformation and societal progress.

More precisely, on one hand, IOT will ultimately achieve multi-agent collaborative intelligence. This cooperative intelligence, with data at its core and digitalization as the means, will profoundly reshape the industrial landscape and operational models of the real economy. On the other hand, carbon neutrality will ultimately give rise to decarbonized/low-carbon industries. Under strong policy guidance, carbon neutrality will become an external constraint and prerequisite for all industrial development. Both IOT and carbon neutrality are closely tied to the automotive industry: it serves both as a crucial domain for digitalization and multi-agent collaboration, and as the key link in achieving carbon neutrality for the transportation sector. Going further, the historic convergence of these two mega-trends will catalyze the emergence of a green and intelligent automotive ecosystem, which essentially constitutes the complete system of automotive intelligent manufacturing: establishing end-to-end connectivity across R&D, production, supply chain, sales and services based on IOT, while simultaneously building a green ecosystem covering the entire product lifecycle through carbon neutrality initiatives. Conversely, advancing automotive intelligent manufacturing will powerfully accelerate the development of both IOT

Fig. 6.12 The development vision of automotive intelligent manufacturing

and carbon neutrality, significantly expanding their value potential. Ultimately, this development will realize three key visions.

The first is to ensure high-quality development of the automotive industry. The innovation-driven automotive intelligent manufacturing system and model will effectively support the creation and delivery of premium products and services, maintaining China's first-mover advantage in electrification and intelligent vehicle technologies. This will solidify the global competitiveness of China's automotive sector while driving the overall upgrade of the industrial system. Simultaneously, it will significantly enhance the flexibility and resilience of automotive supply chains, enabling agile responses to unexpected disruptions. This ensures stable, sustained supply and efficient delivery, equipping the industry to navigate growing uncertainties, both internal and external, with greater robustness.

The second is to pioneer the practical implementation of new industrialization. Automotive intelligent manufacturing will achieve the integrated application of digital and manufacturing technologies, thereby reshaping the entire production chain and product lifecycle to drive the digitally-based intelligentization of both the automotive sector and manufacturing at large. Concurrently, breakthroughs in key intelligent manufacturing technologies and their industrial deployment will lead to the comprehensive adoption of advanced production tools—IoT, big data, cloud computing, and AI foundation models—sparking a revolutionary shift toward large-scale personalized customization as the new manufacturing paradigm. This will substantially strengthen the automotive industry's foundational capabilities, optimize its ecosystem structure, and propel the sector's ascent to higher-value segments of the global supply chain.

Third, we will accelerate the holistic transformation and upgrading of manufacturing. Automotive intelligent manufacturing will drive cross-industry resource integration, deepen platform-based, networked, and ecosystem-oriented development models, and catalyze collaborative innovation across sectors—including ICT, equipment manufacturing, and software development—through specialized division of labor. This will forge a multi-stakeholder, resource-sharing, and tightly coordinated intelligent manufacturing ecosystem, achieving true synergy and co-creation of value among diverse elements and participants. As the pinnacle of advanced manufacturing and the largest foundational ecosystem in the era of ubiquitous connectivity, the automotive industry holds unique strategic value. Once end-to-end intelligent manufacturing—spanning R&D, production, supply chain, sales, and services—achieves comprehensive breakthroughs, it will provide a transformative blueprint and practical roadmap for the entire manufacturing sector's upgrade.

In summary, realizing these visions for future automotive intelligent manufacturing will elevate the comprehensive competitiveness of both the automotive industry and its interconnected sectors, injecting robust momentum into high-quality socioeconomic development.

6.5.2 Overall Goals

The development vision charts the overarching direction for the future advancement of automotive intelligent manufacturing. Based on this, we have further established the overall development goals for automotive intelligent manufacturing by 2040, as illustrated in Fig. 6.13.

The overall development goals consist of the general goals (strategic goals) and key area goals. Among them, the general goals include the following four aspects:

(1) **Improving quality, increasing efficiency, reducing cost and achieving low carbon**. This embodies the intrinsic purpose and ultimate goal of advancing automotive intelligent manufacturing—delivering tangible benefits and substantively improving corporate performance. To this end, we must holistically elevate product and operational quality, significantly enhance efficiency across all manufacturing stages and responsiveness to user demands, drastically streamline intermediate processes and eliminate waste-driven unnecessary costs, while accelerating the transition to low-carbon operations throughout the entire industrial chain and product life cycle.

(2) **Integrating the whole manufacturing process into a single, seamless system**. The goal is to achieve seamless interconnectivity among all information management systems throughout automotive intelligent manufacturing, fostering open sharing of diverse data held by different stakeholders. This ensures the flow and closed-loop circulation of data across the entire automotive value chain, enabling full integration of R&D, production, supply chain, sales, and services.

(3) **Constructing the intelligent manufacturing ecosystem**. A collaborative, multi-stakeholder ecosystem for automotive intelligent manufacturing must be developed, ensuring increasingly complete supporting elements, expanding diversity of participants, growing incorporation of resources, enhanced stability and scalability. This will comprehensively reshape industrial division of labor, collaborative partnerships, and business models

2040

Overall Goals	**Improving quality, increasing efficiency, reducing costs, and achieving low carbon.**	Comprehensively enhancing quality, significantly improving manufacturing efficiency, greatly reducing costs, and effectively achieving a low-carbon approach throughout the life cycle
	Integrating the whole manufacturing process into a single, seamless system	Building interconnected systems, adopting closed-loop data management, and achieving integration of research, production, supply, sales and service.
	Constructing the intelligent manufacturing ecosystem	Building an intelligent manufacturing ecosystem with multi-party collaborative co-creation.
	Supporting the development and upgrading of "new auto"	Creating "new auto" that meets user-specific needs, and supports product upgrades and service optimizations based on data → Experience enhancement.

Fig. 6.13 Overall development goals for automotive intelligent manufacturing

(4) **Supporting the development and upgrading of "new auto."** The automotive intelligent manufacturing system must effectively produce "new auto" products that meet user demands while leveraging data to continuously drive product upgrades and service optimizations. This ensures vehicles improve with use—remaining perpetually refreshed and increasingly superior—thereby supporting user experience enhancements from the manufacturing side.

Under the overarching objectives, each key domain of automotive intelligent manufacturing also has its own development targets. These aim to support the realization of the broader goals while defining priority tasks for their respective areas, as outlined below:

(1) **Digitally-based intelligent R&D**. Driven by data, centered on scenario design, anchored in software development, and empowered by large AI models—focusing on experience development, ecosystem integration, continuous delivery, and full lifecycle OTA (Over-the-Air) updates. Through digitally-based intelligent means, enabling the "new auto" to achieve autonomous evolution—remaining perpetually refreshed and increasingly superior with use.
(2) **Digitally-based intelligent production**. Human–machine collaborative and intelligent unit production lines possess heightened flexibility and resilience. The intelligent production system features self-organization, hyper-flexibility, self-learning, and self-maintenance capabilities, enabling self-optimization to meet diverse complex manufacturing needs—from mass production to personalized and flexible customization.
(3) **Digitally-based intelligent equipment**. Equipped with multi-modal, full-domain environmental perception, devices achieve self-awareness, self-learning, autonomous decision-making, self-execution, and self-optimization. Individual units and equipment groups demonstrate high modularity, reconfigurability, and reuse value to support flexible and resilient production demands.
(4) **Digitally-based intelligent hardware supply**. Deep integration of supply chain management with next-gen digitally-based intelligent and advanced manufacturing technologies fosters an open, collaborative, co-creative, and mutually beneficial ecosystem. This enables high-efficiency, high-resilience, and high-flexibility end-to-end smart supply with continuous self-evolution.
(5) **Digitally-based intelligent software supply**. A robust software ecosystem and collaborative development framework accelerates high-quality automotive software iteration, delivering cutting-edge digital experiences and realizing "software-defined vehicles."
(6) **Digitally-based intelligent marketing and service**. Digital sales channels and upgraded service models align user needs with brand strategy, achieving precision marketing, personalized engagement, and smart, real-time, bespoke services. An interconnected service ecosystem facilitates iterative optimization.
(7) **Digitally-based intelligent management**. A self-evolving management system integrates multi-source data fusion, advanced machine learning, transparent governance, and data-driven decision-making.

(8) **Low-carbon manufacturing**. Decarbonized product structures, energy use, processes, and materials; circular resource utilization; and non-toxic input consumption.

6.6 Overall Technology Roadmap

The overall technology roadmap for automotive intelligent manufacturing is shown in Fig. 6.14.

6.7 Technology Roadmaps in Domains

The automotive intelligent manufacturing technology cluster is centered on building a smart production system for "new auto." By examining key elements—scenarios, technologies, processes, systems, and ecosystems—it systematically outlines cutting-edge practices and future trends across specialized domains, synthesizing them into distinct development directions (each domain distilled into three focal areas). Subsequent technical roadmaps for each domain will elaborate on these directions in detail.

6.7.1 The Development Scheme for Digitally-Based Intelligent Research

The R&D system of the "new auto" presents three major development directions: data-driven R&D, full life cycle iterative development, and collaborative co-creation convergent innovation, as shown in Fig. 6.15.

(1) **Data-driven R&D**. "Software-defined vehicles" (SDVs) have redefined the relationship between hardware and software, shifting from hardware-dominant designs with software adaptation to hardware accommodating software. Hardware evolves toward modularization, standardization, and abstraction, enabling software to flexibly orchestrate hardware components. This transformation gives rise to a data-led, software-first development paradigm. After achieving architecture-level decoupling, software advances through agile, iterative development, while hardware adopts catalog-based ("off-the-shelf") development. Integration testing follows their independent development cycles. This workflow demands novel R&D structures: enterprises must establish collaborative units, software centers, hardware centers, and data centers, with clearly delineated roles and seamless cross-functional synergy.

			2030	2035	2040
OVERALL GOALS	Overall Target		50% of enterprises to reach the iM-1 level 45% of enterprises to reach the iM-2 level 5% of enterprises to reach the iM-3 level	65% of enterprises to reach the iM-2 level; 30% of enterprises to reach the iM-3 level; 5% of enterprises to reach the iM-4 level	15% of enterprises to reach the iM-2 level 45% of enterprises to reach the iM-3 level 40% of enterprises to reach reached the iM-4 level
	Quality		The reliability and safety of automotive products to increase by more than 20% compared to 2024	The reliability and safety of automotive products to increase by more than 40% compared to 2024	The reliability and safety of automotive products to increase by more than 60% compared to 2024
	Efficiency		The overall labor productivity of the automotive manufacturing industry to increase by more than 20% compared to 2024	The overall labor productivity of the automotive manufacturing industry to increase by more than 40% compared to 2024	The overall labor productivity of the automotive manufacturing industry to increase by more than 60% compared to 2024
	Cost		The unit cost output rate of the automotive manufacturing industry to increase by more than 10% compared to 2024	The unit cost output rate of the automotive manufacturing industry to increase by more than 20% compared to 2024	The unit cost output rate of the automotive manufacturing industry to increase by more than 35% compared to 2024
	Low Carbon		The carbon emissions throughout the life cycle of the automotive industry to decrease by more than 15% compared to 2024 The energy consumption per unit of GDP to decrease by more than 10% compared to 2024	The carbon emissions throughout the life cycle of the automotive industry to decrease by more than 40% compared to 2024; The energy consumption per unit of GDP to decrease by more than 20% compared to 2024	The carbon emissions throughout the life cycle of the automotive industry to decrease by more than 60% compared to 2024; The energy consumption per unit of GDP to decrease by more than 30% compared to 2024
KEY DOMAINS	R&D	Overall	40% of enterprises to reach the iM$_{R}$-1 level 50% of enterprises to reach the iM$_{R}$-2 level 10% of enterprises to reach the iM$_{R}$-3 level	50% of enterprises to reach the iM$_{R}$-2 level 30% of enterprises to reach the iM$_{R}$-3 level 20% of enterprises to reach the iM$_{R}$-4 level	10% of enterprises to reach the iM$_{R}$-2 level 40% of enterprises to reach the iM$_{R}$-3 level 50% of the enterprises reach the iM$_{R}$-4 level
		Key Roadmap	Establish a comprehensive open innovation system within the enterprise to enable rapid iterative product development through real-time cross-departmental collaboration. Leverage AI agents for efficient cross-disciplinary review and design optimization. Achieve scaled "mass personalization" product management via full data integration and application—implementing a "thousand users, thousand configurations" model	Build a cross-enterprise open innovation ecosystem enabling full lifecycle and supply-chain management. Reconstruct the software architecture to automate AI model integration and deployment. Utilize mature standards to precisely forecast product performance, market trends, and user needs—implementing a "thousand vehicles, thousand software variants" service model	Realize a high-efficiency prototype ecosystem where AI autonomously drives end-to-end development, validation, and self-iterative updates. Establish co-creation platforms and AI-augmented design for crowdsourced R&D models—implementing an "open innovation" operational paradigm
	Production	Overall	45% of enterprises to reach the iM$_{P}$-1 level 40% of enterprises to reach the iM$_{P}$-2 level 15% of enterprises to reach the iM$_{P}$-3 level	55% of enterprises to reach the iM$_{P}$-2 level 20% of enterprises to reach the iM$_{P}$-3 level 25% of enterprises to reach the iM$_{P}$-4 level	10% of enterprises to reach the iM$_{P}$-2 level 40% of enterprises to reach the iM$_{P}$-3 level 50% of enterprises to reach the iM$_{P}$-4 level
		Key Roadmap	Select enterprises will adopt a "centralized production line + distributed flexible assembly cells" model, achieving full digital process design. This enables reconfigurable production lines for diversified personalized combinations, with some enterprises establishing digital twin factories	The majority of enterprises will implement the "centralized production line + distributed flexible assembly cells" model, while some will transition to a "modular production line + distributed flexible manufacturing cells" approach. This supports dynamic capacity allocation and large-scale customization of multi-variant products	Leading enterprises will possess self-organizing collaborative production capabilities with adaptive capacity allocation. Digital twin factories will become standard infrastructure across the industry
	Equipment	Overall	50% of enterprises to reach the iM$_{E}$-1 level 45% of enterprises to reach the iM$_{E}$-2 level 5% of enterprises to reach the iM$_{E}$-3 level	60% of enterprises to reach the iM$_{E}$-2 level 30% of enterprises to reach the iM$_{E}$-3 level 10% of enterprises to reach the iM$_{E}$-4 level	10% of enterprises to reach the iM$_{E}$-2 level 50% of enterprises to reach the iM$_{E}$-3 level 40% of enterprises to reach the iM$_{E}$-4 level
		Key Roadmap	Enterprise-level modular interfaces achieve full standardization, enabling perception in highly dynamic complex environments. AI-driven reasoning facilitates intelligent fault diagnosis while adaptive rule-based coordination supports single-scenario sequential human-machine collaboration	Breakthroughs in decoupling stamping-welding-painting-assembly processes with functional encapsulation and modular design. AI-enabled autonomous task planning with real-time execution adjustment achieves bidirectional interactive cooperation	Holistic modularization from components to systems. Adaptive equipment morphology/functionality/operation enables seamless multitasking. Realize omni-directional intelligent fusion perception, establishing a self-evolving smart collaboration ecosystem with continuous innovation capabilities
	Supply Chain (Hardware)	Overall	40% of enterprises to reach the iM$_{SH}$-1 level 50% of enterprises to reach the iM$_{SH}$-2 level 10% of enterprises to reach the iM$_{SH}$-3 level	50% of enterprises to reach the iM$_{SH}$-2 level 40% of enterprises to reach the iM$_{SH}$-3 level 10% of enterprises to reach the iM$_{SH}$-4 level	5% of enterprises to reach the iM$_{SH}$-2 level 50% of enterprises to reach the iM$_{SH}$-3 level 45% of enterprises to reach the iM$_{SH}$-4 level
		Key Roadmap	Initially establish cross-industry supply chain ecology platforms, achieving fundamental data sharing and preliminary collaboration among key stakeholders. Supply chain design quality, manufacturing quality, and service quality will improve significantly. Decision intelligence will compensate for human limitations in handling specific granularities and long-cycle requirements	The supply chain ecosystem platform will realize resource circularity and environmentally-friendly operations. Supply chain design quality, manufacturing quality, and service quality will be further enhanced. Decision intelligence will dominate conventional supply chain planning processes, with human intervention reserved solely for emergency contingencies	A mature supply chain ecosystem will take shape, achieving full industry coverage and promoting deep collaboration across all supply chain segments alongside environmental sustainability. All critical domains of intelligent manufacturing coordination will undergo comprehensive digital-intelligence transformation, establishing a complete data-driven decision-making mechanism that commences with decision intelligence and concludes with human judgment
	Supply Chain (Software)	Overall	50% of enterprises to reach the iM$_{SS}$-1 level 45% of of enterprises to reach the iM$_{SS}$-2 level 5% of enterprises to reach the iM$_{SS}$-3 level	60% of enterprises to reach the iM$_{SS}$-2 level 30% of enterprises to reach the iM$_{SS}$-3 level 10% of enterprises to reach the iM$_{SS}$-4 level	10% of enterprises to reach the iM$_{SS}$-2 level 40% of enterprises to reach the iM$_{SS}$-3 level 50% of enterprises to reach the iM$_{SS}$-4 level
		Key Roadmap	Development will be based on SOA, with low-code platforms and automated testing widely adopted. High-frequency OTA updates will focus primarily on enhancing user experience, while effectively detecting and addressing critical software security and quality issues	Open APIs will enable ISPs to deliver richer software services. AI will be extensively applied in software development and testing, enabling deeper synergy between vehicle and cloud software. OTA updates will mainly cater to personalized user demands	Third-party software will flourish, delivering increasingly intelligent user experiences. Software development management will reach ASPICE L5 maturity. AI will be widely used in development, testing, and quality assurance, automatically maintaining security and mitigating risks
	Marketing & Sales and Users Operation	Overall	45% of enterprises to reach the iM$_{MSU}$-1 level 50% of enterprises to reach the iM$_{MSU}$-2 level 5% of enterprises to reach the iM$_{MSU}$-3 level	60% of enterprises to reach the iM$_{MSU}$-2 level 30% of enterprises to reach the iM$_{MSU}$-3 level 10% of enterprises to reach the iM$_{MSU}$-4 level	10% of enterprises to reach the iM$_{MSU}$-2 level 40% of enterprises to reach the iM$_{MSU}$-3 level 50% of enterprises to reach the iM$_{MSU}$-4 level
		Key Roadmap	Achieve full commercialization of autonomous data acquisition systems, seamless user connectivity solutions, integrated data resource management architectures, multi-modal AI algorithms, unified cockpit-ADAS platforms, and edge-cloud convergence frameworks in this domain	Establish industrial maturity for vertical-scenario AI modeling techniques, automotive-grade large language model implementations, regulatory-compliant L4 autonomous driving systems, immersive virtual reality interfaces, and multi-OS single-chip computing platforms	Complete technological realization of self-evolving AI agency mechanisms, artificial general intelligence frameworks, certified L5 autonomous driving ecosystems, and integrated smart city mobility infrastructures
	Management	Overall	50% of enterprises to reach the iM$_{M}$-1 level 45% of the enterprises reach the iM$_{M}$-2 level 5% of enterprises to reach the iM$_{M}$-3 level	60% of enterprises to reach the iM$_{M}$-2 level 30% of enterprises to reach the iM$_{M}$-3 level 10% of enterprises to reach the iM$_{M}$-4 level	10% of enterprises to reach the iM$_{M}$-2 level 40% of enterprises to reach the iM$_{M}$-3 level 50% of enterprises to reach the iM$_{M}$-4 level
		Key Roadmap	Establish a preliminary intelligent ecosystem across the entire value chain, enhancing decision-making efficiency and user experience while demonstrating initial success in data sharing	Develop a mature intelligent ecosystem achieving deep collaboration and high-efficiency decision-making, with data sharing significantly strengthening automakers' competitiveness	Create an industry-leading intelligent ecosystem enabling fully automated decision-making and premium user experiences, with data sharing driving sector-wide innovation
	Low Carbon Manufacturing	Overall	40% of enterprises to reach the iM$_{LC}$-1 level 50% of enterprises to reach the iM$_{LC}$-2 level 10% of enterprises to reach the iM$_{LC}$-3 level	50% of enterprises to reach the iM$_{LC}$-2 level 40% of enterprises to reach the iM$_{LC}$-3 level 10% of enterprises to reach the iM$_{LC}$-4 level	10% of enterprises to reach the iM$_{LC}$-2 level 40% of enterprises to reach the iM$_{LC}$-3 level 50% of enterprises to reach the iM$_{LC}$-4 level
		Key Roadmap	Through key strategies including low-carbon design, sustainable material selection, green supply chain management, and recycling/reuse technologies, the automotive manufacturing industry will achieve continuous reductions in lifecycle carbon emissions and energy consumption per unit GDP compared to 2024 benchmarks, reaching carbon peak before 2030		

Fig. 6.14 Overall technology roadmap for automotive intelligent manufacturing

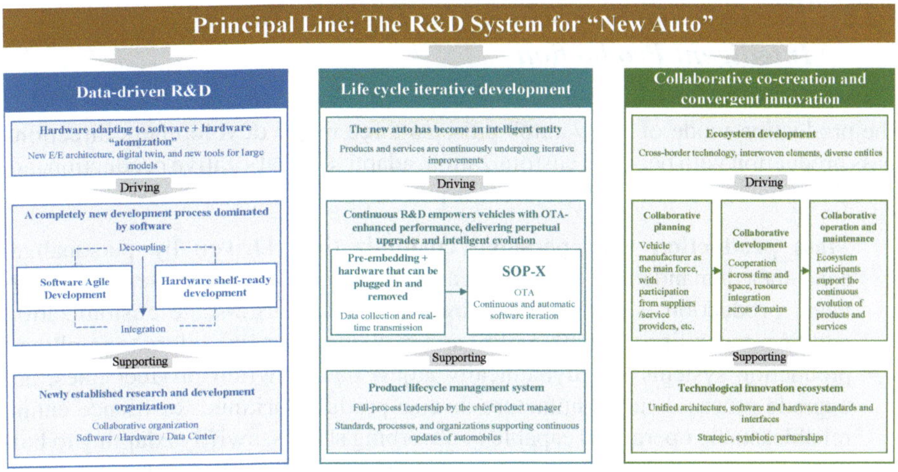

Fig. 6.15 The development direction of digitally-based intelligent R&D

(2) **Full life cycle iterative development**. "New auto" will evolve into an intelligent entity with continuous self-iterative capabilities. This transformation necessitates a shift in the R&D system from one-time development to full-lifecycle continuous development.To enable vehicles with OTA-enhanced performance, delivering perpetual upgrades and intelligent evolution, pre-installed sensors are required to facilitate real-time operational data collection and transmission. Additionally, plug-and-play hardware configurations must be adopted to extend functional upgradability. Post initial SOP (Start of Production), the R&D system must sustain SOP-X, an ongoing, automated product optimization process driven by OTA software updates based on returned data. From an organizational and managerial perspective, enterprises must establish a product lifecycle management system led by senior product managers, formulating standards, processes, and structures to support continuous vehicle and service enhancements.

(3) **Collaborative co-creation and convergent innovation**. Under the trend of ecosystem development, the automotive R&D system will evolve into a new multi-stakeholder collaborative model, characterized by joint planning, co-development, and coordinated operation. Automakers, suppliers, and service providers will integrate cross-domain resources to jointly support innovative product development and continuous iteration. To achieve such integrated innovation, enterprises need to establish a technological innovation ecosystem, unifying architectures, software/hardware standards, and interfaces, while forging strong connections with strategic and symbiotic partners through diversified cooperation models.

6.7.2 The Development Scheme for Digitally-Based Intelligent Production

The production mode of "new auto" presents three major development directions: mass production with personal customization, adaptive collaborative production, and virtual-to-physical control across the entire production process, as shown in Fig. 6.16.

(1) **Mass production with personal customization**. Driven by personalized consumer demands and technological advancements in processes and equipment, production is transitioning toward flexible, large-scale customization, building capabilities in both agility and resilience. Agility refers to intelligent production systems that dynamically adjust plans, switch product lines, and upgrade processes to manufacture diverse product variants. Resilience entails reliable, stable operations capable of absorbing shocks, swiftly adapting to bulk order fluctuations while ensuring on-time delivery. To achieve this dual capability, automakers and suppliers must establish digitalized collaboration and implement risk mitigation mechanisms.

(2) **Adaptive collaborative production**. Digital technologies such as intelligent robots and industrial internet are accelerating swarm collaborative intelligence in production, enabling production resources to gradually develop self-organization, self-decision-making, self-execution, and self-evolution capabilities. Supported by a digitally-based intelligent production management system, enterprises can leverage production-related data to facilitate efficient human–machine and machine-machine collaboration. This merges human creativity and judgment with machines' data processing and precision execution, creating human–machine hybrid augmented intelligence. As a result, optimal allocation and unified scheduling of production resources can be achieved.

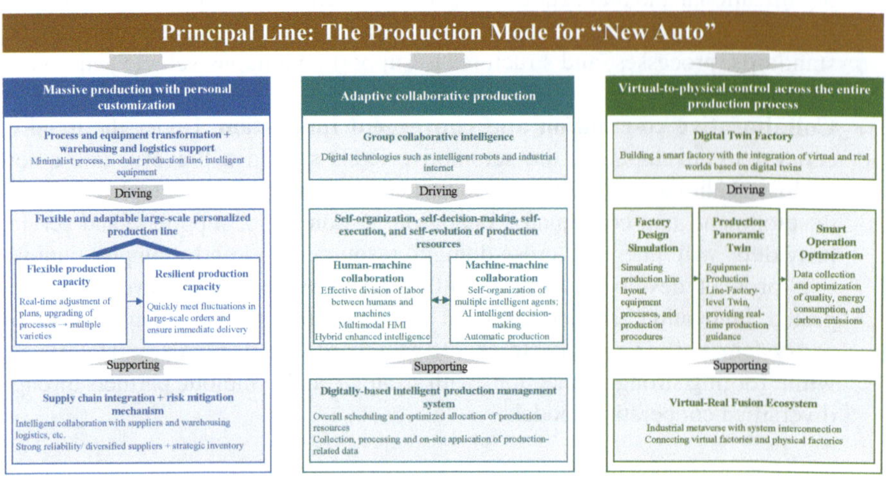

Fig. 6.16 The development direction of digitally-based intelligent production

(3) **Virtual-to-physical control across the entire production process**. Smart factories, powered by digital twin technology, integrate virtual and physical environments to enable design simulation, comprehensive modeling of production line layouts, process equipment, and workflow optimization. Achieving full-scenario digital twins, covering equipment, production lines, and entire factories, allows for real-time monitoring and intelligent guidance across the entire production process. Smart operational optimization further enhances factory efficiency by analyzing data on production quality, efficiency, energy consumption, and carbon emissions. The digital twin factory relies on a virtual-physical integrated industrial ecosystem, facilitating bidirectional interaction between virtual and physical plants, as well as interconnectivity among digital twin factories, ultimately forming a cohesive industrial metaverse ecosystem.

6.7.3 The Development Scheme for Digitally-Based Intelligent Equipment

Digitally-based intelligent equipment is evolving towards equipment agents in the "new auto" production mode, presenting three major development directions: customization of equipment, evolution of equipment into intelligent agents, and evolution of equipment operation to multi-agent collaboration, as shown in Fig. 6.17.

(1) **Customization of equipment**. The development of "new auto" requires new manufacturing systems tailored to their unique production demands. This includes specialized equipment for producing electrified components, intelligent

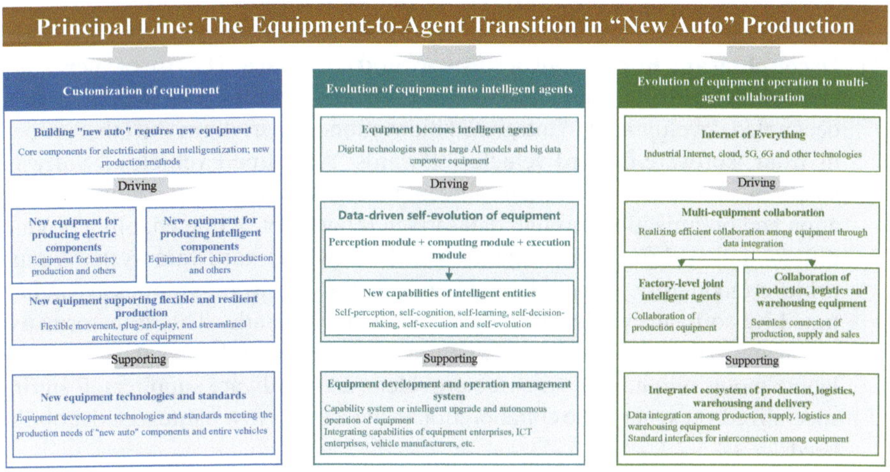

Fig. 6.17 The development direction of digitally-based intelligent equipment

systems, and flexible/resilient production processes. To enable such customization, future efforts must advance equipment R&D and standardization aligned with "new auto" parts and assembly requirements.

(2) **Evolution of equipment into intelligent agents**. In the future, equipment will transform into intelligent entities empowered by large models and big data, developing self-awareness, cognition, learning, decision-making, execution, and evolution capabilities through data. This necessitates collaboration among equipment manufacturers, ICT firms, and automakers to establish a new paradigm for equipment development and operations.

(3) **Evolution of equipment operation to multi-agent collaboration**. Amid the trend of ubiquitous connectivity, collaborative multi-equipment systems, acting as intelligent swarms, will achieve collective intelligence. This manifests as production machinery dynamically interacting to form factory-level networked intelligence, while manufacturing, logistics, and warehousing systems synchronize to enable seamless supply chain integration. The future will see the emergence of integrated production-supply ecosystems, enabled by standardized interfaces and unified operational data flows spanning manufacturing, logistics, warehousing, and delivery systems.

6.7.4 *The Development Scheme for Digitally-Based Intelligent Supply Chains (Hardware + Software)*

The software and hardware supply system of "new auto" presents three major development directions: decoupling and integration of software and hardware, evolution towards full-chain intelligent supply, and evolution towards a networked supply ecosystem, as shown in Fig. 6.18.

(1) **Decoupling and integration of software and hardware**. The rise of "new auto" elevates software to unprecedented importance, marking the transition from decoupled development to integrated innovation—a paradigm shift that propels us from "software-defined vehicles" towards "AI-defined vehicles." Software solutions must account for their inherent uniqueness, ensuring continuous iteration and optimization through data-driven refinement, while enabling product differentiation through intelligent code. Meanwhile, hardware systems must achieve modularity, standardization, and abstraction to be seamlessly orchestrated by software while fulfilling its evolving demands. This transformative landscape calls for a novel supply ecosystem, one that redefines the division of labor among automakers, software providers, and hardware suppliers, fostering specialized yet synergistic collaboration to meet tomorrow's integrated mobility needs.

(2) **Evolution towards full-chain intelligent supply**. Digitally-based intelligent technologies will empower supply chains to achieve comprehensive automation and intellectualization across the entire value chain, transforming both

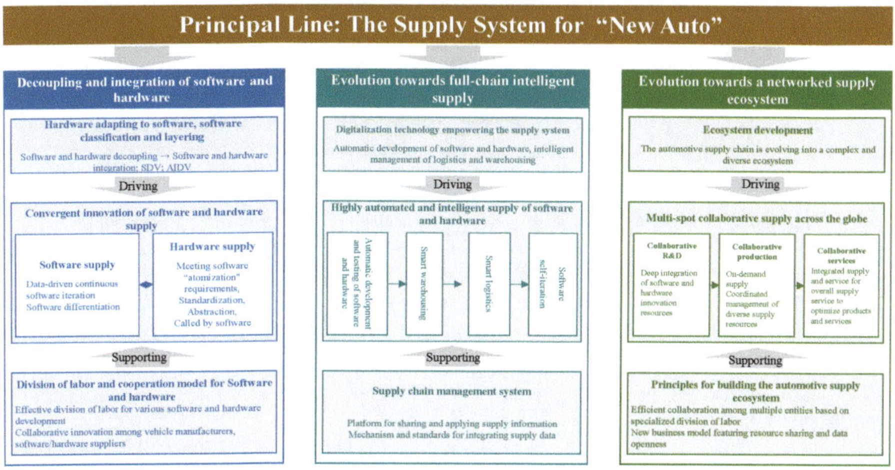

Fig. 6.18 The development direction of digitally-based intelligent supply chain (hardware + software)

hardware and software provisioning. This manifests through automated development and testing of hardware/software components, intelligent warehousing with autonomous inventory management, precision-guided smart logistics, and self-iterating software systems. Fundamentally supporting this transformation, supply chain management systems will undergo synchronous modernization, establishing unified data standards and interconnected mechanisms while building platforms for collaborative supply data utilization and exchange.

(3) **Evolving towards a networked supply ecosystem**. Amid the industry's ecosystem-oriented transformation, automotive supply chains will evolve into complex, dynamic ecosystems. Responding to the global macro environment, they will establish multi-node collaborative supply networks worldwide, enabling joint development, co-production, and integrated services between automakers and diverse suppliers. To achieve this, fundamental principles for ecosystem development must be established, exploring innovative business models that facilitate data openness and resource sharing. This ensures all participants can leverage their professional expertise to engage in efficient, synergistic cooperation.

6.7.5 The Development Scheme for Digitally-Based Intelligent Marketing & Sales and Users Operation

The marketing and services of "new auto" are presented in three major directions: digitally-based intelligent technologies empowering the entire marketing chain,

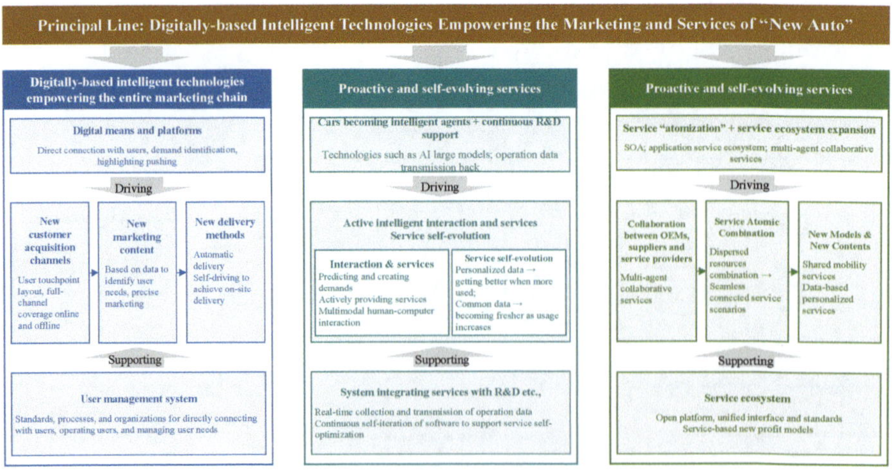

Fig. 6.19 The development direction of digitally-based intelligent marketing & sales and users operation

proactive and self-evolving services, and pervasive and ecosystem-driven services, as shown in Fig. 6.19.

(1) **Digitally-based intelligent technologies empowering the entire marketing chain**. Digital platforms and methodologies comprehensively enhance marketing processes, enabling full-chain innovation supported by advanced user management systems. Key manifestations include novel customer acquisition channels, establishing omnichannel touchpoints for seamless online-to-offline user engagement; data-driven content strategy, leveraging intelligent analytics to identify customer needs and deliver precision-targeted product messaging; next-generation delivery models, pioneering autonomous vehicle-enabled door-to-door delivery services
(2) **Proactive and self-evolving services**. As vehicles transform into intelligent agents with continuous R&D support, the convergence of development and service systems will enable proactive intelligent interactions and self-evoling services. Service proactivity means enterprises will predict and create demand through multimodal human–machine interaction, delivering personalized services preemptively. Service self-evolution refers to leveraging individual user data to enhance products and services through usage ("better with use"), while employing collective user insights to ensure continuous innovation ("new with use").
(3) **Pervasive and ecosystem-driven services**. Future automotive services will exhibit modular ("atomic") and ecosystem-integrated characteristics. On the one hand, automakers, suppliers, and service providers will collectively deliver and enhance interconnected services; on the other hand, dispersed service components will combine dynamically like "atoms" to create seamless service

scenarios. This evolution will enable data-driven personalized service models, such as shared mobility solutions. Realizing pervasive, ecosystem-enabled services requires an extensible open platform with unified standards for service integration, new service-centric revenue models, and continuous ecosystem expansion to support ubiquitous service delivery.

6.7.6 The Development Scheme for Digitally-Based Intelligent Management

The digitally-based intelligent management of enterprise-wide business chain collaboration manifests three key development trends: data sharing, transparent and efficient management, and multi-stakeholder collaborative management, as illustrated in Fig. 6.20.

(1) **Data sharing**. The growing demand for data interoperability and evolving security technologies are jointly maturing data resource management systems. On the one hand, the data of research, production, supply, sales and service within the enterprise need to be closed-loop connected; On the other hand, outside the enterprise, open sharing of data among different enterprises should be achieved based on open platforms and unified data standards. As an important guarantee foundation, data security and data governance systems should be continuously improved to address issues such as cross-border data and data privacy.
(2) **Transparent and efficient management**. Digital technologies are comprehensively transforming enterprise operations, enabling truly transparent and

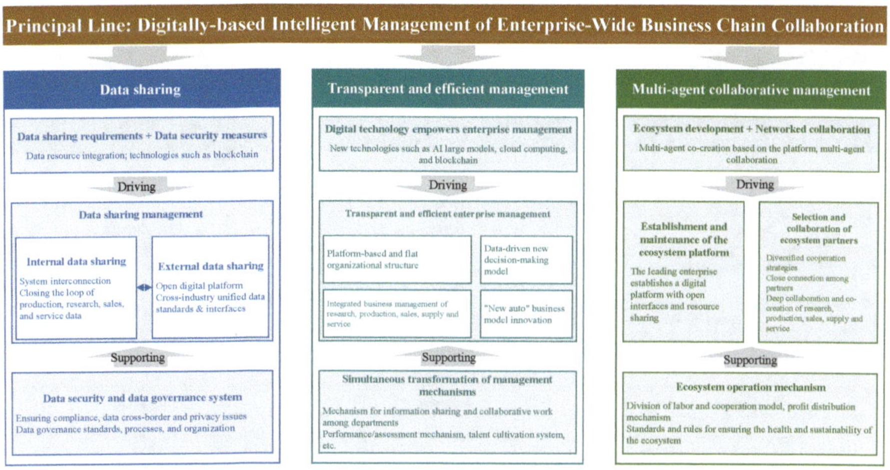

Fig. 6.20 The development direction of digitally-based intelligent management

efficient governance models, including streamlined organizational architecture, data-driven new decision-making paradigm, integrated business operations of research, production, supply, sales and service, and "new auto" business model innovation, etc. Enterprise management mechanisms also need to be transformed simultaneously, including information sharing among departments, collaborative working mechanisms, performance/assessment mechanisms, and talent development systems.

(3) **Multi-stakeholder collaborative governance**. The trend of ecosystem-oriented transformation and networked collaboration are driving the maturation of co-creation frameworks involving multiple entities and intelligent agents. With the support of the ecosystem operation mechanism, multiple stakeholders should jointly establish and maintain open, digital ecosystem platforms for automotive intelligent manufacturing, with diverse partners participating through various cooperation models, thus enabling deep collaboration across R&D, production, supply chain, marketing, and service operations. During the process, operational mechanisms embrace continuous refinement, division-of-labor models and value distribution systems get gradually optimized, ensuring sustainable ecosystem growth.

6.7.7 The Development Scheme for Low Carbon Manufacturing

The low-carbon manufacturing of the "new auto" presents three key development directions, including low-carbon design and R&D, low-carbon production and supply, and low-carbon services, as shown in Fig. 6.21.

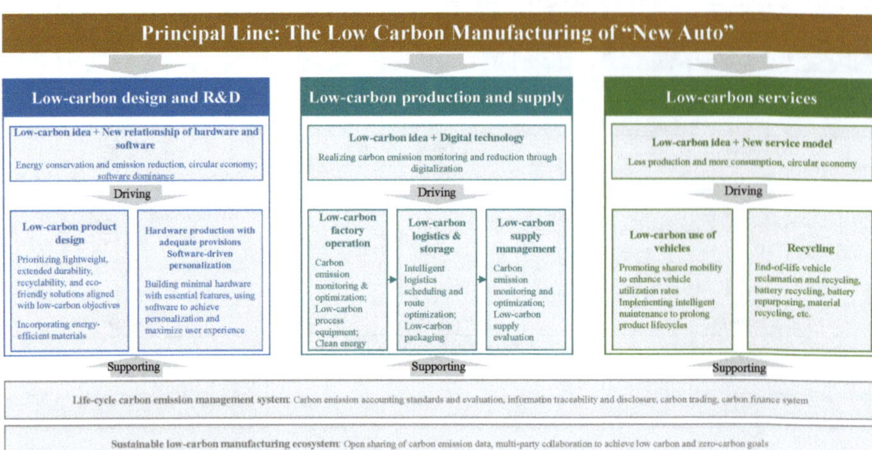

Fig. 6.21 The development direction of low-carbon manufacturing

(1) **Low-carbon design and R&D**. Guided by green principles such as energy conservation, carbon reduction, and circular economy, future automotive design should prioritize lightweight, extended durability, recyclability, and eco-friendly solutions aligned with low-carbon objectives, while incorporating energy-efficient materials. Simultaneously, the new software-dominated dynamic between hardware and software offers novel design approaches for achieving lifecycle carbon neutrality, minimal, judicious hardware production with adequate provisions, complemented by software-driven personalization and experience optimization, thereby fundamentally reducing the carbon footprint of physical component manufacturing.

(2) **Low-carbon production and supply**. Future automotive enterprises must establish green factories targeting carbon neutrality, deploying low-carbon manufacturing technologies and clean energy comprehensively while utilizing digital solutions for real-time emissions monitoring and systemic optimization to achieve sustainable operations. They should develop eco-conscious logistics and warehousing systems, employing intelligent scheduling and route optimization to minimize carbon footprints, alongside widespread adoption of sustainable packaging. Additionally, a supplier carbon assessment framework and emission tracking mechanisms for procurement processes must be implemented to elevate carbon governance across supply chains.

(3) **Low-carbon services**. Enterprises shall adopt service models rooted in circular economy principles, emphasizing "maximized utilization over excessive production." This involves promoting shared mobility to enhance vehicle utilization rates and implementing predictive maintenance to prolong product lifecycles. Concurrently, comprehensive resource circularity must be pursued through end-of-life vehicle reclamation, battery recycling, battery repurposing, and material recovery systems.

These three major development directions all require support from product lifecycle carbon emission management systems and sustainable low-carbon manufacturing ecosystems. The former primarily include carbon emission accounting standards and evaluation systems, information traceability and disclosure systems, as well as carbon trading and carbon finance systems. The latter mainly involve promoting open sharing of carbon emission data across the automotive and related industries, enabling low-carbon and carbon–neutral intelligent manufacturing through multi-stakeholder collaboration.

Bibliography

1. IBM. White Paper on Industry 4.0 and IoT [R]. 2022.
2. Accenture. 2024 Accenture China Enterprise Digital Transformation Index [R]. 2024.
3. iResearch. White Paper on Digital Transformation Solutions for China's Automotive Industry [R]. 2023.
4. Guohai Securities. In-Depth Report on the Automotive Industry: Tesla's Manufacturing Revolution—Integrated Die Casting [R]. 2022.
5. National Industrial Information Security Development Research Center, Shandong University. White Paper on Industrial Equipment Digital Twins [R]. 2021.
6. National Manufacturing Strategy Advisory Committee, Chinese Academy of Engineering. 2023 China Manufacturing Power Development Index Report [R]. 2023.
7. Liu Zongwei. Zhao Fuquan on Automotive Industry (Volume 5) [M]. Beijing: China Machine Press, 2023.
8. McKinsey & Company. "Lost and Found": A Guide to Digital Transformation for Automakers [R]. 2019.
9. Zhao Fuquan, Liu Zongwei, Shi Tianze. Analysis of the Relationship Between Industry 4.0 and Lean Thinking and Coping Strategies for Chinese SMEs [J]. Science and Technology Management Research, 2018, 38(03): 156–160.
10. Zhao Fuquan, Liu Zongwei, Shi Tianze. Comparative Analysis of "Made in China 2025" and Industry 4.0 and the Coping Strategies for China's Automotive Industry [J]. Science & Technology Progress and Policy, 2017, 34(14): 85–91.
11. Zhao Fuquan, Liu Zongwei, Ma Qingzhu. Automotive Technology Ecosystem Innovation [M]. Beijing: China Machine Press, 2023.
12. China Electronics Standardization Institute. Intelligent Manufacturing Maturity Index Report (2022) [R]. 2023.
13. China Academy of Information and Communications Technology. China Intelligent Manufacturing Development Research Report—Smart Factories [R]. 2022.
14. Zhou J, Li P, Zhou Y, et al. Toward New-Generation Intelligent Manufacturing [J]. Engineering, 2018, 4(1): 11–20.

Technology Roadmap for Energy Saving and New Energy Vehicles 3.0,
https://doi.org/10.1007/978-981-95-2502-7

MIX
Papier aus verantwortungsvollen Quellen
Paper from responsible sources
FSC® C105338

If you have any concerns about our products,
you can contact us on
ProductSafety@springernature.com

In case Publisher is established outside the EU,
the EU authorized representative is:
Springer Nature Customer Service Center GmbH
Europaplatz 3, 69115 Heidelberg, Germany

Printed by Libri Plureos GmbH
in Hamburg, Germany